2017 Minutes of the General Assembly Cumberland Presbyterian Church

Office of the General Assembly

Cumberland Presbyterian Church

July 2017

8207 Traditional Place
Cordova (Memphis), Tennessee 38016

©2017 Office of the General Assembly, CPC

All Rights Reserved. No part of this book may be reproduced or transmitted in any form or by any means, electronic or mechanical, including photocopying, recording, or by any information storage or retrieval system, without permission in writing from the publisher. For information address Office of the General Assembly, Cumberland Presbyterian Center, 8207 Traditional Place, Cordova (Memphis), Tennessee, 38016-7414.

Published and distributed by The Discipleship Ministry Team, CPC
Memphis, Tennessee

The Discipleship Ministry Team of the Ministry Council of the Cumberland Presbyterian Church is the successor organization to the Board of Christian Education of the Cumberland Presbyterian Church.

Funded, in part, by your contributions to Our United Outreach.

First Edition 2017

ISBN-13: 978-1945929137
ISBN-10: 1945929138

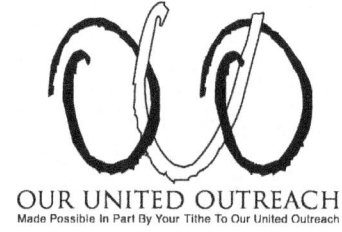

OUR UNITED OUTREACH
Made Possible In Part By Your Tithe To Our United Outreach

Vision of Ministry

Biblically-based and Christ-centered
  born out of a specific sense of mission,
  the Cumberland Presbyterian Church strives to be true to its heritage:
  to be open to God's reforming spirit,
  to work cooperatively with the larger Body of Christ,
  and to nurture the connectional bonds that make us one.
The Cumberland Presbyterian Church seeks—to be the hands and feet of Christ in witness and service to the world and, above all, the Cumberland Presbyterian Church lives out the love of God to the glory of Jesus Christ.

TABLE OF CONTENTS

Vision of Ministry .... Title Page
Program 3
Commissioners 5
Youth Advisory Delegates 6
Committees and Abbreviations 6
Committee Meeting Rooms 6
Committee Assignments 7
Referrals to Committees 8
Recommendations at a Glance 9
Assembly Meetings and Officers 10
By Laws of General Assembly Corporation 13
Memorial Roll of Ministers 23
Living General Assembly Moderators 24
Membership of Boards and Agencies 25

Reports
    Moderator 33
    Stated Clerk 34
    Ministry Council 40
    Board of Stewardship, Foundation and Benefits 46
    Board of the Historical Foundation 77
    Board of Trustees of Memphis Theological Seminary 85
    OUO Committee 98
    Commission on Chaplains and Military Personnel 100
    Permanent Judiciary Committee 103
    Nominating Committee 105
    Place of Meeting Committee 108
    Unified Committee on Theology and Social Concerns 110
    Unification Task Force 118
    Board of Trustees of Bethel University 125
    Board of Trustees of the Cumberland Presbyterian Children's Home 127
    Joint Committee on Amendments 135
    Joint Committee on the Covenant Relationship between the General Assembly Corporation and
        Bethel University 136
    Joint Committee on the Covenant Relationship between the General Assembly Corporation and
        Cumberland Presbyterian Children's Home 140

Memorial 145

Agency Budgets 147

General Assembly Minutes 156

Audits 164

Appendices 306

Church Calendar .... Inside Back Cover

PROGRAM SCHEDULE

Assembly Meetings: Innisbrook Convention Center
General Assembly Office: Edinburgh Boardroom (Salon I)
Women's Ministry Office: Edinburgh Salon II
Retiring Moderator: The Reverend Dwayne Tyus, Nashville Presbytery
Co-Host: Florida Churches of Grace Presbytery (CPC) & General Assembly Executive Committee (CPCA)
Pastor Host: The Reverend Eddie Jenkins, Grace Presbytery
Worship Director: The Reverend Jennifer Newell, Tennessee-Georgia Presbytery
Music Director: The Reverend Chris Warren, Murfreesboro Presbytery

SUNDAY, JUNE 18, 2017

Location	Time	Event	Location
Stirling Hall	3:00 p.m.	Orientation for Commissioners and Youth Advisory Delegates	Salon O-Q
		Orientation for Committee Chairs and Co-Chairs	
		(Commissioner/YAD packets may be picked up before or after the orientation session.)	
		Registration for Women's Ministry Convention	Salon II
		Setup displays	Edinburgh West
Inverness Hall	7:00 p.m.	Joint Opening GA Worship/Communion Service	Inverness Ballroom

FIRST DAY - MONDAY, JUNE 19, 2017

Location	Time	Event	Location
Edinburgh Hall	8:00 a.m.	Registration for Commissioners and Youth Advisory Delegates (for those who did not register on Sunday)	Salon I
	8:00 a.m.	Women's Ministry Registration (open until noon)	Salon II
Inverness Hall	8:30 a.m.	Opening GA Business Session	Ballroom A
	.	Constitution of the CPC General Assembly	
	.	Adoption of the Agenda	
	.	Report of the Credentials Committee	
		Election of Moderator	
		Election of Vice-Moderator	
		Presentation by the Stated Clerk, Mike Sharpe	
		Communications	
		Corrections to Preliminary Minutes	
		Committee Appointments and Referrals to Committees	
		Welcome, Pastor Host, Local Officials	
		Introduction of Board and Agency Representatives	
	10:00 a.m.	Break	
Edinburgh/Stirling	10:30 a.m.	GA Committees meet	Various Locations (see bottom of page 6)
		CP Women's Ministry Regional Council Meeting (for Regional Delegates only)	Stirling West
	12:00 p.m.	CP Women's Ministry Regional Council Luncheon	Stirling West
Inverness Hall	2:00 p.m.	Joint Field Trip to Beth-El Farmworker Ministry (staggered departure times beginning - 2:00, 2:30, 3:00 - departing Inverness Hall)	
Beth-El	3:30 p.m.	Beth-El Open House/Tour/Powerpoint/Music	
	5:00 p.m.	Reception/light meal (finger foods) Joint Moderator's Reception (CPC/CPCA) honoring the Moderator and Vice-Moderator of the General Assembly, the Immediate Past Moderator, the President-Elect and the President of the Cumberland Presbyterian Women's Ministry and National Missionary Society Officers	
	5:30 p.m.	Return trip to Innisbrook (departing @ 5:30, 6:00, 6:30 p.m.)	

SECOND DAY - TUESDAY, JUNE 20, 2017

Location	Time	Event	Location
Edinburgh Hall	7:30 a.m.	Convention Registration	Salon II
Edinburgh Hall	8:30 a.m.	Joint Devotions led by National Missionary Society	Edinburgh East
Edinburgh/Stirling	9:00 a.m.	GA Committee meetings (until 5pm)	Various Locations
Edinburgh Hall	9:00 a.m.	Gathering of CP Women's Ministry	Edinburgh East
Edinburgh Hall	10:30 a.m.	Connecting with Neighbors through Prayer	Edinburgh East
Edinburgh Hall	10:30 a.m.	Connecting with Neighbors through Training	Salon II & III
Inverness Hall	12:00 p.m.	CPCA National Missionary Society Luncheon	Inverness Lobby
Edinburgh Hall	2:00 p.m.	Connecting with Neighbors through Bible Study	Edinburgh East
Edinburgh Hall	2:00 p.m.	Connecting with Neighbors through Service	Salon III & off site locations
Stirling Hall	5:00 p.m.	Bethel University Dinner	Stirling West

EVENING PROGRAM

Location	Time	Event	Location
Inverness Hall	7:00 p.m.	Joint Program/Worship (led by UTF)	Ballroom A
Island Clubhouse	8:30 p.m.	Joint Reception Honoring Women in Ministry	Toscana

THIRD DAY - WEDNESDAY, JUNE 21, 2017

Location	Time	Event	Location
Stirling Hall	7:00 a.m.	CPCH Breakfast	Stirling West
Inverness/Stirling	8:30 a.m.	Joint Devotions/GA Business Presentations by Bethel University & PCCMP	Ballroom A
	9:00 a.m.	Break	
Edinburgh/Stirling	9:30 a.m.	GA Committees Meet (until 5 pm)	Various Locations
Edinburgh Hall	9:30 a.m.	Women's Ministry Convention	Edinburgh East
Osprey Clubhouse	12:00 p.m.	Fellowship Luncheon (reservations required) Sponsored by Discipleship Ministry Team	Market Salamander Grille
Edinburgh Hall	2:00 p.m.	Women's Ministry Convention	Edinburgh East
Edinburgh/Stirling	5:00 p.m.	Conclusion of Committee Meetings	Various Locations

EVENING PROGRAM

Location	Time	Event	Location
Inverness	7:00 p.m.	Evening Worship/Progam (offering for Beth-El Farmworker Ministry, including a collection of school supplies for their backpack program)	Ballroom A

FOURTH DAY - THURSDAY, JUNE 22, 2017

Location	Time	Event	Location
Stirling Hall	8:30 a.m.	Devotional, Ms. Shelby Stover, Youth Advisory Delegate, Presbytery of East Tennessee	Stirling Ballroom
	9:00 a.m.	Break	
Stirling Hall	9:30 a.m.	General Assembly Business	Stirling Ballroom
Edinburgh Hall	9:30 a.m.	Women's Ministry Convention Reconvenes	Edinburgh East
	12:00 noon	Lunch Break	
Inverness Hall	12:00 p.m.	Cumberland Presbyterian Women's Luncheon	Inverness Lobby
Stirling Hall	2:00 p.m.	General Assembly Business	Stirling Ballroom
	5:00 p.m.	Dinner Break	
		Take Down Displays	Edinburgh West

EVENING PROGRAM

Location	Time	Event	Location
Stirling Hall	7:00 p.m.	General Assembly Business Closing Devotion:: Reverend Jennifer Newell, Tennessee-Georgia Presbytery	Stirling Ballroom

(In the event that business is not concluded on Thursday,
the closing worship will be at the conclusion
of business on Friday morning.)

COMMISSIONERS
to the
ONE HUNDRED EIGHTY-SIXTH GENERAL ASSEMBLY

PRESBYTERY	MINISTER	COMMITTEE	ELDER	COMMITTEE
Andes (2)	John Correa	M/PD		
Arkansas (2)	Bruce Hamilton	MC/C/D	Ben Fields	S/E
	Gary Tubb	TSC/UTF	Cathy Remy	MC/C/D
Cauca Valley (3)	Wilson Lopez	M/PD		
Choctaw (1)	Nathan Scott	S/E	Linda Scott	C/HF
Columbia (2)	Tommy Clark	TSC/UTF	Patty Clark	C/HF
	Roger Reid	CH/HE	John Koelz	S/E
Covenant (3)	Fred Fahl	J	Pat Clark	TSC/UTF
	Chris Fleming	MC/C/D	Johnny Jenkins	MC/C/D
	Curtis Franklin	C/HF		
Cumberland (3)	Marc Bell	C/HF	Matthew Blair	CH/HE
	Earl West	M/PD	Diann Phelps	S/E
	Brenda Wilson	CH/HE		
Cumberland East Coast (1)				
Del Cristo (1)	Justin Richter	CH/HE	Sherry Meier	CH/HE
East Tennessee (3)	Jerry Scott	S/E		
	Thomas Sweet	CH/HE	Tom Longmire	J
	Patrick Wilkerson	MC/C/D	Mary McCarter	C/HF
Emaus (1)	Josue Guerrero	M/PD		
Grace (3)	Daniel Barkley	CH/HE	Hedemarrie Dussan	S/E
	Ramon Garcia	M/PD	Billy Gandy	M/PD
			Jim Phillips	J
Hong Kong (2)	(NONE)			
Hope (1)	Susan Parker	TSC/UTF	Jimmie Moore	J
Japan (1)	(NONE)			
Missouri (1)	Andy Eppard	S/E	Judith Steffen-Drake	J
Murfreesboro (4)	Amber Clark	CH/HE	Kathy Powers	S/E
	Larry Green	J	Fred Schramm	CH/HE
	Lanny Johnson	C/HF	Richard Turner	C/HF
	Lisa Oliver	MC/C/D		
Nashville (3)	Kenny Butcher	MC/C/D	Bill Dobbins	TSC/UTF
	Rickey Page	M/PD	Tim Odom	MC/C/D
	Dwayne Tyus	J	Gene Stephens	M/PD
North Central (2)	J C McDuffee	J	Dan Sager	M/PD
	Lisa Scott	TSC/UTF	Roy Shanks	C/HF
Red River (3)	Linda Howell	S/E	Steve Kaneaster	M/PD
	Charles Nelson	C/HF	Burt Hager	CH/HE
	Tom Sanders	CH/HE		
Robert Donnell (1)	Steven Howell-Diamond	TSC/UTF	Lorna Light	CH/HE
Tenn./Georgia (3)	Theresa Martin	C/HF	James Condra	S/E
	Rhonda McGowan	M/PD	George Holland	TSC/UTF
	Jen Newell	J	Christy Miller	J
Trinity (2)	Duane Dougherty	C/HF	Jack Holt	M/PD
	J P Kessie	M/PD	Karen Lock	TSC/UTF
West Tennessee (5)	Rob Harris	C/HF	Eugenia Hancock	MC/C/D
	Tony Janner	S/E	(Patricia) Jo Laster	M/PD
	Peter Jeffrey	TSC/UTF	Bob Tucker	TSC/UTF
	David Lancaster	MC/C/D	Molly Williams	J
	Mike Lavendar	J		

YOUTH ADVISORY DELEGATES
to the
ONE HUNDRED EIGHTY-SIXTH GENERAL ASSEMBLY
(Each Presbytery is eligible to send two Youth Advisory Delegates)

PRESBYTERY	DELEGATE	COMMITTEE
Arkansas	Katelyn Bayless	S/E
	Denver Warren	C/HF
Choctaw	(no youth)	
Columbia	(no youth)	
Covenant	(no youth)	
Cumberland	Carly Bell	J
	Alise Butler	CH/HE
del Cristo	(no youth)	
East Tennessee	Duncan Shelton	M/PD
	Shelby Stover	J
Grace	Alina Ferraz	S/E
Hope	Calee Copely	M/PD
Japan	(no youth)	
Missouri	Whitney Moyers	TSC/UTF
Murfreesboro	Elizabeth Mahoney	S/E
	Brenna Truitt	J
Nashville	Savannah Lamb	MC/C/D
	Austin Womack	J
North Central	Skyler Birch	C/HF
	Macie Clark	CH/HE
Red River	Josh Moore	M/PD
Robert Donnell	Lydia Cook	CH/HE
	Mary Cook	C/HF
Tennessee Georgia	Sarah Rackley	TSC/UTF
	Danny Ruiz	MC/C/D
Trinity	Aldan Webb	TSC/UTF
	Cameron Wilkerson	MC/C/D
West Tennessee	Audrey Adams	C/HF
	David Whalen	CH/HE

COMMITTEES ABBREVIATIONS AND MEETING ROOMS

Stirling Hall

ABBREV.	COMMITTEE	MEETING ROOMS
C/HF	Chaplains/Historical Foundation	Salon O
J	Judiciary	Salon Q
MC/C/D	Ministry Council/Communications/Discipleship	Salon L
M/PD	Missions/Pastoral Development	Salon M
TSC/UTF	Theology & Social Concerns/Unification Task Force	Salon P

Edinburgh

ABBREV.	COMMITTEE	MEETING ROOMS
CHCP/HE	Children's Home/Higher Education	Salon 6
S/E	Stewardship/Elected Officers	Salon 5

COMMITTEE ASSIGNMENTS

1. **CHAPLAINS/HISTORICAL FOUNDATION** *(Stirling Hall - Salon O)*
   Chair: Rev. Theresa Martin   **Co-Chair:** Rev. Duane Dougherty
   Ministers: Marc Bell, Curtis Franklin, Rob Harris, Lanny Johnson, Charles Nelson
   Elders: Patty Clark, Mary McCarter, Roy Shanks, Richard Turner
   Youth Advisory Delegates: Audrey Adams, Skyler Birch, Mary Cook, Denver Warren

2. **CHILDREN'S HOME/HIGHER EDUCATION** *(Edinburgh - Salon 6)*
   Chair: Rev. Thomas Sweet   **Co-Chair:** Rev. Amber Clark
   Ministers: Daniel Barkley, Roger Reid, Justin Richter, Tom Sanders, Brenda Wilson
   Elders: Matthew Blair, Burt Hager, Lorna Light, Sherry Meier, Fred Schramm, Linda Scott
   Youth Advisory Delegates: Alise Butler, Macie Clark, Lydia Cook, David Whalen

3. **JUDICIARY** *(Stirling Hall - Salon Q)*
   Chair: Rev. Dwayne Tyus   **Co-Chair:** Elder Molly Wiliams
   Ministers: Fred Fahl, Larry Green, Mike Lavender, J C McDuffee, Jen Newell
   Elders: Tom Longmire, Christy Miller, Jimmie Moore, Jim Phillips, Judith Steffen-Drake
   Youth Advisory Delegates: Carly Bell, Shelby Stover, Brenna Truitt, Austin Womack

4. **MINISTRY COUNCIL/COMMUNICATIONS/DISCIPLESHIP** *(Stirling Hall - Salon L)*
   Chair: Rev. David Lancaster   **Co-Chair:** Rev. Lisa Oliver
   Ministers: Kenny Butcher, Chris Fleming, Bruce Hamilton, Patrick Wilkerson
   Elders: Eugenia Hancock, Johnny Jenkins, Tim Odom, Cathy Remy
   Youth Advisory Delegates: Savannah Lamb, Danny Ruiz, Cameron Wilkerson

5. **MISSIONS/PASTORAL DEVELOPMENT** *(Stirling Hall - Salon M)*
   Chair: Rev. Rickey Page   **Co-Chair:** Rev. Rhonda McGowan
   Ministers: John Correa, Ramon Garcia, Josue Guerrero, J P Kessie, Wilson Lopez, Earl West
   Elders: Billy Gandy, Jack Holt, Steve Kaneaster, Patricia Laster, Dan Sager, Gene Stephens
   Youth Advisory Delegates: Calee Copely, Josh Moore, Duncan Shelton

6. **STEWARDSHIP/ELECTED OFFICERS** *(Edinburgh - Salon 5)*
   Chair: Rev. Tony Janner   **Co-Chair:** Elder Diann Phelps
   Ministers: James Condra, Andy Eppard, Linda Howell, Jerry Scott, Nathan Scott
   Elders: Hedemarrie Dussan, Ben Fields, John Koelz, Kathy Powers
   Youth Advisory Delegates: Katelyn Bayless, Alina Ferraz, Elizabeth Mahoney

7. **THEOLOGY & SOCIAL CONCERNS/UNIFICATION TASK FORCE** *(Stirling Hall - Salon P)*
   Chair: Rev. Lisa Scott   **Co-Chair:** Rev. Tommy Clark
   Ministers: Stephen Howell-Diamond, Peter Jeffrey, Susan Parker, Gary Tubb
   Elders: Pat Clark, Bill Dobbins, George Holland, Karen Lock, Bob Tucker
   Youth Advisory Delegates: Whitney Moyers, Sarah Rackley, Aldan Webb

8. **CREDENTIALS:**
   Chair: Elder Christy Miller
   Members: Reverend Lanny Johnson, Reverend Roger Reid
   Youth Advisory Delegate: Josh Moore

REFERRALS TO COMMITTEES

Referrals to the Committee on Chaplains/Historical Foundation
Page   Report
- 77   The Report of the Board of Trustees of the Historical Foundation
- 100 The Report of the Commission on Military Chaplains and Personnel

Referrals to the Committee on Children's Home/Higher Education
Page   Report
- 85   The Report of the Board of Trustees of Memphis Theological Seminary
    except Recommendation 4 which is referred to Missions/Pastoral Development
- 125 The Report of the Board of Trustees of Bethel University
- 127 The Report of the Board of Trustees of the Cumberland Presbyterian Children's Home
- 136 The Report of the Joint Committee on the Covenant Relationship between the General Assembly Corporation and Bethel University
- 140 The Report of the Joint Committee on the Covenant Relationship between the General Assembly Corporation and Cumberland Presbyterian Children's Home

Referrals to the Committee on Judiciary
Page   Report
- 103 The Report of the Permanent Committee on Judiciary
- 135 The Report of the Joint Committee on Amendments
- 145 Memorial from Andes Presbytery Regarding Gender Diversity

Referrals to the Committee on Ministry Council/Communication/Discipleship
Page   Report
- 40   The Report of the Ministry Council
    except Section I.B.5 which is referred to Stewardship/Elected Officers,
    except Section I.B.6. which is referred to Theology and Social Concerns/Unification Task Force
    except Section II.C which is referred to Missions/Pastoral Development

Referrals to the Committee on Missions/Pastoral Development
Page   Report
- 43   The Report of the Ministry Council, Section II.C.
- 85   The Report of the Board of Trustees of Memphis Theological Seminary Recommendation 4

Referrals to the Committee on Stewardship/Elected Officers
Page   Report
- 33   The Report of the Moderator
- 34   The Report of the Stated Clerk
- 41   The Report of the Ministry Council, Section I.B.5.
- 46   The Report of the Board of Stewardship, Foundation and Benefits
- 98   The Report of the Our United Outreach Committee
- 108 The Report of the Place of Meeting Committee
- 147 Line Item Budgets Submitted by General Assembly Agencies

Referrals to the Committee on Theology and Social Concerns/Unification Task Force
Page   Report
- 42   The Report of the Ministry Council, Section I.B.6
- 110 The Report of the Unified Committee on Theology and Social Concerns
- 118 The Report of the Unification Task Force

RECOMMENDATIONS AT A GLANCE

Report of the Moderator
(No Recommendations)

Report of the Stated Clerk
Page 36 Recommendation 1

Report of the Ministry Council
Page 41 Recommendation 1
42 Recommendations 2-3
43 Recommendations 4
44 Recommendations 5-7

Report of the Board of Stewardship, Foundation and Benefits
(No Recommendations)

Report of the Board of Trustees of the Historical Foundation
Page 78 Recommendations 1 - 2
79 Recommendation 3
82 Recommendations 4 - 6

Report of the Board of Trustees of Memphis Theological Seminary
Page 86 Recommendation 1
90 Recommendation 2
92 Recommendation 3
94 Recommendation 4
97 Recommendation 5

Report of the Our United Outreach Committee
Page 98 Recommendation 1

Report of the Commission on Chaplains and Military Personnel
(No Recommendations)

Report of the Permanent Judiciary Committee
Page 103 Recommendation 1

Report of the Place of Meeting Committee
(No Recommendations)

Report of the Unified Committee on Theology and Social Concerns
Page 110 Recommendations 1 - 3
Page 111 Recommendations 4-5

Report of the Unification Task Force
Page 122 Recommendations 1
Page 123 Recommendations 2

Report of the Board of Trustees of Bethel University
(No Recommendations)

Report of the Board of Trustees of the CP Children's Home
(No Recommendations)

Report of the Joint Committee on Amendments
Page 135 Recommendations 1-2

Report of the Joint Committee on Covenant Relationship Between GAC/Bethel University
Page 136 Recommendation 1

Report of the Joint Committee on Covenant Relationship Between GAC/CP Children's Home
Page 140 Recommendation 1

Memorial from Andes Presbytery
(Page 145-146)

Budgets of General Assembly Board/Agencies
(Pages 147-155)

ASSEMBLY MEETINGS AND OFFICERS

Historical Review of the Stated Meetings and Officers of:

THE CUMBERLAND PRESBYTERY, 1810-1813

Date	Place	Moderator	Clerk	Members
1810, February	Sam McAdow's House, Dickson Co., TN	Samuel McAdow	Young Ewing	3
1810, March 20	Ridge Meeting-House, Sumner Co., TN.	Samuel McAdow	Young Ewing	14
1810, October 23	Lebanon Meeting-House	Finis Ewing	Young Ewing	16
1811, March 19	Big Spring, Wilson Co., TN	Robert Bell	Young Ewing	19
1811, October 9	Ridge Meeting-House	Thomas Calhoun	David Foster	23
1812, April 7	Suggs Creek Meeting-House	Hugh Kirkpatrick	James B. Porter	28
1812, November 3	Lebanon, KY	Finis Ewing	Hugh Kirkpatrick	22
1813, April 6	Beech Meeting-House, Sumner Co. TN	Robert Bell	James B. Porter	34

THE CUMBERLAND SYNOD, 1813-1828

Date	Place	Moderator	Clerk	Members
1813, October 5	Beech Meeting-House	William McGee	Finis Ewing	13
1814, April 5	Suggs Creek	David Foster	James B. Porter	27
1815, October 17	Beech Meeting-House	William Barnett	David Foster	15
1816, October 15	Free Meeting-House, TN	Thomas Calhoun	David Foster	22
1817, October 21	Mt. Moriah, KY	Robert Donnell	Hugh Kirkpatrick	27
1818, October 20	Big Spring, TN	Finis Ewing	Robert Bell	27
1819, October 19	Suggs Creek, TN	Samuel King	William Barnett	24
1820, October 17	Russellville, KY	Thomas Calhoun	William Moore	30
1821, Third Tues. in Oct.	Russellville, KY	Minutes not recorded		
1822, October 15	Beech Meeting-House	James B. Porter	David Foster	47
1823, October 21	Russellville, KY	John Barnett	Aaron Alexander	48
1824, October 19	Cane Creek, TN	Samuel King	William Moore	68
1825, October 18	Princeton, KY	William Barnett	Hiram McDaniel	76
1826, Third Tues. in Oct.	Russellville, KY	Minutes not recorded		
1827, November 20	Russellville, KY	James S. Guthrie	Laban Jones	63
1828, October 21	Franklin, TN	Hiram A. Hunter	Richard Beard	94

THE GENERAL ASSEMBLY, 1829-

Date	Place	Moderator	Clerk	Members
1829, May 19	Princeton, KY	Thomas Calhoun	F. R. Cossitt	26
1830, May 18	Princeton, KY	James B. Porter	F. R. Cossitt	36
1831, May 17	Princeton, KY	Alex Chapman	F. R. Cossitt	34
1832, May 15	Nashville, TN	F. R. Cossitt	F. R. Cossitt	36
1833, May 21	Nashville, TN	Samuel King	F. R. Cossitt	35
1834, May 20	Nashville, TN	Thomas Calhoun	James Smith	48
1835, May 19	Princeton, KY	Sam King	James Smith	42
1836, May 17	Nashville, TN	Reuben Burrow	James Smith	43
1837, May 16	Lebanon, TN	Robert Donnell	James Smith	49
1838, May 15	Princeton, KY	Hiram A. Hunter	James Smith	47
1840, May 19	Elkton, KY	Reuben Burrow	James Smith	55
1841, May 18	Owensboro, KY	William Ralston	C. G. McPherson	56
1842, May 17	Owensboro, KY	Milton Bird	C. G. McPherson	57
1843, May 16	Owensboro, KY	A. M. Bryan	C. G. McPherson	68
1845, May 20	Lebanon, TN	Richard Beard	C. G. McPherson	95
1846, May 19	Owensboro, KY	M. H. Bone	C. G. McPherson	86
1847, May 18	Lebanon, Ohio	Hiram A. Hunter	C. G. McPherson	71
1848, May 16	Memphis, TN	Milton Bird	C. G. McPherson	100
1849, May 16	Princeton, KY	John L. Smith	C. G. McPherson	75
1850, May 21	Clarksville, TN	Reuben Burrow	Milton Bird	102
1851, May 20	Pittsburgh, PA	Milton Bird	Milton Bird	71
1852, May 18	Nashville, TN	David Lowry	Milton Bird	107
1853, May 17	Princeton, KY	H. S. Porter	Milton Bird	108
1854, May 16	Memphis, TN	Isaac Shook	Milton Bird	112
1855, May 15	Lebanon, TN	M. H. Bone	Milton Bird	101
1856, May 15	Louisville, KY	Milton Bird	Milton Bird	99
1857, May 21	Lexington, MO	Carson P. Reed	Milton Bird	106
1858, May 20	Huntsville, AL	Felix Johnson	Milton Bird	124
1859, May 19	Evansville, IN	T. B. Wilson	Milton Bird	131
1860, May 17	Nashville, TN	S. G. Burney	Milton Bird	168
1861, May 16	St. Louis, MO	A. E. Cooper	Milton Bird	51
1862, May 15	Owensboro, KY	P. G. Rea	Milton Bird	58
1863, May 21	Alton, IL	Milton Bird	Milton Bird	73
1864, May 19	Lebanon, OH	Jesse Anderson	Milton Bird	65
1865, May 18	Evansville, IN	Hiram Douglas	Milton Bird	78
1866, May 17	Owensboro, KY	Richard Beard	Milton Bird	155
1867, May 16	Memphis, TN	J. B. Mitchell	Milton Bird	176
1868, May 21	Lincoln, IL	G. W. Mitchell	Milton Bird	184
1869, May 20	Murfreesboro, TN	S. T. Anderson	Milton Bird	173
1870, May 19	Warrensburg, MO	J. C. Provine	Milton Bird	167

Date	Place	Moderator	Clerk	Members
1871, May 18	Nashville, TN	J. B. Logan	Milton Bird	173
1872, May 16	Evansville, IN	C. H. Bell	Milton Bird	182
1873, May 15	Huntsville, AL	J. W. Poindexter	John Frizzell	165
1874, May 21	Springfield, MO	T. C. Blake	John Frizzell	185
1875, May 20	Jefferson, TX	W. S. Campbell	John Frizzell	169
1876, May 18	Bowling Green, KY	J. M. Gill	John Frizzell	184
1877, May 17	Lincoln, IL	A. B. Miller	John Frizzell	171
1878, May 16	Lebanon, TN	D. E. Bushnell	John Frizzell	205
1879, May 15	Memphis, TN	J. S. Grider	John Frizzell	143
1880, May 20	Evansville, IN	A. Templeton	John Frizzell	194
1881, May 19	Austin, TX	W. J. Darby	John Frizzell	187
1882, May 18	Huntsville, AL	S. H. Buchanan	John Frizzell	188
1883, May 17	Nashville, TN	A. J. McGlumphey	T. C. Blake	204
1884, May 15	McKeesport, PA	John Frizzell	T. C. Blake	148
1885, May 21	Bentonville, AR	G. T. Stainback	T. C. Blake	185
1886, May 20	Sedalia, MO	E. B. Crisman	T. C. Blake	193
1887, May 19	Covington, OH	Nathan Green	T. C. Blake	187
1888, May 17	Waco, TX	W. H. Black	T. C. Blake	217
1889, May 16	Kansas City, MO	J. M. Hubbert	T. C. Blake	217
1890, May 15	Union City, TN	E. G. McLean	T. C. Blake	220
1891, May 21	Owensboro, KY	E. F. Beard	T. C. Blake	213
1892, May 19	Memphis, TN	W. T. Danley	T. C. Blake	229
1893, May 18	Little Rock, AR	W. S. Ferguson	T. C. Blake	226
1894, May 17	Eugene, OR	F. R. Earle	T. C. Blake	167
1895, May 16	Meridian, MS	M. B. DeWitt	T. C. Blake	208
1896, May 21	Birmingham, AL	A. W. Hawkins	J. M. Hubbert	200
1897, May 20	Chicago, IL	H. S. Williams	J. M. Hubbert	224
1898, May 19	Marshall, MO	H. H. Norman	J. M. Hubbert	221
1899, May 18	Denver, CO	J. M. Halsell	J. M. Hubbert	181
1900, May 17	Chattanooga, TN	H. C. Bird	J. M. Hubbert	230
1901, May 16	West Point, MS	E. E. Morris	J. M. Hubbert	226
1902, May 15	Springfield, MO	S. M. Templeton	J. M. Hubbert	255
1903, May 21	Nashville, TN	R. M. Tinnon	J. M. Hubbert	247
1904, May 19	Dallas, TX	W. E. Settle	J. M. Hubbert	251
1905, May 18	Fresno, CA	J. B. Hail	J. M. Hubbert	249
1906, May 17	Decatur, IL	Ira Landrith	J. M. Hubbert	279
1906, May 24	Decatur, IL	J. L. Hudgins	T. H. Padgett	106
1907, May 17	Dickson, TN	A. N. Eshman	J. L. Goodknight	140
1908, May 21	Corsicana, TX	F. H. Prendergast	J. L. Goodknight	136
1909, May 20	Bentonville, AR	J. T. Barbee	J. L. Goodknight	142
1910, May 19	Dickson, TN	J. H. Fussell	J. L. Goodknight	144
1911, May 18	Evansville, IN	J. W. Duvall	J. L. Goodknight	109
1912, May 16	Warrensburg, MO	J. D. Lewis	J. L. Goodknight	119
1913, May 15	Bowling Green, KY	J. H. Milholland	J. L. Goodknight	112
1914, May 21	Wagoner, OK	F. A. Brown	J. L. Goodknight	105
1915, May 20	Memphis, TN	William Clark	D. W. Fooks	116
1916, May 18	Birmingham, AL	J. L. Price	D. W. Fooks	125
1917, May 17	Lincoln, IL	F. A. Seagle	D. W. Fooks	102
1918, May 16	Dallas, TX	C. H. Walton	D. W. Fooks	117
1919, May 15	Fayetteville, AR	J. H. Zwingle	D. W. Fooks	101
1920, May 15	McKenzie, TN	J. E. Cortner	D. W. Fooks	123
1921, May 19	Greenfield, MO	Judge John B. Tally	D. W. Fooks	108
1922, May 18	Greeneville, TN	Hugh S. McCord	D. W. Fooks	102
1923, May 17	Fairfield, IL	P. F. Johnson, D. D.	D. W. Fooks	105
1924, May 15	Austin, TX	D. M. McAnulty	D. W. Fooks	93
1925, May 21	Nashville, TN	W. E. Morrow	D. W. Fooks	114
1926, May 20	Columbus, MS	I. K. Floyd	D. W. Fooks	111
1927, May 19	Lakeland, FL	T. A. DeVore	D. W. Fooks	97
1928, May 21	Jackson, TN	J. L. Hudgins	D. W. Fooks	97
1929, May 16	Princeton, KY	H. C. Walton	D. W. Fooks	98
1930, May 15	Olney, TX	O. A. Barbee	D. W. Fooks	92
1931, May 21	Evansville, IN	J. L. Elliot	D. W. Fooks	98
1932, May 19	Chattanooga, TN	G. G. Halliburton	D. W. Fooks	104
1933, June 14	Memphis, TN	W. B. Cunningham	D. W. Fooks	94
1934, June 14	Springfield, MO	A. C. DeForest	D. W. Fooks	103
1935, June 13	McKenzie, TN	C. A. Davis	D. W. Fooks	104
1936, June 18	San Antonio, TX	E. K. Reagin	D. W. Fooks	100
1937, June 16	Knoxville, TN	George E. Coleman	D. W. Fooks	109
1938, June 16	Russellville, AR	D. D. Dowell	D. W. Fooks	117
1939, June 15	Marshall, MO	E. R. Ramer	D. W. Fooks	126
1940, June 13	Cookeville, TN	Keith T. Postlethwaite	D. W. Fooks	116
1941, June 19	Denton, TX	L. L. Thomas	D. W. Fooks	120
1942, June 18	McKenzie, TN	George W. Burroughs	D. W. Fooks	108
1943, June 17	Paducah, KY	A. A. Collins	D. W. Fooks	94
1944, June 15	Bowling Green, KY	I. M. Vaughn	D. W. Fooks	94
1945, May 31	Lewisburg, TN	S. T. Byars	Wayne Wiman	103
1946, June 13	Birmingham, AL	C. R. Matlock	Wayne Wiman	105
1947, June 12	Knoxville, TN	Morris Pepper	Wayne Wiman	108

Date	Place	Moderator	Clerk	Members
1948, June 17	Nashville, TN	Paul F. Brown	Wayne Wiman	105
1949, June 16	Muskogee, OK	Blake Warren	Wayne Wiman	109
1950, June 15	Los Angeles, CA	L. P. Turnbow	Wayne Wiman	98
1951, June 14	Longview, TX	John E. Gardner	Wayne Wiman	105
1952, June 12	Memphis, TN	Emery A. Newman	Wayne Wiman	120
1953, June 18	Gadsden, AL	Charles L. Lehning, Jr.	Wayne Wiman	107
1954, June 17	Dyersburg, TN	John S. Smith	Wayne Wiman	124
1955, June 16	Lubbock, TX	Ernest C. Cross	Shaw Scates	118
1956, June 21	Cookeville, TN	Hubert Morrow	Shaw Scates	118
1957, June 21	Evansville, IN	William T. Ingram, Jr.	Shaw Scates	119
1958, June 18	Birmingham, AL	Wayne Wiman	Shaw Scates	116
1959, June 17	Springfield, MO	Virgil T. Weeks	Shaw Scates	120
1960, June 15	Nashville, TN	Arleigh G. Matlock	Shaw Scates	130
1961, June 21	Florence, AL	Ollie W. McClung	Shaw Scates	126
1962, June 20	Little Rock, AR	Eugene L. Warren	Shaw Scates	126
1963, June 19	Austin, TX	Franklin Chesnut	Shaw Scates	117
1964, June 17	Chattanooga, TN	Vaughn Fults	Shaw Scates	123
1965, June 16	San Francisco, CA	Thomas Forester	Shaw Scates	114
1966, June 15	Memphis, TN	John W. Sparks	Shaw Scates	124
1967, June 21	Paducah, KY	Raymon Burroughs	Shaw Scates	123
1968, June 19	Oklahoma City, OK	Loyce S. Estes	Shaw Scates	115
1969, June 18	San Antonio, TX	J. David Hester	Shaw Scates	116
1970, June 17	Knoxville, TN	L. C. Waddle	Shaw Scates	116
1971, June 16	Jackson, TN	E. Thach Shauf	Shaw Scates	116
1972, June 19	Kansas City, MO	Claude D. Gilbert	Shaw Scates	110
1973, June 18	Ft. Worth, TX	Thomas H. Campbell	Shaw Scates	101
1974, June 17	Bowling Green, KY	David A. Brown	Shaw Scates	116
1975, June 16	McKenzie, TN	Roy E. Blakeburn	Shaw Scates	120
1976, June 21	Tulsa, OK	Hubert W. Covington	T. V. Warnick	115
1977, June 30	Tampa, FL	Fred W. Bryson	T. V. Warnick	122
1978, June 19	McKenzie, TN	Jose Fajardo	T. V. Warnick	120
1979, June 18	Albuquerque, NM	James C. Gilbert	T. V. Warnick	126
1980, June 16	Evansville, IN	Robert L. Hull	T. V. Warnick	126
1981, June 15	Denton, TX	W. Jean Richardson	T. V. Warnick	126
1982, June 21	Owensboro, KY	W. A. Rawlins	T. V. Warnick	124
1983, June 20	Birmingham, AL	Robert G. Forester	T. V. Warnick	127
1984, June 11	Chattanooga, TN	C. Ray Dobbins	T. V. Warnick	125
1985, June 17	Lexington, KY	Virgil H. Todd	Roy E. Blakeburn	125
1986, June 23	Odessa, TX	James W. Knight	Roy E. Blakeburn	125
1987, June 15	Louisville, KY	Wilbur S. Wood	Roy E. Blakeburn	125
1988, June 6	Tulsa, OK	Beverly St. John	Robert Prosser	119
1989, June 12	Knoxville, TN	William Rustenhaven, Jr.	Robert Prosser	96
1990, June 25	Ft. Worth, TX	Thomas D. Campbell	Robert Prosser	88
1991, June 24	Paducah, KY	Floyd T. Hensley, Jr.	Robert Prosser	106
1992, June 22	Jackson, TN	John David Hall	Robert Prosser	102
1993, June 21	Little Rock, AR	Robert M. Shelton	Robert Prosser	100
1994, June 20	Albuquerque, NM	Donald C. Alexander	Robert Prosser	100
1995, June 19	Nashville, TN	Clinton O. Buck	Robert Prosser	102
1996, June 17	Huntsville, AL	Merlyn A. Alexander	Robert Prosser	95
1997, April 11	Nashville, TN	Merlyn A. Alexander	Robert Prosser	80
1997, June 16	Louisville, KY	W. Lewis Wynn	Robert Prosser	95
1998, June 15	Chattanooga, TN	Masaharu Asayama	Robert Prosser	97
1999, June 21	Memphis, TN	Gwendolyn Roddye	Marjorie Shannon	96
2000, June 19	Bowling Green, KY	Bob G. Roberts	Robert D. Rush	96
2001, June 18	Odessa, TX	Randolph Jacob	Robert D. Rush	88
2002, June 17	Paducah, KY	Bert L. Owen	Robert D. Rush	95
2003, June 23	Knoxville, TN	Charles McCaskey	Robert D. Rush	96
2004, June 21	Irving, TX	Edward G. Sims	Robert D. Rush	87
2005, June 27	Franklin, TN	Linda H. Glenn	Robert D. Rush	91
2006, June 18	Birmingham, AL	Donald Hubbard	Robert D. Rush	87
2007, June 18	Hot Springs, AR	Frank Ward	Robert D. Rush	84
2007, December 7	Nashville, TN	Frank Ward	Robert D. Rush	62
2008, June 7	Japan	Jonathan Clark	Robert D. Rush	82
2009, June 15	Memphis, TN	Sam Suddarth	Robert D. Rush	86
2010, June 13	Dickson, TN	Boyce Wallace	Robert D. Rush	88
2011, June 20	Springfield, MO	Don M. Tabor	Michael Sharpe	82
2012, June 18	Florence, AL	Robert D. Rush	Michael Sharpe	90
2013, June 17	Murfreesboro, TN	Forest Prosser	Michael Sharpe	93
2014, June 16	Chattanooga, TN	Lisa Anderson	Michael Sharpe	86
2015, June 20	Colombia, South America	Michele Gentry	Michael Sharpe	91
2016, June 20	Nashville, Tennessee	Dwayne Tyus	Michael Sharpe	84
2017, June 19	Palm Harbor, Florida	David Lancaster	Michael Sharpe	77

BYLAWS

Bylaws of the Cumberland Presbyterian Church General Assembly Corporation
A Non-profit Religious Corporation Organized and Existing
Under the Laws of the State of Tennessee

ARTICLE 1-RELIGIOUS CORPORATION

1.01 Purpose. The Cumberland Presbyterian Church is a spiritual body comprised of a portion of the universal body of believers confessing Jesus Christ as Lord and Savior. As an ecclesiastical body, the Cumberland Presbyterian Church is a connectional Church which includes all of the judicatories of the Church. The highest judicatory of this ecclesiastical body is the General Assembly of the Cumberland Presbyterian Church (referred to in these Bylaws as "the Church"). This corporation has been formed to serve and support the Church by holding real and personal property of the Church, employing staff to serve the Church, and performing other secular and legal functions.

1.02 Ecclesiastical Authority Not Limited by Corporate Powers. The enumeration in state statutes or these Bylaws of specific powers which may be exercised by the Commissioners, Board of Directors, or the officers of the corporation when acting in their corporate capacity shall not limit their authority when acting in their ecclesiastical capacity for the Church.

1.03 Church Authorities. The doctrine of the Cumberland Presbyterian Church, expressed in the Confession of Faith, Constitution, Rules of Discipline, and Rules of Order of the Cumberland Presbyterian Church, shall have precedence over any inconsistent provision of these Bylaws.

ARTICLE 2-TERMINOLOGY

2.01 Delegates. The corporation's delegates shall be called "Commissioners."
2.02 General Assembly. A meeting of the Commissioners shall be called a "General Assembly."
2.03 President. The corporation's president shall be called the "Stated Clerk."
2.04 Ecumenical Representative. A person who is not a member of a Cumberland Presbyterian Chuch or presbytery but who supports the mission of a denominational entity and is elected to a term of service on that entity shall be called an "Ecumenical Representative."

ARTICLE 3-OFFICES

3.01 Location. The principal office of the corporation in the State of Tennessee shall be located in Shelby County, Tennessee. The corporation may have such other offices, either within or outside the State of Tennessee, as the General Assembly or the Board of Directors may direct from time to time.

ARTICLE 4–COMMISSIONERS

4.01 Commissioners. The Commissioners shall have the powers and authority described in the corporation's charter and these Bylaws. Included among them are the power to:

   a. Elect the elected members of the Board of Directors.
   b. Approve any amendment to the corporation's charter except an amendment to delete the names of the original directors; to change the name of the registered agent, or to change the address of the registered office;
   c. Elect and remove the Moderator, Stated Clerk, and the Engrossing Clerk.
   d. Fill vacancies on the corporation's various boards, agencies and committees, and on the boards of any subsidiaries;
   e. Approve the merger or dissolution of the corporation, or the sale of substantially all of the corporation's assets; and
   f. Transact such other business of the corporation as may properly come before any meeting of the Commissioners.

4.02 Selection of Commissioners: Number and Qualifications. Commissioners shall be selected by the presbyteries. A presbytery shall be entitled to send one minister and one elder for each 1,000, or fraction thereof, active members (including ordained clergy) in the presbytery. Each elder selected as a Commissioner must be serving as a member of a session at the time of the General Assembly at which he or she will serve. A Commissioner shall continue to serve until no longer qualified or until his or her successor is selected and qualified. The clerk of each presbytery shall certify the presbytery's duly elected commissioners, youth advisory delegates, and alternates to the Stated Clerk in a manner provided by the Stated Clerk.

4.03 Youth Advisory Delegates. Each presbytery may select not more than two youth advisory delegates who should be from 15 through 19 years of age. Advisory delegates may serve as members with full rights on General Assembly committees, but shall not vote as Commissioners.

4.04 Annual Meeting and Notice. The Commissioners shall meet annually at a date and time established by the General Assembly. The meeting shall be continued from day to day until adjournment. Written notice of the meeting shall be mailed to the stated clerks of all presbyteries and published in the Cumberland Presbyterian at least sixty (60) days prior to the proposed meeting.

4.05 Special Meetings and Notice. The Moderator, or in case of the Moderator's absence, death, or inability to act, the Stated Clerk, may with the written concurrence or at the written request of twenty Commissioners, ten of whom shall be ministers and ten elders, representing at least five presbyteries, call a special meeting of the Commissioners. If warranted by a change of circumstances, a called special meeting may be cancelled by the Moderator, or in case of the Moderator's absence, death, or inability to act, the Stated Clerk, with the written concurrence of at least ten of the Commissioners who requested or concurred in the call of the special meeting. Written notice of any special meeting shall be mailed to the stated clerks of all presbyteries, to all Commissioners, and to their alternates at least sixty (60) days prior to the meeting. The notice shall specify the particular business of the special meeting, and no other business shall be transacted.

4.06 Place of Meeting. The General Assembly may designate any place within or outside the state of Tennessee as the place for an annual meeting. If the Commissioners fail to designate a place for an annual meeting, or if an emergency requires the place to be changed, the Board of Directors may designate a place for the annual meeting. The Moderator or the Stated Clerk, as the case may be, when calling a special meeting shall designate the time and place of the meeting in the notice of the meeting.

4.07 Quorum. Any twenty or more Commissioners, of whom at least ten are ministers and ten elders, entitled to vote shall constitute a quorum at any General Assembly. When a quorum is once present to organize a meeting, business may continue to be conducted and votes taken despite the subsequent withdrawal of any Commissioner. A meeting may be adjourned despite the absence of a quorum.

4.08 Voting. Every Commissioner shall be entitled to one vote, which must be cast by the Commissioner in person; no proxies are permitted. All corporate actions shall be taken by majority vote except as otherwise provided by the corporation's parliamentary authority. Voting for members of the Board of Directors shall be non-cumulative.

ARTICLE 5-BOARD OF DIRECTORS

5.01 Authority. The Board of Directors shall manage the business and affairs of the corporation except for any power or authority which is reserved to the Commissioners or delegated to any other agency of the corporation. The Board of Directors is authorized to amend the corporation's charter only to delete the names of the original directors; to change the name of the registered agent; or to change the address of the registered office.

5.02 Composition of the Board of Directors. The Board of Directors shall consist of seven (7) members, who shall be the directors of the corporation. Six (6) members shall be elected by the Commissioners and the Stated Clerk shall serve by virtue of office. All members, whether elected or ex officio, shall have all of the privileges of office.

5.03 Qualification for Election. Each person elected to the Board of Directors shall be a natural person who is a person in good standing of a presbytery or local Cumberland Presbyterian Church. No two directors shall be from the same presbytery, provided, however, that a director who moves from one presbytery to another may continue to serve until the expiration of his or her term of office.

5.04 Election and Tenure. The elected members of the Board of Directors shall serve terms of three (3) years each. The terms shall be staggered so that two (2) directors shall be elected each year. Each person elected shall serve until his or her successor has been elected and qualified.

5.05 Action of Board in Emergency or By Default. If, for any reason, the General Assembly fails to fill a vacancy on the Board of Directors at the next General Assembly, then the Board of Directors may fill the vacancy by majority vote of the members then in office.

5.06 Meetings. The Board of Directors shall meet annually or more often at such time and place as it may set. Special meetings may be called by or at the request of the Stated Clerk or any three directors at any place, either within or outside the state of Tennessee.

5.07 Notice. Notice of any meeting shall be given at least five (5) days before the date of the meeting, except that notice by mail shall be given at least ten (10) days before the date of the meeting. Notice may be communicated in person; by telephone, fax, or electronic mail; or by first class mail or courier. Except as specifically provided by these Bylaws, neither the business to be transacted at nor the purpose of any special or regular meeting of the Board of Directors need be specified in the notice of the meeting.

5.08 Notice of Special Actions. Any meeting of the Board of Directors at which one or more of the following actions shall be considered must be preceded by seven (7) days written notice to each member that the matter will be voted upon, unless notice has been waived. Actions requiring such notice are: amendment or restatement of the corporate charter; approval of a plan of merger for the corporation; sale of all or substantially all of the corporation's assets; and dissolution of the corporation.

5.09 Officers of the Board of Directors. The Board of Directors may have such officers of the board as it may deem appropriate.

5.10 Quorum and Voting. A majority of the members shall constitute a quorum for the transaction of business at any meeting of the Board of Directors. When a quorum is once present to organize a meeting, it is not broken by the subsequent withdrawal of any of those present. A meeting may be adjourned despite the lack of a quorum. The vote of a majority of the members present at a meeting at which a quorum is present shall be the act of the Board of Directors unless a greater vote is specifically required by the Charter or the Bylaws.

5.11 Conference Meetings. Any or all the members of the Board of Directors or any committee designated by it may meet by means of conference telephone or similar communications equipment which permits all persons participating in the meeting to hear each other simultaneously. A member who participates in a meeting by such means is deemed to be present in person at the meeting.

5.12 Action by Written Consent. Whenever the members of the Board of Directors are required or permitted to take any action by vote, such action may be taken without a meeting on written consent, setting forth the action so taken and signed by all of the members entitled to vote,

5.13 Emergency Actions. If the Board of Directors determines by a vote of three-fourths of all its members that an emergency exists of such magnitude as to threaten the work of the whole Church, or of all boards and other agencies of the Church, and that the emergency requires action before the next meeting of the General Assembly, then the Board of Directors shall exercise the powers of the Commissioners in such emergency.

5.14 Compensation. Members of the Board of Directors shall receive no compensation in their capacity as members of the Board of Directors. Members may be paid their expenses, if any, of attendance at each meeting of the Board of Directors.

5.15 Removal of Directors. An elected member of the Board of Directors may be removed by the Commissioners for misfeasance or if he or she is no longer qualified to be elected to the Board of Directors.

ARTICLE 6-WAIVER OF NOTICE

6.01 Written Waiver. Any notice required to be given to any member of the Board of Directors or a Commissioner under these Bylaws, the Charter, or the laws of Tennessee may be waived. The waiver shall be in writing, signed (either before or after the event requiring notice) by the person entitled to the notice, and delivered to the corporation.

6.02 Waiver by Attendance. The attendance of a member of the Board of Directors or a Commissioner at any meeting shall constitute a waiver of notice of the meeting, unless the person attends a meeting for the express purpose of objecting to the transaction of any business because the meeting was not properly called or convened.

ARTICLE 7-MODERATOR AND VICE-MODERATOR

7.01 Nomination and Election. At the beginning of each annual meeting the General Assembly shall elect a Commissioner to serve as Moderator until the next annual meeting. Nominations for Moderator shall come from the floor. One nominating speech, not to exceed ten minutes, shall be permitted on behalf of each nominee. If there is more than one nominee, the election shall be conducted by written ballot. A committee appointed and supervised by the Stated Clerk shall receive the ballots, count them, and certify the election. If no nominee receives a majority of the votes cast, a run-off election shall be conducted. Only those leading nominees who together received a majority of the votes cast on the preceding ballot shall be included in the run-off election.

7.02 Nature of Office. The Moderator of the General Assembly is the ecclesiastical head of the Cumberland Presbyterian Church during the tenure of the office and a spiritual representative of the Cumberland Presbyterian Church wherever God leads. The Moderator receives a precious gift and great opportunity for service in the Church: the freedom to go anywhere and to listen to the mind, heart and spirit of the denomination and to speak with and to the Church. The office of Moderator has great honor and respect, and the person elected to the Office is a priest, prophet, and pastor of the Church at large. The Moderator prays with and for the work of the Spirit of God in the life of the denomination at every opportunity. The Moderator participates in the life and work of the Church as far as possible, and pays particular attention to ecumenical relations, especially with the Cumberland Presbyterian Church in America. Judicatories, congregations, and others are urged to invite the Moderator, and the Moderator is encouraged to attend meetings of Church entities and judicatories to observe the life and work of the Church at every level.

7.03 Duties and Privileges of Office.
- a. The Moderator shall preside at all meetings of the General Assembly.
- b. The Moderator shall appoint, with the consent of the General Assembly, such special committees as are needed;
- c. The Moderator shall serve as chairperson of the General Assembly Program Committee and as a member of the Place of Meeting Committee;
- d. The Moderator shall perform such other duties as may be assigned by the General Assembly.
- e. The Moderator shall serve as an advisory member of the Ministry Council during tenure in office and for the year following tenure.
- f. The Moderator shall observe the places and times God is calling the Church to service, assess the need for a Denominational response to God's call, and report items that concern the General Assembly.
- g. The Moderator shall wear the official cross and stoles of office during the term of office.

7.04 Expenses of Office. Any allowance budgeted by the General Assembly to offset the expenses of the Moderator shall be administered by the Stated Clerk. Persons issuing an invitation to the Moderator are encouraged to agree in advance on arrangements for the payment of travel expenses. Upon the Moderator's retirement from office, a gavel and a replica of the Moderator's cross shall be presented to the Moderator.

7.05 Vice-Moderator. The General Assembly shall elect a Vice-Moderator in like manner. The Vice-Moderator shall perform such duties as may be assigned by the Moderator of the General Assembly and perform the duties of the Moderator in the event of the Moderator's disability or absence from office for any reason.

7.06 Removal. The Moderator or Vice-Moderator may be removed by the General Assembly whenever in its judgment the removal would serve the best interests of the corporation.

ARTICLE 8-STATED CLERK

8.01 President. The Stated Clerk is the principal executive officer of the corporation and shall also have the titles of "president" and "treasurer".

8.02 Nomination and Election. The Nominating Committee may nominate the serving Stated Clerk for re-election. If the Nominating Committee declines to nominate the serving Stated Clerk for re-election, or if the Stated Clerk has vacated the office, resigned, or declined to be re-nominated, then the Corporate Board shall conduct a search for and nominate a candidate to the General Assembly. In either event, further nominations may be made by the Commissioners. The Commissioners shall elect the Stated Clerk by majority vote.

8.03 Term of Office. The Stated Clerk shall be elected to a term of four (4) years. The regular term of office begins on January 1 and ends on December 31. There is no limit on the number of terms which may be served by an individual Stated Clerk.

8.04 Duties. The Stated Clerk shall be concerned with the spiritual life of the Church and with maintaining and strengthening a united witness for the Church. The Stated Clerk shall also generally supervise and control the business affairs of the corporation and see that all orders and resolutions of the General Assembly are carried into effect. In fulfillment of these duties, the Stated Clerk shall:
- 01. Have responsibility to provide for the orderly governance of the Church in accordance with the Constitution, Rules of Order and Rules of Discipline.
- 02. Maintain records of the corporation and respond to requests for official records of General Assembly actions and interpretations of its actions.

03. Represent the Church when an official of the General Assembly is needed.
04. Represent the Cumberland Presbyterian Church in establishing and maintaining relations with other Churches, particulary those of the Presbyterian and Reformed tradition, and in addressing common concerns.
05. Sign all documents on behalf of the corporation or the Cumberland Presbyterian Church.
06. Represent the corporation or the Church in litigation or other legal matters affecting the Cumberland Presbyterian Church, including the selection and employment of legal counsel.
07. Make suitable arrangements for General Assembly meetings, including researching possible meeting sites, contracting for facilities, and arranging space for committee meetings and sessions of the General Assembly;
08. Provide for printing and other communication needs of the General Assembly while in session.
09. Call meetings of the Place of Meeting Committee and the Program Committee.
10. Prepare and distribute an information form to be completed by Commissioners for the Moderator's use in making committee appointments.
11. Advise the Moderator in the appointment of committees.
12. In consultation with the Moderator, refer all matters to come before the next General Assembly; and provide copies of all such referrals to the Commissioners and advisory delegates before the General Assembly convenes.
13. Prepare and distribute preliminary minutes and an agenda for General Assembly meetings which shall provide time for the consideration of any appropriate business, including memorials from a judicatory or denominational entity delivered to the Stated Clerk in writing by April 30.
14. Supervise the recording and publication of minutes and a summary of actions taken by each General Assembly.
15. Make copies of General Assembly minutes available to ordained ministers, licentiates, candidates, commissioners, clerks of sessions, members of denominational entities, schools of the Church, synod, and presbytery clerks, to the Stated Clerk's exchanges and other interested persons in order to encourage lower judicatories and persons in the Church to implement the actions of the General Assembly.
16. File the minutes of each General Assembly with the Historical Foundation as a permanent record.
17. Maintain and update annually the Digest of the General Assembly actions.
18. Represent the Church at large on the Ministry Council.
19. Provide support services for the Moderator and all denominational entities.
20. Receive and make any appropriate response to communications to the Cumberland Presbyterian Church or General Assembly.
21. Maintain a name and address file on congregations, session clerks, pastors, and other leadership of congregations with statistical information about congregations, presbyteries, and synods.
22. Solicit, receive, publish, and disseminate annual reports from churches.
23. Review reports by denominational entities and assist them in complying with correct reporting and budgeting procedures and in avoiding duplication of work.
24. Hold, report annually, and distribute as authorized by the General Assembly or the Ministry Council the Contingency Fund and all other General Assembly Funds not entrusted to the care of a denominational entity.
25. Call the Judiciary Committee into session or by other means secure the advice of the committee on appropriate matters.
26. Communicate with presbyteries and synods on behalf of the General Assembly and attend their meetings from time to time.
27. Provide training for presbytery and synod clerks and orientations for General Assembly commissioners.
28. Generally perform duties as are prescribed in the Constitution or directed by the General Assembly.

8.05 Removal. The Stated Clerk may be removed by the General Assembly whenever in its judgment the removal would serve the best interests of the corporation.

ARTICLE 9-OTHER OFFICERS

9.01 Secretary. The chief executive officer of the Ministry Council shall, by virtue of office, be the secretary of the corporation, and shall in general perform all duties incident to the office of secretary.

9.02 Engrossing Clerk. The Engrossing Clerk shall be elected by the General Assembly to a term of four (4) years. The regular term of office begins on January 1 and ends on December 31. There is no limit on the number of terms which may be served by an individual Engrossing Clerk. The Engrossing Clerk shall serve as Stated Clerk pro tempore during the meeting of the General Assembly in the event the Stated Clerk is absent or unable to serve. The Engrossing Clerk shall perform such other duties as may from time to time be prescribed by the Board of Directors or the General Assembly.

9.03 Additional Officers. The corporation may have such additional officers as it may from time to time find necessary or appropriate.

ARTICLE 10-ORGANIZATION AND RELATIONSHIPS

10.01 Generally. The following are denominational entities related to the Cumberland Presbyterian Church:

01. Subsidiary corporations: Board of Stewardship, Foundation and Benefits of the Cumberland Presbyterian Church; Memphis Theological Seminary of the Cumberland Presbyterian Church; Ministry Council of the Cumberland Presbyterian Church.
02. Related corporations: Bethel University; Cumberland Presbyterian Children's Home; Historical Foundation of the Cumberland Presbyterian Church and the Cumberland Presbyterian Church in America.
03. Commissions: Chaplains and Military Personnel.
04. Committees: Committee on Nominations; Joint Committee on Amendments; Judiciary, Our United Outreach; Place of Meeting Committee; Program Committee; Unified Committee on Theology and Social Concerns.

10.02 Election and Tenure. The following qualifications and rules relate to service on any denominational entity.

01. Unless elected as an Ecumenical Representative, no person shall be qualified to serve except a member in good standing in a presbytery or local congregation of the Cumberland Presbyterian Church.
02. No person who is employed in an executive capacity including Chief Executive, Vice-President, Team Leader, Director, or equivalent in the Cumberland Presbyterian Church is eligible to serve on a denominational entity. No employee of a denominational entity is eligible for service on the same denominational entity.
03. Each person shall be elected for a term of three years unless elected to fill the remainder of an unexpired term. However, if a person elected to serve on a denominational entity where residence in a particular synod is a qualification for election shall move to another synod while in office, the term to which he or she was elected shall terminate at the close of the next meeting of the General Assembly. When nominating persons to boards and agencies, priority consideration be given to persons whose individual life and/or church involvement demonstrates a commitment to support Our United Outreach.
04. Members of the Committee on Nominations may not be elected to a consecutive term. All other persons may serve up to three consecutive terms for a total not to exceed nine years in office.
05. A Cumberland Presbyterian who has served on any entity is not eligible to serve on the same entity (except for an authorized consecutive term) until at least two (2) years have elapsed since the conclusion of the previous service.
06. A Cumberland Presbyterian who is serving on any entity is not eligible to serve on another entity until at least one (1) year has elapsed since the conclusion of the previous service.
07. An Ecumenical Representative who is serving or has served on any entity is not eligible to serve on any other entity (except for an authorized consecutive term on the same entity) until at least one (1) year has elapsed since the conclusion of the previous service.

10.03 Resignation or Removal.

01. Any person serving on a denominational entity who is no longer qualified or eligible

to serve shall be deemed to have resigned.
- 02. Any person serving on an incorporated denominational entity may resign by delivering written notice of resignation to the secretary or an executive officer of the denominational entity, who shall promptly report the resignation to the Stated Clerk. Any person serving on an unincorporated denominational entity may resign by delivering written notice of resignation to the Stated Clerk. A resignation is effective when delivered unless some other effective date is specified in the written resignation.
- 03. No member who continues to meet the standard requirements for election or appointment to any denominational entity shall be removed from office except for misfeasance. Removal of a person elected by the General Assembly shall be by vote of the General Assembly.

10.04 Board of Stewardship, Foundation and Benefits. The corporation shall elect the eleven (11) directors of the Board of Stewardship as provided in its charter.

10.05 Cumberland Presbyterian Children's Home. The corporation shall elect the fifteen (15) directors of Children's Home as provided in its corporate articles. The corporation shall elect the directors in such a manner that, immediately following any election, there shall be at least six (6) directors who are members of ecumenical partners of the Children's Home.

10.06 Historical Foundation. The corporation shall elect six (6) of the twelve (12) directors of the Historical Foundation as provided in its charter. The corporation shall elect the directors of the Historical Foundation in such a manner that, immediately following any election, there shall be at least one (1) member from each synod and no person shall be elected if the election would cause two directors from the same presbytery to be serving simultaneously. The remaining six (6) directors shall be elected by the Cumberland Presbyterian Church in America.

10.07 Memphis Theological Seminary. The corporation shall elect the twenty-four (24) directors of Memphis Theological Seminary as provided in its charter. The corporation shall elect the directors in such a manner that, immediately following any election, there shall be at least eleven (11) directors who are members of ecumenical partners of the Seminary.

10.08 Ministry Council.
- 01. The corporation shall elect the fifteen (15) directors of the Ministry Council as provided in its charter.
- 02. The corporation shall elect the directors of the Ministry Council in such a manner that immediately following any election, there shall be three (3) directors from each synod; at least six (6) but no more than nine (9) directors who are ordained clergy; and no more than nine (9) directors of the same gender.
- 03. The Stated Clerk, Moderator, and Immediate Past Moderator shall be designated as Advisory Members to the board of directors of the Ministry Council. In addition, the corporation shall elect three (3) Youth Advisory Members who shall be between the ages of 15 – 17 be elected for 1-year terms, with eligibility for re-election for one additional term.

10.09 Commission on Chaplains and Military Personnel. The commission shall consist of three (3) members elected by the corporation.

ARTICLE 11-COMMITTEES

11.01 General. The corporation shall have the committees provided for in these Bylaws and such other standing or special committees as the General Assembly may create from time to time. Except as otherwise provided in these Bylaws, the Moderator, in consultation with the Stated Clerk, shall appoint all committees.

11.02 Committees of Commissioners and Youth Advisory Delegates. Prior to each General Assembly, the Moderator, in consultation with the Stated Clerk, shall organize the Commissioners and Youth Advisory Delegates into the following committees: Chaplains/Missions/Pastoral Development, Children's Home/Historical Foundation, Higher Education, Judiciary, Ministry Council/Communications/Discipleship, Stewardship/Elected Officers, and Theology and Social Concerns. Each committee shall consider such matters expected to come before the General Assembly as are referred to it by the Stated Clerk. Any denominational organization, the work of which is affected by a matter before a committee, shall be entitled to address the committee.

11.03 Committee on Nominations.

01. The committee shall consist of ten (10) persons elected by the corporation in such a manner that, immediately following any election, the committee shall have at least one minister and one lay person from each synod. It is preferred but not required that no two members shall be from the same presbytery.
02. Approximately one third of the members of the committee shall be elected each year by the General Assembly and shall serve one term not to exceed three years.
03. The committee shall meet not earlier than February 15 each year and shall nominate to the General Assembly qualified persons to fill all vacancies to be filled by vote of the General Assembly, including vacancies on the Committee on Nominations, unless another method of nomination is provided in these Bylaws. The report of the committee shall list the names of nominees, the presbytery if a minister, and the presbytery and the local congregation if a lay person. The Committee on Nominations shall be intentional in nominating persons who represent the global nature of the Church.
04. Presbyteries and synods and their moderators and stated clerks are requested to assist the Committee on Nominations by recommending persons for any position by providing the name and qualifications of the potential nominees to the Stated Clerk no later than February 1 on a form to be provided by the Stated Clerk. Nominations from the floor shall also be in order.
05. No person shall be nominated for election by the General Assembly unless the nominee has within the past year given his or her consent to the nomination.

11.04 Joint Committee on Amendments. The Judiciary Committee shall appoint as many as five of its members to act in committee with an equal number of members of the Judiciary Committee of the Cumberland Presbyterian Church in America. Upon the request of the General Assembly of the Cumberland Presbyterian Church or the General Assembly of the Cumberland Presbyterian Church in America, this Joint Committee shall prepare for the consideration of both general assemblies proposed amendments to the Confession of Faith, Catechism, Constitution, Rules of Discipline, Directory for Worship, and Rules of Order.

11.05 Judiciary Committee.
01. The committee shall consist of nine (9) persons elected by the corporation in such a manner that, immediately following any election, the committee shall have at least four members (4) who are ordained ministers and at least three (3) members who are licensed attorneys-at-law. The Stated Clerk shall be staff liaison to the committee, attending its meetings and providing resources and counsel.
02. The committee shall meet at least annually upon the call of its chairperson or the Stated Clerk.
03. The committee shall provide advice and counsel to the Stated Clerk. Upon the written request of any judicatory or denominational entity made to the chairperson or Stated Clerk, the committee shall render an advisory opinion on matters of church law or procedure. The chairperson shall secure the views of all members of the committee and write the advisory opinion based on the majority view of the members. The committee shall not render legal opinions on matters of civil law nor otherwise engage in the practice of law.
04. At least one member of the committee shall attend each meeting of the General Assembly to advise with its officers and Commissioners on matters of church law or procedure. At the Moderator's request a member of the committee shall be available to advise the Moderator during the business sessions of the General Assembly.
05. The committee shall be a commission within the meaning of section 2.5 of the Rules of Discipline to hear and determine appeals from synods.

11.06 Our United Outreach Committee.
01. The committee shall consist of five (5) persons elected by the corporation in such a manner that, immediately following any election, the committee shall have one person from each synod. Seven (7) additional members will include a member of the Ministry Council, a member of the Corporate Board, a member of the Board of Stewardship, Foundation and Benefits, a member of the Board of Trustees of the Historical Foundation, and a Cumberland Presbyterian member of the Boards of Trustees of Bethel University, the Cumberland Presbyterian Children's Home, and Memphis Theological Seminary. The executives of the above named denominational entities

shall serve as non-voting, Resource/Advocacy members.
: 02. The Office of the General Assembly will be responsible for the expenses of the representative of each synod. The represented denominational entities will be responsible for the expenses of their representatives and executives.

11.07 Place of Meeting. The committee shall consist of the Moderator, the Stated Clerk and a representative of the Cumberland Presbyterian Women's Ministries.

11.08 Program Committee. The committee shall consist of the Moderator, Stated Clerk, Director of Ministries, Assistant to the Stated Clerk who serves as secretary, the pastor of the host church, four elected representatives designated by the Ministry Council from among its ministry teams, and one representative designated by each of the following: Bethel University, Board of Stewardship, Foundation, and Benefits, Cumberland Presbyterian Children's Home, Historical Foundation, Memphis Theological Seminary, and the Cumberland Presbyterian Women's Ministry. The committee will begin planning for two years prior to the meeting of a particular General Assembly.

11.09 Unified Committee on Theology and Social Concerns. The committee shall consist of eight (8) members elected by the corporation, the Stated Clerk, and the President of Memphis Theological Seminary. At least one member of the committee other than the Seminary's president shall be a Cumberland Presbyterian member of the faculty of Memphis Theological Seminary.

ARTICLE 12-INDEMNIFICATION

12.01 Indemnification. The corporation shall indemnify any director, officer or employee who is, or is threatened to be, made a party to a completed, pending, or threatened action or proceeding from any liability arising from the director's, officer's or employee's official capacity with the corporation. This indemnification shall extend to the personal representation of a deceased person if the person would be entitled to indemnification under these Bylaws if living.

12.02 Costs and Expenses Covered by Indemnification. Indemnification provided under these Bylaws shall extend to the payment of a judgment, settlement, penalty, or fine, as well as attorney's fees, court costs, and other reasonable and necessary expenses incurred by the director or officer with respect to the action or proceeding.

12.03 Limitation on Indemnification. No indemnification shall be made to or on behalf of any person if a judgment or other final adjudication adverse to that person establishes his or her liability:
: 01. for any breach of the duty of loyalty to the corporation;
: 02. for acts or omissions not in good faith or which involve intentional misconduct or a knowing violation of law; or
: 03. for any distribution of the assets of the corporation which is unlawful under Tennessee law.

ARTICLE 13-TRUSTEE FOR THE CORPORATION

13.01 Trustee. The Board of Stewardship, Foundation and Benefits of the Cumberland Presbyterian Church, a nonprofit corporation existing under the laws of the state of Tennessee, holds certain real property and other assets of the Church as trustee for the use and benefit of the Church. The Board of Stewardship may continue to hold such real property and other assets, but after the adoption of these Bylaws, it shall hold those assets as trustee for the use and benefit of the Cumberland Presbyterian Church General Assembly Corporation.

13.02 Other Assets. Other, additional property may from time to time be conveyed to the Board of Stewardship to be held by it as trustee for the corporation. All assets held by the Board of Stewardship as trustee for the corporation shall be held at the pleasure and direction of the General Assembly.

ARTICLE 14-PARLIAMENTARY AUTHORITY

14.01 Designation. The parliamentary authority of the corporation in all meetings shall be the latest revised edition of the Rules of Order as set out in the Confession of Faith and Government of the Cumberland Presbyterian Church. In matters not provided for in the Rules of Order, the parliamentary authority shall be Robert's Rules of Order, latest revised edition.

14.02 Standing Rules. The following shall be Standing Rules for meetings of the General Assembly and may be suspended as provided in the parliamentary authority. (see Rules of Order 8.34c)

Standing Rules

1. Unless otherwise determined by the General Assembly or by the Stated Clerk in the event of an emergency, the annual General Assembly shall meet on the third or fourth Monday of June at two o'clock in the afternoon to organize, elect a moderator and transact business, and shall close on Thursday or Friday of the same week.

2. Reports of all standing and special committees shall be considered in the order established by the Moderator in consultation with the Stated Clerk. Committee reports may be presented orally or in writing provided to all Commissioners and youth advisory delegates. Those presenting committee reports shall have the opportunity to make remarks and give explanation, such presentations not to exceed ten minutes unless time is extended by two-thirds vote taken without debate. All committee recommendations shall be submitted in writing.

3. All materials from denominational entities for consideration or action by a General Assembly shall be submitted to the Stated Clerk at least thirty (30) days before the meeting of General Assembly.

4. Resolutions and memorials proposed for adoption by individual commissioners rather than denominational entities or judicatories of the Cumberland Presbyterian Church shall be introduced no later than the close of business on the second day of a meeting of General Assembly, and, when introduced, shall be referred by the Moderator, in counsel with the Stated Clerk, to the appropriate committee or committees for report and recommendations to the Assembly.

ARTICLE 15-REPORTS AND AUDITS

15.01 Congregational Reports. Annually by December 1, the Stated Clerk shall send to session clerks statistical forms for reporting congregational data. Session clerks shall mail the completed forms to presbytery clerks by February 1. The presbytery clerk shall mail the composite statistical report for all congregations of a presbytery to the Stated Clerk by February 10.

15.02 Institutional Reports. In order to be considered for inclusion in the General Assembly budget, all denominational entities shall deliver to the Stated Clerk an annual report including a concise description of the organization's work during the previous year and a line item budget for the forthcoming year. Financial reports should be condensed as much as possible while conveying all essential information on the organization's operations. All denominational entities except academic institutions on a fiscal year are requested to maintain their books on a calendar year.

15.03 Reporting Schedule. An electronic copy and two written copies of the annual report signed by two officers of the organization shall be delivered to the Stated Clerk by March 15 each year. Organizations requesting funds from Our United Outreach shall submit multi-year program budgets to the Our United Outreach Committee.

15.04 Audits. Organizations and operations included in the General Assembly budget shall be audited annually by a certified public accountant. Copies of the auditor's report, including any recommendations for changes in the procedures relating to internal financial controls, shall be delivered to the Stated Clerk. Organizations with total receipts of $100,000 or less are not required to have an audit but shall submit their books and financial statements to the Stated Clerk annually.

15.05 Bonds. Each organization or person whose financial records are required to be audited shall have a fidelity bond in an amount adequate to protect all funds held by the organization or person.

ARTICLE 16-AMENDMENTS

16.01 Manner of Amendment. Except as provided below, these Bylaws may be amended or repealed only by the affirmative vote of two-thirds of the votes cast in a duly constituted meeting of the General Assembly. No portion of the Bylaws may be amended or repealed by the Board of Directors. Fair and reasonable notice of any proposed amendment shall be provided as required by state law.

16.02 Extraordinary Actions. In order to be effective the following actions must be approved by (1) the affirmative vote of two consecutive General Assemblies, or (2) a ninety percent (90%) vote of a single General Assembly.

01. Terminating the existence of a denominational entity named in Bylaw 10.01
02. Creating a new denominational entity other than a temporary committee or task force.
03. Decreasing the Our United Outreach budget allocation to a denominational entity by more than 40% of the amount distributed to it during the previous calendar year; or
04. Taking any other actions which would cause a drastic change in the mission or structure of the Cumberland Presbyterian Church.

MEMORIAL ROLL OF MINISTERS

IN MEMORY OF
MINISTERS LOST BY DEATH

NAME	PRESBYTERY	AGE	DATE
Benson, William	Grace	69	11/06/16
Blakeburn, Roy E.	East Tennessee	87	04/14/16
Fleming, Patrick T.	Arkansas	53	08/07/16
Gross, Ronald	North Central	86	01/15/17
Hatcher, Carlton	Cumberland	87	01/01/16
Hom, Paul	del Cristo	85	03/14/17
Jacob, Randy	Choctaw	80	01/29/17
Lunn, Calvin	Columbia	70	06/06/17
Malone, Michael	Murfreesboro	49	05/28/16
Maynard, Terrell	Grace	72	03/14/17
Murrie, Willard	Covenant	97	04/20/17
Neafus, Kenneth	Cumberland	71	08/08/16
Ortiz, Jaime	Andes	83	03/29/16
Phelps, Earl	West Tennessee	87	04/20/16
Reid, Richard	West Tennessee	52	07/13/16
Shelton, Robert E.	Red River	75	11/01/16
Smith, Albert J	North Central	87	02/10/17
Smith, Billy T.	Nashville	86	06/16/16
Talley, James E.	Cumberland	89	03/15/16
Vasseur, Terry	Covenant	78	02/05/17
Wallace, Andrew	North Central	56	08/14/16
Wallace, Boyce	Cauca Valley	87	01/04/17
Westfall, Charles	Covenant	89	03/12/17
Wooten, Wallace	Arkansas	88	12/28/16

LIVING GENERAL ASSEMBLY MODERATORS

2017—REV. DAVID LANCASTER, 426 Fuqua Road, Martin, TN 38237
2016—REV. DWAYNE TYUS, 426 Old Hickory Boulevard, Madison, TN 37115
2015—REV. MICHELE GENTRY, Urb San Jorge casa 28, Km 8 via a La Tebaida Armenia, Quindio, COLOMBIA, SA
2014—REV. LISA HALL ANDERSON, 1790 Faxon Avenue, Memphis, TN 38112
2013—REV. FOREST PROSSER, 1157 Mountain Creek Road, Chattanooga, TN 37405
2012—REV. ROBERT D. RUSH, 12935 Quail Park Drive, Cypress, TX 77429
2011—REV. DON M. TABOR, 9611 Mitchell Place, Brentwood, TN 37027
2009—ELDER SAM SUDDARTH, 206 Ha Le Koa Court, Smyrna, TN 37167
2008—REV. JONATHAN CLARK, 88 Woodcrest Drive, Winchester, TN 37398
2007—REV. FRANK WARD, 8207 Traditional Place, Cordova, TN 38016
2006—REV. DONALD HUBBARD, 2128 Campbell Station Road, Knoxville, TN 37932
2005—REV. LINDA H. GLENN, 49 Mason Road, Threeway, TN 38343
2004—REV. EDWARD G. SIMS, 2161 N. Meadows Drive, Clarksville, TN 37043
2003—REV. CHARLES MCCASKEY, 679 Canter Lane, Cookeville, TN 38501
1999—ELDER GWENDOLYN G. RODDYE, 3728 Wittenham Drive, Knoxville, TN 37921
1998—REV. MASAHARU ASAYAMA, 3-15-9 Higashi, Kunitachi-shi, Tokyo, JAPAN
1996—REV. MERLYN A. ALEXANDER, 80 N. Hampton Lane, Jackson, TN 38305
1995—REV. CLINTON O. BUCK, PO Box 770068, Memphis, TN 38117
1993—REV. ROBERT M. SHELTON, 7128 Lakehurst Avenue, Dallas, TX 75230
1992—REV. JOHN DAVID HALL, 109 Oddo Lane SE, Huntsville, AL 35802
1990—REV. THOMAS D. CAMPBELL, PO Box 315, Calico Rock, AR 72519
1989—REV. WILLIAM RUSTENHAVEN, Jr., 703 W. Burleson, Marshall, TX 75670
1981—REV. W. JEAN RICHARDSON, 7533 Lancashire, Powell, TN 37849

IN MEMORY OF:

Moderator of the 180th General Assembly
REV. BOYCE WALLACE
Died January 4, 2017

Moderator of the 171st General Assembly
REV. RANDY JACOB
Died January 29, 2017

Moderator of the 158th General Assembly
ELDER BEVERLY ST. JOHN
Died May 18, 2017

GENERAL ASSEMBLY OFFICERS

MODERATOR
THE REVEREND DAVID LANCASTER
426 Fuqua Road
Martin, TN 38237
lancasterd@bethelu.edu
(731)588-5895

VICE MODERATOR
THE REVEREND LISA SCOTT
(address on file in GA office)
lascott1979@att.net
(816)332-0604

STATED CLERK AND TREASURER
THE REVEREND MICHAEL SHARPE
8207 Traditional Place
Cordova, TN 38016
(901)276-4572
FAX (901)272-3913
msharpe@cumberland.org

ENGROSSING CLERK
THE REVEREND VERNON SANSOM
7810 Shiloh Road
Midlothian, TX 76065
(972)825-6887
vernon@sansom.us

THE BOARD OF DIRECTORS OF THE GENERAL ASSEMBLY CORPORATION

(Members whose terms expire in 2018)
(1)MS. CALOTTA EDSELL, 7044 Woodsong Cove, Germantown, TN 38138
    cedsell@hotmail.com
(1)REV. NORLAN SCRUDDER, 29688 S 534 Road, Park Hill, OK 74451
    ndscrudder@gmail.com

(Members whose terms expire in 2019)
(2)MR. TIM GARRETT, 150 Third Avenue South, Suite 2800, Nashville, TN 37201
    tgarrett@bassberry.com
(2)REV. BOBBY COLEMAN, 704 E Webb Street, Mountain View, AR 72560
    bobby.coleman@gmail.com

(Members whose terms expire in 2020)
(2)REV. JOHN BUTLER, 501 Cherokee Drive, Campbellsville, KY 42718
    jbutler@iccable.com
(2)MS. BETTY JACOB, PO Box 158, Broken Bow, OK 74728
    chocpres@pine-net.com

*Ecumenical Partners   +Cumberland Presbyterian Church in America

MINISTRY COUNCIL

(Members whose terms expire in 2018)
(2)MR. KENNETH BEAN, 1035 Stonewall Street N, McKenzie, TN 38201
(1)REV. KENNY BUTCHER, 4608 Cather Court, Nashville, TN 37214
(1)REV. PHILLIP LAYNE, 10699 Griffith Highway, Whitwell, TN 37397
(2)REV. RON MCMILLAN, 675 Kimberly Drive, Atoka, TN 38004
(1)MS. VICTORY MOORE, 17388 Chandlerville Road, Virginia, IL 62691

(Members whose terms expire in 2019)
(1)MS. KAREN AVERY, 9420 Layton Court NE, Albuquerque, NM 87111
(1)MS. CARLA BELLIS, 19264 Law 2170, Aurora, MO 65605
(3)REV. TROY GREEN, 105 Cobb Hollow Lane, Petersburg, TN 37144
(1)MS. TSURUKO SATOH, 8710 Hickory Falls Lane, Pewee Valley, KY 40056
(1)REV. MIKE WILKINSON, 1504 Clear Brook Drive, Knoxville, TN 37922

(Members whose terms expire in 2020)
(3)REV. DONNY ACTON, 1413 Oakridge Drive, Birmingham, AL 35242
(1)MR. DAVID CORREA, Calle 76 #87-14, Medellin, COLOMBIA, SOUTH AMERICA
(1)MS. SAMANTHA HASSELL, 510 N Main Street, Sturgis, KY 42459
(3)REV. LANNY JOHNSON, 120 S Mill Street, Morrison, TN 37357
(1)MS. CHARELLE WEBB, 3507 Pickering Lane, Pearland, TX 77584

YOUTH ADVISORY MEMBERS
(2)MR. CAMERON ALDERSON, 122 E Cherry Street, Chandler, IN 47610
(1)MS. LEIGHANN MORGAN, 1468 Williams Cove Road, Winchester, TN 37398
(2)MS. CHARLI UHLRICH, 250 County Road 1950 N, Bethany, IL 61914

ADVISORY MEMBERS
REV. DAVID LANCASTER, 426 Fuqua Road, Martin, TN 38237
REV. MICHAEL SHARPE, 8207 Traditional Place, Cordova, TN 38016

COMMUNICATIONS MINISTRY TEAM

(Members whose terms expire in 2018)
(3)REV. MICHAEL CLARK, 80 Bryan Drive, Winchester, TN 37398
(3)REV. JAMES D. MCGUIRE, 220-2 Southwind Circle, Greeneville, TN 37743

(Members whose terms expire in 2019)
(2)REV. NICHOLAS CHAMBERS, 11300 Road 101, Union, MS 39365
(2)REV. STEVEN SHELTON, 7886 Farmhill Cove, Bartlett, TN 38135

(Members whose terms expire in 2020)
(1)MS. FREDERICKA JOHNS, PO Box 234, Calico Rock, AR 72519
(2)MS. DUSTY LUTHY, 2026 Washington Street, Paducah, KY 42003

*Ecumenical Partners   +Cumberland Presbyterian Church in America

DISCIPLESHIP MINISTRY TEAM

(Members whose terms expire in 2018)
(3)MS. JOANNA WILKINSON, 1174 Tanglewood Street, Memphis, TN 38114
(2)MS. RACHEL COOK, 210 Bynum Street, Scottsboro, AL 35768
(2)REV. CHRISTIAN SMITH, 475 State Street, Cookeville, TN 38501
(Members whose terms expire in 2019)
(2)REV. NANCY MCSPADDEN, 120 Roberta Drive, Memphis, TN 38112
(2)REV. JOSEFINA SANCHEZ, 7 Hancock Street, Melrose, MA 02176
(1)REV. JESSE THORNTON, 1016 S Fly Avenue, Goreville, IL 62939
(Members whose terms expire in 2020)
(2)MS. LE ILA DIXON, 4406 John Reagan Street, Marshall, TX 75672
(2)REV. DREW GRAY, 8220 Timberland Drive, West Paducah, KY 42086
(1)REV. BILLY PRICE, 12510 Buttermilk Road, Knoxville, TN 37932

MISSIONS MINISTRY TEAM

(Members whose terms expire in 2018)
(2)MR. TIM CRAIG, 8958 Carriage Creek Road, Arlington, TN 38002
(2)REV. CARDELIA HOWELL-DIAMOND, 1580 Jeff Road NW, Huntsville, AL 35806
(3)MS. SHERRY POTEET, P.O. Box 313, Gilmer, TX 75644
(2)MS. MELINDA REAMS, 10 W Azalea Lane, Russellville, AR 72802
(Members whose terms expire in 2019)
(2)REV. VICTOR HASSELL, 510 N Main Street, Sturgis, KY 42459
(2)MR. DOMINIC LAU, 3820 Anza Street, San Francisco, CA
(2)REV. BRITTANY MEEKS, 710 N Avalon Street, Memphis, TN 38107
(2)REV. CHRIS WARREN, 906 Prince Lane, Murfreesboro, TN 37129
(Members whose terms expire in 2020)
(1)MS. DONNA CHRISTIE, 3221 Whitehall Road, Birmingham, AL 35209

PASTORAL DEVELOPMENT MINISTRY TEAM

(Members whose terms expire in 2018)
(2)REV. DUAWN MEARNS, 15347 County Road 3537, Ada, OK 74820
(3)REV. LINDA SNELLING, PO Box 61, Waxahachie, TX 75168
(Members whose terms expire in 2019)
(2)REV. SANDRA SHEPHERD, 1432 Wexford Downs Lane, Nashville, TN 37211
(Members whose terms expire in 2020)
(2)REV. AMBER CLARK, 80 Bryan Drive, Winchester, TN 37398
(2)REV. DREW HAYES, 6322 Labor Lane, Louisville, KY 40291

*Ecumenical Partners +Cumberland Presbyterian Church in America

GENERAL ASSEMBLY BOARD OF:

I. TRUSTEES OF BETHEL UNIVERSITY

(Members whose terms expire in 2017)
(2)*MS. LISA COLE, PO Box 198615, Nashville, TN 37219
(2)MR. CHESTER (CHET) DICKSON, 24 W Rivercrest Drive, Houston, TX 77042
(1)REV. NANCY MCSPADDEN, 120 Roberta Drive, Memphis, TN 38112
(3)MR. BOBBY OWEN, 1625 Cabot Drive, Franklin, TN 37064
(2)DR. ED PERKINS, 721 Paris Street, McKenzie, TN 38201
(1)MR. KENNETH (KEN) D. QUINTON, 2912 Waller Omer Road, Sturgis, KY 42459
(3)REV. ROBERT (ROB) TRUITT, 1238 Old East Side Road, Burns, TN 37029
(1)REV. ROBERT (BOB) WATKINS, 10950 West Union Hills Drive #1356, Sun City, AZ 85373
(Members whose terms expire in 2018)
(3)MR. CHARLIE GARRETT, 107 Willow Green Drive, Jackson, TN 38305
(2)+REV. ELTON C. HALL, SR., 305 Tiffton Circle, Hewitt, TX 76643
(2)MS. DEWANNA LATIMER, 1077 Jr. Jones Road, Humboldt, TN 38343
(1)*DR. E. RAY MORRIS, PO Box 924628, Norcross, GA 30010
(1)MR. STEVE PERRYMAN, 535 Ranch Road, Rogersville, MO 65742
(Members whose terms expire in 2019)
(2)MR. JEFF AMREIN, 11711 Paramont Way, Prospect, KY 40059
(3)*JUDGE BEN CANTRELL, 1485A Woodmont Boulevard, Nashville, TN 37215
(1)*MR. SCOTT CONGER, 551 Westmoreland Place, Jackson, TN 38301
(3)+DR. ARMY DANIEL, 3125 Searcy Drive, Huntsville, AL 35810
(2)MR. BILL DOBBINS 5716 Quest Ridge Road, Franklin, TN 37064
(3)DR. ROBERT LOW, c/o New Prime, Inc., 2740 W Mayfair Avenue, Springfield, MO 65803
(1)*DR. BROCK MARTIN, 419 Browning Avenue, Huntingdon, TN 38344

Trustee Emeritus – Dr. Vera Low, 3653 Prestwick Court, Springfield, MO 65809 (deceased)

II. TRUSTEES OF CUMBERLAND PRESBYTERIAN CHILDREN'S HOME

(Members whose terms expire in 2017)
(1)MS. CAROLINE BOOTH, 2200 Westview Trail, Denton, TX 76207
(3)MS. MAMIE HALL, 305 Tiffton Circle, Hewitt, TX 76643
(1)MR. CHARLES HARRIS, 3293 Birch Avenue, Grapevine, TX 76051
(1)MR. KNIGHT MILLER, 1035 Garden Creek Circle, Louisville, KY 40223
(3)REV. DON TABOR, 9611 Mitchell Place, Brentwood, TN 37027
(Members whose terms expire in 2018)
(1)REV. DUANE DOUGHERTY, 212 County Road 4705, Troup, TX 75789
(1)MRS. CAROLYN HARMON, 4435 Newport Highway, Greeneville, TN 37743
(1)DR. ROBIN HENSON, 8220 Westwind Lane, North Richland Hills, TX 76182
(1)REV. JOYCE MERRITT, 3929 Snail Shell Cove, Rockvale, TN 37153
(Members whose terms expire in 2019)
(2)*MR. RICHARD DEAN, 2140 Cove Circle North, Gadsden, AL 35903
(1)MRS. KAY GOODMAN, 1042 Bobcat Road, Sanger, TX 76266
(2)REV. MELISSA KNIGHT, 5730 Haley Road, Meridian, MS 39305
(2)MS. PATRICIA LONG, 525 E Oak Street, Aledo, TX 76008
(Members whose terms expire in 2020)
(1)MR. PETE CARTER, 306 Jackson Hills Drive, Maryville, TN 37804
(1)MR. CAMERON MARONE, 3933 Park Haven Drive, Denton, TX 76210
(1)MR JAY THOMAS, 3301 Cooperbranch E, Denton, TX 76209

*Ecumenical Partners   +Cumberland Presbyterian Church in America

III. TRUSTEES OF HISTORICAL FOUNDATION

(Members whose terms expire in 2018)
(1)REV. LISA OLIVER, 110 Allen Drive, Hendersonville, TN 37075
(3)DR. SIDNEY L. SWINDLE, 4407 Swann Avenue, Tampa, FL 33609
(Members whose terms expire in 2019)
(1)MS. ROBIN MCCASKEY HUGHES, 1205 Olde Bridge Road, Edmond, OK 73034
(3)REV. MARY KATHRYN KIRKPATRICK, 401 1/2 Henley-Perry Drive, Marshall, TX 75670
(1)MS. ASHLEY LINDSEY, 2090 Claypool Boyce Road, Alvaton, KY 42122
(Members whose terms expire in 2020)
(3)+MS. EDNA BARNETT, 7 Breezewood Cove, Jackson, TN 38305
(2)MR. MICHAEL FARE, 401 E Deanna Lane, Nixa, MO 65714
(2)*MS. DOROTHY M. HAYDEN, 3103 Carolina Avenue, Bessemer, AL 35020
(1)+MS. PAT WARD, 2620 Rabbit Lane, Madison, AL 35756
(3)+REV. RICK WHITE, 124 Towne West, Lorena, TX 76655

IV. TRUSTEES OF MEMPHIS THEOLOGICAL SEMINARY OF THE CUMBERLAND PRESBYTERIAN CHURCH

(Members whose terms expire in 2018)
(3)REV. KEVIN BRANTLEY, 308 A Chestnut Street, Sacramento, KY 42372
(1)REV. KEVIN HENSON, 1101 Bear Creek Parkway, Ste 3210, Keller, TX 76248
(1)REV. LINDA HOWELL, PO Box 80050, Keller, TX 76244
(3)MR. MARK MADDOX, 225 Oak Drive, Dresden, TN 38225
(2)MS. SONDRA RODDY, 2583 Hedgerow Lane, Clarksville, TN 37043
(3)MR. TAKAYOSHI SHIRAI, 25 Minami Kibogaoka Asahi-ku, Yokohama, Kanagawa-ken 241-0824 JAPAN
(2)*REV. MELVIN CHARLES SMITH, 1263 Haynes Street, Memphis, TN 38114
(2)*MS. LATISHA TOWNS, The Med, 877 Jefferson Avenue, Memphis, TN 38103
(Members whose terms expire in 2019)
(3)MR. MICHAEL R. ALLEN, 149 Windwood Circle, Alabaster, AL 35007
(3)MS. DIANE DICKSON, 24 West Rivercrest, Houston, TX 77042
(1)*MS. JANE ASHLEY FOLK, 4405 Dunwick Lane, Fort Worth, TX 76109
(1)*MR. HARRY HILLIARD, 206 E Bankhead Street, New Albany, MS 38652
(2)*DR. RICK KIRCHOFF, 2044 Thorncroft Drive, Germantown, TN 38138
(3)*DR. INETTA RODGERS, 1824 S Parkway E, Memphis, TN 38114
(1)*DR. DEBORAH SMITH, 584 E McLemore Avenue, Memphis, TN 38106
(1)MS. MARIANNA (MOLLY) WILLIAMS, 947 Troy Avenue, Dyersburg, TN 28024
(Members whose terms expire in 2020)
(1)*REV. NANCY COLE, 3346 Arcadia Drive, Tuscaloosa, AL 35404
(2)REV. ANNE HAMES, 118 Paris Street, McKenzie, TN 38201
(1)*REV. JIMMY JOHNATHAN MOSBY, PO Box 45843, Little Rock, AR 72214
(3)REV. JENNIFER NEWELL, 2322 Marco Circle, Chattanooga, TN 37421
(2)REV. SUSAN PARKER, 655 York Drive, Rogersville, AR 35652
(1)*MR. REGINALD PORTER, JR., 4458 Whitephine Cove, Memphis, TN 38109
(1)REV. KIP RUSH, 516 Franklin Road, Brentwood, TN 37027
(1)+MR. CRAIG WHITE, 134 McEntire Lane SW A36, Decatur, AL 35603
(1)*MS. RUBY WHARTON, 1183 E Parkway South, Memphis, TN 38114

V. STEWARDSHIP, FOUNDATION AND BENEFITS

(Members whose terms expire in 2018)
(3)MR. ANDREW B. FRAZIER, JR., 107 Doris Street, Camden, TN 38320
(1)MR. JAMES SHANNON, 2307 Littlemore Drive, Cordova, TN 38016
(2)MR. MICHAEL ST. JOHN, 324 Carriage Place, Lebanon, MO 65536

*Ecumenical Partners   +Cumberland Presbyterian Church in America

(Members whose terms expire in 2019)
(2)REV. CHARLES (BUDDY) POPE, 2391 Fairfield Pike, Shelbyville, TN 37160
(3)MS. SUE RICE, 1301 Brooker Road, Brandon, FL 33511
(3)MS. DEBBIE SHELTON, 1255 MG England Road, Manchester, TN 37355
(1)MS. ANDREA SMITH, 1715 Water Cure Road, Winchester, TN 37398
(Members whose terms expire in 2020)
(2)MR. RANDY DAVIDSON, PO Box 880, Ada, OK 74821
(1)REV. MARK HESTER, 763 Finn Long Road, Friendsville, TN 37737
(1)REV. GARY TUBB, 103 Forest Drive, Mountain Home, AR 72653
(1)REV. DWAYNE TYUS, 426 W Old Hickory Boulevard, Madison, TN 37115

GENERAL ASSEMBLY COMMISSIONS:

I. MILITARY CHAPLAINS AND PERSONNEL

(1) Term Expires in 2018–REV. TONY JANNER, 104 Northwood Drive, McKenzie TN 38201

(2) Term Expires in 2019–REV. CASSANDRA THOMAS, 1920 Dancy Street, Fayetteville, NC 28301

(1) Term Expires in 2020–REV. CHARLES MCCASKEY, 679 Canter Lane, Cookeville, TN 38501

These three persons and the Stated Clerk represent the denomination as members of the Presbyterian Council for Chaplains and Military Personnel, 4125 Nebraska Avenue NW, Washington, DC 20016

GENERAL ASSEMBLY COMMITTEES

I. JUDICIARY

(Members whose terms expire in 2018)
(2)REV. ANNETTA CAMP, 2263 Mill Creek Road, Halls, TN 38040
   anetta@cumberlandchurch.com
(3)MS. KIMBERLY SILVUS, 1128 Madison Street, Clarksville, TN 37040
   kgsilvus@gmail.com
(1)MR. BILL TALLY, 907 Tipperary Drive, Scottsboro, AL 35768
   wtally@scottsboro.org
(Members whose terms expire in 2019)
(3)REV. ANDY MCCLUNG, 919 Dickinson Street, Memphis, TN 38107
   scubarev@att.net
(1)MS. RACHEL MOSES, 1138 Blaine Avenue, Cookeville, TN 38501
   coachrach@aol.com
(1)REV. JAN OVERTON, 3320 Pipe Line Road, Birmingham, AL 35243
   jan@crestlinechurch.org
(Members whose terms expire in 2020)
(1)MS. PAMELA BROWN, 6400 North Grove Avenue, Warr Acres, OK 73012
   pambrownlaw@cox.net
(2)REV. HARRY CHAPMAN, 4908 El Picador Court SE, Rio Rancho, NM 87124
   wrightrev2gmail.com
(1)REV. GEOFFREY KNIGHT, 2119 Avalon Place, Houston, TX 77019
   geoff@cphouston.org

*Ecumenical Partners   +Cumberland Presbyterian Church in America

II. JOINT COMMITTEE ON AMENDMENTS

The committee consists of five members of the Judiciary Committee of the Cumberland Presbyterian Church in America and the Cumberland Presbyterian Church.

III. NOMINATING

(Members whose terms expire in 2018)
(1)REV. THOMAS CAMPBELL, PO Box 343, Calico Rock, AR 72519
    tdcampbellar@gmail.com
(1)MS. HEATHER MORGAN, 1468 Williams Cove Road, Winchester, TN 37398
    htmorgan87@gmail.com

(Members whose terms expire in 2019)

(1)MS. FAYE DELASHMIT, 2705 Garrett Drive, Bowling Green, KY 42104
    steve.delashmit@twc.com
(1)REV. DEREK JACKS, 341 Shadeswood Drive, Hoover, AL 35226
    pastorderek@homewoodcpc.com
(1)REV. STEPHEN LOUDER, 98 Gallant Court, Clarksville, TN 37043
    pastorsteve@clarksvillecpc.com
(1)MS. JANIE STAMPS, 4008 Logan Lane, Fort Smith, AR 72903
    bjstamps@msn.com

(Members whose terms expire in 2020)
(1)REV. BRIAN HAYES, 69 Cactus Drive, Benton, KY 42025
    cprevbhayes@gmail.com
(1)MR. LEE HOLDER, 6589 County Road 747, Cullman, AL 35055
    lholder@tvpine.com
(1)REV. TOM SPENCE, PO Box 802, Burns Flat, OK 73624
    tomspence0302@gmail.com
(1)MS. JENANN LESLIE, 300 Henley Perry Drive, Marshall, TX 75670
    jenann.leslie@gmail.com

IV. OUR UNITED OUTREACH COMMITTEE

(Members whose terms expire in 2018)
(2)MR. RANDY WEATHERSBY, 6130 US Highway 278 E, Cullman, AL 35055
(2)MS. ROBIN WILLS, 4607 E Richmond Shop Road, Lebanon, TN 37090

(Members whose terms expire in 2019)
(1)REV. BRUCE HAMILTON, 1037 Binns Drive, Monticello, AR 71655

(Members whose terms expire in 2020)
(1)MS. MARY ANN COLE, 1726 Karen Circle, Bowling Green, KY 42104
(1)MR. MIKEL DAVIS, 102 Willow Wood Lane, Ovilla, TX 75154

V. PLACE OF MEETING

THE STATED CLERK OF THE GENERAL ASSEMBLY
THE MODERATOR OF THE GENERAL ASSEMBLY
A REPRESENTATIVE OF WOMEN'S MINISTRIES OF THE MISSIONS MINISTRY TEAM

---

*Ecumenical Partners   +Cumberland Presbyterian Church in America

VI. UNIFIED COMMITTEE ON THEOLOGY AND SOCIAL CONCERNS

(Members whose terms expire in 2018)
(2)REV. GEORGE ESTES, 7910 Cloverbrook Lane, Germantown, TN 38138
    geoestes@gmail.com; (901)755-6673
(2)REV. SHELIA O'MARA, PO Box 170, Gadsden, TN 38337
    chaplainshelia@aol.com; (443)699-2321; (443)370-7218 cell
(2)MR. DAVID PHILLIPS-BURK, 3325 Bailey Creek Cove N, Collierville, TN 38017
    dlphillipsburk@aol.com; (256)520-1380

(Members whose terms expire in 2019)
(3)+MRS. JIMMIE DODD, c/o Hopewell CPCA, 4100 Millsfield Highway, Dyersburg, TN 38024
    dodd125@gmail.com
(3)REV. BYRON FORESTER, 2376 Eastwood Place, Memphis, TN 38112
    bforester@bellsouth.net; (901)246-1242
(1)REV. MARCUS HAYES, 2901 Sandage Avenue, Apt 304, Fort Worth, TX 76109
    marcus.hayes@att.net
(2)REV. JOHN A. SMITH, 916 Allen Road, Nashville, TN 37214
    john.a.smith.81@gmail.com; (615)545-6486
(3)+ELDER JOY WALLACE, 6940 Marvin D Love Freeway, Dallas, TX 75237
    jwallace@wlgllc.net

(Members whose terms expire in 2020)
(1)+MS. SHARON COMBS, PO Box 122, Sturgis, KY 42459
    (270)860-4175
(1)+REV. EDMOND COX, 249 Mimosa Circle, Maryville, TN 37801
    (865)789-6161
(2)+DR. NANCY FUQUA, 1963 County Road 406, Towncreek, AL 35672
    fuq23@bellsouth.net; (256)566-1226
(1)REV. RICHARD MORGAN, 1468 Williams Cove Road, Winchester, TN 37398
    icthuse@charter.net
(1)REV. LISA SCOTT, (address on file in GA office)
    lascott1979@att.net
(1)+REV. ROBERT E THOMAS, 1017 N Englewood, Tyler, TX 75702
    (903)592-0238

President of Memphis Theological Seminary - Ex-officio Member
    REV. JAY EARHEART-BROWN, 866 N McLean Boulevard, Memphis, TN 38107
        jebrown@memphisseminary.edu; (901)278-0367

OTHER DENOMINATIONAL PERSONNEL

REPRESENTATIVES TO:
American Bible Society: REV. MICHAEL SHARPE, 8207 Traditional Place, Cordova, TN 38016

Caribbean and North American Area Council, World Communion of Reformed Churches: STATED CLERK MICHAEL SHARPE, 8207 Traditional Place, Cordova, TN 38016

(Member whose terms expire in 2020)
(1)MS. SHERRY POTEET, PO box 313, Gilmer, TX 75644
    spoteet1@aol.com

THE REPORT OF THE MODERATOR

First of all, I express my gratitude to the commissioners who elected me to serve as Moderator of the 186th General Assembly. I have enjoyed all aspects of my term as Moderator, and I hope and pray that my work in this role was satisfactory. I really wish to express my gratitude to the Reverend Michael Sharpe, Stated Clerk, and to Elizabeth Vaughn, who serves as Assistant to the Stated Clerk, for their invaluable help and guidance during my term of office. I thank the Reverend Nobuko Seki, Vice-Moderator, for her help and her service, and I wish we could have had some more time together during our travels.

I chose, this year, to meet with as many stateside presbyteries as possible, especially those who have perhaps been under served in the past. I attended meetings of the following presbyteries: del Cristo, Missouri, North Central, East Tennessee, Hope, Murfreesboro, Arkansas, Tennessee-Georgia, East Coast Cumberland, Nashville, Trinity, Red River, and West Tennessee. In addition, I also preached at a Denomination Day celebration of the Robert Donnell Presbytery. Other preaching assignments included del Cristo, Missouri, West Tennessee, and Nashville presbyteries.

The Office of Moderator also has other duties besides meeting with presbyteries. It was my pleasure to meet with the Ministry Council; the Board of Stewardship, Foundation, and Benefits; the Board of Trustees of Memphis Theological Seminary; and a special meeting to review the Denomination's covenant relationship with the Children's Home in Denton, Texas.

One other thing really kept me busy during this year. I was able to write an article each month for the Cumberland Presbyterian Magazine. Thanks to Editor Mark Davis for being patient with me in this exciting chore. I pray that the joy I received from relating to friends old and new in the meetings of the presbyteries and Boards was evident in the small articles I wrote. I hope my enthusiasm about the good news I found in all the various places I visited came through on the written page.

There is a lot to excite us in our church. We have growth in our institutions like Memphis Theological Seminary, Bethel University, the Children's Home, and we added a new presbytery, Emaus, in Colombia. I thank the Reverend Leslie Johnson, who serves as Moderator of Mission Synod, for his tireless work representing the Synod, not only at the beginning of Emaus Presbytery, but also in the meetings of other presbyteries in the United States. The Cumberland Presbyterian Church is reaching a lot of new persons in a lot of new places with the gospel of Jesus Christ. Although in our minds we may lump these places together, each new preaching point, each new church building, is a victory for the church. Each of these new places represents a goal, a dream, an accomplishment of someone led by the Holy Spirit to preach the gospel in new places.

Last, but not least, I thank my wife of 42 years, Guin, for her help, patience, and her driving of long distances to the meetings. She was with me at almost all the presbyteries.

Finally, I encourage each congregation's continued giving to Our United Outreach, as well as to the Stott-Wallace Fund, so that your congregation may share in all that God is doing through a people called Cumberland Presbyterian.

Respectfully submitted,

Reverend Dwayne Tyus
Moderator of the 186th General Assembly

THE REPORT OF THE STATED CLERK

I. THE OFFICE OF THE STATED CLERK

The Constitution, the Rules of Discipline, the Rules of Order, and the General Assembly Bylaws (found in the front of the General Assembly Minutes) list the many responsibilities for the person who holds the position of Stated Clerk, the primary task is to maintain and strengthen a united witness for the Church. The Stated Clerk shall also generally supervise and control the business affairs of the Corporation, and see that all directives of the General Assembly are implemented.

The Office of the General Assembly also provides budgeting, accounting, and support services for commissions, committees, agencies and task forces without executive assistance.

Additional services and activities provided through the office of the Stated Clerk this past year include:
- Providing assistance to the Unification Task Force
- Developing and maintaining a web presence for the following General Assembly Committees/Commissions without staff: Nominating Committee, Unified Committee on Theology and Social Concerns, Commission on Military Chaplains and Personnel, Our United Outreach Committee and the Unification Task Force.
- Creation of spring and fall Denominational News Updates, a compilation of talking points obtained from each board and agency that may be shared by visiting denominational staff and the moderator when making visits to presbyteries and in other settings. The updates are also shared with presbytery clerks.
- Development of a Travel Chart, to assist with the coordination of travel plans by denominational staff to meetings of presbyteries. The travel chart is also shared with presbytery clerks.
- Hosted the annual conference for Presbytery and Synod Clerks.

A significant portion of the Stated Clerk's time has been spent responding to various judicial and legal questions affecting local churches and presbyteries. The Clerk is appreciative for advice provided to this office from both the Permanent Judiciary Committee and from Mr. Jamie Jordan who serves as legal counsel for the Office of the General Assembly.

The Stated Clerk is grateful to the Church for calling him to serve in this position and appreciates the support of the Church for the Office and for the person who holds this position.

II. STAFF

Ms. Elizabeth Vaughn serves as the Assistant to the Stated Clerk, a position that requires her to maintain accurate records of ministers, probationers, congregations, record income and expenses and to authorize payment of all items in the Office of the General Assembly budget. The Church is fortunate to have a person with such knowledge, efficiency and dedication to work. The Stated Clerk and the Assistant to the Stated Clerk are currently the only employees of the Office of the General Assembly.

Reverend Vernon Sansom continues to serves as Engrossing Clerk and is to be commended for the accuracy in recording the minutes of the General Assembly. Vernon also leads the orientation session for those who serve as chairperson and co-chairperson for each General Assembly appointed Committee and provides valuable assistance in the preparation of committee reports at each meeting of the General Assembly.

III. ECUMENICAL RELATIONSHIPS

The Cumberland Presbyterian Church has historically been involved in ecumenical relationships. Through co-operative ministries, chaplains for the military and veteran's hospitals are endorsed, migrant workers and persons in Appalachia are served, and missionaries are sent into a variety of countries. Through ecumenical partnerships disaster relief funds are distributed. Through working co-operatively church school and camping materials are developed. The Cumberland Presbyterian witness is more effective through participation with other Christians in these and various other ministries.

A. CUMBERLAND PRESBYTERIAN CHURCH IN AMERICA

The Cumberland Presbyterian Church in America and the Cumberland Presbyterian Church have one heritage, one Confession of Faith and share in several co-operative relationships and ministries such as the Historical Foundation, the United Board of Christian Discipleship, youth ministry, and the Unified Committee on Theology and Social Concerns. The Cumberland Presbyterian Church in America and the Cumberland Presbyterian Church also participate with other Reformed bodies in ministry. Although working through partnerships, the witness of the Cumberland Presbyterian Church in America and the Cumberland Presbyterian Church would be greatly enhanced through a union of the two denominations.

B. WORLD COMMUNION OF REFORMED CHURCHES

Both the Cumberland Presbyterian Church and the Cumberland Presbyterian Church in a America are members of World Communion of Reformed Churches (WCRC). The WCRC was formed in 2010 by a merger of the World Alliance of Reformed Churches and the Reformed Ecumenical Council. The WCRC represents approximately eighty million members of two hundred thirty denominations from one hundred seven countries, including Reformed, Congregationalists, Presbyterian and United Churches. Resources and updates from the World Communion of Reformed Churches are available on their website: (www.wcrc.ch).

Reverend Christopher Ferguson serves as general secretary of the WCRC and offices in Hanover, Germany where the headquarters for WCRC is located.

The WCRC meets every seven years. The next meeting of the general Council will be held in Erfurt, Germany, June 2017 and will coincide with the 500th Anniversary of the Reformation. The theme for the 26th general Council is Living God, Renew and Transform Us (based on Romans 12:2 and Luke 4:16-19).

IV. REVIEW OF THE COVENANT RELATIONSHIPS

The Covenant Relationship between the Cumberland Presbyterian Church and both Bethel University and the Cumberland Presbyterian Children's Home were reviewed this past year, as required by the covenant agreement currently in place with both institutions. Separate reports regarding the review and recommendations pertaining to each of the covenant agreements is included in this year's preliminary minutes.

V. THE CORPORATE BOARD

In the called meeting in December 2007, the General Assembly elected a new board of directors for the General Assembly Incorporation, thus the Corporate Board was formed. The responsibilities for the Corporate Board are listed in the General Assembly Bylaws, Article 5.

The Corporate Board met once this past year, which included a biennial review of the Stated Clerk. The Center Interagency Team (CIT) comprised of the Center's Principle Executive Officers, continues to be responsible for oversight of the day-to-day maintenance and property needs at the Denominational Center. Current CIT members include: Mike Sharpe (Office of the General Assembly), Robert Heflin (Board of Stewardship, Foundation and Benefits), Susan Gore (Historical Foundation), and Edith Old (Ministry Council). The Shared Services budget covers the cost for maintaining the Center offices and property (see page 133).

VI. LEGAL ISSUES

Last year the Stated Clerk reported on a lawsuit brought against the Milburn Chapel Church, Coventry Presbytery, Synod of the Midwest, the General Assembly, and certain individual defendants. That suit has been resolved by the agreement of all the parties and is concluded. The terms of the settlement are confidential, but included a financial contribution from the General Assembly's liability insurance carrier. This experience is a reminder to all Cumberland Presbyterian churches and higher judicatories of the importance of adopting and following policies to protect minors and other vulnerable populations in our churches. The suit also serves as a reminder of the importance of both insurance coverage and incorporation for all judicatories of the church.

VII. MINUTES OF THE GENERAL ASSEMBLY

The Office of the General Assembly continues to make the minutes of the General Assembly available on a CD, and mailing them to persons requesting them. The resource center also prints and sells a few printed copies of the General Assembly Minutes each year. For information contact Matthew Gore, mhg@cumberland.org. It is permissible to download and print a copy of the minutes from the website (www.cumberland.org/gao).

VIII. STATISTICAL INFORMATION

The annual congregational report forms are sent to the session clerk on December 1, and due in the office of the Stated Clerk of the Presbytery on February 1, and all reports are to be in the Office of the General Assembly by February 10.

In 2016 a hundred and thirty-one congregations failed to report, thus statistics are not accurate. The statistics for a non-reporting congregation may be several years old, but it is the latest information available. The General Assembly Office continues to shorten and simplify the reporting process. Efforts also continue to further simplify online reporting for those able to utilize the technology. Hard copies of the report forms will still be made available for those congregations who do not have access to the internet.

The 178th and 179th General Assembly directed "that each presbytery request that its Board of Missions or similar agency, as they minister to the needs of the churches within their presbyteries, remind the churches that it is important that they submit annual reports which are part of our history and offer assistance when needed in preparation of these reports." If a congregation fails to receive a report, a duplicate form can be requested from the Office of the General Assembly or one may be printed from the web site (www.cumberland.org/gao), and going to the section on congregational reports.

Compiled statistical information is available in the annual Yearbook available online (www.cumberland.org/gao) or in print format, available through Cumberland Resource Distribution – resources@cumberland.org (901-276-4581)

VIII. CHURCH CALENDAR 2017-2018

The 182nd General Assembly, directed the Office of the General Assembly to be responsible for reporting the "Church Calendar" to the General Assembly for adoption. Listed below are the dates received from the Boards and Agencies of the denomination.

RECOMMENDATION 1: That the 187th General Assembly approve the following dates for the 2017-2018 Church Calendar:

CHURCH CALENDAR 2017-2018

July-2017
8	Children's Fest, Bethel, McKenzie, Tennessee
8	Program of Alternate Studies Graduation
8-22	PAS Summer Extension School, Bethel, McKenzie, Tennessee

August-2017
1-Sept 30	Christian Education Season
5	Bethel University Commencement
6-Sept 24	Christian Education Season
19	MTS Fall Semester Begins
20	Seminary/PAS Sunday
21	Bethel University Fall Semester Begins
29	Bethel University Spring Convocation
30	MTS Opening convocation

September-2017
10	Senior Adult Sunday
17	Christian Service Recognition Sunday
17	International Day of Prayer and Action for Human Habitat

October-2017
	Clergy Appreciation Month
1	Worldwide Communion Sunday
8	Pastor Appreciation Sunday
22	Native American Sunday

November-2017
	Any Sunday Loaves and Fishes Program
1	All Saints Day
4	World Community Day (Church Women United)
5	Bethel University Sunday
5	Stewardship Sunday
12	Day of Prayer for People with Aids and Other Life-Threatening Illnesses
19	Bible Sunday
26	Christ the King Sunday

December-2017
	Any Sunday Gift to the King Offering
3-25	Advent in Church and Home
9	Bethel University Commencement
24	Christmas Eve
25	Christmas Day

January-2018
6	Epiphany
8	BU Spring Semester Begins
8-9	Stated Clerks' Conference
7	Human Trafficking Awareness Day
15	Deadline for receipt of 2017 Our United Outreach Contributions

February-2018
	Black History Month
1	Annual congregational reports due in General Assembly office
4	Denomination Day
4	Historical Foundation Offering
4	Souper Bowl Sunday
11	Our United Outreach Sunday
14	Ash Wednesday, the beginning of Lent
14–March 31	Lent to Easter
18	Youth Sunday

March-2018
	Women's History Month (USA)
18	Children's Home Sunday
25	Palm/Passion Sunday
25-31	National Farm Workers Awareness Week
29	Maundy Thursday
30	Good Friday

April-2018
1	Easter
1-7	Family Week
8	One Great Hour of Sharing

May-2018
5   Bethel University Commencement
6   Friendship Day (Church Women United)
12   MTS Closing Convocation & Graduation
20   Pentecost
27   Memorial Day Offering for Military Chaplains & Personnel for USA churches

June-2018
3   Stott-Wallace Missionary Fund Offering/World penMission Sunday
17-21   General Assembly, Norman, Oklahoma
18-20   CPWM Convention, Norman, Oklahoma
24-29   Cumberland Presbyterian Youth Conference, Bethel University, McKenzie, Tennessee

July-2018
14   Children's Fest
7   Program of Alternate Studies Graduation
7-21   PAS Summer Extension School, Bethel, McKenzie, Tennessee

August-2018
4   Bethel University Commencement
5-Sept 30   Christian Education Season
18   MTS Fall Semester Begins *(tentative)*
19   Seminary/PAS Sunday
22   Bethel University Fall Semester Begins
25   MTS Fall Semester Begins *(tentative)*
28   MTS Opening convocation *(tentative)*
30   Bethel University Spring Convocation

September-2018
4   MTS Opening convocation *(tentative)*
9   Senior Adult Sunday
16   Christian Service Recognition Sunday
16   International Day of Prayer and Action for Human Habitat

October-2018
    Clergy Appreciation Month
7   Worldwide Communion Sunday
7   Pastor Appreciation Sunday
21   Native American Sunday

November-2018
    Any Sunday Loaves and Fishes Program
1   All Saints Day
2   World Community Day (Church Women United)
4   Bethel University Sunday
4   Stewardship Sunday
11   Day of Prayer for People with Aids and Other Life-Threatening Illnesses
18   Bible Sunday
25   Christ the King Sunday

December-2018
    Any Sunday Gift to the King Offering
2-24   Advent in Church and Home
8   Bethel University Commencement
24   Christmas Eve
25   Christmas Day

XI. CONTINGENCY FUND

The Stated Clerk is to hold, distribute and report annually the General Assembly Contingency Fund (see Bylaws 8.04, #24). Below is a summary Contingency Fund Activity for the 2016 Calendar Year.

Summary of 2016 Activity

Balance Forward 1/1/2016 $ 16,475.95

Income in 2016:
    Our United Outreach/Contributions $16,859.52
    Interest   1,366.33
    Total Income: **$18,225.85**

There were no expenditures in 2016:

Total Fund Balance as of 12/31/16 *$34,701.80

***Restricted Funds:**

$ 4,100.00	The current balance designated by the 178th General Assembly to print the Catechism in the various languages represented in the church.
1,011.51	Pastoral Development Ministry Team/General Assembly Ordination Task Force

Total Amount of *Restricted Funds: $ 5,111.51 (12/31/16)

Total Amount of Unrestricted Amount: $45,341.55 (12/31/16)

Total Fund Balance: $50,453.06 (12/31/16)

Respectfully submitted,
Michael Sharpe, Stated Clerk

THE REPORT OF THE MINISTRY COUNCIL

To the 187th General Assembly of the Cumberland Presbyterian Church meeting in session in at the Innisbrook Resort and Conference Center, near Tampa, Florida on June 19-23, 2017.

I. MINISTRY COUNCIL

A. INTRODUCTION

The Ministry Council (MC) serves as the primary long- and short-range program planning agency of the Church, striving to ensure that all segments work on a unified mission and human and material resources are utilized to carry out ministries of the Church in an effective manner. The Ministry Council is accountable to the General Assembly (GA).

Due to the scope of the work related to denominational ministries under the MC, our report has historically been quite lengthy, necessitating the division of the report to multiple GA committees. At the urging of the Stated Clerk, and with the intention of providing crucial information in a concise manner, we made significant changes to our report format last year. This condensed report focuses on recommendations to the GA. A more detailed annual report of the work of the MC and Ministry Teams is available to commissioners and guests at this GA and on our web page https://cpcmc.org/mc/ga17-supplement/. We encourage commissioners and others to visit the Ministry Council booth to meet elected members and staff and to share ideas for enhancing ministries.

1. Ministry Council (MC) Elected Membership and Terms

MC elected members are subject to GA requirements of endorsement by presbytery (clergy) or church (laity), as well as geographical (synodic) and gender representation. It is our belief that God calls people from across the denomination to serve in leadership roles, and that the limited number of Personal Data Forms and related endorsements on file in the Office of General Assembly does not reflect the abundance of qualified leaders within the Church. The Ministry Council respectfully reminds all Commissioners of an action of the 186th General Assembly that urged each presbytery "to proactively recruit and encourage qualified leaders to prayerfully consider opportunities to serve as elected board members at the denominational level, to include the Ministry Council and all other denominational entities."

The terms of Reverend Donny Acton, Reverend Michele Gentry, Reverend Lanny Johnson, Mr. Adam McReynolds, and Reverend Tom Sanders expire in 2017. Acton, Johnson, McReynolds and Sanders are eligible for an additional term of service. Gentry has completed three terms and is ineligible for re-election. McReynolds and Sanders asked not to be nominated for a successive term. Reverend Paula Louder resigned following General Assembly 2016. The Council wishes to express appreciation to Reverend Gentry, Reverend Louder, Mr. McReynolds and Reverend Sanders for their faithful service. The one-year terms of Youth Advisory Members Mr. Cameron Alderson, Mr. Caleb Davis and Ms. Charli Uhlrich expire in 2017. Alderson and Uhlrich are eligible for an additional one-year term. Davis has served two terms and is ineligible for re-election. We express our appreciation to Mr. Davis for his service. The Ministry Council is the only denominational entity board with Youth Advisory Members.

2. Ministry Teams plan and implement the program ministries of the Church and are made up of both Staff and Elected Team Members. Ministry Teams report to the Ministry Council. Elected Team Members are elected by the MC and reflect the GA model to ensure representation among gender, laity and clergy.

Communications Ministry Team (CMT) elected member Denise Adams has completed three terms of service. The CMT and Ministry Council are grateful for her tenacity and creativity which will be sorely missed.

Discipleship Ministry Team (DMT) elected member, Samantha Hassell, has also completed three terms. DMT and Ministry Council are grateful for her diligent and faithful service. The MC elected Reverend Billy Price to replace Ms. Hassell on DMT.

The MC re-elected Donna Christie to a second term on Missions Ministry Team (MMT). Elected members, Reverend Jimmy Byrd and Reverend Ricardo Franco have completed three 3-year terms. Karen Tolen completed a 3-year term vacated by Nancy Gordon. We are grateful for their passionate heart for missions and for their faithful service on the MMT.

Reverend Patrick Wilkerson resigned from the Pastoral Development Ministry Team (PDMT) to accept the call to missionary service in Colombia. We are thankful for Reverend Wilkerson's exemplary service to PDMT and for his call to the Mission Field.

A complete list of Ministry Team members appears at https://cpcmc.org/mc/.

Staff Team Members are employees of the Ministry Council:
- **CMT:** Senior Art Director Sowgand Sheikholeslami and CMT Leader Mark J. Davis.
- **DMT:** Coordinator of Resource Development and Distribution Matt Gore; Coordinator of Adult and Third-Age Ministry Cindy Martin; Shipping Clerk Greg Miller; Coordinator of Children and Family Ministry Jodi Hearn Rush (Nashville, Tennessee office); Coordinator of Youth and Young Adult Ministry Reverend Nathan Wheeler; and DMT Leader Reverend Elinor S. Brown.
- **MMT:** Coordinator for Women's Ministry and Congregational Ministry Reverend Pam Phillips-Burk; Cross-Culture Immigrant USA Ministry Reverend Johan Daza; Manager, Finance and Administration Jinger Ellis; Evangelism and New Church Development Reverend T. J. Malinoski; Bilingual English/Korean Administrative Assistant Julie Min; Director Global Missions Reverend Lynn Thomas (Birmingham, Alabama office); and MMT Leader Reverend Milton Ortiz.
- **PDMT:** PDMT Leader Rev. Chuck Brown.

3. The Global Ministries Leadership Team (GMLT) is made up of the four Ministry Team Leaders and Director of Ministries. This body works together to apply the vision/mission of the MC to the many varied programs and resource materials planned and produced by the Ministry Teams, coordinating ministries in a unified, collaborative manner. GMLT meets monthly and minutes are disseminated to all members of the MC and Ministry Teams.

4. Administration: Director of Ministries Edith Busbee Old gives executive leadership to the MC in accomplishing duties defined by its Bylaws and supervises the GMLT. The Director of Ministries is under direct employment of and is responsible to the MC. The Assistant to the Executive Director position is vacant due to budget constraints.

B. GENERAL INFORMATION

1. Meetings: The MC met twice in regular session since the 186th General Assembly. A Summary of Action for meetings appears at https://cpcmc.org/mc/soa/.

2. Future Meeting Dates: August 17, 2017 (Thursday) – Orientation for newly elected MC and newly elected Ministry Team Members at the Denominational Center, Cordova, Tennessee.

August 18–19, 2017 (Friday and Saturday) – MC and Teams meet concurrently at Faith Cumberland Presbyterian Church, Bartlett, Tennessee (10 minutes from the Denominational Center).

February 17–18, 2018 (Saturday and Sunday) – MC Corporation Annual Meeting of the Board of Directors with Team Leaders and Director of Ministries at the Denominational Center.

RECOMMENDATION 1: That the 187th General Assembly amend the Ministry Council Bylaws, ARTICLE III, BOARD OF DIRECTORS, AUTHORITY, AND MEETINGS, Section E., Meetings to add "5. Meetings. A special meeting of the Ministry Council shall be called when requested by five or more Directors. (Bylaws online at https://cpcmc.org/mc/bylaws/)

3. Elected member accountability and training: Elected MC members and elected Ministry Team members receive orientation prior to their first MC/MT meeting. In 2016, we introduced a mentoring approach, partnering current MC members with newly elected members. The response has been favorable. Each year, all elected members sign a Covenant reinforcing their commitment to answering the call to serve God through service to the Church. Elected members set individual annual goals and complete annual self-evaluations reflecting on their service. These tools serve as metrics to help guide the MC and Ministry Teams. The MC Covenant may be seen at https://cpcmc.org/mc/covenant/.

4. Human Resources: When a staff position becomes vacant, the MC invests time in a thorough revision of that job description. Input is gathered from elected members, GMLT and relevant staff. As budget allows, resources are invested in staff development.

5. The Global Church in the Digital Age: An aging denomination and travel costs are often cited as real challenges to individuals/groups desirous of attending General Assembly. Widespread availability of and growing demand for online participation at meetings coupled with affordable cost of providing audio and video streaming has prompted a growing number of denominations to include these to broaden access to persons wanting to attend (virtually/ remotely) their annual conferences/assemblies. Providing audio and video streaming offers accessibility to those unable to attend GA, including those outside the US.

RECOMMENDATION 2: That the 187th General Assembly calls for all future General Assembly sites to have high speed, hard-wired internet access in the main meeting room, and that this condition be included in the contract negotiations with the host venue.

6. Unification: The Unification Task Force's revised plan recommends that some boards and agencies of the Cumberland Presbyterian (CP) Church be merged and expanded, and some be restructured. Merging two denominations and all their boards and agencies is a momentous task. As a reference, the 177th GA consolidated four boards into the MC, in that case the GA named a special Organizational Task Force (OTF) that worked with professional consultants and conducted numerous interviews with church leaders, boards, agencies and the Office of General Assembly. The goal of merging two denominations at the General Assembly and synodical level, reforming (unifying) all boards and agencies, creating new agencies and positions, and restructuring some of those agencies is more involved than merging four ministry boards. In order to facilitate a unification that is realistic, based on actual operational facts, and not disruptive to the ministries of the Church(es), the General Assembly's boards and agencies should be asked to outline what unification looks like from their board, agency perspective. The CP Church's boards and agencies should do an assessment of unification from their perspective and report to General Assembly how they see unification being implemented with respect to their board or agency. They should explain what changes or new structures they believe should be made to their board or agency, and what costs they anticipate based on the changes they suggest. The General Assembly can then use this information as follows: to assess and anticipate the potential impact and costs on its boards and agencies, to give informed information to the Unification Task Force of what the boards and agencies believe unification should look like from their perspective, and ultimately to help develop an informed process of unification that is not disruptive to the ministries of the Church.

RECOMMENDATION 3: That the Cumberland Presbyterian General Assembly instruct boards and agencies listed in the Unification Task Force's revised plan to provide a report to the next General Assembly (188th) asking these boards and agencies to provide: 1.) Their ideas with respect to the best ways to implement unification within their board or agency, 2.) Their assessment explaining if their board or agency needs structural changes as part of unification and what those changes should be, and 3.) What the board or agency anticipates will be the approximate costs implementing unification and or restructure of their board or agency.

II. MINISTRIES

A. PARAMETERS – The MC created "Parameters to Guide the Work of Our Ministry Teams" as a standard for all work done by the Ministry Teams. Parameters appear on the MC website https://cpcmc.org/mc/mt-work-params/ and in the 2016/2017 MC Annual Report.

B. SAFE SANCTUARY

The MC promotes the Safe Sanctuary initiative through its DMT in order to accomplish its purpose to encourage and support the ministry of all CP churches and to provide Christian education to all Cumberland Presbyterians through resources and events. Safe Sanctuary highlights the desire to create a safe environment for all people who walk through the doors of our churches and participate in the activities and events associated with our churches.

Three of the last four General Assemblies recognized the importance of having all CP congregations, presbyteries, and synods do their part to protect children and any other vulnerable people to whom we minister by considering and adopting policies like the Safe Sanctuary initiative (183rd General Assembly, 184th General Assembly, and 186th General Assembly). Our system of government places the burden of protecting our congregants on the Session, with the presbytery exercising pastoral oversight and jurisdiction by calling on the sessions within its bounds to attend to this important issue.

DMT staff have led a number of training events to educate congregations as to the information needed for writing their own policies. These training events included subjects and policies to consider as sound practices. Examples of what a safe sanctuary policy might look like are on the MC website (https://cpcmc.org/safe-sanctuary/). These are educational examples which may need to be tailored for the needs of each church or denominational body.

The commitment to safe sanctuaries must take hold at the grassroots of our denomination, in the churches themselves. Presbyteries must exercise their oversight responsibilities to see that Sessions shoulder this burden.

RECOMMENDATION 4: That the 187th General Assembly continue to encourage congregations, presbyteries, synods, and denominational groups to adopt and practice a written safe sanctuary plan; encourage presbyteries to maintain a copy of the safe sanctuary plan of every church and denominational entity within its jurisdiction; and encourage the Ministry Council to continue offering training and sample policies to congregations, presbyteries, synods and denominational groups about subjects to consider and include when writing a safe sanctuary plan.

C. MISSIONS

1. Reverend Harry Boyce Wallace – Boyce Wallace died in January 2017 after more than 50 years as a missionary in Colombia. Just before Boyce's death he and Beth were traveling in the US and actively promoting the Stott-Wallace Missionary Support Fund. They visited churches and individuals, encouraging them to faithfully support all our missionaries. For information about Boyce's missionary career, a limited number of copies of the February 2017 issue of THE CUMBERLAND PRESBYTERIAN magazine and the Spring 2017 issue of The Missionary Messenger are available at the MC booth. The booth also has information about the Stott-Wallace Missionary Support Fund. Beth continues to live in Cali, Colombia as a missionary emeritus.

2. Reverend Randy Jacob – Randy Jacob died in January 2017, 3 days after his 80th birthday. He was an ordained minister in the CP Church serving primarily in Choctaw Presbytery. Reverend Jacob served as Moderator of General Assembly as well as on several denominational boards. The denomination has lost a great leader and he will be greatly missed by the CP Church. For more information about Randy's ministry, a limited number of copies of the Summer 2017 issue of The Missionary Messenger are available at the Ministry Council booth. That issue includes expanded features on Randy and Betty Jacob.

3. The Stott-Wallace Missionary Fund gained new donors over the past two years. The chart below labels SW (donations to specific missionaries and general donation with no missionary designation); and Setup, (money new missionaries raise to pay their initial setup expenses when they move to the mission field including but not limited to airfare, visa/legal expenses, furniture, car, office equipment).

In order to sustain the 15 missionaries the Cumberland Presbyterian Church supports through the SW Missionary Fund we need $31,669 each month, or $380,028 annually in donations. We can only maintain our missionaries and deploy new ones if enough donors contribute to this fund. A new pledge and donation link are on the MC website https://cpcmc.org/mmt/sw.

Annual giving spikes are the result of Pentecost Sunday offerings, our Mission Sunday.

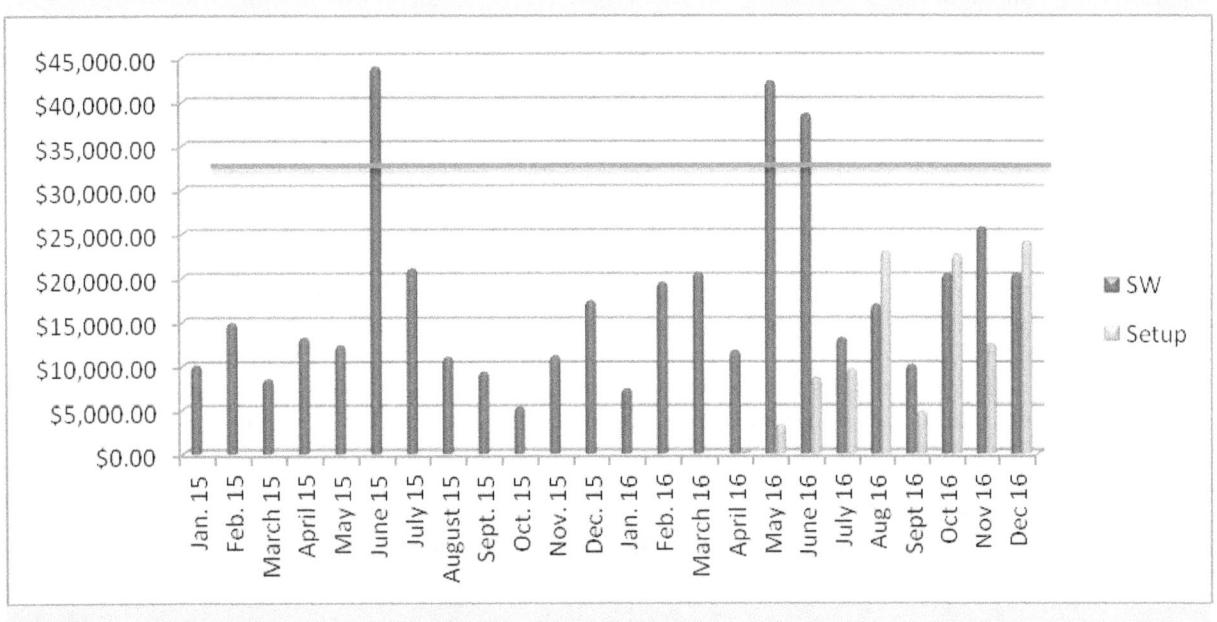

RECOMMENDATION 5: That the 187th General Assembly encourages presbyteries in attendance to promote the Stott-Wallace Missionary Support Fund among the churches of their presbytery. That each presbytery stated clerk provides the presbytery with the promotional video to be shown at presbytery and provides brochures for presbytery delegates to take back to their churches.

4. **New Church Development (NCD):** MMT is committed to starting new churches as an effective means of evangelism and church growth, providing regular contact, administrative and financial support, and supervision. MMT currently assists 19 NCDs in the US, nine of which are Cross-Culture, and three NCDs overseas.

Much of the activity of NCD is in giving encouragement and guidance to the initial exploration, studies and planning necessary for a successful new church development. At times, this is requested or initiated by a presbyterial board of missions, a NCD task force or by the MMT itself. Not all initial explorations, studies or planning result in NCDs or in viable CP congregations. However, efforts and attempts to start new churches are vital to sharing the gospel and for the building of God's kingdom. Places being explored for NCDs as future possibilities include Nashville, Tennessee area; Denver, Colorado; greater Dallas, Texas area; and central Oklahoma. MMT is open to exploring new areas and securing leadership for potential projects.

RECOMMENDATION 6: That the 187th General Assembly calls the Cumberland Presbyterian Church to be in diligent prayer for new exploration initiatives (formerly known as Mission Probes), and new church development as a means of evangelism and denominational growth in the United States. For individuals, both lay and ordained, to answer the call to church planting and for all judicatories of the Church to emphasize starting new exploration initiatives and/or new churches by identifying individuals and geographical areas where a Cumberland Presbyterian presence is needed and desirable.

5. **Intercultural Internship Opportunities:** The 2016 Intercultural Internship was hosted by Cristo Salva CP Fellowship in Memphis, Tennessee. Miss Adriana Rodriguez, a member of Casa De Fe CPC served as an intern for four weeks in Memphis, supporting the English-speaking ministry of Cristo Salva CP Fellowship. She served in a variety of ways: developed and led a curriculum for Vacation Bible School; served as an interpreter to assist Latino parents with their children's school enrollment; and served as an interpreter for sermons preached in English in the congregation. This year's internship is a joint effort among three Latino ministries in Memphis. Miss Karen Tejada, a covenant member of a NCD in Hialeah, Florida, will serve as an intern for three weeks in Memphis, working with three Latino ministries. Funding required for this internship is $2,000.00, and will only be made possible by donations from presbyteries, local churches, and individuals.

RECOMMENDATION 7: That the 187th General Assembly encourages presbyteries, local churches, and individuals to support Intercultural Internship opportunities through praying for the interns, and also through financially support the ongoing internship opportunities throughout the country.

III. FUNDING

Since the inception of the "new structure" in 2007, the MC and Teams have shared in planning new and ongoing ministries. Each year the collegial environment has grown stronger, enabling the reality of a truly comprehensive budget. Funding sources include Our United Outreach, other donations, grants, the Investment Loan Program (ILP) and endowments (listed within the Board of Stewardship section of the preliminary minutes). The endowment program is an important part of our funding, however small endowments do not generate usable funds until they reach sufficient size to generate interest payments that can be used.

Ministry Council and Ministry Teams hope donors will contribute directly to programs of the Church, thus providing us with funds to meet immediate programming needs.

IV. MINISTRY COUNCIL CONCLUSION

The 52 MC/Ministry Team elected and advisory members and 17 staff members are committed to serving as conduits of information to and from the MC. We remain committed to serving God through the CPC and ask that the Church remain in prayer for our collaborative work. We are thankful for the sustaining guidance of the Holy Spirit as we work to enhance and implement ministries that draw people to Christ. We encourage Commissioners to the 187th General Assembly and guests to learn about our neighbors at the MC booth. Learn about the MC's many diverse programs while you recharge your cell phone. Pick up print materials to share with your congregation, groups and presbytery. Booth hosts are MC and Ministry Team staff and elected members, eager to listen to ideas and to answer questions.

Like other denominations, ours is an aging denomination. We yearn to see a new generation of Cumberland Presbyterians serving in leadership roles throughout the Church. We yearn for Cumberland Presbyterians everywhere to commit to actively sharing in the work of the Church, for leaders to rise up from across the globe to further the work of the Church around the world.

Respectfully Submitted,
The Ministry Council of the Cumberland Presbyterian Church
Reverend Troy Green, President
Reverend Michele Gentry, First Vice President
Reverend Lanny Johnson, Second Vice President
Reverend Phillip Layne, Secretary
Edith B. Old, Director of Ministries/Treasurer

THE REPORT OF THE
BOARD OF STEWARDSHIP,
FOUNDATION, AND BENEFITS

I. GENERAL INFORMATION

A. BOARD MEETINGS AND ORGANIZATION
The Board of Stewardship, Foundation and Benefits under the direction of its officers, President Randy Davidson, Vice-president Mike St. John, Secretary Debbie Shelton, and Treasurer Robert Heflin, met two times in regular session.

B. BOARD MEMBERS WHOSE TERMS EXPIRE
Members whose terms expire at the 2017 General Assembly, with their years of service, are as follows: Boyd Day, nine years; Sylvia Hall, nine years; Jackie Satterfield, nine years; and Randy Davidson, three years. Boyd Day, Sylvia Hall and Jackie Satterfield are not eligible to serve another term. We want to thank them for their service and dedication to the Board of Stewardship, Foundation and Benefits. Randy Davidson is eligible and has agreed to serve another three year term.

C. BOARD REPRESENTATIVE TO THE 186TH GENERAL ASSEMBLY
The board's representative to the 187th General Assembly is Boyd Day.

D. STAFF
Kathryn Gilbert Craig serves as Administrative Assistant, Mark Duck serves as Coordinator of Benefits and Robert Heflin serves as Executive Secretary. Carolyn Harmon serves as the Planned Giving Coordinator for the Presbytery of East Tennessee. The Board appreciates the work Carolyn Harmon does in educating congregations of the legacy ministry that can be accomplished as individuals make planned gifts to their local congregations.

E. 2018 BUDGET
The 2018 line-item budget has been filed with the Office of the General Assembly.

F. 2016 AUDIT
Certified copies of the 2016 audit reports from Fouts and Morgan will be filed with the Office of the General Assembly in compliance with General Regulations E.5. and E.6. The 2016 audit will be printed in the audit section of the 2017 minutes.

II. FINANCIAL FOUNDATION DEVELOPMENT AND MANAGEMENT

A. PURPOSE
One area of the work of the board is in financial foundation development and management. The purpose of this program is as follows:
To secure a firm financial undergirding for the ongoing ministry of congregations and the agencies of presbyteries, synods, and the General Assembly as they bear witness to the saving love of God, the grace of our Lord Jesus Christ, and the fellowship and communion of the Holy Spirit.

B. 2016 IN REVIEW
The year 2016 can be viewed as a series of distinctly different investment environments. The first six weeks were marked by fears of a deflationary slowdown and hedge fund deleveraging before a Fed-inspired relief rally. The first quarter was very challenging for investors. The second and third quarters were more friendly to fundamental investors and proved fruitful for our diversified approach. The U.S. Presidential election's outcome dominated the fourth quarter, as the U.S. equity market initially dropped, then euphorically rose.

We need to continue to be cautious about looking too far down the road. Sentiment and emotion rule the short term. We are confident that our investment manager, Gerber/Taylor can continue to help us navigate the sometimes turbulent ups and downs of the market. Since October 1981, Gerber/Taylor has done a wonderful job for the Cumberland Presbyterian Church.

C. BOARD OF STEWARDSHIP

The Board of Stewardship is ever mindful of expenses incurred and try to be good stewards of what has been entrusted to the Board. We are grateful for the faithful support from congregations and individuals through their contributions to Our United Outreach.

1. PaperSave

In an effort to be better stewards, the Board of Stewardship has implemented a paperless document management system. In excess of ten thousand pages of over 850 endowment files, over 300 retirement files, over 280 Investment Loan Program account files and about 50 loan files have been scanned. Future reports and documents will become a part of the paperless system. The staff enjoys the paperless system as it provides quicker response and better service to those who call with questions.

D. MANAGEMENT OF FUNDS

In January 2013, we combined the Growth/Income Endowment Fund and the Total Return Endowment Fund with a focus on not only interest and dividends but also growth in realized and unrealized gains/losses.

At the end of 2016 the Endowment Fund portfolio was under the co-management of Gerber/Taylor Management, RREEF America II, Clarion, Headlands Capital and Eagle MLP. The funds of the Retirement Program were co-managed by Gerber/Taylor Management, RREEF America II, Headlands Capital and Eagle MLP.

The church loan portion of the endowment portion of the endowment portfolio and the investments of the Cumberland Presbyterian Church Investment Loan Program, Inc. were under the management of board staff with the help of Hilliard Lyons.

III. ENDOWMENT PROGRAM

Since 1836, the board and its corporate predecessors have sought to be faithful trustees of the funds given into their hands to provide a permanent financial foundation for the work of congregations, presbyteries, synods, and General Assembly agencies. The work of the Endowment Program is the oldest responsibility of the board and fulfills a portion of that task to which all Cumberland Presbyterians are called: "Christian stewardship acknowledges that all of life and creation is a trust from God, to be used for God's glory and service."—Confession of Faith for Cumberland Presbyterians 6:10.

A. COMMUNICATION

The Endowment Program report will be distributed to all endowment program participants, general assembly board members, churches, and individual contributors.

Agencies, other participants, and interested parties received quarterly detailed reports on the postings to all their endowments. With the addition of names supplied by the agencies during the year, the number of persons receiving these reports continues to expand. In addition, special reports were made as requested.

B. ASSETS, INVESTMENT MIX, AND PERFORMANCE

1. Assets and Investment Mix

The assets of the Endowment Fund totaled $55,377,108 for 2016 at market value. The following table provides a breakdown of the investment mix:

INVESTMENT MIX		
Securities & Investments		
14.3%	US Equity	$ 7,918,926
14.6%	Real Assets	$ 8,085,058
14.1%	Fixed Income	$ 7,808,172
18.5%	Hedged Equity	$10,244,765
15.3%	Multi-Strategy	$ 8,472,698
2.6%	Opportunistic	$ 1,439,805
12.0%	International Stocks	$ 6,645,253
7.3%	Emerging Markets	$ 4,042,529
1.3%	Private Equity	$ 719,902
100.0%	Total	$55,377,108

2. Performance of the Endowment Fund

The Endowment Fund generated $3,508,422 in investment earnings during 2016. Net contributions and withdrawals were a negative $34,800. The change in market value was a positive of $3,473,622.

With the combining of the Growth/Income Fund and the Total Return Fund in January 2013, we also began paying out 5% (annualized) to the congregations, presbyteries and agencies. Previously agencies had difficulty in preparing budgets because of the unknown amount they would receive from endowment income. Now, they realize they will receive 5% in endowment income over a twelve-month period. With this information, they have a better idea how much endowment income they can expect. Earnings paid to congregations, presbyteries and agencies totaled $1,478,865 for 2016.

3. Total Rate of Return for the Endowment Fund

The following table gives the annualized rates of return as contained in the report from Gerber/Taylor Associates for year end 2016:

	One Year Period 01/01/16 - 12/31/16	Five Year Period 01/01/12 - 12/31/16	Since Inception 09/30/81 - 12/31/16
Endowment Fund	6.7%	7.5%	9.8%

C. ESTABLISHING AN ENDOWMENT AS A LEGACY

The Board of Stewardship, Foundation and Benefits manages over 800 endowments established for the benefit of congregations, presbyteries, synods, agencies and other special ministries of the Cumberland Presbyterian denomination. Many of these endowments were established by individuals as a legacy to continue to benefit long after they are no longer with us. Some of the endowments were established by congregations, presbyteries and synods to help further their specific ministries. Some of the endowments were started with very little. Through the years these endowments have grown and the beneficiaries are reaping the gifts of the endowment income and using it in ministry in their local area or worldwide. Please consider establishing an endowment.

List of Endowments

Board of Stewardship

Endowment	Ending Balance 2015	Ending Balance 2016
Grace J. Beasley Memorial	$29,897.34	$30,153.47
Donald Bierhaus Trust	$70,376.12	$70,979.03
C. C. Brock Endowment Fund	$4,879.10	$4,920.87
Lavenia Campbell Cole Annunity Endowment	$66,408.31	$66,977.22
Lavenia Cole Testamentary Trust 25%	$581,419.01	$587,966.51
Lavenia Campbell Cole Trust 20%	$49,327.13	$49,750.00
Lavenia Campbell Cole Finance Endowment	$9,965.66	$10,051.02
Foundation & Finance Trust	$9,146.45	$9,226.65
Freeman Trust	$108,123.78	$109,050.04
Floyd Hensley Trust	$27,956.52	$28,196.03
P. F. Johnson Memorial Endowment	$9,450.98	$9,531.94
Robert H. Jordan Endowment Fund	$6,696.04	$6,753.39
Della Campbell Lowrie 20%	$448,889.26	$452,734.68
J. Richard Magrill, Jr. Endowment	$45,300.91	$45,905.65
Sam B. Miles Endowment	$83,094.54	$83,807.86
M. Dale Orr Endowment	$38,665.73	$38,996.99
William Dana Shriver Fund	$212,760.42	$214,583.04
Maymie Stovall - Frontier Press 25%	$30,940.49	$31,205.52
Evelyn & Gene Walpole Endowment	$26,120.66	$27,742.87
Eugene Warren Endowment Fund	$24,987.82	$25,201.88
Dixie Campbell Zinn Memorial	$15,165.31	$15,295.35
Total	**$1,899,571.58**	**$1,919,030.01**

Ministerial Aid

Endowment	Ending Balance 2015	Ending Balance 2016
Ministerial Aid Endowment	$793,336.10	$805,699.24
Ministerial Aid Surplus Endowment	$30,512.53	$32,407.47
CPWM Endowment for Minister Care	$6,551.54	$6,958.40
Jesse W. Hipsher Endowment	$41,580.01	$44,162.31
Annie Lee Hogue Endowment	$39,526.16	$41,980.85
Herschel E. Jones Ministers' Trust	$11,588.51	$12,308.27
Kate H., Robert E. & Robert M. King	$156,418.39	$166,132.61
Della Campbell Lowrie Endowment 20%	$1,708,210.52	$1,814,297.60
Special Reserve Retirement Program	$86,005.50	$90,871.73
Sue Stiles Endowment Fund 50%	$96,117.11	$102,086.39
Total	**$2,969,846.37**	**$3,116,904.87**

Ministry Council - Missions Ministry Team

Endowment	Ending Balance 2015	Ending Balance 2016
Church Loan Fund - General	$1,344,826.15	$1,356,346.70
McKenzie Endowment	$41,506.90	$41,862.48
Advance in Missions Trust Fund	$434,076.91	$437,795.55
Missions & Evangelism Endowment	$112,990.68	$113,958.76
Grace Johnson Beasley Memorial	$36,937.34	$37,253.77
Grace Beasley - Small Rural Church	$49,909.06	$50,336.59
Bennett & Mildred Brown Trust	$55,783.25	$59,247.65
David Brown Endowment	$11,648.86	$12,372.30
CPW Leadership Trust Fund	$95,378.81	$101,302.23
CPWM Bethel College Scholarship	$172,702.34	$181,965.81
Lavenia Campbell Cole Annuity Endowment	$61,379.17	$61,904.98
Lavenia Cole Testamentary Trust (25%)	$610,642.40	$617,440.89
Lavenia Campbell Cole Trust Endowment 20%	$21,782.16	$21,968.78
Rouine Vodra Coleman Endowment	$1,422.87	$1,511.23
Winnifred M. Dixon Endowment	$57,505.60	$57,998.19
Joseph B. Dungy Endowment	$89,846.85	$90,616.55
Louise & Sam R. Estes Endowment	$13,964.03	$14,090.44
Clifford Gittings Endowment	$6,218.98	$6,605.17
Lelia B. Goodman for Missions	$3,196.05	$3,394.55
P. F. Johnson Memorial End.	$18,913.74	$19,075.74
Finis Ewing & Bessie Keene Memorial	$147,534.56	$148,798.44
Chow King Leong Endowment	$50,746.49	$51,181.20
Mary Katherine Mize Longwell Endowment	$719.32	$763.99
Della Campbell Lowrie Trust 20%	$449,172.36	$453,020.26
Jamie Roy Chaffin Endowment	$2,203.19	$2,340.01
Mark G. Lynch Choctaw Presbytery	$10,726.88	$11,393.05
Clifford W. & Sarah C. McCall NCD	$7,232.39	$11,340.10
Joe E. Matlock Endowment	$51,496.69	$51,951.09
Robert E. Matlock Endowment	$161,988.67	$163,376.39
Robert T. & Dona Milam Endowment	$6,872.46	$7,511.92
Nancy J. Orr Bequest	$4,725.37	$5,018.83
New Church Development Endowment	$96,222.01	$97,046.32
S. Q. Proctor Home Mission Endowment	$11,444.68	$11,542.73
Marguerite D. Richards Rural Church	$24,370.17	$24,578.94
Maymie Stovall - Home Missions 25%	$12,014.28	$12,117.17
Paul & Geneva Richards Memorial	$12,143.88	$12,247.92
William A. & Beverly St. John Endowment	$13,038.20	$13,321.09
Madge Sprague Memorial Endowment	$6,095.94	$6,474.55
Lela Swanson Stricklen NCD	$64,276.80	$64,827.43
Cornelia Swain Endowment	$62,169.69	$64,300.70
Marguerite D. Richards MM Magazine	$8,935.32	$9,490.25

Walkerville CPC Memorial Endowment	$7,307.56	$7,761.38
Brown & Julia Welch Missions Endowment	$31,534.61	$31,804.77
Marvin O. Clement & Clement E. Wilkins Memorial Endowment	$0.00	$1,749.79
Gina Marie Benzel Ableson Memorial	$10,963.90	$11,644.81
Ashburn-Graf Educational Endowment	$148,448.61	$157,926.16
Maree Blackwell Endowment	$2,674.54	$2,840.65
James A. Brintle II Scholarship	$6,564.51	$6,972.19
Mattie Ree Suddarth Brown Endowment - Missions	$20,681.40	$20,858.57
Gladys H. Bryson Scholarship Fund	$118,426.62	$125,987.44
Davis O. & Gladys H. Bryson Missionary	$84,488.66	$85,212.46
Mary Frances & William Carpenter	$11,888.87	$11,986.40
Mildred Chandler Scholarship Endowment	$146,134.71	$155,330.89
Colombian CPW Elementary Scholarships	$39,993.62	$40,522.42
Helen Deal Endowment	$51,419.55	$51,860.07
John A. Deaver Mission	$11,059.96	$11,746.84
Chester E. Dickson Endowment	$44,730.22	$45,113.37
Jose & Fanny Fajardo Endowment	$10,573.81	$11,128.03
Foreign Missions Endowment	$340,476.65	$343,393.35
Mrs. G. W. Freeman Bible Woman Trust	$6,958.29	$7,390.44
McAdow and Mae Gam Endowment	$15,617.92	$16,175.56
Samuel King Gam	$28,590.34	$28,992.91
Freda Mitchell Gilbert Endowment (MMT)	$8,621.35	$9,233.31
Bernice Barnett Gonzalez Endowment	$1,518.81	$1,613.12
Gleniel Grounds Endowment	$2,334.08	$2,479.04
Holzer Trust	$87,539.55	$93,128.35
Hong Kong Mission	$40,261.85	$40,606.77
Marvin C. & Ruth M. Kinnard Trust	$16,941.40	$17,993.51
Warren and Carline Lowe Trust	$2,954.00	$3,137.44
Mamie McAdoo Endowment	$2,902.32	$3,082.54
McClung/Fowler Memorial Endowment	$93,466.13	$101,894.06
Holly Katelyn McClurkin	$730.79	$776.18
Rubye Johnson May Memorial 50%	$8,270.88	$8,784.51
Lucie C. Mayhew Fund for U-P Children	$16,789.05	$17,996.76
Elizabeth A. & James W. Morrow Trust	$24,173.77	$24,380.87
Richard Nicks Memorial Endowment	$57,829.78	$61,421.25
Hamilton & Merion S. Parks Family Trust #2	$26,838.72	$28,505.50
Patron Membership	$810,401.05	$821,245.80
Myra Patton Foreign Mission Endowment	$163,003.51	$164,399.89
Perpetual Membership Fund	$1,006,161.53	$1,017,821.02
Don & Gwen Peterson Endowment Fund	$114,075.09	$116,836.30
Rose Ella Porterfield Scholarship	$20,214.76	$21,470.14
Carl Ramsey Scholarship Fund	$36,058.20	$35,454.72
Marguerite D. Richards Japan	$16,273.10	$16,412.52

Endowment	Ending Balance 2015	Ending Balance 2016
Elise Sanders Endowment	$300,712.73	$303,288.79
Scholarship-Universidad Evangelica	$11,790.86	$12,523.12
Buddy & Beverly Stott Endowment	$27,502.53	$27,736.55
Maymie Stovall - Foreign Mission 25%	$12,015.37	$12,118.26
Irvin & Annie Mary Draper Swain	$30,234.37	$32,378.65
Walter Swartz - Jose Fajardo Scholarship Fund	$46,025.13	$48,963.15
William B. & Emma Jo Denson Todd Endowment	$7,243.11	$7,692.94
Boyce & Beth Wallace Endowment	$50,059.18	$50,488.49
Robert J. & Marilee B. Watkins	$2,119.07	$2,250.67
Bill & Kathryn Wood	$69,680.61	$74,510.25
Forester World Missions Endowment	$3,544,780.14	$3,575,146.89
Bill & Iona Wyatt Endowment	$12,985.78	$13,097.00
Rev. & Mrs. Tadao Yoshizaki Memorial	$690.14	$733.02
Total	**$12,256,494.59**	**$12,455,690.62**

Ministry Council - Communications Ministry Team

Endowment	Ending Balance 2015	Ending Balance 2016
Masaharu Asayama/CPWM Endowment	$11,029.88	$11,714.86
Ky Curry Publishing Endowment	$39,091.92	$41,519.71
C. Ray Dobbins Endowment	$36,675.31	$38,952.99
Dennis H. Kiefer Endowment	$992.55	$1,054.19
Marguerite D. Richards CP Magazine	$19,788.22	$21,017.17
Pat White Endowment	$7,808.61	$8,293.52
Total	**$115,386.49**	**$122,552.44**

Ministry Council - Discipleship Ministry Team

Endowment	Ending Balance 2015	Ending Balance 2016
Paul Allen Endowment for C E	$11,323.82	$11,427.75
Grace Johnson Beasley Mem.	$10,828.54	$10,921.30
Bennett & Mildred Brown for C E	$25,192.01	$25,407.83
Christian Education Mid-Century	$247,287.21	$249,405.65
Christian Education Season Endowment	$183,965.59	$185,755.10
Carl Cook Outdoor Ministry Endowment	$4,822.45	$4,864.37
Lavenia Campbell Cole Annuity End.	$35,600.25	$35,905.20
Jill Davis Carr - Leadership Development	$11,473.55	$11,577.33
Consultant Training Fund	$57,380.91	$57,872.49
C. P. Youth Conference	$163,464.55	$164,950.71
H. Harold Davis Endowment Fund	$163,877.51	$165,281.59
Jack W. Ferguson, Jr. C E Endowment	$10,830.98	$10,923.77
Ira & Rae Galloway for C E	$14,106.06	$14,226.90
Jean Garrett Endowment for C E	$4,088.65	$4,129.07

Louise Adams Heathcock Memorial	$10,880.92	$10,974.10
John Gilbert Horsley - Youth Leaders	$13,230.83	$13,346.48
Donald & Jane Hubbard Endowment for C E	$11,379.97	$11,477.44
Into the Nineties for C E	$273,493.76	$275,836.70
Reverend Gayle J. Keown for C E	$3,544.60	$3,574.92
Earl King Memorial	$10,833.52	$10,926.33
Virginia Malcom Christian Education	$113,068.84	$114,037.46
Wesley & Jackie Mattonen Endowment	$34,146.73	$34,439.24
David & Mary McGregor C E Endowment	$55,027.42	$55,502.12
James D. McGuire Endowment for C E	$16,088.92	$16,332.13
Howell G. & Martha Jo Mims CPYC	$28,337.11	$29,107.77
Morris & Ruth Pepper for C E	$51,496.76	$51,937.97
Bill & Hazel Phalan Endowment	$14,471.00	$14,599.43
Claudette Hamby Pickle C E Endowment	$20,451.63	$20,626.79
Publishing House Endowment 33%	$142,108.44	$143,326.11
Dr. & Mrs. E. K. Reagin Endowment	$56,366.84	$56,849.67
Jodi Hearn Rush Endowment	$11,164.69	$11,260.42
Rev. Rusty Rustenhaven Youth Ministry	$13,511.69	$13,627.44
Give for Good Endowment	$2,530.12	$2,687.27
John W. Speer Endowment for C E	$19,703.15	$19,871.92
Cornelia Swain Endowment for C E	$19,447.46	$20,954.50
Irvin & Annie Mary Swain Endowment	$23,458.86	$25,000.63
Jake Tyler Children's Ministry	$2,432.70	$3,848.24
Frank & Linda Ward Endowment (CE)	$35,878.42	$36,197.83
William Warren Endowment for C E	$11,624.82	$11,727.60
Clark Williamson Memorial	$40,943.50	$41,294.27
Helen Wiman Memorial	$4,241.45	$4,277.79
Young Adult Ministry Endowment	$23,332.49	$23,532.39
Terence R. McCain, Sr. Endowment	$6,130.08	$6,192.52
Total	**$2,013,568.80**	**$2,036,016.54**

Ministry Council - Pastoral Development Ministry Team

Endowment	Ending Balance 2015	Ending Balance 2016
Awards for CP Ministers & Spouses	$25,595.19	$25,832.84
Roosevelt and Ruth Baugh	$4,922.50	$5,228.20
LaRoyce Brown Endowment	$1,532.18	$1,627.35
James & Helen Knight Endowment	$26,384.62	$26,629.56
Ministerial Endowment	$13,885.12	$14,014.06
Ministers Conference	$19,258.91	$19,437.86
Melvin & Naomi Orr Endowment	$21,619.88	$21,820.59
James Lee Ratliff Endowment	$11,323.74	$11,569.19
Norlan & Ellie Scrudder Endowment	$21,935.76	$22,139.39
James & Geneva Searcy Endowment	$33,413.54	$33,723.74

Endowment		Ending Balance 2015	Ending Balance 2016
E. G. & Joy Sims Endowment		$23,272.95	$23,489.00
Leonard & Mary Jo Turner Endowment		$14,189.33	$14,320.93
Lyon Walkup Endowment		$14,703.16	$15,366.19
Arturo & Carmen Ortiz Endowment		$14,139.49	$15,017.63
Louisa M. Woosley Endow. for Sustaining Women in Ministry		$11,529.67	$12,245.69
	Total	**$257,706.04**	**$262,462.22**

Office of the General Assembly

Endowment		Ending Balance 2015	Ending Balance 2016
D. W. Fooks Memorial Endowment		$18,465.84	$18,624.05
Publishing House Endowment (33%)		$32,013.41	$31,847.15
Robert & Olene Rush Endowment		$18,830.51	$18,991.87
Trustee Endowment		$363,181.23	$366,292.37
	Total	**$432,490.99**	**$435,755.44**

Historical Foundation

Endowment	Ending Balance 2015	Ending Balance 2016
Anne Elizabeth Knight Adams Heritage Fund	$3,919.18	$6,224.76
Rosie Magrill Alexander Trust	$16,984.93	$17,130.59
Paul H. & Ann Middleton Allen Heritage Fund	$7,176.08	$7,237.52
Grace J. Beasley Birthplace Shrine	$57,050.76	$57,539.75
Birthplace Shrine Fund	$162,534.53	$178,260.93
James L. & Louise M. Bridges Heritage Fund	$18,126.15	$18,281.44
Mark and Elinor Swindle Brown Heritage Fund	$4,869.42	$5,769.00
*Sydney & Elinor Brown Heritage Fund	$8,179.14	$8,577.62
Centennial Heritage Endowment	$86,600.93	$87,342.81
Walter Chesnut Endowment	$16,167.35	$16,325.65
Lavenia Campbell Cole Heritage Fund	$68,080.41	$68,663.69
C. P. Church in America Heritage Fund	$14,279.18	$14,401.50
CPW Archival Supplies Endowment	$30,294.07	$30,553.60
Bettye Jean Loggins McCaffrey Ellis Heritage Fund	$1,339.25	$2,007.56
Samuel Russell & Mary Grace Barefoot Estes	$23,542.06	$23,743.74
Family of Faith Endowment	$14,734.32	$14,861.25
Gettis & Delia Snyder Gilbert Heritage Fund	$6,730.63	$6,788.26
James C. & Freda M. Gilbert Heritage Fund	$23,048.07	$23,252.42
James C. & Freda M. Gilbert Trust (HF)	$62,884.42	$63,423.13
Mamie A. Gilbert Trust	$14,541.16	$14,665.73
Henry Evan Harper Endowment CP History	$1,945.88	$2,035.35
Ronald W. & Virginia T. Harper	$4,163.79	$4,422.39
Historical Foundation Trust	$95,153.79	$98,150.87
Donald & Jane Hubbard Heritage Fund	$14,361.84	$15,754.29

Cliff & Jill Hudson Heritage Fund	$5,963.19	$6,015.67
Robert & Kathy Hull Endowment	$16,528.71	$16,678.49
Into the Nineties Endowment	$39,053.63	$39,388.22
Joe Ben Irby Endowment	$6,492.68	$7,390.03
P. F. Johnson Memorial Endowment (HF)	$18,967.70	$19,130.21
Irene A. Kiefer Endowment	$1,629.67	$1,730.87
Mr. & Mrs. Chow King Leong Heritage Fund	$5,619.15	$5,667.26
Dennis L. & Elmira Castleberry Magrill 50%	$23,599.09	$23,801.28
J. Richard Magrill, Jr. Heritage Fund	$6,179.19	$10,528.65
Joe R. & Mary B. Magrill Trust	$168,799.37	$170,245.41
Jimmie Joe McKinley Heritage Fund	$8,422.70	$8,497.23
Edith Louise Mitchell Heritage Fund	$4,268.99	$4,534.12
Lloyd Freeman Mitchell Heritage Fund	$4,268.98	$4,534.15
Snowdy C. & Lillian Walkup Mitchell Heritage Fund	$6,730.72	$6,788.35
Rev. Charles & Paulette Morrow Endowment	$1,266.85	$1,345.54
Virginia Sue Williamson Morrow Heritage Fund	$12,849.62	$12,959.68
Anne E. Swain Odom Heritage Fund	$22,792.52	$24,549.46
Martha Sue Parr Heritage Fund	$33,635.58	$33,931.60
Florence Pennewill Heritage Fund	$4,678.25	$4,718.41
Morris & Ruth Pepper Endowment (HF)	$16,399.45	$16,549.79
Publishing House Endowment 33% (HF)	$78,837.24	$79,895.09
Mable Magrill Rundell Trust	$16,979.24	$17,124.68
Samuel Callaway Rundell Heritage Fund	$11,468.08	$11,566.33
Paul & Mary Jo Schnorbus Heritage Fund	$8,223.42	$8,293.87
Shiloh CPC Ellis County Texas Endowment	$7,506.76	$7,571.06
Hinkley & Vista Smartt Heritage Fund	$7,317.51	$7,386.71
John W. Sparks Heritage Fund	$97,641.70	$98,481.63
Irvin S. Annie Mary Draper Swain Heritage Fund	$27,565.84	$29,161.12
F. P. (Jake) Waits Heritage Fund	$12,011.61	$12,116.47
Roy & Mary Seawright Shelton Heritage Fund	$3,523.53	$3,958.96
Gwendolyn McCaffrey McReynolds Hertiage Fund	$10,696.73	$10,806.23
Total	**$1,446,625.04**	**$1,490,760.42**

Our United Outreach

Endowment	Ending Balance 2015	Ending Balance 2016
George F. Battenfield Memorial	$51,275.97	$51,715.82
Daisy Bray Freeman Trust	$55,738.64	$56,216.27
Bertha Feazel Hammons Memorial	$47,379.54	$47,785.38
Kenneth & Myrtle Holsopple Memorial	$234,096.46	$236,101.89
Cliff & Jill Hudson OUO Endowment Fund	$11,834.54	$12,227.34
Knights of Honor Association Trust	$3,302.66	$3,330.94
Lowrie Estate Oil Royalties	$1,669,729.96	$1,715,551.32
Robert L. McReynolds Endowment 50%	$41,575.58	$41,931.73

The Moderators' Endowment for Our United Outreach	$31,701.47	$33,329.95
Santa Anna Church Memorial Fund	$20,633.02	$20,809.74
Tithing and Budget Endowment	$369,157.59	$372,319.98
Total	**$2,536,425.43**	**$2,591,320.36**

Cumberland Presbyterian Children's Home

Endowment	Ending Balance 2015	Ending Balance 2016
Merlyn & Joann Kitterman Alexander	$1,395.35	$1,031.45
W. A. & Elizabeth Bearden Trust	$15,886.68	$11,743.07
Grace Johnson Beasley Mem	$36,989.28	$27,341.50
Bethlehem CPC, Maury County, TN	$6,045.65	$4,468.71
James L. & Louise Bridges Scholarship	$41,319.92	$30,757.79
J. T. & Dorothy Britt Trust	$11,185.53	$8,267.91
Children's Home Endowment	$322,681.83	$238,520.54
Lavenia Campbell Cole Annuity Endow	$82,633.58	$61,079.52
Lavenia Cole Testamentary Trust - 25%	$612,119.09	$470,037.67
Lavenia Campbell Cole Trust (20%)	$20,346.96	$15,039.67
Mrs. A. L. Colvin Memorial Fund	$1,054.77	$1,120.29
John H. & Eva Cox Trust Fund	$30,970.08	$22,891.84
Steve Currie Trust	$543,640.55	$401,837.88
Daniel Class, Morningside CPC	$31,983.96	$23,641.28
Donnie Curry Davis Memorial	$187,161.48	$138,342.45
Mary Elberta Davis Memorial	$19,970.91	$14,761.75
Fred & Mattie Mae Dwiggins Memorial	$80,188.26	$59,271.99
J. S. Eustis Memorial Trust Fund	$12,659.86	$9,357.67
Winnie & Clester H. Evans, Sr. Trust	$21,136.12	$15,622.97
John M. Friedel Trust	$21,863.25	$16,160.47
Joyce C. Frisby Memorial Endowment	$28,117.20	$20,815.23
Vaughn & Mary Elizabeth Fults Trust	$20,167.28	$14,906.83
Garner-Miller Memorial Trust	$12,441.98	$9,196.66
James C. & Freda M. Gilbert Endowment (CPCH)	$113,803.58	$85,393.03
Henry & Jayne Glaspy Memorial Fund	$8,253.56	$6,100.67
Rev. W. J. Gregory Memorial	$103,738.27	$76,679.31
Glenn Griffin Endowment 33%	$44,225.00	$32,689.42
Rev. & Mrs. Henry M. Guynn Memorial	$4,595.27	$3,396.60
Chad Evan Harper Memorial Endowment	$11,618.37	$12,417.87
Newsome & Imogene Harvey Endowment	$2,536.64	$1,874.99
Clarence & Lula Herring Endowment	$6,038.23	$4,463.22
Kenneth & Clara M. Holsopple Trust	$53,454.57	$39,511.53
George & Lottie M. Hutchins Trust	$1,136,843.86	$840,310.52
Norma K. Johnson Memorial Library	$11,408.94	$8,433.04
P. F. Johnson Memorial Endow	$18,939.27	$13,999.19
Robert H. & Genevie Johnson Endowment	$4,805.02	$4,029.20

Mr. & Mrs. Robert L. Johnson	$11,933.62	$8,820.83
Violet Louise Jolly Endowment	$1,204.89	$890.62
Eulava Joyce Memorial Trust	$9,957.88	$7,360.47
Ruth Cypert & Harlie Kugler Memorial	$20,052.88	$14,822.35
Blanche R. Lake Endowment	$14,451.69	$10,682.12
Wade P. Lane & Maude Dorough Memorial	$9,512.03	$7,030.93
Adolphus M. Latta Memorial Trust	$51,324.41	$37,936.97
Mr. & Mrs. Robert F. Little (CPCH)	$35,504.98	$26,653.36
Charles E. Addie Mae Lloyd Endowment	$22,606.93	$16,710.16
Tony & Ann Martin Endowment	$2,509.24	$2,665.06
Mrs. Lucille (Lucy) Mast Endowment	$2,550.74	$2,709.17
W. B. & Azalee McClurkan, Sr. Memorial	$19,328.08	$14,286.52
William J. McCall Memorial Trust	$9,957.83	$7,360.45
McEwen Church Trust	$7,650.13	$5,654.70
J. C. McKinley Endowment (CPCH)	$18,856.28	$13,937.82
Velma McKinley Trust Fund	$18,856.42	$13,937.94
McKinley & Barnett Families 33%	$821,798.54	$617,113.33
Mary McKnight Memorial Trust	$10,616.74	$8,294.59
Kenneth & Mae Moore Endowment Fund	$7,040.70	$5,203.97
Operational Trust Fund	$148,142.93	$109,496.12
Bert & Pat Owen Endowment for CPCH	$1,566.19	$1,157.59
^Martha Sue Parr Endowment	$1,598.18	$1,181.46
Mary M. Poole Endowment Fund	$957,753.96	$707,913.54
Jack & Mary Lou Proctor Memorial Trust	$63,858.62	$47,199.52
Mary Acenal Prewitt Trust Fund	$90,276.57	$66,725.70
S. Q. & K. Maurine Proctor Trust	$5,656.11	$4,180.55
Rev. & Mrs. Joe Reed Memorial	$2,867.14	$3,045.20
Marguerite D. Richards Endowment	$25,433.44	$18,798.71
Agnew Durbin Richardson Trust	$30,168.99	$22,298.66
Pat N. & Essie H. Roberts Memorial	$58,884.79	$43,524.12
Frances Benefield Roberts Trust	$2,332.47	$1,724.01
Rev. & Mrs. John A. Russell Memorial	$4,553.90	$3,365.44
John, Ann & Mary Elizabeth Shimer	$14,990.31	$11,079.95
Rev. W. B. & Lydia Snipes Memorial	$19,864.76	$21,098.44
Don M. & Nancy E. Tabor Trust	$34,437.88	$25,466.23
Townsend Trust Fund	$38,432.10	$28,407.27
Hattie E. Wheelis Fund	$19,770.29	$14,613.17
Whitfield Family Endowment	$12,031.27	$8,905.67
Porter & Hattie S. Williamson Memorial	$171,481.46	$126,746.24
Helen and Lewis Wynn Endowment Fund	$11,013.00	$11,696.95
Maxie & Will Young Memorial Endowment	$20,756.97	$15,342.17
Dixie Campbell Zinn Memorial Trust	$6,240.08	$4,612.22
Joe Parr Trust Fund	$78,284.57	$57,861.91
Hamilton & Merion S. Parks Family Trust #3	$16,146.86	$13,483.26

Dr. John P. Austin Endowment	$20,224.82	$19,628.42
Total	**$6,634,701.82**	**$4,957,137.61**

Memphis Theological Seminary

Endowment	Ending Balance 2015	Ending Balance 2016
African-American Studies Chair	$8,341.39	$8,859.46
Emerson A. Alburty Endowment	$5,977.98	$6,028.75
John W. Aldridge Memorial Scholarship	$8,175.09	$8,259.31
Merlyn A. & Joann K. Alexander	$8,696.11	$8,770.71
Alston Family Evangelistic Association	$51,835.71	$53,664.78
Polly Atterbury Aldridge Scholarship	$10,257.27	$10,344.78
Alternate Studies Endowment	$9,583.55	$9,789.05
Virgil R. Anderson Memorial Endowment	$10,228.58	$10,347.67
Baird-Buck Chair of CP Studies	$355,785.62	$394,211.74
Walter & Eula Baker Memorial Fund	$11,647.28	$11,745.10
O. A. Barbee Endowment	$1,680.49	$1,703.44
Richard M. & Martha Carol Barker Scholarship	$10,891.11	$10,515.32
Barnes Seminary Endowment	$61,014.23	$61,529.13
Isaac R. Barnes Scholarship Endowment	$16,008.98	$16,162.89
George B. Bates Trust	$3,497.39	$3,527.32
Grace Johnson Beasley Endowment	$90,126.98	$91,513.78
Joseph E. Bedinger Memorial Library	$4,852.52	$4,894.03
Tarlton M. Belles Fund	$23,043.19	$23,255.98
Marie Blackwell Endowment	$470.06	$482.67
Larry A. Blakeburn Endowment	$2,649.55	$2,672.23
Roy E. Blakeburn Scholarship	$5,623.52	$10,720.23
Bowen Chapel Church Trust	$28,297.21	$15,595.28
Bowen Lecture Fund	$20,084.90	$21,332.27
Kyle D. Brantley, M. D. Memorial	$22,305.25	$24,978.74
Wes & Susan Brantley Endowment	$12,999.99	$19,232.47
Brockwell Library Endowment	$11,046.38	$11,244.15
Evelyn Brodeur	$22,989.11	$23,205.36
Brooksville CPC Endowment	$21,762.89	$21,972.81
Beth-Helen-Peggy Brown Endowment	$28,082.45	$29,211.55
Paul B. Brown Endowment - MTS	$16,957.74	$17,827.60
Paul F. & Mattie Suddarth Brown - MTS	$36,112.99	$36,418.42
W. W. Brown Scholarship	$4,376.29	$4,422.21
Finis McAdoo Bruington Board-Designated Endowment	$41,391.51	$22,668.53
Davis & Gladys Bryson Education 50%	$25,234.42	$26,925.78
Henry & Alfreda Bunton Scholarship	$23,896.84	$24,999.33
Hal & Gladys Burks Memorial Fund	$7,306.17	$7,376.58
Thomas H. Campbell Library Endowment	$4,538.19	$4,585.52
Thomas H. & Margaret E. Campbell	$30,621.80	$30,944.10
Campbell-Todd Trust	$10,684.56	$11,410.23

Carlock Memorial Trust	$1,205.51	$1,215.84
Cawthon Memorial Fund	$4,002.75	$4,036.92
Mildred Chandler Endowment	$3,863.61	$4,165.69
Rev. Walter & Mrs. Sarah Chesnut Scholarship Endowment	$9,838.63	$10,876.17
Gladys Chumbler Endowment	$6,986.14	$7,045.84
Marian Lisenbee Clark Endowment	$5,106.59	$5,158.46
Sallie H. Clay & Alice J. Cooksey	$263,644.25	$280,638.69
Faye E. & Ford F. Claytor Endowment	$7,503.24	$7,567.78
Lavenia Campbell Cole Annuity Endow.	$54,652.88	$58,295.44
Lavenia Campbell Cole Testamentary Trust 25%	$480,909.74	$510,776.24
Lavenia Campbell Cole Trust	$19,296.40	$19,461.42
George E. & Rouine V. Coleman Endowment	$8,656.75	$8,737.81
George E. Coleman Scholarship	$56,377.23	$55,793.48
Willene Cooper Scholarship	$30,888.67	$32,476.52
Hubert & Dortha Covington Memorial	$3,699.67	$3,730.56
James Covington Scholarship	$8,732.43	$9,274.73
Thelma Craig Scholarship	$29,398.23	$29,648.35
Cora Hawkins Crutchfield Scholarship Endowment	$31,427.38	$43,838.35
Cumberland Hall Endowment	$4,811.24	$4,895.13
Cumberland Presbyterian Women	$31,155.88	$33,277.11
Sallie Stacy Davenport	$6,703.50	$7,181.95
Mary Elberta Davis Memorial (MTS)	$5,657.19	$5,714.12
Paul & Nancy Dekar/Immersion Studies	$6,670.24	$5,525.37
James W. & Gladys Murray Diamond	$3,118.78	$3,145.40
Margaret M. Dirks	$8,169.22	$8,232.85
Houston Dixon Memorial	$6,991.48	$7,059.21
Winifred M. Dixon Endowment	$28,193.22	$30,130.40
C. Ray Dobbins Endowment (MTS)	$1,984.70	$2,001.68
Jesse R. & Virginia R. Durham Endowment	$866,624.15	$849,769.79
Rev. Dr. Loyce Estes Endowment Fund	$7,879.20	$8,368.52
Expansion & Development Fund	$3,055.68	$3,090.05
Faith CPC, Tulsa, OK - Scholarship	$45,272.21	$42,741.27
Alice Fay Finley	$5,324.74	$5,370.04
H. Glenn Finley Library Fund	$2,819.29	$2,843.44
E. H. & Millie Finley	$2,300.15	$2,319.83
Linda Hester Fooks Memorial	$15,751.90	$15,886.80
Jere B. Ford Family Endowment	$11,312.54	$12,015.13
Rev. J. C. & Willie Mae Forester Library	$5,701.90	$6,742.73
Vaughn Fults Endowment	$10,452.13	$10,541.13
Gadsden Area Churches Trust<	$41,605.32	$42,755.42
McAdow Gam Endowment Fund	$29,345.59	$30,711.44
John E. & Anna B. Gardner Endowment	$15,878.03	$16,013.56
Jessie B. & Noella Garner	$1,282.28	$1,293.23
W. L. & Dot Lacey Gaston Endowment	$7,537.78	$9,083.10

Louis E. & Millie Coats Gholson	$155,097.93	$164,916.50
James C. & Freda M. Gilbert Endowment (MTS)	$14,279.01	$15,165.79
James & Martha Gill Sacred Theology	$11,798.85	$11,906.15
David E. Glasgow Endowment	$1,453.90	$1,466.35
James A. & Lenora Greer Endowment	$3,237.89	$3,438.94
Mary Guice Memorial	$13,190.98	$14,010.19
Margaret I. Gunn Memorial	$24,685.62	$26,218.73
Hamilton Chapel Fund	$558,189.58	$592,855.53
Carlton & Margaret Ann Harper Endowment Fund	$10,890.63	$11,566.99
Mrs. George N. Harris Library Memorial	$3,397.89	$3,426.97
Newsome & Imogene Daniel Harvey	$6,682.18	$7,097.16
Bettye & Dick Hendrix Scholarship	$15,996.94	$15,432.45
Henshaw Family Endowment Fund	$5,575.93	$5,623.52
Frank & Margaret Henshaw Endowment 1	$13,479.43	$13,617.09
J. David & Barbara Hester Endowment	$53,134.28	$49,402.04
Rev. E. Samuel Hicks Endowment Fund	$4,474.28	$4,512.46
Dr. Alfred D. Hill Scholarship	$7,391.54	$7,915.87
Cortis E. Hill Library	$3,660.16	$3,691.51
David & Patsy Hilliard	$10,502.89	$11,155.19
Francis A. Hobgood Trust	$26,958.65	$28,632.85
William Clarence Hodge Memorial	$3,276.89	$3,304.99
B. L. & Jewel Looper Holder	$11,546.06	$11,273.04
Lee Hollowell Trust	$13,770.40	$13,904.93
Barbara A. Holmes Lectures	$9,017.66	$9,577.73
Mr. & Mrs. J. S. Holmes Trust	$4,991.40	$5,034.14
Kenneth & Myrtle Holsopple Endowment	$26,847.28	$28,700.95
Jack & Gwen Hood Scholarship	$54,283.88	$70,999.61
Rev. John William Howell Memorial	$2,237.26	$2,264.93
Cardelia Howell-Diamond Scholarship	$74,734.92	$71,441.39
Donald & Jane Hubbard Endowment for MTS	$10,317.10	$10,957.89
Bernice A. Humphreys Endowment	$16,693.90	$16,835.61
Charles E. & Helen Humphreys Endowment	$10,469.91	$10,590.07
Gerald S. & Louise Felts Hunter	$2,772.15	$2,795.82
George & Lottie M. Hutchins 33%	$213,659.20	$213,895.24
Mattie Hutchison Seminary Fund	$1,653.73	$1,667.87
Eugenia Turner Ingram Endowment	$3,069.68	$3,104.47
Lillian Johnston Ingram Library	$5,616.85	$5,673.42
Tom & Barbara Ingram Student Asst.	$43,413.40	$46,374.72
Virginia Howell Ingram Endowment Fund	$83,165.00	$85,295.33
Rev. W. T. Ingram, Sr. & Family Scholarship	$98,838.81	$98,654.26
William T. & Virginia H. Ingram Lectures	$117,705.44	$121,363.86
Joe Ben Irby Trust	$4,092.84	$4,127.91
Joe Ben & Julia Irby Endowment Fund	$84,745.83	$85,461.95
Virginia Irwin Memorial Endowment	$4,808.09	$4,849.27

Johns Lectures	$15,422.35	$16,380.14
P. F. Johnson Memorial	$48,570.23	$49,025.77
Robert A. & Jo S. Johnson (MTS)	$61,643.22	$61,953.08
Roby M. Johnston Endowment	$82,167.57	$82,866.84
Joiner Ministerial Scholarship	$5,977.20	$6,028.27
V. A. Jones Library Memorial	$4,022.27	$4,056.62
Kiningham-Kuehn Endowment	$10,493.67	$10,591.89
Franklin W. Latta Memorial Scholarship	$14,451.74	$14,592.06
Ruth Fumbanks Latta Endowment	$14,598.39	$14,731.07
Randal (Randy) Leslie Endowment Fund	$15,362.57	$16,692.14
C. S. Lewis & His Friends Lecture	$31,676.48	$29,336.36
Library Reserve - Seminary Development	$2,406.53	$2,435.70
Mr. & Mrs. Robert F. Little (MTS)	$28,769.82	$29,082.35
James & Louella Lively Family Endowment	$8,242.58	$8,313.35
Inez Lovelace Endowment	$32,380.43	$34,515.62
Virgil L. & Della M. Lowrie Lectures	$105,068.02	$109,809.30
Della Campbell Lowrie Endowment 20% (MTS)	$405,485.12	$332,304.05
Dennis L. & Elmira C. Magrill 50%	$28,530.82	$28,775.76
Rev. George Malone / Rev. Edmong Weir	$78,207.97	$83,189.22
W. A. Johnson Family Endowment	$14,935.02	$15,559.68
Dessa Jane Manuel Scholarship 50%	$41,131.93	$39,466.70
Marshall (Texas) CPW Endowment	$10,002.98	$10,099.09
Dr. & Mrs. Arleigh G. Matlock Scholarship	$32,770.52	$33,084.43
Charles R. Matlock Library Endowment	$5,042.38	$5,085.47
Walter L. Mayo Endowment Fund	$5,693.27	$5,742.03
Mr. & Mrs. David M. McAnulty Memorial	$13,477.97	$13,591.48
Doris McCall Memorial Endowment	$12,138.41	$12,440.36
James W. & Mary H. McCulloch Memorial	$13,418.75	$14,252.13
Margaret McCulloch Scholarship	$9,304.24	$9,165.16
F. Dwight & Bernice K. McDonald	$178,096.54	$164,537.34
McGuinness-Wood Endowment	$20,308.81	$20,482.48
Jack B. McKamey Endowment Fund	$5,353.41	$5,414.69
^Velma McKinley Memorial Endowment	$4,495.27	$4,533.82
McKinley & Barnett Families 33% (MTS)	$275,173.41	$278,404.87
Wesley McKinney Memorial Endowment	$11,795.99	$12,590.66
Maude McLin Memorial Endowment	$4,237.56	$4,273.86
Robert W. McReynolds Memorial	$5,279.39	$5,332.72
Mr. & Mrs. W. J. McReynolds Trust	$5,862.37	$5,912.18
John E. Meeks Family Endowment Fund	$22,764.76	$25,616.71
Memphis Methodist Conference Fund	$30,142.54	$32,014.53
Ed Mikel Doctoral Scholarship Memorial	$10,024.59	$10,120.87
Sam B. & Naurine W. Miles Endowment	$4,768.72	$4,809.47
Sam B. Miles Board Designated Endowment	$76,605.58	$45,089.36
Mary Elliott Miller Endowment	$8,725.26	$9,267.13

Rev. & Mrs. W. E. Miller Scholarship	$5,511.79	$5,567.45
Robert Lynn & Elizabeth P. Mills	$8,439.75	$8,513.34
Ministerial Scholarship Endowment 40%	$17,961.51	$14,450.27
Missouri-Arkansas CO-OP PCUSA	$4,476.06	$4,754.03
John L. Mize Scholarship	$8,466.38	$8,547.01
Clinton & Eva B. Moore Endowment	$30,360.41	$32,308.00
Frank C. Moore Endowment Fund	$10,690.84	$11,416.89
Mary E. Morefield Memorial 40%	$5,093.49	$5,136.74
Hubert W. Morrow Endowment PAS	$33,897.72	$36,127.10
Virginia Sue Williamson Morrow MT	$31,091.59	$33,146.72
Ruby Page Morton Endowment	$10,785.17	$11,348.33
William Taylor Morton Endowment	$11,557.48	$11,961.62
John & Gail Moss Endowment	$6,564.43	$6,972.11
Dr. Arthur Murrell Memorial Scholarship	$4,380.50	$4,426.22
Walter & Anna Murrie Endowment	$6,189.79	$6,242.65
Willard & Bettie Murrie Endowment	$10,179.29	$10,392.69
Gladys Teter Nichols	$95,815.48	$96,644.43
North Central Texas Presbytery Scholarship	$5,099.26	$5,143.02
Northside Presby. Church, Cleveland, TN Seminary Ed.	$0.00	$101,507.05
Northside Presby. Church, Cleveland, TN PAS End.	$0.00	$50,753.56
William H. & Nola A. Oliver Scholarship	$5,418.24	$5,473.04
Bert & Pat Owen - Shepherd's Rest	$100,415.04	$106,651.23
Palestine CPC Endowment at MTS	$3,688.52	$3,720.03
Walter G. (Pete) Palmer Endowment (PAS)	$143,848.10	$259,429.83
Paskell & Bernice Parker Endowment	$4,326.52	$4,363.58
Parr Scholarship Endowment	$52,529.03	$48,966.04
Rev. G. F. Phelps Memorial Scholarship	$16,914.18	$15,239.85
John W. Piper Endowment Fund	$23,395.38	$23,601.49
Platte-Lexington Seminary	$20,469.48	$20,659.05
Pleasant Hill CP Endowment	$6,405.14	$7,003.83
Bernice A. Humphreys Scholarship Endowment	$139,979.48	$146,649.50
Bettie Press Library Fund	$4,576.13	$4,614.78
S. Q. Proctor Ministerial Scholarship	$7,950.51	$8,035.73
Klahr & Iris Raney Endowment Fund	$18,241.71	$18,413.03
Eugene & Agnes Richardson Endowment	$7,296.25	$7,375.28
Evelyn B. Crick Richmond Endowment	$51,812.10	$55,029.81
Roy Roberts Memorial Endowment	$1,601.75	$1,615.47
Mrs. W. H. Rochelle Endowment Fund	$9,642.21	$9,724.50
Hudson & Robbie C. Roseberry	$78,154.52	$83,008.26
W. L. & Mary K. Rolman Scholarship	$19,292.26	$16,314.28
William & Dolores Rustenhaven Endowment	$5,280.62	$5,325.83
Beverly St. John/Theology & Arts	$8,392.14	$8,603.59
Saint Timothy CPC	$3,343.34	$3,371.91
Herschel A. & Iris L. Schultz	$126,269.05	$127,341.21

Clara Scott Family Chair - Part I	$333,427.06	$336,280.50
Clara Scott Family Chair - Part II	$207,353.36	$208,883.83
George W. Scott Endowment Fund	$6,617.15	$6,796.49
W. H. Scott Family Endowment	$10,518.14	$10,616.27
Marie C. Scrudder Memorial	$4,238.73	$4,275.04
Seminary Commitment Campaign	$2,958.60	$3,000.87
Seminary Development Fund Endowment	$784.72	$791.46
Seminary Scholarship Fund	$8,639.02	$8,728.55
Ed Shannon Endowment	$8,142.31	$8,710.08
E. Thach & Jerry Shauf Endowment	$15,466.50	$15,598.35
Robert E. Shelton Scholarship	$3,941.14	$4,185.86
Robert M. Shelton Scholarship	$3,340.55	$3,369.17
Ruby Burris Shelton Endowment	$4,940.88	$4,983.22
Dick & Virginia Singellton Endowment	$13,337.68	$13,449.98
Esther Smith & Search Parish Endowment	$2,083.77	$2,101.61
Odus H. Smith Memorial Endowment	$4,691.15	$4,731.37
Katherine Hinds Smythe Endowment	$5,697.83	$6,051.69
W. B. Snipes Memorial Scholarship	$15,077.85	$13,960.86
Truman Barrett Snowden Memorial	$4,784.74	$5,144.03
Dorothea Snyder Endowment	$4,922.62	$5,228.32
L. D. & Dathel Jones Stacey Endowment	$630.22	$635.62
Henry L. Starks Scholarship	$177,268.82	$186,380.35
Anne Stavely Endowmet Fund	$2,261.68	$2,281.04
Eva Jane Stewart Trust 50%	$47,785.95	$50,877.85
J.W. Stiles Lectures	$35,946.87	$38,346.24
Rev. Elizabeth Stone Mem. Schol.	$2,018.28	$2,035.54
Lela Stricklen Endowment	$42,875.45	$43,230.35
Maymie Stovall Memorial Trust 25%	$11,458.64	$11,556.59
Roy Stucker Scholarship Fund 50%	$37,681.47	$40,145.89
Charles Studdard Memorial	$17,584.38	$17,751.54
Emma Elizabeth Suddarth Memorial	$6,644.36	$6,701.27
Robert H. & Lois Went Taylor Endowment	$11,374.58	$11,480.59
Thomas V. Taylor Seminary Student	$5,881.22	$5,940.18
Verdys E. Taylor Trust	$2,243.98	$2,263.19
A. J. Terry Scholarship	$2,136.18	$2,154.48
Theological Seminary General Endowment	$74,414.35	$72,389.42
Virgil H. & Irene R. Todd - OT EXCL	$77,985.43	$82,828.69
Tri-Mu Bible Class Scholarship	$63,610.64	$66,189.47
R L Truax, M L Truax, R L Truax, Jr Award for Academic Ach	$8,065.96	$8,566.87
Carl Walker Endowment	$7,912.25	$7,988.57
Mr. & Mrs. Carl Forbis Ward Memorial	$5,266.90	$5,311.45
Tom V. Warnick Memorial	$40,821.65	$45,374.12
Geneverette Warr Endowment	$5,502.56	$5,557.68

Warren, MI, First CPC Endowment	$7,574.84	$8,045.26
Rev. David & Leota Watson Scholarship Endowment	$4,611.39	$5,496.14
The Rev. Harlon & Mary Edith Watson Endowment	$43,500.27	$49,449.52
Virgil T. & Sue B. Weeks	$7,325.76	$7,388.35
Lynn Westbrook Memorial Endowment	$8,716.76	$8,799.78
Mae Westbrook Memorial Endowment Fund	$4,178.89	$4,214.62
The Weston Endowment	$14,154.95	$14,275.01
J. W. Wilder Scholarship	$188,369.78	$192,494.59
Alline Williams Endowment	$8,564.15	$8,637.50
Wayne Wiman Scholarship	$28,816.04	$29,131.94
Davis/Winston Scholarship for National Baptist Students	$1,367.49	$4,214.83
Lamar & Ellen Wilson Memorial Scholarship	$19,845.23	$20,004.33
Women's Issues in Ministry Endowment	$5,568.02	$5,913.84
Louisa Woosley Endowment Fund	$73,733.61	$79,326.05
Rev. Charles W. Hall Endowment for Pastoral Excellence	$17,308.37	$19,950.03
Dr. Thomas D. Campbell Endowment	$9,637.92	$10,236.49
Rev. Matthew Miller Endowment	$2,059.83	$2,187.74
Total	**$9,891,168.18**	**$10,313,095.72**

Miscellaneous

Endowment	Ending Balance 2015	Ending Balance 2016
Lavenia Cole Test. Trust Temp.	$17,677.81	$42,473.81
CP Retirement & Health Maintenance (Sue Galey)	$14,168.08	$15,048.02
Lillie M. Dickerson Memorial Fund	$72,135.49	$73,530.05
Verna Fillius Green Charities Endowment	$8,614.12	$5,197.34
Hodgeville Cemetery Association	$13,989.13	$14,857.91
Laddie Lollar Scholarship	$20,923.52	$19,560.67
McKinley & Barnett Families Temp.	$4,621.72	$16,691.34
Matching Gift Endowment Fund	$49.89	$53.02
Terrell D. and Jacqueline C. Maynard Endowment	$18,644.73	$18,874.35
Anay Ortega Montroy Missionary Endowment Fund	$5,193.11	$15,148.49
Ethel Phillips Endowment	$52,630.15	$57,912.49
Premium Stabilization	$1,972,103.90	$1,878,548.54
Thomas P. & Barbara J. Semmens Scholarship	$1,718.24	$1,824.94
Stobbe Mathematics Scholarship	$48,599.55	$50,553.47
Maymie Stovall Trust	$276,542.63	$284,795.05
Mary Ann Walton Trust	$2,297,308.67	$2,314,784.96
Parr Estate/Mission Synod Ministerial Aid	$139,956.92	$148,648.80
Total	**$4,964,877.66**	**$4,958,503.25**

Bethel University

Endowment	Ending Balance 2015	Ending Balance 2016

J. E. Ash Memorial	$7,689.71	$7,755.74
Daisy J. Barger & Lena J. Davis	$19,502.09	$19,669.20
Grace Johnson Beasley (Memorial)	$17,169.23	$17,316.30
Herman Osteen Beasley Memorial	$42,377.57	$42,740.59
Bethel CPC, Columbia Presbytery	$1,950.29	$1,967.04
Boyett Trust	$34,304.05	$34,597.92
Rev. & Mrs. C. L. Bruington Library	$11,460.39	$11,558.56
Davis O. & Gladys Bryson Educ. 50%	$42,752.55	$43,118.84
Lavenia Campbell Cole Annuity End	$77,018.99	$77,678.78
Lavenia Campbell Cole Trust - 20%	$18,751.52	$18,912.18
Cumberland Presbytery Scholarship	$12,581.99	$12,689.75
J. Claud & Mary L. Dickinson Fund	$7,736.65	$7,802.93
Mary L. Claud Dickinson Educ.	$439,762.33	$443,529.66
Rev. & Mrs. Walter E. Dillow Memorial	$24,344.04	$24,552.59
Winifred M. Dixson Endowment	$48,875.75	$49,294.42
Jack & Ewie Freeman Trust	$20,028.29	$20,199.90
Vaughn & Mary E. Fults Min. Scholarship	$38,720.29	$39,052.01
Samuel K. Gam & Mamie S. Gam Endowment	$24,647.68	$25,016.44
Greensburg CPC Memorial Scholarship	$7,836.43	$7,903.56
Glenn Griffin Endowment - 33%	$37,537.77	$37,859.36
Fenner Heathcock Memorial Fund	$80,344.98	$81,033.27
Roy Hickman & Ruth Hughes Hickman	$42,130.86	$42,491.76
Francis A. Hobgood Trust 25%	$32,989.26	$33,271.87
George & Lottie M. Hutchins (Trust)	$270,430.43	$272,747.14
Dr. P. F. Johnson Memorial Endowment	$59,796.23	$60,308.49
Joiner Ministerial Scholarship (Bethel)	$6,479.78	$6,535.26
Rev. E. R. & Forest Ladd Memorial	$2,544.55	$2,566.39
Robert F. & Jane L. Little (BC)	$28,636.85	$28,926.03
Della Campbell Lowerie 20%	$386,567.45	$389,879.12
Dessa Jane Manuel Scholarship 50% (Bethel)	$180,705.37	$182,253.42
Albert & Belle McDonald Trus	$485,322.12	$489,479.72
Cliff McElroy Memorial Trust	$20,625.28	$21,906.18
Nyta Miller Scholarship	$7,232.79	$7,294.79
Nell Miller Scholarship	$3,235.71	$3,263.42
Ministerial Scholarship Endowment 60%	$127,215.28	$128,305.09
Bert & Pat Owen Endowment for Bethel	$2,158.51	$2,176.98
Max & Ethel Mize Parker Scholarship	$20,983.32	$21,163.12
S. Q. Proctor Ministerial Scholarship	$12,466.68	$12,573.46
Agnes D. Richardson Endowment Fund	$9,870.50	$9,955.04
Pauline Rucker Memorial	$4,434.17	$4,472.16
Rev. & Mrs. J. Howard Scott Memorial	$10,825.23	$10,917.96
Esther M. Smith Trust	$7,337.40	$7,400.24
Martha S. & W. Horace Snipes Scholarship	$2,473.77	$2,502.45
Eva Jane Stewart Trust - 50%	$61,777.71	$62,306.95

Roy Stucker Scholarship 50%	$52,208.28	$52,655.56
Richard Swain Memorial Scholarship	$23,964.90	$24,170.17
Weigel Bible CLass	$10,331.63	$10,420.15
Total	**$2,888,136.65**	**$2,914,191.96**

Cumberland Presbyterian Church in America

Endowment	Ending Balance 2015	Ending Balance 2016
CP Church in America Min. Education	$4,417.62	$4,691.96
CP Church in America World Mission	$9,009.50	$9,569.04
Total	**$13,427.12**	**$14,261.00**

Congregational

Endowment	Ending Balance 2015	Ending Balance 2016
Kate Maxwell Allen Trust	$6,103.50	$6,155.81
Grace Bright Circle Missions	$10,034.98	$10,658.21
Brunswick Cumberland Presbyterian Church Trust	$13,257.26	$14,080.58
Jane and Ed Chapman Endowment	$3,312.18	$2,434.30
Chinese Mission of San Francisco	$27,502.39	$27,738.27
Christ (FL) Tom W. Kelley Ed Fund	$30,515.24	$30,940.91
Christ (FL) Mary Beth Swindle Scholarship	$87,641.77	$90,272.75
Calico Rock CPC - Christian Service Center End	$5,821.13	$6,182.62
The Mary Cloud Fund	$42,772.62	$43,139.12
Lavenia Campbell Cole Endowment	$262,396.17	$220,510.12
Dyersburg - Charles F. Moore C/T	$52,636.38	$55,905.32
Dyersburg - Jenny Edwards Endowment	$31,501.97	$33,458.37
Elliottsville - Gillis Endowment	$10,593.79	$11,251.72
Elliottsville - Kent Endowment	$7,931.69	$8,424.26
Fairfield C P Church Trust	$87,787.94	$57,936.63
Frankie Floyd Fund for Education	$13,502.15	$14,340.67
Faith-Hopewell CPC Ministries Endowment	$1,006.15	$1,068.65
Germantown - Christian Education Ministry	$27,758.05	$29,508.20
Germantown - Outreach Ministry	$6,728.52	$7,146.35
Germantown - Worship Ministry	$2,147.06	$2,280.39
Germantown - Eugene/Rosa Mae Warren	$13,879.66	$13,478.37
Germantown - William Pickle Member Care	$5,695.97	$6,069.92
Basil & Gertrude Green Scholarship Fund	$61,460.28	$63,436.04
Glenn Griffin Endowment 33% (Congregational)	$44,522.96	$44,904.45
Francis A. Hobgood Trust 50%	$66,771.96	$67,344.04
Hohenwald CPC (Congregational)	$340,853.20	$343,773.00
Hopewell Cumberland Presbyterian Church Endowment	$503.10	$534.35
Albert M. & Delia Jackson Memorial	$4,888.39	$4,936.55
Albert S. Johnston Trust	$59,637.87	$60,148.80

Orn/Laughlin Trust	$6,585.44	$6,641.86
Lawrenceburg CPC - Jack & Marjorie Anderson Endowment	$133,154.79	$141,424.29
Lawrenceburg CPC - Mason/Jennings	$95,600.36	$96,419.41
Della Campbell Lowrie Trust	$80,760.94	$81,452.88
Lucado Endowment	$666,118.63	$707,487.38
Manchester CPC - Christian Education Endowment	$11,562.50	$13,268.05
Marshall (MO) David Guthrie Youth	$6,294.86	$6,685.82
Marshall (MO) 50 Year Church Member Rec	$7,377.39	$7,835.53
CPC of Marshall (TX) Endowment	$211,073.89	$164,413.40
Marshall (TX) Ewing Chapel Cemetery	$62,638.81	$66,582.18
McKenzie CPC - Beasley Endowment	$72,136.86	$72,754.89
McKenzie CPC - Julia Patterson Irby	$12,977.76	$13,088.94
Medina CPC Trust	$2,616.05	$2,778.55
Mesquite CPC - Every Member Endowment	$11,447.80	$0.00
Louise Moffitt Trust Fund	$294,513.26	$297,036.07
Mount Moriah Cemetery Fund (W. TN Presbytery)	$325,623.46	$336,480.02
Murfreesboro First CPC Trust	$1,747.30	$0.00
New Salem Cemetery Fund	$100,550.24	$104,468.39
Oliver's Chapel Cemetery Trust	$96,596.58	$102,595.65
Trimble CPC - Horace J. Coffer Memorial Trust	$5,481.98	$5,529.18
Trimble CPC - Howard Glasgow Memorial Trust	$5,481.98	$5,529.18
Trimble CPC - Bob & Chris Page Family Trust	$3,420.17	$3,449.80
Carolyn Smythe Parks Memorial Trust	$161,882.01	$163,269.32
E. E. Parks Memorial Trust	$4,196.76	$4,232.72
Hamilton & Merion S. Parks Family	$42,440.95	$53,053.64
Rev. Hamilton Parks Memorial Trust	$11,817.92	$12,116.05
W. H. Parks Memorial Trust	$6,659.53	$6,716.59
Franklin Pierce Memorial Trust	$9,595.15	$9,677.36
William W. & Lou W. Pierce Memorial	$1,917.65	$1,934.08
J. Dixie Johnson Primm Endowment	$1,724.51	$1,831.66
Red Bank CPC Endowment	$29,668.69	$31,763.29
Robinson Cemetery Endowment	$35,862.79	$38,090.02
Saint Timothy CPC Trust	$28,616.11	$28,865.72
Short Creek CPC Memorial Fund	$19,473.59	$21,032.29
Swan Cumberland Presbyterian Church	$14,390.28	$15,284.03
Inman & Mildred Swain Memorial	$64,506.49	$65,059.11
Thomas D. & Mary Jo (Adams) Vaughan	$541,709.97	$546,350.33
Thomas & Mary Jo Vaughan Outreach	$54,487.94	$54,954.69
West Union Cemetery - Old Committee	$62,410.46	$61,228.28
Rev. Jonathan Clark Endowment	$685.43	$728.01
Calico Rock CPC - Mildred B. Curless Danielson	$1,766.27	$1,875.96
Calico Rock CPC - Every Member Endowment	$9,059.25	$9,621.88
Calico Rock CPC -Dixie Jennings Gray Endowment	$8,181.61	$8,689.71
Calico Rock CPC - Ernie Horton Gray Endowment	$7,206.28	$7,653.82

Calico Rock CPC - Willis Newton Hankins End.	$729.32	$774.60
Calico Rock CPC - Joann Smith Hudson Endowment	$2,041.28	$2,168.05
Calico Rock CPC - Zelda Killian Endowment	$1,554.42	$1,650.97
Calico Rock CPC - James & Ariel Utt-Landrus End	$7,271.93	$7,723.57
Calico Rock CPC- John & Ernette "Ernie" Parker	$1,627.93	$1,728.99
Calico Rock CPC - Ray & Velma Perryman End	$8,023.16	$8,521.43
Calico Rock CPC - Beatric Virginia Pino End	$637.93	$677.56
Calico Rock CPC - Pietro "Pete" Pino Endowment	$5,024.18	$5,336.20
Calico Rock CPC - Muriel Thompson Ryan End	$1,563.79	$1,660.91
Calico Rock CPC - Sean Vann Endowment	$4,227.46	$4,490.00
Calico Rock CPC - Wayland - Seay Endowment	$14,106.31	$15,087.30
Calico Rock CPC - Wayne & Gaye Wood End	$11,341.96	$12,046.33
Calico Rock CPC - Trimble House Maintenance Endowment	$6,873.21	$6,295.34
Calico Rock CPC - Pete & Betty Riggins	$1,924.80	$2,044.37
Total	**$4,728,132.70**	**$4,728,214.42**

Presbyterial

Endowment	Ending Balance 2015	Ending Balance 2016
Arkansas Presbytery - Camp Peniel	$25,891.25	$26,135.07
Arkansas Presbytery - Higher Education	$62,883.21	$63,421.93
Rev. Leo E. Smith Min. Memorial Scholarship	$11,949.69	$12,800.88
Daisy Bell Belcher Estate	$31,128.44	$33,061.63
Cauca Valley Presbytery - Hogar Samaria	$100,669.85	$123,553.80
Columbia Presbytery Endowment	$439,649.00	$485,807.37
Crystal Springs Camp - Fred Ramsey	$30,800.80	$32,713.66
East Tennessee - Philip Norris Jones	$9,929.06	$10,545.67
William J. Eldredge Trust Fund	$11,537.19	$11,636.08
Ephraim McLean Sr. Memorial Fund	$54,270.37	$57,640.75
Missouri Presbytery - Education Fund	$38,155.47	$43,263.42
Missouri Presbytery - Church Development & Revitalization	$22,112.47	$26,224.06
Missouri Presbytery - Missions Growth	$23,939.27	$25,426.01
Oklahoma/Kansas/Nebraska Mission (Red River Presbytery)	$829,097.63	$1,414,115.86
Red River Presbytery - Camp	$44,744.97	$47,523.82
Red River Presbytery Christian Ed. General	$8,439.81	$8,963.94
Tennessee Georgia Presbytery Capital	$26,679.68	$29,357.97
Tennessee Georgia Presbytery Candidate Education	$12,128.79	$19,217.78
Trinity Presbytery - Trinity Investment Fund	$745,895.81	$811,205.22
Trinity Presbytery - Trinity Church Development Fund	$96,710.49	$111,978.71
W. Tennessee Presbytery - Grace Beasley Fund	$157,870.45	$123,744.85
W. Tennessee Presbytery - Camp Clark Williamson	$17,948.00	$19,062.67
Covenant Presbytery - Russ Milton Scholarship Endowment	$12,346.81	$13,113.56
Cumberland Presbytery -Missions - McInteer End	$62,791.14	$63,329.03
Cumberland Presbytery - Missions - Millwood	$5,341.01	$5,385.77

Cumberland Presbytery -Missions - Ray A. Morris	$1,962.15	$1,978.96
Cumberland Presbytery - Missions - NCD	$136,817.19	$138,627.13
Cumberland Presby Missions - Reid's Chapel End	$45,131.03	$45,517.61
Cumberland Presbytery - Missions-Royal Oak End	$43,168.88	$43,543.06
Cumberland Presby - Scholarships - Freeman End	$131,468.75	$132,594.89
Cumber Pres Scholarships - E. L. Freeman Farms	$184,835.75	$186,419.12
Cumberland Presby - Scholarships - Howard End	$49,055.53	$49,475.72
Cumberland Presby - Min. Educ - Bremen CPC 25%	$50,936.86	$51,373.20
Cumberland Presby - Cont. Educ - Hampton End	$117,733.45	$118,741.94
Cumberland Presbytery - Cont. Edu - KY Synod	$4,893.06	$4,934.99
Cumberland Presby - Gen. Prog - Bremen CPC 75%	$152,810.53	$154,119.53
Cumberland Presby - General Program - KY Synod	$9,811.16	$9,895.20
Cumberland Presby -Gen Prog - Eugene A. Leslie	$2,855.77	$2,880.26
Cumberland Presby - Gen Prog - Wilcoxson End.	$3,924.42	$3,958.03
Cumberland Presby Christian Ed - Camp Koinonia	$32,012.88	$32,287.10
Cumberland Presby - Christian Ed - Cecil Huff	$4,159.30	$4,194.96
Cumberland Presby - Christian Ed - Sam Macy	$1,443.05	$1,457.68
Cumberland Presby Higher Ed - Joseph H. Butler	$1,825.76	$1,841.37
Cumberland Presby - Higher Ed - Sharon Church	$26,549.55	$26,776.98
Cumberland Presbytery -Robert L. McReynolds 50%	$41,776.56	$42,134.47
Total	**$3,926,082.29**	**$4,671,981.71**

D. ENDOWMENT PROGRAM LOANS
Historical Review

Through investing up to 40% of the assets of the Endowment Program in the witness of the Church, the message of good news concerning Christ is strengthened both in the United States and overseas. A survey of old files in the Historical Foundation and in the vault of the Board of Stewardship reveals the important role played by this aspect of the investment policy. Over the past sixty-five years from 1944 to 2009, 841 loans were made to congregations, presbyteries, and synods. From 2010 through 2016 an additional 17 loans have been made. Through these loans, $42,714,405 has been provided in financing for expansion of facilities and extension of witness.

A look at the different periods during which loans have been made provides a picture of growing endowments (and of post World War II inflation!).

Period	Loans	Total Loaned	Average
1944-49	35	$ 145,755	$ 4,164
1950-59	171	$ 1,360,441	$ 7,955
1960-69	208	$ 3,056,891	$ 14,697
1970-79	166	$ 3,609,084	$ 21,741
1980-89	101	$ 4,349,120	$ 43,061
1990-99	102	$ 14,440,837	$ 141,577
2000-09	58	$ 10,571,723	$ 182,271
2010-16	17	$ 5,180,554	$ 304,738

While looking at the table, it should be noted that the Cumberland Presbyterian Church Investment Loan Program began January 1, 2001. Since its creation most of the larger loans are made through the Investment Loan Program. At the end of the year the Endowment Loan Balance was $2,242,093.

Down through the years, donors to endowments have found satisfaction in the knowledge that the prudent investment of their gifts strengthened not only the work of the particular churches, institutions, and causes which they designated to receive the income but also the broader witness of the Church.

E. OTHER CHURCH LOANS

In addition to loans from the Investment Loan Program and the Endowment Program there is another source available to the board for loans to churches.

1. Small Church Loan Fund

This fund, formerly known as the Revolving Church Loan Fund, was created through an endowment established by Lavenia Cole and gifts to the "Into the Nineties" Capital Gifts Campaign. All interest earned by the loans is added to the fund to increase the amount available for loans. There were seven loans from the Small Church Loan Program at the end of 2016 totaling $176,054.

The rate of interest for the Small Church Loans made during 2016 was based on the loan rate established by the Cumberland Presbyterian Church Investment Loan Program at the beginning of each quarter. These loans are generally small loans of $70,000 or less, most are amortized over five years.

F. REGIONAL PLANNED GIVING COORDINATORS
1. History

In 1993, the 163rd General Assembly commended the Board of Stewardship for "its vision in developing a program of planned giving in local congregations" and urged congregations "to be open to this new program and to take advantage of the assistance being offered" by the Board.

Further, it adopted recommendations to:

Approve a church-wide annual emphasis on planned gifts as a complementary part of the observation of the Family Week focus provided by the Board of Christian Education during May of each year; and

Urge each congregation to recognize the importance of promoting planned gifts as a part of its overall nurture of Christian stewardship among its members.

In response to the 1993 action, staff of the Board of Stewardship have made presentations to more than 150 congregations on the need to develop congregational endowments and encourage planned giving by church members.

At one time there were four Regional Planned Giving Coordinators. At the moment Carolyn Harmon is the only Regional Planned Giving Coordinators. She is an elder in the Cedar Hill Church,

Greeneville, Tennessee, serving the Presbytery of East Tennessee. The other coordinators can no longer serve due to health conditions or other reasons. Though Carolyn is employed by the Presbytery of East Tennessee she has made presentations beyond her presbytery.

She can educate congregations and individuals regarding stewardship opportunities in planned giving. Often times the results of her work is not easily measured. It may be several years before her work bears fruit. Presentations can plant seeds which may bear fruit immediately or years down the road. What is of utmost importance is that the seeds are being planted.

The Board of Stewardship works to continue efforts of educating local congregations about the opportunities available through planned giving. It is through planned giving that current Cumberland Presbyterians can provide for effective ministry long after they are gone.

It is our prayer that God will bless the work of encouraging Cumberland Presbyterians to give generously to enhance the future ministry of all our churches.

IV. CUMBERLAND PRESBYTERIAN CHURCH INVESTMENT LOAN PROGRAM, INC.

In 1976, the board began a program to provide an opportunity for flexible investment of current temporary cash assets of congregations and agencies of the church. The primary purpose of the program is to provide income to participants as a foundation for ministry. On January 1, 2001, the assets of the original program, Cash Funds Management, were transferred to the new Cumberland Presbyterian Church Investment Loan Program, Inc.

For the year ending 2016, the assets for the Investment Loan Program were $22,407,583 compared to $16,853,197 in 2015. This is a 33% increase in assets in one year. There were 309 individual, congregation and agency accounts. At year end, deposits on account totaled $14,788,707. The total loans were $7,618,876 at year end.

For 2016, the corporation complied with the regulatory requirements in the states of Tennessee and Kentucky and was able to offer investment opportunities to individual Cumberland Presbyterians in the states of Tennessee, Kentucky, Texas, Missouri and New Mexico.

The board of directors is composed of the following: Mike St. John, president; Sue Rice, vice-president and Debbie Shelton, secretary, and Jackie Satterfield. Robert Heflin serves as Treasurer and Executive Secretary. During the past year, the board met twice in regular session.

In order to simplify administration and focus on the strengths of the Investment Loan Program, the board took action to limit the offering of notes and depository accounts to "ready access accounts." All note holders (individuals) and depository account holders (churches and church agencies) with funds invested in these "on demand" accounts participated in the $504,923 which the program paid in interest. For 2016 the interest rate paid to account holders was 3%. The interest rate paid to account holders can fluctuate from one quarter to the next. In recent years there has been renewed interest for congregations to open new accounts because the interest paid is higher than current CD rates.

The table below provides a breakdown of the investment mix.

INVESTMENT LOAN PROGRAM		
Securities & Investments		
20.5%	Cash Equivalents	$ 3,104,855
9.9%	Preferred Stocks	$ 1,495,872
0.9%	U. S. Equity Bond Funds	$ 139,512
68.5%	Taxable Fixed Income	$10,394,755
0.2%	Multi Asset	$ 42,164
100.0%		$15,177,158

At the end of 2016 there were 23 loans to congregations made through the Investment Loan Program. The loan balance was $8,617,980. Every accountholder is investing in the future ministry of the Cumberland Presbyterian Church as well as receiving interest on that investment.

VIII. EMPLOYEE BENEFITS ADMINISTRATION AND RESEARCH

A. PURPOSE
The second of two broad areas of the work of the board is in employee benefits administration and research. The purpose of this program is as follows:

To support the lay and ordained employees of the church as they venture to be faithful under the call of Christ and the Church to the daily demands of providing leadership to congregations and Church agencies whom are the incarnation of the Body of Christ, the family of God at work in the world.

B. VISION
The board has a vision of uniform benefits for all Cumberland Presbyterian clergy, including group health insurance, group long-term disability coverage, and participation in the General Assembly's retirement plan. Ministers would then know what to expect when they are called to another church. No longer would some ministers have to do without what is considered in the secular world to be basic employee benefits. No longer would ministers and their families have to settle for being relegated to second class status. The reality is, as several General Assemblies have recognized, that this is possible if we work together in much the same manner that we send out missionaries and do a lot of other ministry. Good employee benefit plans are in place and they would be healthier and stronger if used and supported by all employees of the Cumberland Presbyterian Church.

IX. RETIREMENT PROGRAM

Since 1952, the board has provided a retirement program open to all church employees of the Cumberland Presbyterian Church. The program gives opportunity for churches and their employees to provide a source of retirement income based on voluntary contributions. In 1987, a new Cumberland Presbyterian Retirement Plan No. 2 was established as a qualified 403(b) defined contribution plan and in 1990 the General Assembly amended the plan to include the churches and employees of the Second Cumberland Presbyterian Church, now known as the Cumberland Presbyterian Church in America.

A. PLAN AMENDMENTS
As new needs arise or deficiencies in the original plan document for Cumberland Presbyterian Retirement Plan No. 2 become apparent, the General Assembly has the authority under Article IX Section 9.01 of the Plan to amend the same. In 2012 a revised plan document was approved by the General Assembly.

B. YEAR END REPORT
On December 31, 2016, there were 310 active participants in the Retirement Plan. There were 10 receiving direct monthly payments as a result of their elections. In addition to these participants, there were 14 persons who were receiving annuity payments purchased through the Plan and for whom the Plan issues 1099-R's.

During 2016, $1,578,924 was dispersed to or for participants, an increase of 8% over 2015s $1,461,432. Contributions totaled $686,942 and were up 3.6 % over 2015s $663,084. Realized and unrealized gain on investments totaled $1,256,899 compared to a loss in 2015 of $310,078. The rate of return credited to the accounts for the year was 6.5% compared to -0.8% for 2015. (Comparative annual rates of return for: previous three years +3.7%, previous five years +7.3%, and from the beginning of professional management in March, 1982 +9.3%.)

Effective January 1, 2011, Gerber/Taylor Management was retained to manage our stock portfolio. We have continued our relationship with Met West, a bond manager, and RREEF, a private real estate investment trust manager. Matt Robbins and Stacy Miller of Gerber/Taylor continue to be very helpful with keeping the board updated on market conditions and investment strategies.

X. MINISTERIAL AID PROGRAM

A. MINISTERIAL AID
1. Full Benefit Recipients
As of March 2017 there are 5 Cumberland Presbyterian Church recipients of the full benefit of $519 (adjusted for inflation yearly) per month (increased from $300 on July 1, 2010). The monthly total of these

payments is $2,595.00; annually, $31,140.00 is paid. Beginning May 1, 2015, the method of distributing funds to overseas presbyteries was revised with the help of the Missions ministry team. Ministerial aid will now be offered in overseas presbyteries on an individual basis. Presently there are 5 recipients in Cauca Valley Presbytery and 5 recipients in Andes Presbytery that are receiving aid in the amount of $300 a month, for a total of $3,000 a month or $36,000 annually.

In October 2005, the board decided to distribute 75% of the previous year's surplus to the remaining recipients. No distribution was made December 2016 due to negative performance of endowments for 2015. The Board of Stewardship has approved a cap of a maximum of $4,000 in lieu of large distributions that may have a negative effect on other benefits received, such as SSI, or state assistance.

2. Basic Requirements.

The new basic requirements and amount for stateside recipients for the Ministerial Aid program were approved at the General Assembly of the Cumberland Presbyterian Church in June 2010. The poverty levels have been updated to the latest available figures. They are as follows:

Full Benefit of $519 a month for State Side Recipients

1. Minimum age is full retirement age set forth by the Social Security Administration.
2. Minimum years of service to the church - 15.
3. Can qualify for aid if a participant in the Cumberland Presbyterian Retirement Plan if income is below poverty level as established by the US Census Bureau.
4. Physical and/or mental disability (doctor's statement required) at any age, however, a minimum of ten years of service is required if less than 60 years of age.
5. Individuals' income cannot exceed federal poverty guidelines set forth for the year by the US Census Bureau. Poverty level is $12,060 a year or $1005 a month for 2017.
6. Couples income cannot exceed federal poverty guidelines set forth for the year by the US Census Bureau. Poverty level is $16,240 a year or $1,353.33 a month for 2017.
(The GA Board of Stewardship is authorized to look at each case in light of unusual financial hardship; thus, application may be made even if income levels exceed the ceiling.)
7. Presbytery obtains information and approves (approval can be given by the committee or board charged by presbytery with this responsibility); certification of approval is sent to the General Assembly Board of Stewardship.
8. Surviving spouse is eligible if above items 2, 3 and 4 have been met.

**Note: Recipient is responsible to verify if receiving Ministerial Aid would affect his or her SSI, Social Security or other benefits.

Cumberland Presbyterian Church applicants must submit to the board a listing of assets and liabilities so the net worth can be determined. The board urges presbyteries to maintain contact with persons under the Ministerial Aid Program who live within their bounds. Should there be serious unmet needs, the presbytery is urged to contact the board so that it may determine how the Ministerial Aid program can be of assistance in meeting those needs.

3. Cumberland Presbyterian Church in America

The CPCA currently has 3 participants who receive monthly payments. As of June 1, 2015, the aid amount increased from $109 a month to $510 a month and the CPCA contributes 50% of the yearly aid and the CP Ministerial Aid Endowments 50%. The current amount received monthly per participant is $519. The CPCA normally pays its share in June or July following their General Assembly.

4. Ministers in Overseas Presbyteries

As of May 1, 2015, with the help of the Missions Ministry Team, aid is available to those in overseas presbyteries who qualify on an individual basis. The Cumberland Presbyterian Church is present in 13 different countries and each country presents its unique legislation of how they manage pension plans according to laws and standards for salaries. The Mission Ministry Team will be the liaison between the Board of Stewardship and the Presbyteries outside of the United States aiding the Board in identifying the needs overseas and interpreting pension laws and standards for salaries. At present, aid is being sent to the Cauca Valley Presbytery and Andes Presbytery in Colombia, South America.

B. SPECIAL FINANCIAL NEEDS AID

At the Spring 2014 Board of Stewardship meeting, the Board approved the use of funds from the Ministerial Aid Cash Fund ILP to be used in special situations where illness has caused a financial hardship for those that are not eligible for Ministerial Aid. There were no funds disbursed in 2015 and 2016.

XI. INSURANCE PROGRAMS

The insurance programs of the board have been assigned by the General Assembly beginning in the middle of the previous century. Dental and Vision Insurance is the newest, begun in December 2008. Property and casualty insurance is the oldest, begun in 1951. While all of the insurance programs are important, group life and health insurance, begun in 1961, touches many lives in a personal way and often at times of deep anxiety. In all, about 204 men, women, and children depend on this program to meet their health care needs.

A. PROPERTY & CASUALTY INSURANCE

The Board of Stewardship, Foundation and Benefits secures property and casualty insurance coverage against accidental loss for the General Assembly Corporation, Board of Stewardship, Discipleship Ministry Team, Missions Ministry Team, Ministry Council, Communications Ministry Team, Pastoral Development Ministry Team, Memphis Theological Seminary, and Historical Foundation.

Our broker is Lipscomb & Pitts of Memphis, Tennessee. For 2017, Travelers Insurance carries our Property & Casualty policy and $2,500,000 in earth quake coverage, Evanston Insurance Company provides an additional $16,797,258 in earthquake coverage. Philadelphia carries our Directors & Officers coverage and Hanover carries our General Liability, Professional Liability, Crime, Automobile, and Umbrella policies. Workers Compensation coverage as of 10/23/2014 is with Bridgefield Casualty.

B. GROUP LONG TERM DISABILITY INSURANCE

The presbyteries of Arkansas, Columbia, Covenant, Cumberland, del Cristo, East Tennessee, Missouri, Murfreesboro, Nashville, North Central, Red River, Robert Donnell, Trinity, West Tennessee and The Center have now established non-contributory long term disability programs insured currently through Cigna. This leaves only four stateside presbyteries (Choctaw, Hope, Grace and Tennessee Georgia) without a program. The quarterly rate applied to participant's salaries is .45 per $100 of salary.

There are three primary reasons for ministers to want the coverage and for presbyteries to want to provide the protection. The group rate is significantly lower than individual policy rates and does not require a large cash outlay to cover all full-time ministers in a presbytery; housing allowance and/or the fair rental value of a manse is included in the definition of salary for ministers; and, there is no medical qualification requirement in order to enroll. These advantages over individual policies make this coverage very attractive, especially to those who have previously purchased their own policies. In addition, a provision was negotiated with Cigna by the Board's consultant, whereby ministers, upon leaving a participating presbytery to serve in a non-participating presbytery, may continue the coverage if he or she so desires. The new employing church is then billed for the quarterly premium. There are now 8 ministers and two employees who are receiving or have received benefits from this insurance program. There are 174 participants as of January 1, 2017.

C. GROUP TRAVEL ACCIDENT INSURANCE

This policy provides twenty-four hour coverage on "named employees" for accidental death, dismemberment, or loss of sight while on business travel. The maximum benefit is $50,000 and there is also a $1,000 medical benefit. The annual premium is $900. We renew this policy every 3 years. Thirty-one named positions are covered under this policy.

D. GROUP HEALTH & LIFE INSURANCE

The board has used a fully-insured, managed care approach to provide group health insurance for Cumberland Presbyterian clergy and lay employees since March 1, 1999. Blue Cross / Blue Shield of Tennessee is our insurance carrier in 2017. In 2016, the group plan was split into 4 separate community rated groups which provided more competitive rates. For 2017, the plans realized a 10% increase due to premium increase of 5.4% and less funds being used from the Premium Stabilization Reserve due to lower returns of the endowments. Lipscomb & Pitts, a Memphis based insurance company, is our insurance broker, and Craig Wright, our agent.

1. Loss Ratio
Due to the change to community rated plans, the insurer does not provide loss information for the groups.

2. Premiums
Efforts to maintain affordable premiums and comprehensive coverage are the biggest challenges we face. Premiums for 2017 are listed below and reflect the assistance from the Premium Stabilization Reserve. The goal for 2017 is to utilize approximately $123,000 from the Premiums Stabilization Reserve to help reduce the premiums participants pay for health insurance. In 2016 we utilized $185,191 from the Premium Stabilization Reserve.

Health Insurance Premiums for 2017		
	Option 1	Option 2
Employee Only	$ 686	$ 550
Employee & Spouse	$1,361	$1,087
Employee & Child(ren)	$1,256	$1,003
Family	$1,953	$1,562

The Health Plans are on a calendar year as far as deductible and pricing is concerned. It is our objective to have the renewal pricing by no later than September 1 so presbyteries and agencies can have the figures for their fall meetings and better plan their budgets for the coming year. Periodically we seek bids from other carriers in an effort to keep premiums competitive. When this is done, we may not have the new premium information by September 1.

Open enrollment period is the month of December. It is during this time that an employee can enroll or change their health insurance coverage unless there are special circumstances.

3. Participation
As of February 1, 2017, 123 employees and 81 dependents for a total of 204 people depend on the Cumberland Presbyterian Church Health Insurance Program. A breakdown of family units by size at February 1, 2017 is listed below.

FAMILY UNITS BY SIZE		
	Number of Units	Total
Employee Only	78	78
Spouse Only	0	0
Employee & 1	1	2
Employee & 2	5	15
Employee & 3	0	0
Employee & Spouse	22	44
Families of 3	4	12
Families of 4	12	48
Families of 5	1	5
Families of 6	0	0
Families of 7	0	0
Total	123	204

The following table shows the enrollment figures from January 2016 to December 2016. As one can see the numbers fluctuate from month to month.

MONTHLY GROUP INSURANCE ENROLLMENT			
	EMPLOYEE COVERAGE	DEPENDENT COVERAGE	TOTAL
January	90	45	135
February	87	45	132
March	88	44	132
April	86	44	130
May	85	45	130
June	85	45	130
July	85	45	130
August	84	46	130
September	81	47	128
October	79	49	128
November	80	48	128
December	78	47	125

4. Premium Stabilization Reserve (Formerly Emergency Reserve)

The Premium Stabilization Reserve is invested in the Endowment Program Total Return Fund account which had a balance of $1,857,625 as of December 31, 2016. The Emergency Health Insurance Reserve was established in compliance with the 1992 General Assembly directive to be used in "emergency" situations to match presbyterial emergency fund disbursements. The 1998 General Assembly approved the Board's recommendation to allow the Board to use the Emergency Reserve to maintain the stability of the group health and life insurance plan. This allows these funds to be used for purposes outside of the original scope of the reserve. In 2016, the Board of Stewardship used $185,191 to help offset some of the cost of the health insurance premiums and have estimated that approximately $123,000 will be used in 2017 to help in reducing premiums for the health insurance participants.

5. Dental and Vision Insurance

On December 1, 2008, we began offering Dental and Vision insurance, on a voluntary basis, for anyone working at least 30 hours or more for any Cumberland Presbyterian Church, its agencies, boards, and institutions. Peter Whitely is the agent of record. At present there are 79 participating employees.

6. Jessie W. Hipsher Health Insurance Endowment

The Jesse W. Hipsher Health Insurance Endowment was created as the first step in the board's goal to raise $10,000,000 in endowments for the support of the Cumberland Presbyterian Health and Life Insurance Program. The endowment was established on March 6, 2004. At its establishment $11,450 had been raised. The balance of the endowment as of December 31, 2016 was $44,162.31.

7. Health Education / E-Mail Newsletter

To further educate participants in matters concerning healthcare, participants receive a monthly e-newsletter entitled, TopHealth, published by Oakstone Publishing. The monthly e-newsletter is full of health related tips that can be easily implemented by readers. The two page newsletter can be read within a matter of minutes. Doctor Ann tips on healthy eating are also included with the e-newsletter monthly. Also initiated in 2008 is the E-Mail newsletter that is designed as an information tool to help the participants of the Health and Retirement programs.

8. Wellness Program

Blue Cross offers a Preventive Health Guide and the Blue 365 discount program for a range of item from fitness, healthy eating, personal care and wellness and even information on financial health. Also offered are the Nurse chat 24/7/365 and Physician Now where you can speak to a physician on call.

Respectfully submitted,
Boyd Day, Board Member
Robert Heflin, Executive Secretary.

THE REPORT OF THE HISTORICAL FOUNDATION

I. GENERAL INFORMATION

A. OFFICERS OF THE BOARD
The officers of the board are as follows: Reverend Rick White, president; Pat Ward, vice-president; and Michael Fare, secretary. Susan Knight Gore is the director and treasurer of the Historical Library and Archives.

B. BOARD REPRESENTATIVES TO THE CPC & CPCA GENERAL ASSEMBLIES
The board's representative to the 187th General Assembly of the Cumberland Presbyterian Church is Robin McCaskey Hughes. The alternate is Reverend Lisa Oliver.

The board's representative to the 142nd General Assembly of the Cumberland Presbyterian Church in America is Reverend Rick White. The alternate is Edna Barnett.

C. MEMBERSHIP AND MEETINGS OF THE BOARD
The board is currently composed of the following members: from the Cumberland Presbyterian Church in America—Edna Barnett, Dorothy Hayden, Willie Lynk, Pat Ward, and Rick White, from the Cumberland Presbyterian Church—Michael Fare, Robin McCaskey Hughes, Mary Kathryn Kirkpatrick, Ashley Lindsey, Lisa Oliver, and Sidney Swindle.

The Board of Trustees met, September 16, 2016, and February 24, 2017.

D. MEMBERS WHOSE TERMS EXPIRE
The second term of Michael Fare expires with the 2017 meeting of the Cumberland Presbyterian General Assembly, and he is eligible for reelection.

The third terms of Edna Barnett and Rick White expire with the 2017 meeting of the Cumberland Presbyterian Church in America General Assembly, and they are not eligible for reelection. The second term of Dorothy Hayden expires with the 2017 meeting of the Cumberland Presbyterian Church in America General Assembly, and she is eligible for reelection. The first term of Pat Ward expires with the 2017 meeting of the Cumberland Presbyterian Church in America General Assembly, and she is eligible for reelection.

E. STAFF
Susan Knight Gore serves as the Archivist of the Historical Foundation. Missy Rose is the archival assistant for the Foundation.

II. ASSEMBLY REPORTING

As a matter of official structure, relative to the CPC, there is a Board of Trustees composed of members from both the CPC and CPCA, and relative to the CPCA, there is a committee composed of members from the CPCA.

III. PROGRAMS AND ACTIVITIES

A. HISTORY INTERPRETATION AND PROMOTIONAL ACTIVITIES

1. The 1810 Circle
In order to enlist the financial support of interested members of our churches in the work of the Foundation, the 1810 Circle was created. Membership is based on a financial contribution of $25 or more per year. Income through such gifts enables the Foundation to meet expenditures and is vital to the continued work of the Foundation.

We appreciate the support given to the Foundation by all members of the 1810 Circle and encourage other members of the Cumberland Presbyterian Church and the Cumberland Presbyterian Church in America to join this donor group.

RECOMMENDATION 1: That the General Assembly make congregations and presbyteries aware of the 1810 Circle and encourage new members to support this endeavor annually.

2. Patrons
Persons who contribute $100 or more to one of the endowments of the Historical Foundation become patron members and receive a certificate. Patron memberships may also be given in honor or in memory of an individual.

3. Heritage Churches
Congregations contributing a minimum of $1,000 to an endowment of the Historical Foundation become Heritage Churches and receive a framed certificate. There are six categories of recognition and churches can move from one level to another.

Heritage Church $1,000 - $4,999
Silver Heritage Church $5,000 to $9,999
Golden Heritage Church $10,000 to $24,999
Platinum Heritage Church $25,000 to $49,999
Diamond Heritage Church $50,000 to $99,000
Jubilee Heritage Church $100,000 and up

4. Presbyterial Heritage Committees/Presbyterial Historians
To promote interest in the work of the Foundation and to nurture work in history on the presbyterial level, the Historical Foundation seeks to work cooperatively with the Presbyterial Heritage Committees/Presbyterial Historians of both general assemblies. The brochure, *Suggestions for Heritage Committees and Presbyterial Historians*, is available from the Foundation. The board expresses its appreciation to the presbyteries that have Heritage Committees/Presbyterial Historians.

5. Denomination Day Offering
The 2017 Denomination Day Offering was designated to fund the conversion of fragile and deteriorating analogue media to digital formats in order that it might better be preserved.

The Foundation expresses appreciation to congregations and others groups who received special offerings for the work of the Historical Foundation on Denomination Day. This special offering provides an opportunity for congregations to directly contribute to the support of the Historical Foundation as well as the Foundation supplying educational materials to each congregation.

RECOMMENDATION 2: That congregations be encouraged to have a special offering on the Sunday designated as Denomination Day to help support the special project designated for that year.

B. PUBLICATIONS

1. Promotional Materials
The Historical Foundation provides promotional materials describing its purpose and work, the various means of financially supporting this work, and listings of available publications and prints for sale through the Foundation. These materials are available on the Foundation's website.

2. Publication Series
The Foundation has a number of titles and prints available for purchase. Income from the sale of these items goes into the Historical Foundation Trust, a permanent endowment supporting the Foundation's work. Titles available are:

1883 Confession of Faith.
1895 Cumberland Cook Book.
Cumberland Presbyterianism and Arminianism Compared/Contrasted on Selected Doctrines by Joe Ben Irby.
Faith Once Delivered; Some Indispensable Doctrines of the Christian Faith by Joe Ben Irby.
Family of Faith: Cumberland Presbyterians in Harrison County [Texas], 1848-1998 by Rose Mary Magrill.

God So Loved by Roy Hall.
History of East Side Cumberland Presbyterian Church, Memphis, Tennessee, Memphis Tennessee: 1926-1986, by the Historical Committee.
History of the Cumberland Presbyterian Church by B. W. McDonnold.
Jerusalem Cumberland Presbyterian Church: A Documentary and Pictorial History by Anne Elizabeth Swain Odom.
Legacy of Grace: Louisiana and Texas Cumberland Presbyterian People & Places of Trinity Presbytery by Rose Mary Magrill.
Life and Thought of Finis Ewing by Joe Ben Irby.
Life and Thought of Milton Bird by Joe Ben Irby.
Life and Thought of Reuben Burrow by Joe Ben Irby.
Life and Thought of Robert Verrell Foster by Joe Ben Irby.
Life and Thought of Stanford Guthrie Burney by Joe Ben Irby.
Life and Times of Finis Ewing by F. R. Cossitt.
Soundings by Morris Pepper.
Theological Snippets by Joe Ben Irby.
This They Believed by Joe Ben Irby.
What Cumberland Presbyterians Believe by E. K. Reagin.
Women Shall Preach: Celebrating 125 Yeas of Ordained Women in Ministry in the Cumberland Presbyterian Church.
Prints of the *Samuel McAdow Home* and the *First Meeting of Cumberland Presbytery*.
These items are available for sale from Cumberland Presbyterian Resources.

RECOMMENDATION 3: That the General Assembly make presbyteries, congregations, and individuals aware that the Historical Foundation is interested and has funds to publish books on topics concerning the Cumberland Presbyterian Church and Cumberland Presbyterian Church in America.

3. Denomination Day Resources
All the Past is but the Beginning of Beginning (Denomination Day resource) is available on the Foundation's web site under the Resources section: http://www.cumberland.org/hfcpc/resource/
It includes eight dramas intended to present the birth of the Cumberland Presbyterian Church and the Cumberland Presbyterian Church in America. A hard copy may be requested from the Foundation office.

4. Online Promotion
Recognizing the increasing value of emerging social media, the Historical Foundation employs a Facebook group, "Historical Foundation of the CPC & CPCA," to engage an expanding audience of Cumberland Presbyterians in denominational history and heritage. By showcasing collection acquisitions, the Foundation expands the knowledge of those materials sought for preservation as well as the nature of archival development.

C. HISTORICAL FOUNDATION AWARDS

1. Award in Cumberland Presbyterian History
The Foundation encourages the writing and publication of papers on all aspects of the history of the Cumberland Presbyterian Church in America and the Cumberland Presbyterian Church. One means of promoting such writing is the Historical Foundation Award in Cumberland Presbyterian History. A $300 prize is awarded to the author entering the best paper on any CPC or CPCA history subject which meets in form and content the requirements set by the Board of Trustees and judged by the board appointed awards committee. All manuscripts submitted to the competition become property of the Foundation and are added to the Historical Library and Archives.

The contest follows the calendar year, and entries for the 2017 competition are encouraged. All entries will be accepted through December 2017 for this year's contest. Any entries received following the deadline of December 31st will be automatically entered in the 2018 competition.

Guidelines and entry forms for submitting manuscripts to the competition are available from the Foundation office as well as on the internet, http://www.cumberland.org/hfcpc/Awards.htm. The Historical

Foundation appreciates the participation of past and future CPCA and CP historians in this program.

The 2016 Award went to Courtney Krueger of Cleveland, Tennessee for the paper "Devil With a Blue Dress On: What History Teaches About How Cumberland Presbyterians Can Live in Unity with Widely Divergent Perceptions of Truth and God's Will."

2. Awards of Recognition

Awards of recognition are certificates given to organizations or individuals in recognition of historic events or contributions to the preservation of our heritage as Cumberland Presbyterians. Appropriate applications for the award are: particular churches celebrating anniversaries of their organization; any judicatory or agency celebrating publication of a written history; celebrations of history or historic event in a creative or unusual manner; individuals who have provided continued service for 50 years or more as members of a local congregation or presbytery; individuals who have served for 40 years or more in a continuing leadership role (including pastors) within a local church. Individuals, churches, or presbyterial heritage committees may make application for the issuing of an award by contacting the Foundation office. Application forms are supplied by the Foundation office as well as the internet, http://www.cumberland.org/hfcpc/Awards.htm.

D. RELATIONSHIPS

Presbyterian Historical Society of the Southwest

The Presbyterian Historical Society of the Southwest is an agency of The Synod of the Sun, Presbyterian Church (USA) and Cumberland Presbyterian Churches in Arkansas, Louisiana, Oklahoma and Texas. Members of the Cumberland Presbyterian Church who serve on the board of this organization are Reverend Norlan Scrudder, Reverend Perryn Rice, and Doctor Rose Mary Magrill.

IV. HISTORICAL LIBRARY AND ARCHIVES

A. RESEARCH SERVICE

The Foundation's main research commitment is to the agencies, local congregations, and members of the Cumberland Presbyterian Churches. Since the Historical Library and Archives of the Historical Foundation serves as the official repository for the Cumberland Presbyterian General Assemblies, this is our focus. Although the separation of research into two types designated by their mode of access has been rapid and dramatic, both the traditional and "cyber" mode contribute to and enhance the other.

1. Traditional/Physical Access

Hands on access to primary source material remains the vital heart of historic and theological research. Rather than being diminished by increased electronic resources, traditional research has broadened due to heightened awareness of primary sources in an expanding information age. The Foundation receives research requests by personal visitors, mail, e-mail, and telephone. As time permits, requests are researched. Responses are sent to the requestor, as well as pertinent information on ministers, congregations, presbyteries and synods being placed on our website for future researchers.

2. Electronic Access

The Foundation's website continues to expand in order to provide greater access to the materials in the Historical Library and Archives. As well as being a research tool, the internet provides an invaluable and inexpensive means of promotion for the physical collections of the Historical Library and Archives, the activities of the Historical Foundation, and for the greater community of faith called Cumberland Presbyterians. Information at the site includes: general information about the Foundation, entire texts of important historical documents, historical information on particular congregations, ministers, presbyteries, and synods. The gateway URL to the Foundation's website is http://www.cumberland.org/hfcpc/.

B. ACQUISITIONS

The Historical Library and Archives regularly receives items published by the two denominations, *Minutes of the General Assembly of the Cumberland Presbyterian Church, Preliminary Minutes of the General Assembly of the Cumberland Presbyterian Church, Yearbook of the General Assembly of the Cumberland Presbyterian Church, The Cumberland Presbyterian, Missionary Messenger, Minutes of the General Assembly of the Cumberland Presbyterian Church in America, Preliminary Minutes of the General*

Assembly of the Cumberland Presbyterian Church in America, and *The Cumberland Flag.* Synods and presbyteries deposit four copies of their printed minutes in the Historical Library and Archives. In addition, books, pamphlets, theses, dissertations, records and publications of general assembly, boards, agencies, institutions, and task forces; records and publications of synods and presbyteries, session records and other materials of particular churches, biographical material of Cumberland Presbyterian and Cumberland Presbyterian Church in America ministers, photographs, audiovisual materials, and museum items were among the accessions received. The 2016 Accession List closed with 102 accession groups.

Some of the highlights added to the collection in 2016 include:

Audiovisual Items

Chinese Cumberland Presbyterian Church. San Francisco, California. Worship Services.

Books

Agudelo, Gildardo. *Un Misionero Sin Elogios.* Cali, Colombia, 2015.

Announcement and Catalogue of Mrs. M. E. Clark's Select School for Young Ladies, Nashville, Tennessee. 1885-1886. Nashville, Tenn.: Cumberland Presbyterian Publishing House, 1886.

The Constitution of the Cumberland Presbyterian Church, In the United States of America: Containing the Confession of Faith, A Catechism, the Government and Discipline, and the Directory for the Worship of God. Nashville, Tennessee: Printed by M. & J. Norvell, for the Publishers, 1815.

Mink, Ken. *The Rag Tag Gang: The Hilarious Story of America's Zaniest College Football Game: Ga. Tech 222, Cumberland 0.* CreateSpace, 2011.

Psalms and Hymns, Adapted to Social, Private, and Public Worship, in the Cumberland Presbyterian Church. "Authorized and Adopted by the General Assembly, at her Sessions in Lebanon, Tennessee, A.D. 1845." Stereotyped by J. A. James, Cincinnati, Ohio. Cumberland Presbyterian Board of Publication, 1848.

Wallace, Boyce. El Cristianismo Básico. Primera edición. Cali, Valle, Colombia, Octubre de 2013.

Periodicals

Ladies' Pearl. (1872).

Our Little Children. Volume 12, Part 3 (November 18, 1917).

The Cumberland Flag, 1995-1999.

The Cumberland Presbyterian, 1896-1909.

Institutions

Cumberland Female College. McMinnville, Tennessee. Autograph book, 1885.

Cumberland University. Lebanon, Tennessee. *The Phoenix.* 1908.

Missouri Valley College. Marshall, Missouri. *The Sabiduria.* 1915.

Museum Items

Cloverdale CPC, Obion, Tennessee. Baptismal font.

Hopkinsville CPC, Hopkinsville, Kentucky. Commemorative plate.

St. Timothy CPC, Bedford, Texas. Shirt, 40th Anniversary, 1870-2010.

Trinity University. Waxahachie, Texas. Toothpick holder, Wheelock pottery.

Other Congregational Records

Caney Fork CPC. Sumner County, Tennessee. Organization Document, March 20, 1827.

Goodlettesville CPC. Goodlettesville, Tennessee. Church Directory, 1989.

Halls Creek CPC. Waverly, Tennessee. Cookbook.

Newton Chapel CPC. Star City, Arkansas. Guest Book 1975-2008.

Photographs

Bethel College. McKenzie, Tennessee. 1886.

McKenzie CPC. McKenzie, Tennessee. Young People's Society for Christian Endeavor, about 1895.

New Hope Cumberland Presbyterian Church. Paducah, Kentucky.

Southern Illinois College. Enfield, Illinois.

Postcards

Erin CPC. Erin, Tennessee.

Loudon CPC. Loudon, Tennessee.

Princeton CPC. Princeton, Kentucky.

Punxsutawney CPC. Punxsutawney, Pennsylvania.

Presbyterial Records

Ohio Valley Presbytery. Colored Cumberland Presbyterian Church. Minutes. 1932-1947 & 1957-1963.

Japan Presbytery CPC. Minutes. 2006-2016.

Holly Grove CPC (Princeton, Alabama). 1965-1997.

Mangum CPC (Mangum, Oklahoma). 1990-2015.
Mount Hebron CPC (Goreville, Illinois) 1989-2012.
Mount Joy CPC (Parsons, Tennessee) 1881-1947
New Providence CPC (Clarksville, Tennessee) 1963-1985, 1987-2005.
Paris CPC (Paris, Arkansas) 1987-2009.
Shiloh CPC (Palmyra, Tennessee) 1972-2012.
St. Andrew CPC (El Dorado, Arkansas) 1958-2001.

Sermons
James Hilmon "Pete" Hegwood (1939-2012)
Lawrence Earl Phelps (1928-2016)

Session Records
Hopewell CPCA. Leighton, Alabama. 1997-2016.
Cloverdale CPC. Obion, Tennessee. 1900-1931
Salt Fork CPC. Nelson, Missouri. 1871-1901
Silverdale CPC. Chattanooga, Tennessee. 1984-2000

Synodical Records
Alabama Synod. Colored Cumberland Presbyterian Church. Minutes. 1953.

In all judicatories, from the session of the congregation through presbytery, synod, and the General Assemblies of both the Cumberland Presbyterian Church and the Cumberland Presbyterian Church in America, minutes form the legal record of the judicatory. Without these records there is often nothing to document persons joining the church, ordination as elder and clergy, disciplinary actions, etc. It is important to be aware that legally original minutes are always the property of the judicatory for which they are created. Should that judicatory cease to exist, the next higher judicatory becomes custodian responsible for securing and preserving the records of the extinct body. It can be difficult to convince persons that records kept by their relative are not family property but the General Assemblies of both denominations have ruled the only legal repository for the records of extinct judicatories is the Historical Foundation.

RECOMMENDATION 4: That the General Assembly encourage all congregations to preserve their session records by depositing them in the Historical Foundation.

RECOMMENDATION 5: That the General Assembly instruct each synod and presbytery to deposit their minutes in a timely fashion with the Historical Foundation.

The Historical Foundation can provide on-site assistance to both presbyteries and individual congregations. On the presbyterial level, we can assist the appropriate agency to evaluate materials left when a church has ceased to be viable and has been closed. This can eliminate speculation on the presbytery's part as to what is, or is not, material to be preserved. For congregations we can provide a similar service helping them to determine what can and should be archived.

RECOMMENDATION 6: That the General Assembly instruct presbyteries to locate the session records when closing a church and then deposit them in the Historical Foundation.

V. BIRTHPLACE SHRINE

The Birthplace Shrine located at Montgomery Bell State Park near Dickson, Tennessee was dedicated June 18, 1960. This site consists of the Memorial Chapel and a replica of the Reverend Samuel McAdow's log house. Since 1994, the Foundation has been responsible for the preservation of the Birthplace Shrine. Four endowments provide funds for maintenance and repairs: the Grace Johnson Beasley Birthplace Shrine Fund, the Birthplace Shrine Fund, the Henry Evan Harper Endowment for Cumberland Presbyterian History, and the P.F. Johnson Memorial Endowment. Gifts to these endowments provide for the continued preservation of the Birthplace Shrine. Interested donors are encouraged to contact the Foundation office. Another means of support are the fees collected from couples who use the chapel for their wedding ceremony. These funds are added to the Birthplace Shrine Fund and earnings are used for maintenance and special projects. The Board encourages individuals and groups to visit the Birthplace Shrine as an act of remembering our heritage and envisioning our future as Cumberland Presbyterians.

Groups and individuals are encouraged to contact the Foundation to set up work days and special projects. The Foundation thanks the Heritage Committee of Nashville Presbytery and the Charlotte Cumberland Presbyterian Church for their continuing volunteer upkeep of the property.

VII. FINANCIAL CONCERNS AND 2018 BUDGET

A. BUDGETS
The 2018 line-item budget of the Historical Foundation has been filed with the CPC General Assembly Office.

B. ENDOWMENTS
Anne Elizabeth Knight Adams Heritage Fund
Rosie Magrill Alexander Trust
Paul H. and Ann M. Allen Heritage Fund
Grace Johnson Beasley Birthplace Shrine Fund
Birthplace Shrine Fund
James L. and Louise M. Bridges Heritage Fund
Mark and Elinor Swindle Brown Heritage Fund
Sydney and Elinor Brown Heritage Fund
Centennial Heritage Endowment
Walter Chesnut Heritage Fund
Lavenia Campbell Cole Heritage Fund
Cumberland Presbyterian Church in America Heritage Fund
Cumberland Presbyterian Women Archival Supplies Endowment
Bettye Jean Loggins McCaffrey Ellis Heritage Fund
Samuel Russell & Mary Grace (Barefoot) Estes Endowment
Family of Faith Endowment
Gettis and Delia Snyder Gilbert Heritage Fund
James C. and Freda M. Gilbert Heritage Fund
James C. and Freda M. Gilbert Trust
Mamie A. Gilbert Trust
Henry Evan Harper Endowment for Cumberland Presbyterian History
Ronald Wilson and Virginia Tosh Harper Endowment
Historical Foundation Trust
Donald and Jane Hubbard Heritage Fund
Cliff and Jill Hudson Heritage Fund
Robert and Kathy Hull Endowment
Into the Nineties Endowment
Joe Ben Irby Heritage Fund
P. F. Johnson Memorial Endowment
Irene A. Kiefer Endowment
Chow King Leong Endowment
Dennis Lawrence & Elmira Castleberry Magrill Trust
J. Richard Magrill Heritage Fund
Joe Richard and Mary Belle Magrill Trust
Gwendolyn McCaffrey McReynolds Heritage Fund
Jimmie Joe McKinley Heritage Fund
Edith Louise Mitchell Heritage Fund
Lloyd Freeman Mitchell Heritage Fund
Snowdy Clifton and Lillian Walkup Mitchell Heritage Fund
Rev. Charles and Paulette Morrow Endowment
Virginia Sue Williamson Morrow Heritage Fund
Anne Elizabeth Swain Odom Heritage Fund
Martha Sue Parr Heritage Fund
Florence Pennewill Heritage Fund
Morris and Ruth Pepper Endowment
Publishing House Endowment
Mable Magrill Rundell Trust

Samuel Callaway Rundell Heritage Fund
Paul and Mary Jo Schnorbus Heritage Fund
Roy and Mary Seawright Shelton Heritage Fund
Shiloh CPC Ellis County Texas Endowment
Hinkley and Vista Smartt Heritage Fund
John William Sparks Heritage Fund
Irvin Scott and Annie Mary Draper Swain Heritage Fund
F. P. Waits Historical Trust

Respectfully submitted,
Rick White, President
Susan Knight Gore, Archivist

THE REPORT OF THE BOARD OF TRUSTEES OF MEMPHIS THEOLOGICAL SEMINARY

Introduction

Memphis Memphis Theological Seminary is the only seminary of the Cumberland Presbyterian Church. Our history is traced back through the Cumberland Presbyterian Theological Seminary in McKenzie to the organization of the graduate School of Theology at Cumberland University and the Theological Department at Bethel College, both of which began in 1852. Those two schools of theology continued the legacy begun in the work of founder Finis Ewing, who educated candidates for the ministry in his home, and many other ministers, who trained young candidates in homes, churches, and on the trail. For one hundred fifty seven years, Cumberland Presbyterians have been providing formal theological education for the church's ministers. For almost two hundred years, the Cumberland Presbyterian Church has valued the importance of an educated ministry.

With the denomination's decision to move its seminary to Memphis in 1964, Memphis Theological Seminary of the Cumberland Presbyterian Church began to serve a larger and more diverse student body. Though students from other denominations were admitted during the McKenzie years, the move to a major metropolitan area opened the opportunity to attract more students from more denominations. Today, Memphis Theological Seminary has one of the most diverse student populations, in terms of denomination and race, of any seminary in the United States. This theological and denominational diversity provides a rich environment for educating pastors, chaplains, Christian educators, and other leaders for the church of Jesus Christ. The sign on our campus that faces Union Avenue reads: "Memphis Theological Seminary: an Ecumenical Mission of the Cumberland Presbyterian Church." Every Cumberland Presbyterian can be proud of the mission our seminary fulfills of educating our own church leaders, and leaders from more than 25 other denominations.

We, the trustees and administration of Memphis Theological Seminary, are privileged to be a part of this legacy, born out of and guided by the ecumenical and evangelical spirit of the Cumberland Presbyterian Church. We look forward to what God has in store for our ministry in the future. With gratitude for God's grace, guidance and provision in the past year, we make the following report to the 187th General Assembly of the Cumberland Presbyterian Church, meeting June 19-23 in Palm Harbor, Florida.

I. BOARD OF TRUSTEES

A. OFFICERS

The following officers were elected by the Board of Trustees to serve during the past academic year: Moderator – Reverend Jennifer Newell (Cumberland Presbyterian minister, Tennessee-Georgia Presbytery); Vice-moderator – Reverend Kevin Henson (Cumberland Presbyterian minister, Red River Presbytery); Secretary – Mrs. Sondra Roddy (Cumberland Presbyterian elder, Clarksville, Tennessee); Treasurer – Mrs. Cassandra Price-Perry (Vice President of Operations and CFO, MTS).

B. BOARD REPRESENTATIVE

Reverend Susan Parker, Hope Presbytery, was elected to serve as the Board's representative to this meeting of the General Assembly. Mrs. Sondra Roddy was elected alternate.

C. MEETINGS

The Board of Trustees has met twice since the last meeting of General Assembly: October 6-7, 2016 and February 9-10, 2017. The Board is scheduled to meet one more time before the meeting of General Assembly, on May 11-12, 2017. In addition to full Board meetings, standing committees meet on a regular schedule between Board meetings, usually by conference call.

Members of our Board of Trustees devote significant time and resources to their work on behalf of the seminary. By rule of the General Assembly, thirteen of the twenty-four members are Cumberland Presbyterians. The other eleven members of the Board represent six different denominations.

D. EXPIRATION OF TERMS

The terms of eight of twenty-four members of the Board of Trustees expire each year. Five of the eight whose terms expire this year are eligible to succeed themselves and have agreed to serve another three year term: Reverend Nancy Cole (United Methodist, Tuscaloosa, Alabama); Reverend Anne Hames (Cumberland Presbyterian, McKenzie, Tennessee); Reverend Jennifer Newell (Cumberland Presbyterian, Chattanooga, Tennessee); Reverend Susan Parker (Cumberland Presbyterian, Rogersville, Alabama), and Reverend Stewart Salyer (Cumberland Presbyterian, Clarksville, Tennessee). All have served faithfully and contributed greatly to the life of the seminary. We are grateful for their willingness to continue serving if re-elected.

One trustee who was eligible to serve for another term had declined to serve. Reverend Robert Marble (United Methodist, Little Rock, Arkansas) will be unable to serve a third term. Two trustees have completed their eligibility having served three terms: Doctor Joe Ward (Cumberland Presbyterian in America, Huntsville, Alabama) and Mrs. Ruby Wharton (Roman Catholic, Memphis, Tennessee).

Trustee Mr. Johnny Coombs (United Methodist, Ripley, Mississippi) submitted his resignation effective May of 2017 because of expanded work responsibilities.

RECOMMENDATION 1: That the General Assembly express its gratitude to trustees Marble, Ward, Wharton, and Coombs for their faithful service to Memphis Theological Seminary and the Cumberland Presbyterian Church.

E. WORK OF THE BOARD

The trustees continue to develop their administrative procedures and practices to provide the best possible governance to the life of the seminary. For the past ten years we have had 100% participation by trustees in giving to the Annual Fund, and in participating actively in the work of MTS.

The Board has prioritized strategic planning and the development of alternate revenue streams for the coming year. We will be considering a strategic plan for the next 3 to 5 years at our May Board of Trustees meeting. The plan has been developed with guidance and input from our Board and our broad constituency, and specific goals have been identified by seminary administrators in all areas of the seminary's life.

F. "MINISTRY FOR THE REAL WORLD"

The 183rd General Assembly approved a recommendation from our Board granting us permission to engage in a major capital campaign for Memphis Theological Seminary. After two years in the quiet phase, the Board authorized a comprehensive campaign, titled, "Ministry for the Real World," which was launched publicly in October of 2015. The Board authorized a goal of $25 million to be raised through 2020, with approximately $10 million committed to operations, $10 million to capital improvements, including the construction of a new chapel, and $5 million for endowment.

As of the writing of this report, we have secured approximately $14 million in gifts and pledges toward the goal, including an additional gift of $2 million in the past year for the Hamilton Chapel project. We anticipate breaking ground for the chapel before the end of 2017. What follows is the case statement for the campaign.

MINISTRY FOR THE REAL WORLD
Scholarship, Piety and Justice
MEMPHIS THEOLOGICAL SEMINARY

March 24, 2014

MINISTRY FOR THE REAL WORLD
TWO CENTURIES OF MAKING A DIFFERENCE.

"Academic scholarship is a major hallmark of Memphis Theological Seminary. The school feeds both the minds and spirits of its students. Rigorous scholastic study and intellectual discussion of the Bible from different points of view are encouraged." "The goal is to foster informed critical thinkers. It is not to promote the agenda of Memphis Theological Seminary. When students graduate, they have the knowledge and practical tools to be effective ministers. They live their lives according to the teachings and values of the Bible. Graduates are well prepared to positively impact individuals, congregations and society." – Mrs. Ruby Wharton, Esq., Trustee

In 1821, a pastor's dedication to theological education and inclusiveness gave rise to the first theological school west of the Mississippi. Thirty years later, out of the same Spirit, a theological department was established at Bethel College (now Bethel University) in McKenzie, Tennessee, an institution of the

Cumberland Presbyterian Church.

Over one hundred years later, in 1964, in order to reach more ministers for the Gospel, the seminary was moved to Memphis and renamed Memphis Theological Seminary. It was intentionally opened as an ecumenical seminary that welcomes men and women of all faiths, cultures and ages. The philosophy and values of the seminary are as meaningful today as they were two centuries ago. The school focuses on scholarship, piety and justice. Inherent in these three words are powerful concepts that differentiate MTS from other seminaries.

• Scholarship implies disciplined, traditional study, but it also involves becoming a discerning critical thinker. Graduates are compelling spiritual servant leaders and thoughtful ministers. They are able to explain Biblical passages within both their historical context and their relevancy in today's world—and in such a way that lives are transformed.

• Piety involves our heart-felt devotion to God. True piety leads to compassion, selflessness, universal love and respect for all of God's creation. As Dr. Martin Luther King Jr. described so eloquently when he wrote, "Our goal is to create a beloved community, and this will require a qualitative change in our souls as well as a quantitative change in our lives."

• Justice does not refer to civil law. It is much more. Without the practice of justice as described in the Bible, love, liberty and even life cannot flourish. Love alone does not ensure equality. Biblical justice involves care for the poor and powerless and leads to inclusiveness, understanding and compassion. It is respecting all people, even those who are very different from you. It is actively participating in righting wrongs whenever and however they present themselves.

Our student population is very diverse and reflects the real world. There are no age, gender, economic, cultural, theological or racial barriers here. Our graduates will be ministering to many different populations and denominations. Their experience at MTS helps them understand how to work toward a beloved community.

Some of the most respected and influential ministers in the Mid-South are graduates of Memphis Theological Seminary. They are acknowledged for their depth of Biblical and religious knowledge and their ecumenism. They are respected for their ability to influence both religious and secular communities.

Wherever our graduates serve, they impact the lives of those they touch. They are formed to be ministers in the real world.

Our graduates touch thousands of lives in their chosen ministry. They become pastors, youth ministers, educators and chaplains in hospitals, prisons and the military.

For over fifty years, the seminary has occupied the magnificent turn-of-the-century Newburger Mansion in midtown Memphis. We have worked hard to maintain the original beauty of this grand home. Warmth and intimacy are created by cascading stairways, arched doorways, and handcrafted woodwork. It is the beautiful face we show to the public. In more recent years, we have added two adjoining mansions in response to a growing student body and the faculty and staff hired to serve them.

The three homes have served us well, but with enrollment reaching 325 students, we have outgrown them. Because of the reputation and impact of our graduates, our enrollment continues to grow. We believe we can reach an enrollment of 450 students in the not-too-distant future. Together students will represent over 30 denominations, several states and a few countries.

The Newburger Mansion's prized Ballroom is our makeshift chapel. Unfortunately it can only seat one-fifth of our student body. We are grateful to have resided in the homes on beautiful East Parkway during our time of growth. We will always maintain them. They will continue to serve us well as library space, offices and intimate gathering spaces for small discussion groups. But it is urgent that we expand our campus and construct a chapel and an academic building. We have acquired property adjacent to our campus for both structures. Now we must build. Our future depends on it.

PREPARING FOR ANOTHER TWO HUNDRED YEARS OF MINISTRY FOR THE REAL WORLD

The Board and administration of Memphis Theological Seminary have thought long and hard about the future of the seminary. We have prayed for God to guide us in our decision making. In order to ensure our future, we must undertake three important and much-needed projects without delay.

1. A new chapel is a top priority. We have made do with a small converted ballroom for too long.

2. We need a building to house our new, groundbreaking Methodist House of Studies. Methodists represent the single largest contingent of students at MTS. With faculty offices and meeting space, the Methodist House of Studies will relieve pressure on MTS's limited academic facilities.

3. Significantly increasing our endowment and underwriting an important faculty chair will enable MTS to prosper and grow. It will help us become financially stable and ready to withstand any potential financial crises for the next two hundred years. Like most seminaries, we are tuition dependent. At last report our endowment was $9.2 million. This does not generate sufficient interest income to meet the growing demands of our expanding student body. It is crucial that we double the endowment immediately. It will allow us to meet the increasing need for scholarships and financial aid. And it will be a cushion to protect MTS from unforeseen emergencies.

While MTS serves a variety of denominations, its' roots extend back to the Cumberland Presbyterian tradition. By fully endowing the Baird-Buck Chair in Cumberland Presbyterian Studies, we will ensure that our Cumberland Presbyterian students are fully prepared to serve the congregation to which they are sent.

Successfully completing these projects will enable MTS to aggressively pursue its mission well into the twenty-first century: To educate men and women for ordained and lay Christian ministry in the church and the world by shaping and inspiring lives devoted to scholarship, piety and justice.

Project One: Construct a new free-standing chapel

We are blessed to have already received two wonderfully generous gifts designated for our new chapel. The first is an extraordinary cash donation of $1 million. This significant gift is a vote of confidence in Memphis Theological Seminary. It recognizes the difference our graduates make in the world.

The second is one of the oldest and finest pipe organs in the South. It was donated to us by the Union Avenue United Methodist Church. It is an acknowledgement of the role we play in preparing strong spiritual leaders. The pipe organ was manufactured in 1924 by the M.P. Moller Organ Company. In today's dollars, it is estimated to be worth $550,000—a valuable and prestigious gift. Moller pipe organs are also installed in the chapels at Camp David and Lincoln Center.

Both gifts are true blessings and will enable MTS to construct a chapel that
• Reflects our identity, purpose and excellence.
• Is large and adaptable enough for different denominations within the seminary to conduct worship services reflective of their cultures and expressions of faith.
• Provides a place of worship that will accommodate our entire student body.
• Replicates in a small way the churches in which graduates will preach. This will give students the experience of speaking from a real pulpit rather than a small podium.
• Has the proper acoustics to showcase the beautiful Moller pipe organ.
• Will allow us to offer certificates or degrees in church music and organ music.

Project Two: Construct a home for the Methodist House of Studies

There has long been a perceived gap between "the academy" and "the church." We at MTS have become convinced that such a binary way of thinking is deeply flawed. The relationship between seminary and church ought to be marked by an organic, mutually beneficial partnership. Within that partnership, it is the seminary's calling to be in service to the church—preparing women and men for pastoral leadership and resourcing the current ministry needs of pastors and congregations.

We at MTS believe that there is a point of intersection between the mission of the seminary and the mission of the church. Our commitment is to focus our resources and attention at that point of intersection. We are planning a major new initiative in the life of MTS—the Methodist House of Studies. Under the direction of faculty member Dr. Andrew C. Thompson, the Methodist House of Studies will serve as a "community within a community" where our Methodist students can take advantage of the best in Wesleyan theological formation within MTS' richly ecumenical context. The House of Studies will also serve as a vehicle for connecting the resources of MTS with the needs of the wider church. This link will offer pastors and congregations new avenues and contexts for mission and ministry.

The proposed building will house professors' offices and provide meeting space for this groundbreaking program. Given our facilities limitations, the additional space will contribute to the success of this important program.

The ecumenical partnership between Memphis Theological Seminary and the United Methodist Church goes back for decades. And from a strong foundation we believe a vital future can be cultivated and grown. At this crucial juncture in the life of both seminary and church, we are excited to anticipate advancing the relationship between the two with the creation of a home at MTS for the Methodist House of Studies.

Project Three: Significantly increase our endowment and endow the Baird-Buck Chair in Cumberland Presbyterian Studies

Without a larger endowment, we cannot fully execute our mission. Cassandra Price-Perry, Vice President of Operations/CFO, explains this very well.

"I am here to use my financial skills to help students respond to their call by God to ministry. Because of our small endowment, the number and size of our scholarships and financial aid packages are limited. We are not able to enroll as many highly qualified and motivated students as we would like because they can't afford the cost of attendance—books, fees, travel, food and other miscellaneous expenses."

Our tuition is certainly not exorbitant, but nor is it cheap. Many students find it difficult to fund the entire three years required to receive a degree.

Sadly, this compromises our commitment to being an ecumenical school that welcomes everyone who meets our academic requirements. We have cut our operating expenses to the bone during the economic downturn. Still, we can only offer financial assistance to just a portion of the students who apply. Only with philanthropy will it be possible to provide financial assistance to the many motivated and qualified students who are called to serve.

Founded by the Cumberland Presbyterian Church, Memphis Theological Seminary has proclaimed the inclusiveness of the Gospel message for more than 150 years. A fully endowed Baird-Buck Chair in Cumberland Presbyterian Studies will ensure that the vibrant tradition which has guided MTS for eight generations will inspire seminarians for many years to come.

MAKING A REAL DIFFERENCE: MINISTRY FOR THE REAL WORLD

The graduates of Memphis Theological Seminary proclaim and embody God's message of redemption, justice and peace in service to others. Our graduates guide people in their faith and help them understand why they believe. This is powerful. They ignite people's hearts in love for Jesus Christ and support them in walking in His way. They model Christ-like behavior, and in doing so they transform the lives of those they touch—in church, in the grocery store, on a bus or in prisons. They shatter prejudice. They stand in the face of desperation and offer hope. They provide for those with nothing, and they teach others to do the same. The world is a better place because of their real world ministry—a ministry that is persuasive, practical and purposeful.

"Today, mainline religions are grappling with retaining membership. Our emphasis is on academics, practical application and an inclusive approach to theology. This prepares our graduates to be relevant and meaningful ordained and lay ministers in the real world today. This is the only way they can serve and embody God's mission of redemption, justice and peace in service to the New Creation of Jesus Christ. "My father attended this seminary, so it was only natural that I followed in his footsteps. Now that I am president, I am blessed to be leading the initiative to bring our facilities into the twenty-first century. We cannot wait. Our campus must reflect the extraordinary academic excellence within its walls." – Dr. Daniel J. Earheart-Brown, President

Angel, must I give again, I ask in dismay. And must I keep giving and giving and giving it away? Oh no, said the angel, his glance pierced me through. Just keep giving 'til the Lord stops giving to you.

THIS MINISTRY FOR THE REAL WORLD CAMPAIGN IS NOT REALLY ABOUT NEW BUILDINGS

It is about the people.

It is about the highly qualified professors who work inside them. It is about the committed and passionate students who are following God's call to ministry. Sometimes they leave successful careers. Their families make significant economic and lifestyle changes. They do this to serve God, humanity and all of creation. Their lives are transformed. And as a result, our lives are changed. And the world is a better place because of them. Adequate classrooms and a student center will support students on their rigorous academic and spiritual journey. They deserve a real chapel in which to pray, preach, meditate and seek God's further counsel. A chapel filled with the music of a real pipe organ. And joyous voices joined in praise. Finally, Memphis Theological Seminary deserves facilities that truly reflect the excellence of its high academic standards. Its commitment to forming extraordinary ministers for the real world must be celebrated with quality facilities.

You have the power make a real and powerful difference. Your support ensures the success of our campaign. It also secures the future of Memphis Theological Seminary. With your support we will be able to continue to graduate outstanding ministers for the real world. Prayerfully consider your role in supporting our important undertaking. And as you do, please consider the wisdom of this poem. It reflects the insights of a very generous philanthropist.

YOUR SUPPORT HAS A POWERFUL RETURN

A donation to Memphis Theological Seminary means that your investment will be leveraged in extraordinary ways.

A message from Tim Orr, former Chair of the Board Trustees, Memphis Theological Seminary:

Dear Friends,

As you consider your participation in the Ministry for the Real World Campaign, you can rest assured that your investment will be leveraged in extraordinary ways. The check I write to Memphis Theological Seminary is multiplied many times over. I am not just writing a check for the seminary. My donation impacts global society.

Here is what I mean. People come here because they are called to ministry. MTS forms them into leaders—Christian leaders with Christian values. Their lives are changed forever. But it doesn't stop there. Everyone touched by one of our graduates is changed also. MTS prepares ministers to be relevant and compelling in the real world. In a world that is spiritually bankrupt, they are effective in their congregation and in all of society. Their lives are transformed, and they are given the tools and skills to transform the spirit of our global society— and they do. I ask you, 'what investment has this powerful a return?'

I hope you will join me at this turning point in the life of Memphis Theological Seminary. Your prayers and generosity will ensure that MTS continues to prepare men and women for transformation ministry to the real world.

Faithfully,
Tim Orr

RECOMMENDATION 2: That the General Assembly encourage individuals, churches, and groups across the Cumberland Presbyterian Church to consider investing in the development of future leaders through the "Ministry for the Real World" campaign.

II. Administration

A. PRESIDENT

Daniel J. (Jay) Earheart Brown, Ph.D., became the seventh President of Memphis Theological Seminary August 1, 2005. Jay had served on the faculty of MTS since August, 1997, having previously served as a pastor in Nashville, Tennessee, and Lexington, Kentucky. He is a life-long Cumberland Presbyterian and son of a Cumberland Presbyterian minister. He is a graduate of Bethel College (B.A.), Memphis Theological Seminary (M.Div.), and Union Theological Seminary in Richmond, VA (Ph.D.). He will complete his twelfth year in this position at the end of the current academic year.

B. VICE PRESIDENT OF ACADEMIC AFFAIRS/DEAN

Reverend R. Stan Wood, D.Min., was appointed to serve as Interim Vice President of Academic Affairs and Dean in May, 2010. Dr. Wood had previously served MTS as Clara Scott Associate Professor of Ministry and Director of the Doctor of Ministry Program. He is an ordained minister in the Cumberland Presbyterian Church in America and currently serves as Pastor of the Mt. Tabor CPCA in Jackson, Tennessee. Dr. Wood has announced his retirement effective at the end of next academic year July 31, 2017.

The Board began an open search in the fall of 2016 for our next VP of Academic Affairs and Dean. Members of the search committee identified three candidates to interview, two external and one internal. After interviewing the candidates, the search committee recommended, and the Board confirmed the election of Dr. Peter Gathje, Professor of Ethics at MTS, to serve as our next Vice President of Academic Affairs and Dean beginning in the summer of 2017.

D. VICE PRESIDENT OF ADVANCEMENT

In October 2014, Doctor Keith Gaskin began work as Vice President of Advancement, coming to MTS after over twenty years of experience in development work for higher education, including service at Mississippi State University and the University of Alabama. He is a layman in the Presbyterian Church (USA). Keith holds a Ph.D. in higher education leadership from Mississippi State University.

Keith has brought to his work at MTS a proven track record of higher education fundraising, a commitment to the mission of MTS, and the ability to manage and build on the efforts of those who have gone before him. He has worked well with faculty and staff to encourage participation across the seminary in the work of development.

E. VICE PRESIDENT OF OPERATIONS/CFO

Ms. Cassandra Price-Perry began work with MTS in August 2010 as Vice President of Operations and Chief Financial Officer. She is a Certified Public Accountant with over 20 years of experience in business and accounting. Cassandra is an active laywoman in her Roman Catholic Church in Southaven, Mississippi. She has received high praise from our auditors and our Board for her work over the past almost seven years.

III. INSTRUCTION

A. DEGREE PROGRAMS

Memphis Theological Seminary offers four degree programs and three certificate programs, including the certificate offered through the Program of Alternate Studies. The Master of Divinity is the basic degree program for persons preparing for ordained ministry in many denominations. It continues to be our largest degree program, with over 70% of students enrolled. The M.Div. requires 84 semester hours and takes three years of full-time study to complete.

The Master of Arts (Religion) degree is an academic degree for persons seeking to pursue further graduate studies. The M.A.R. requires 36 semester hours and takes two years of full-time study to complete. The faculty launched a major revision to the MAR in the fall of 2015 to clarify its role as an academic degree.

The Doctor of Ministry degree is a professional degree designed for pastors and other ministers who have at least three years of full-time work in ministry after their M.Div. and who want to engage in further theological reflection on the practice of ministry. The D.Min. is designed around five two-week residencies, in January and July, and the implementation of and report on a major project in ministry. It usually takes 3-5 years to complete.

In the spring of 2013, we awarded our first new degree in several years: the Master of Arts in Youth Ministry (MAYM). Through our partnership with the Center for Youth Ministry Training in Brentwood, Tennessee, and the new certificate program in youth ministry through the Cumberland Presbyterian Church, we have over 40 students enrolled in this degree program. MTS currently has, we believe, the largest master's program in youth ministry in the United States.

In the spring of 2016, we were approved by our accrediting bodies (The Southern Association of Colleges and Schools, and the Association of Theological Schools in the United States and Canada) to offer a new degree, the Master of Arts in Christian Ministry (MACM). This degree program began in the fall of 2016 with concentrations offered in Christian Education, Urban Ministry, and Social Justice Ministry. The MACM is a 42 hour degree for persons interested in pursuing specialized ministries. We plan to offer additional concentrations in the future (possibly rural ministry, counseling, etc.)

At Commencement in May of 2016, Memphis Theological Seminary awarded the Master of Arts in Youth Ministry degree to ten graduates. Three persons were awarded the Master of Arts (Religion) degree. Thirty-two persons were awarded the Master of Divinity degree, and ten were awarded the Doctor of Ministry degree. Seven students were awarded the Graduate Certificate in Addiction Counseling Studies. Of these sixty-two graduates, seven were Cumberland Presbyterians.

Cumberland Presbyterian Master of Divinity graduates were:
- Lynette Hamilton Dalton, West Tennessee Presbytery
- Johan Esteban Daza Rivera, Andes Presbytery
- Emily K. Fowler, Red River Presbytery
- William McKinley Price, West Tennessee Presbytery
- Michael D. Reno, Missouri Presbytery
- Anna Sweet-Brockman, Presbytery of East Tennessee
- Brandon Taylor Young, Nashville Presbytery

B. CERTIFICATE PROGRAMS

In addition to the five degree programs, MTS offers the following certificates:
Program of Alternate Studies of the Cumberland Presbyterian Church
Drug and Alcohol Addiction Counseling Graduate Certificate
James Netters Certificate in Ministry
Certificate in Wesleyan Studies

C. FACULTY

For the current academic year, Memphis Theological Seminary has fifteen full-time teaching faculty and two administrative faculty members who teach part-time. In addition, the seminary curriculum is greatly enhanced by the work of twenty-five to thirty adjunct professors, most of whom are active in pastoral or other ministries.

Members of the MTS faculty continue to publish books and articles both for the academy and the church. Many faculty members preach in area churches on a regular basis, deliver lectures for local churches and judicatories, deliver papers at academic conferences, and write articles for a wide range of readers.

Two new tenure track faculty members joined the MTS community for the current academic year. Doctor Michael Turner (Ph.D. from Vanderbilt University) is Associate Professor of Wesleyan Studies. Doctor Paula McGee (Ph.D. from Claremont Graduate University) serves as Assistant Professor of African American Church Studies.

Under the leadership of VP/Dean Wood, the faculty has implemented our new M.Div. curriculum in the fall of 2016. Under the new curriculum, there will be greater emphasis on integration of learning for pastoral leadership. It will also continue to strengthen our focus on the practice of ministry as imaginative leadership drawing from the resources of scripture and tradition in particular cultural contexts.

D. ENROLLMENT

Total enrollment in Memphis Theological Seminary for the fall term of 2015 was 329, including all degree and certificate programs. We continued to see a slight drop in enrollment in our largest degree program, the Master of Divinity. This dip in our enrollment in the fall led to budget adjustments during the year, and an increased effort to recruit new students. We invested in a new recruiter to focus on our African American constituency. Our largest number of students come from the United Methodist Church, with 25% of total enrollment. Cumberland Presbyterians are the second largest denomination represented in the student body with just under 15% of all students.

We continue to work to recruit Cumberland Presbyterian students, and to lift up the call of God to ordained ministry in the church. We call on all Cumberland Presbyterians to pray that God will continue to call men and women to the office of ministry, and that they will be well prepared through our educational institutions to lead growing and vibrant congregations in the ministry of Jesus Christ to the world.

RECOMMENDATION 3: That the General Assembly urge all probationers to consider Memphis Theological Seminary and the Program of Alternate Studies as their first options for meeting educational requirements for ordained ministry.

E. PROGRAM OF ALTERNATE STUDIES

The Program of Alternate Studies (PAS) is a non-degree program of educational preparation for ministry authorized by the General Assembly of the Cumberland Presbyterian Church. Its chief purpose is to enable persons who are prevented from accessing a traditional theological education to adequately prepare for ordained ministry. It is administered by Memphis Theological Seminary. With the ongoing support of MTS the Program of Alternate Studies has faithfully filled a vital niche for the Cumberland Presbyterian denomination for over thirty years.

There are currently 112 students active in our files. This number includes 58 traditional PAS students, 21 seeking CP studies-only certification, 27 enrolled in PAS-Colombia, and 6 students in the recently formed Haiti Council of the Cumberland Presbyterian Church.

SUMMER EXTENSION SCHOOL

The annual SES held on the campus of Bethel University in McKenzie, Tennessee, continues to be the mainstay of our program. SES 2017 will be held July 8-22 with graduation on the first day, Saturday

July 8th. Retiring Dean of Memphis Theological Seminary, Dr. Stan Wood, will bring our commencement address. The courses offered and the faculty are:

    Block I
Min. In Residence – Steve and Teresa Shauf
CP History – Matt Gore
The Pentateuch – Pat Pickett
The Gospels – Anne Hames
CP Theology I – Jay Earheart-Brown
Christian Ministry – Clinton Buck & Michael Qualls
Introduction to the Bible – William Montague
CP Polity – Andy McClung
Pastor & Public Worship – Tiffany McClung
Ministerial Ethics – Milton Ortiz

    Block II
Min. In Residence – Jason Mikel
Wisdom Literature – Pat Pickett
Evangelism – T. J. Malinoski
Work of the Elder – Robert Watkins
Ministry in the Small Church – Joe Butler
Conflict in the Church – Bruce Hamilton
The Art of Public Speaking – Susan Parker
World Missions – Robert Watkins
History of the Christian Church I – Ron McMillan
Message of the Old Testament – Roy Hall

    Block III
Min. In Residence – William Robinson
Race & Reconcilliation   Michael Qualls & Mitchell Walker
Pastoral Care & Counseling – Tom Sanders
Biblical Exegesis – Marcus Hayes
Epistles of the Early Church – David Lancaster
Principles of Preaching – Perryn Rice
Message of the New Testament – Jon Carlock
Practicum in Pastoral Counseling – Tom Sanders

CPCA/CP COOPERATIVE WORK
    At the request of the General Assembly the Program of Alternate Studies Director, Dr. Michael Qualls, and MTS president, Dr. Jay Earheart-Brown, met with representatives of the School for Continuing Education of the CPCA in Huntsville, Alabama. Those in attendance from CPCA were Dr. Lynne Herring and Dr. Mitchell Walker. The intent was to begin to understand the alternate education processes in the sister denominations and begin searching for synergies and brainstorming what the future might look like with (or without) unification. The meeting was productive and informative, with much information being shared about the respective programs. Further relationship building steps are being taken including:
1) open a position on the advisory board of each program to the Director of the sister program;
2) pursue reciprocal agreements that allow students in one program to receive credit for approved courses in the sister program and pay the tuition to their original certifying program;
3) initiate sharing and standardizing forms and certification procedures; and
4) investigate strengthening relationship between MTS and the School of Continuing Education.
    While tentative, these are promising movements. We will continue to build on these initial steps. A report was made to the Joint Unification Task Force.

RACE AND RECONCILIATION: A CASE STUDY
    We are very excited to feature a special course available to MDiv. students, traditional PAS students, and the two Cumberland Presbyterian denominations at large during our summer school at Bethel University. This course will engage in close examination of the current "Plan for Unification of the Cumberland Presbyterian Church and the Cumberland Presbyterian Church in America" and the issues of

race and reconciliation surrounding the process. It will dig beneath the surface of the current proposal to unify these historically "white" and historically "black" denominations and facilitate an honest, respectful dialogue across the difficult barriers that divide. We believe this will be a valuable and timely learning experience. It is important to include a broad spectrum of perspectives in the conversation.

MTS Administration has approved ten (10) auditor scholarships to be made available from the regular distributions of the Pete Palmer Scholarship Endowment for PAS. A minimum of five (5) will be reserved for representatives of the CPCA due to its under-representation in PAS. Including 5 nights room and board the cost will be $350 per student ($3500).

REQUEST PROCEDURAL CHANGE

When a presbytery approves a candidate to prepare for ministry through the Alternate Studies route the vote must be by two-thirds and the reasons for the exception are noted in the minutes of presbytery. An additional step has emerged over the years which involves notification (now) to the Pastoral Development Ministry Team. We include a form for this in our application process and get the necessary signature for the student's file. It has become a perfunctory and unnecessary step which has outlived its usefulness. Currently, there is no one in the PDMT office and the administrative detail falls to others within the Ministry Council. The Ministry Council office would favor reprieve. Change would require a General Assembly action.

RECOMMENDATION 4: That the General Assembly approve discontinuance of the process of requiring PDMT to review exceptions made for candidates to prepare for ministry through the Program of Alternate Studies.

Respectfully,
Michael Qualls, Director

F. NEW ACADEMIC INITIATIVES

In Fall 2010, we began offering courses toward a certificate in drug and alcohol addiction counseling. This new program, which was initially led by Cumberland Presbyterian minister and counselor Dr. Johnie Welch, promises to meet an important need in our society and in our region. Due to health concerns, Dr. Welch was unable to continue in this role after the 2012 academic year. Currently, Reverend Terry Kinnaman, a Cumberland Presbyterian minister from Columbia Presbytery and licensed counselor working for the State of Tennessee, is coordinating this program in a part-time capacity.

In the spring of 2012, we began a new certificate program targeted for African American ministers in the Memphis area who do not have the educational background to enroll as degree students at MTS. The James Netters Certificate Program, we believe that there is a need for such certificate level education for many in our area and hope to expand this work in the future.

In the spring of 2016 we received word from our accreditors that we have been approved for a new degree program, the Master of Arts in Christian Ministry. This degree is designed for persons who are called to ministries other than ordained pastoral ministry. The new two-year degree will begin enrolling students in the fall of 2016. Students will choose between concentrations in Christian Education, Urban Ministry, and Social Justice. Additional concentrations to be added may include Children and Family Ministries, Rural Ministry, and other specialized ministries.

Our Master of Arts in Youth Ministry degree is, we think, now the largest graduate degree program in youth ministry in the United States. We continue to cooperate with the Center for Youth Ministry Training in Brentwood, Tennessee to offer a graduate residency in youth ministry.

In the fall of 2016 we implemented a major revision to our Master of Divinity curriculum. The revised curriculum will provide more opportunity for team teaching and cross-disciplinary work focused on integration of theology and practice for ministry.

With assistance from Bethel University leaders, we are planning to expand significantly our distance education offerings in the 2017-2018 academic year. New classroom technology will enable us to provide educational services far beyond our geographic base.

G. ACCREDITATION

Memphis Theological Seminary holds dual accreditation by the Association of Theological Schools in the United States and Canada (ATS), and the Southern Association of Colleges and Schools (SACS). Every ten years, member schools go through an extensive process of re-accreditation review.

Our last accreditation visit occurred in 2008, at which time we were fully affirmed for the next ten years by both accrediting bodies. We will be submitting our decennial reaffirmation reports to SACS and ATS in the fall of this year in preparation for our site visits in the spring of 2018.

IV. FACILITIES

A. LEADERSHIP

Since the fall of 2015, our facilities and safety department has been ably led by Mr. Greg Spencer and a dedicated staff of facilities technicians. Mr. Spencer has more than twenty years of experience in construction and facilities management. He served in this role for two years previously, and after a brief stint in facilities management in corporate environment, Greg returned to our MTS leadership. We are grateful for his service.

B. DEBT ON PROPERTY

In 2015 we were able to secure a commercial loan to repay our debt to the Board of Stewardship for the purchase of properties adjacent to our campus. That long term debt now stands at less than $1.5 million, less than a third of our annual budget amount. This low debt allows us to operate as efficiently as possible.

C. COMMUTER HOUSING

MTS began to convert its student housing from individual rentals to commuter housing in the 1998. Currently, MTS provides commuter housing, with very reasonable nightly rates, for about fifty students each week of the regular term. The need for such commuter housing has continued to grow, as has income from such rentals. Our ability to serve students from about a 250 mile radius around Memphis, through block scheduling of classes and provision of affordable commuter housing, has had a significant impact on the growth of the student body over the past ten years.

D. CAMPUS WORK GROUPS

We have been blessed in recent years by adult and youth work groups who have come to MTS during the summer months to help repair and maintain our campus housing. Groups have come from Trilla, Illinois; Greeneville, Tennessee; Florence, Alabama; Bowling Green, Kentucky; and Collierville, Tennessee, and the youth from West Tennessee Presbytery to volunteer their time in a variety of areas. We encourage work groups who would be willing to help the seminary in this way to contact Mr. Greg Spencer in the Facilities Office of the seminary.

E. SAFETY

The Office of Safety of MTS continues to explore ways to enhance the safety of our students in the context of our urban campus. Through the use of lighting, security officers, secure locks, and well articulated safety plans, the seminary seeks to provide a safe environment for students and visitors to our campus.

During past seven years, MTS has contracted with a local security company to provide regular patrols around our neighborhood. This additional safety measure has been well received by our students and by our neighbors. We continue to seek ways to provide a safe environment for our campus community.

V. ADVANCEMENT AND FINANCE

A. BUDGET

Our Board of Trustees will approve a budget for the 2013-2014 academic year at its May meeting. Copies of that budget will be provided at the meeting of General Assembly.

After two years of significant budget reductions in the worst of the recession, we have begun to restore some of the cuts as income has improved the past two years. We continue to be very conservative in our budget planning as we work to recover from the effects of the recession. We were able to give modest raises to our employees last year. Our employees deserve much credit for hanging in with us through some tough economic times.

B. SCHOLARSHIPS AND GRANTS

We continue to cultivate relationships with foundations whose mission closely aligns with ours.

The following grants for scholarships and other projects have been received in recent years:

1. The Wilson Family Foundation

The Wilson family, founders of the Holiday Inn hotel chain and great philanthropists in Memphis, has renewed their funding of the Wilson Scholarships at $15,000 for 2013-14.

2. The H.W. Durham Foundation

In 2013, the Memphis-based H.W. Durham Foundation renewed its gift of $5,000 to provide 5 $1,000 scholarships for students who are 55+ years of age. These Durham Scholars will represent much of our student body who are second-career students.

3. The Lilly Endowment (2013-2018)

With a three-year grant totaling $249,371, followed by a second grant of $140,000 MTS is creating a unique program to increase financial literacy and decrease debt among our student population, and long term, the congregations they serve. We have just received word that we have been approved for a new Lilly Endowment planning grant of $50,000 for the 2017-2018 academic year to develop a program to help encourage and sustain younger ministers in the early post-seminary years of their ministry.

C. ENDOWMENTS

1. The Baird-Buck Chair of Cumberland Presbyterian Studies

Dr. Clinton Buck, Professor Emeritus of Christian Education at MTS, knowing the need for more focused teaching in CP heritage, has converted an existing endowment that was originally begun with the hopes of endowing a chair in Christian Education. Subsequent to Dr. Buck's decision, the late Mrs. Thalia Baird, widow of former President and Professor Dr. Colvin Baird, converted an endowment they had designated for general operations. Together with The Rev. J.T. Buck Scholarship Endowment Fund established in 1979 to provide scholarship assistance for Cumberland Presbyterian students at Memphis Theological Seminary, the new endowment was established with an initial principal balance of approximately $112,000. To-date, the fund has grown to more than $350,201, thanks to generous contributions from many Cumberland Presbyterians. The purpose of this endowment is to strengthen the Cumberland Presbyterian Church by establishing an endowed professorship with a primary focus of teaching Cumberland Presbyterian history, theology, church administration and the practice of ministry that is particular to the Cumberland Presbyterian Church. The goal is to raise $1.5 million to fully fund this endowed chair.

2. Rev. Hillman and Lorene Moore Endowed Scholarship Fund

Hillman Moore established this endowment fund on October 10, 2013, to be funded with a future gift of a bequest from his estate. It will be used to provide scholarship funds for training Cumberland Presbyterian students at Memphis Theological Seminary.

3. Wes and Susan Brantley Endowment

On October 15, 2013, the Brantley family of Ada, OK, was deeply saddened by the death of Susan Brantley, wife of former MTS trustee Wes Brantley, and mother of current trustee Kevin Brantley. In her memory, Wes has established the Wes and Susan Brantley Endowment to support general operating expenses of the seminary.

4. The Davis/Winston Scholarship for National Baptist Students

In the waning days of the spring semester 2013, one CP and one United Methodist student listened as three fellow students talked about the struggles they have in paying their seminary tuition. For these two students, all or most of their tuition is paid by their denomination. For the others, all National Baptists, humble servants with sweet spirits, the story is completely different.

Moved by the Holy Spirit through their student colleagues, they sought a way to establish a scholarship to help future National Baptist students. In recognition of the blessing received when seminary education is paid in full or in part by scholarship and/or denominational assistance, and in honor of exemplary and invigorating teaching by professors Dr. Christopher B. Davis and Dr. Eric Winston, they established a scholarship to support National Baptist students at MTS.

5. Rev. David and Leota Watson Scholarship Endowment Fund

A new endowment has been established to honor the ministry of the late Reverend David Watson. His widow, Mrs. Leota Watson, has chosen to direct the endowment earnings to support scholarships for Cumberland Presbyterian students attending MTS. Those who knew and loved Reverend Watson and appreciate his and Leota's ministry are invited to send a gift to fully establish the Reverend David and Leota Watson Scholarship Endowment Fund. Every gift matters. Perhaps in the Fall semester 2014, a David Watson Scholar will be announced.

6. Rev. Walter (Pete) Palmer Endowment for the Program of Alternate Studies

This endowment was funded from a significant bequest from Reverend Palmer. The endowment will provide program support for the PAS summer extension school and scholarship aid for needy students.

7. Paul Blankenship Endowed Scholarship

Mrs. Nancy Blankenship, widow of former MTS Professor Dr. Paul Blankenship, has given a generous gift to endow a new scholarship for a United Methodist student in the Master of Divinity program, with preference to a student from the Memphis Annual Conference.

8. Other Endowment funds

Many Cumberland Presbyterians and others continue to support endowments that have been established through the years to fund our work. Currently, the total MTS endowment, managed by the Board of Stewardship of the Cumberland Presbyterian Church, is just over $10.5 million. The Advancement Office and President are available at any time to discuss endowment gifts with potential donors.

D. ESTATE GIFTS

We continue to have conversations with friends and donors about the importance of remembering MTS (and their local churches, and other ministries they care deeply about) in their estate plans. We publish a list of those who have informed our office that they have included MTS in their will. That group is known as the Heritage Society. The Heritage Society is listed in every issue of The Lamp, our magazine for alumni and friends.

F. SEMINARY/PAS SUNDAY

We have many churches in our denomination, and in other denominations we serve who recognize Seminary Sunday in their local churches. This provides time for education of members about the work of MTS and the Program of Alternate Studies and provides an opportunity for members to make a special one-time gift to support the work of the seminary. Please contact the seminary for more information on how you can recognize Seminary Sunday in your local church, and to request a speaker for the occasion.

RECOMMENDATION 5: That the third Sunday in August, (August 20, 2017 and August 19, 2018) be included in the General Assembly Calendar as Seminary/PAS Sunday, and that the General Assembly encourage all churches to share information about MTS and PAS and receive a special offering on that day, or on a more convenient day of the session's choosing.

G. ANNUAL FUND

Memphis Theological Seminary could not operate without the faithful contribution of its alumni and friends. Annual Fund contributions help us keep the cost of tuition down, so that students do not leave seminary with a large burden of debt to have to pay during their early years in ministry. Annual Fund contributions have grown steadily over the past fifteen years, as income from Our United Outreach has declined.

In some respects, the income we receive from OUO puts us in a better position than many theological seminaries, whose income from denominational sources has declined significantly over the past twenty years. Our income from OUO has remained relatively steady and over that time period. However, as a percentage of our total income, OUO has fallen from almost 20% to about 3% of our operating budget. We are grateful for the commitment of Cumberland Presbyterians to the ministry of MTS, and all our common ministries, expressed so tangibly through giving to Our United Outreach.

At the same time, we do not expect income from denominational contributions to increase significantly in the future. This means that we are required to put more time and energy into fund raising than ever before. We are grateful for the many alumni who have made a financial contribution to our ministry this year. We are also grateful for all the faithful laypersons who have given to the Annual Fund because they know the importance of an educated ministry to the life and health of our denomination.

H. AUDIT REPORT

The auditing firm of Zoccola Kaplan, P.C. has audited the books of Memphis Theological Seminary for the 2014-2015. The audit was unqualified, and noted several significant improvements in the financial position of MTS. Copies of that report have been filed with the office of the Stated Clerk.

Respectfully submitted,
Jennifer Newell, Moderator of the Board of Trustees
Daniel J. Earheart-Brown, President
Memphis Theological Seminary

THE REPORT OF THE
OUR UNITED OUTREACH COMMITTEE

The 2009 General Assembly established a denominational Our United Outreach Committee to be made up of 12 voting representatives, one from each Synod and the rest from the church programs and institutions. Executives from the church programs and institutions participate on the Committee as advisory members. This Committee meets annually unless there is a needed called meeting.

A goal of the Our United Outreach Committee is to encourage ALL churches to contribute to Our United Outreach. Approximately 30 percent of the churches do not give anything with a high percentage of other churches not giving at the 10 percent level. This past year, 2016, the budgeted goal for Our United Outreach was $2,800,000 – 89% giving was achieved. While this was an admirable achievement, the Committee seeks to involve ALL churches with Our United Outreach giving and at a greater level of giving.

I. OUR UNITED OUTREACH FUNDS ALLOCATION

The Our United Outreach Committee met March 3, 2017, to allocate the Our United Outreach funds for the 2018 year. The Our United Outreach allocation basis for 2018 is $2,800,000.

A line item of $25,000 for Legal Fees has been continued for 2018. These requests, along with the Development Coordinator's salary/benefits, have been approved as guaranteed amounts and are deducted from the goal amount prior to allocation purposes.

RECOMMENDATION 1: That General Assembly adopt the following Our United Outreach allocations for 2018:

The allocation is to be as follows:		$2,800,000.00	
Development Coordinator			92,044.00
Legal Fees			25,000.00
Unification Task Force			35,000.00
Sub-total		152,044.00	
(Amount to be allocated)		2,647,956.00	
Ministry Council		$ 1,323,978.00	50%
Bethel University		132,398.00	5%
Children's Home		79,439.00	3%
Stewardship		158,877.00	6%
General Assembly Office		211,836.00	8%
Memphis Theological Seminary/		185,357.00	7%
Program of Alternate Studies			
Historical Foundation		79,439.00	3%
Shared Services		436,913.00	16.5%
Contingency		13,240.00	.5%
(Next four items total 1%)			
Comm. on Chaplains		10,247.00	.387%
Judiciary Committee		9,665.00	.365%
Theology/Social Concerns		3,601.00	.136%
Nominating Committee		2,966.00	.112%
		2,647,956.00	
Our United Outreach Goal		$2,800,000.00	

From the agencies listed above, all should be self-explanatory except maybe Shared Services. Maintenance, utilities, mowing, trash pick-up, pest extermination, and custodial are all examples of Shared Services for agencies sharing the Cumberland Presbyterian Center.

II. OUR UNITED OUTREACH COMMITTEE

The Our United Outreach Committee is made up of individuals who possess the leadership abilities to identify the focus of the entities of the denomination. The denominational nominating committee always strives to find the best candidate for vacancies on denominational boards and agencies. At General Assembly 2017, three new members will be placed in nomination for the Committee. The existing committee would like to express appreciation to the out-going members, who have served since the inception of the Our United Outreach Committee, for their dedication and support of the goals of the Committee. The out-going members being:

* Rev. Don Tabor – Children's Home
* Rev. Rusty Rustenhaven – Mission Synod
* Dr. Sharon Resch – Midwest Synod

The Our United Outreach Committee members are enthusiastic in their approach to the development of total participation in this program of the church.

Respectfully submitted,
Rev. Rusty Rustenhaven, Chairperson
Randy Weathersby, Vice-Chairperson
Dr. Sharon Resch, Secretary
and the Our United Outreach Committee

THE REPORT OF THE COMMISSION ON MILITARY CHAPLAINS AND PERSONNEL

The Commission on Military Chaplains and Personnel represents the Cumberland Presbyterian Church on the Presbyterian Council for Chaplains and Military Personnel (PCCMP). The commission does its work through the Council which has its headquarters in Washington D.C. and represents also the Cumberland Presbyterian Church in America, Presbyterian Church (USA) and the Korean Presbyterian Church Abroad. The Cumberland Presbyterians who are members of the Commission for the Cumberland Presbyterian Church and hence the broader group known as the PCCMP include the Reverend Mary McCaskey Benedict (Class 2017), the Reverend Cassandra (Sandy) Thomas (Class 2019), the Reverend Doctor Tony Janner (Class 2018), and Stated Clerk, the Reverend Michael Sharpe.

I. REPRESENTATION

For 2017, the Reverend Cassandra (Sandy) Thomas is Chairperson of the Operations Area that oversees personnel, finance, and development. The Reverend Mary McCaskey Benedict is the Chairperson of the Personnel Committee. The Reverend Tony Janner is member on the Chaplaincy Committee. The Chair of the PCCMP is the Reverend Don Nisbet (PCUSA) and the Vice-Chair is the Reverend John Kim (KPCA).

II. RESPONSIBILITY OF THE PCCMP

1. Provide ecclesiastical endorsement for chaplains of the United States Armed Forces who are serving on active duty or in the Reserves/National Guard. The PCCMP also endorses chaplains for the Department of Veterans Affairs. In addition, the PCCMP endorses CPC and PCUSA teaching elders into chaplaincy positions with the Civil Air Patrol and the Federal Bureau of Prisons.
2. Provide training to chaplains and pastoral support to chaplains and their families.
3. Provide a unified and influential voice for member denominations to the National Council on Ministry to the Armed Forces in matters relating to the ministry and welfare of PCCMP-endorsed clergy.
4. Provide representation to denominational agencies and ecumenical bodies with respect to matters relating to United States military personnel, veterans and their families.
5. Promote closer communications between chaplains and denominational judicatories.
6. Carry out other duties as may be requested by the member denominations.

III. ANNUAL PCCMP MEETING AND OTHER UPDATES

The annual meeting of the PCCMP takes place in the fall, with representatives of the member denominations in attendance. In 2016, the Council met at the PCUSA Headquarters in Louisville, Kentucky. The Reverend Cassandra Thomas and the Reverend Mike Sharpe represented the CPC at this meeting. During this meeting, the Council discussed the renewal of the Missional Agreement Partnership between the PCCMP and the PCUSA. The new PCUSA Stated Clerk, Reverend J. Herbert Nelson, and PCUSA staff with the Presbyterian Mission Agency, under which the PCCMP is assigned, met with the council to discuss the history, current agreement, and current challenges that face the internal structuring of the PCUSA as pertains to the PCCMP. Positive dialogue occurred and a special committee was formed to work on the agreement beyond the meeting. The CPC does not have any type of missional agreement with the PCCMP and may want to look into this aspect of ecumenical partnership. Reverend Mike Sharpe, CPC Stated Clerk, was instrumental and insightful in representing the CPC in this predominantly PCCMP/PCUSA discussion. The PCCMP's director, the Reverend Lawrence (Larry) P. Greenslit, guided the staffing and programming reductions needed to sustain primary missions and ministries in the face of denominational budget cuts and lower denominational offerings. Due to family needs, he tendered his resignation in February 2017 to take effect no later than September 1, 2017. There will be a search for a new director with a CPC representative as part of the search committee. There will be a Chaplains Training in Montreat, NC in August 2017 to provide training to chaplains and support to family members. In October 2017, the Council will meet in Huntsville, Alabama for its annual meeting to be hosted by CPCA members and supported by CPC members.

IV. SUPPORT FOR THE COUNCIL

The Council receives financial support from the four denominations, as well as individuals, judicatories, and churches. The current economic challenges in our country are creating a need to redesign how to minister to our chaplains and their families. We will be faithful stewards as we care for our chaplains and their families.

The Cumberland Presbyterian Churches support this ministry by taking an annual Memorial Day Offering. The PCCMP has also developed resources (a 2½ minute video and a bulletin insert) for congregations that may wish to conduct an offering on Four Chaplains Sunday, which is traditionally held on the first Sunday in February. Congregations may conduct a special offering at a time it deems convenient, such as the Sundays closest to Independence Day or Veteran's Day. In this way, CPC congregations can show support for all men and women, who serve or have served in the United States Armed Services, Reserves, Guard, VA, Federal Bureau of Prisons and CAP, as well as their families. The offerings are sent to the General Assembly Stated Clerk and are then forwarded to the Council for its outreach, mission, and maintenance efforts. The Commission would like to express its deepest appreciation to all churches that collected offerings for the PCCMP during 2016 and 2017 to date. All Cumberland Presbyterian Churches are urged to consider their involvement in this vital ministry to God, country, and Presbyterians.

V. CUMBERLAND PRESBYTERIAN CHAPLAINS

Total Number of CPC Ministers serving as Federal Chaplains = 18

Active Duty Military = 5

Army – Captain Tim Baranoski
Colonel Gale Cotton
Major Ramon Santillano

Air Force – Captain Zachary Nash

Navy – Lieutenant Glyn Turner

Reserve Military = 4

Army – Captain James Messer (National Guard)
Colonel William "Curtis" Prewitt

Air Force – Captain John Smith

Navy – Lieutenant Jason Chambers

Chaplain Candidates = 3

Army – Jin Ho Park

Navy – John Phelps
Garrett Burns

VA = 5

Reuben Ferrol
Tony Headrick
Darren Kennemer
David LeFavor
Lisa Scott

DOJ (Federal Bureau of Prisons) = 1

    David McBeth

2016 CPC Endorsements:

6/6/16 - The Reverend David McBeth was endorsed for service as chaplain within the Department of Justice (Federal Bureau of Prisons). He is now serving as a staff chaplain at FCI La Tuna, in Anthony. Texas.

11/5/16 - The Reverend Jacqueline DeBerry was endorsed for service as a VA chaplain.

2016 CPC Retirements: None

2017 CPC Endorsements (to date):

2/18/17 - The Reverend Lisa Scott was endorsed for continued service within the VA. This is an updated endorsement that she needed in preparation for applying for another position.

2/20/17 - The Reverend John Phelps was endorsed for service as an active duty chaplain in the Navy.

3/2/17 - The Reverend Gale Cotton was endorsed for service as a VA chaplain.

2017 CPC Retirements:

The Reverend Gale Cotton will retire this year; exact date TBD.

    Please remember to pray for those servings in this important ministry and their loved ones. Names and addresses are included in the Yearbook of the Cumberland Presbyterian Church. Anyone desiring more information can check the CPC website: www.cumberland.org/ ccmp or the PCCMP website: www.pccmp.org.

Respectively Submitted,
Reverend Cassandra (Sandy) Thomas

THE REPORT OF THE PERMANENT JUDICIARY COMMITTEE

The Judiciary Committee met February 24, 2017, in Huntsville, Alabama. Present were Annetta Camp, Harry Chapman, Robert Rush, Kimberly Silvus, Bill Tally, Wendell Thomas, Andy McClung, and Rachel Moses. Also present were Mike Sharpe, stated clerk of General Assembly, and Jaime Jordan, legal counsel. Jan Overton was excused.

I. ORGANIZATION OF THE COMMITTEE

Kimberly Silvus was elected chairperson and Andy McClung was elected secretary.

II. REFERRAL

The 186th General Assembly referred to this committee and the Missions Ministry Team a proposed constitutional amendment intended to addresses the need to provide judicatory services where there is no presbytery as the Cumberland Presbyterian Church expands around the world. This committee, in consultation with the Missions Ministry Team, developed a new proposed constitutional amendment and recommended it to the Joint Committee on Amendments.

III. JOINT COMMITTEE ON AMENDMENTS

This committee appointed Robert Rush and Harry Chapman to represent the Cumberland Presbyterian Church on the Joint Committee on Amendments, meeting February 24 in Huntsville, Alabama. This committee also recommended to the joint committee a proposed amendment to the Rules of Order.

IV. AMENDMENT TO GENERAL ASSEMBLY BYLAWS

The constitutional amendment recommended by the Joint Committee on Amendments will allow General Assembly to empower its missions entity to act in place of a presbytery when doing ministry outside the United States and outside the bounds of any existing presbytery. If the amendment is adopted we need to amend the Cumberland Presbyterian Church's General Assembly Bylaws to insure that the missions entity so tasked has oversight analogous to a presbytery's oversight by a synod.

RECOMMENDATION 1: That the General Assembly Bylaw 11.05, which refers to the Judiciary Committee, be amended by inserting 11.05.06. "The committee shall have oversight of and responsibility for ecclesiastical decisions made by a body acting in the place of a presbytery with respect to mission work and mission fields. The oversight and responsibility exercised by the committee shall be the same as that exercised by a synod with respect to a presbytery under its care, specifically Constitution 8.5, a, b and c.

V. PROTECTION

In order to protect God's people, this committee re-emphasizes the 184th General Assembly's encouragement for each congregation to adopt and practice a Safe Sanctuary plan. Help for developing such a plan can be found at cpcmc.org/safe-sanctuary/. A copy of each congregation's plan should be placed on file with the presbytery's clerk.

In order to protect God's property, this committee additionally encourages all congregations, presbyteries, and synods both to incorporate and to secure liability insurance. Help for incorporating can be found at cumberland.org/gao/incorporation/.

For further protection, presbyteries are encouraged to ensure that any actions and events occurring within their constituent congregations are in accordance with our Constitution, as a presbytery may be legally liable for any such actions or events.

VI. REVIEW OF SYNOD MINUTES

The committee reviewed the minutes of all five synods and found the following:

Mission Synod's 2016 minutes seemed to be in order, but no appendices were attached. It was also noted that someone named as a member of the General Board is no longer Cumberland Presbyterian.

Synod of Great Rivers' 2016 minutes were in order, with the exception that no Disciplinary Commission or Judiciary Committee are named. The committee was concerned that West Tennessee Presbytery submitted no minutes for several of its meetings.

Synod of the Midwest's 2016 minutes were in order.

Synod of the Southeast's 2016 minutes were in order.

Tennessee Synod's 2016 minutes were in order, with one exception: a nominating committee's report should place nominees' names in nomination, not present recommendations.

VII. PRESERVING MINUTES

Minutes of sessions, presbyteries, synods, and General Assemblies are both historical records and legal documents. As affirmed by our Cumberland Presbyterian Constitution 3.08 such minutes belong to the judicatory and not to any individual. Properly recording and preserving these minutes is important. This committee encourages all Cumberland Presbyterians to help ensure that no minutes are lost and that all minutes, or copies thereof, are given to the Historical Foundation for safekeeping. On its website, cumberland.org/hfcpc/, the Historical Foundation maintains a list of minutes it has on file, under each judicatory's name.

VIII. GENERAL ASSEMBLY REPRESENTATIVES

Andy McClung will serve as this committee's representative to the 187th General Assembly and Harry Chapman will serve as the alternate.

Respectfully submitted,
The Judiciary Committee

THE REPORT OF THE NOMINATING COMMITTEE

The Nominating Committee consists of a minister and a lay person from each synod, preferably from different presbyteries. Members may serve a three year term, but cannot succeed themselves. Cumberland Presbyterian members of any board or committee can be re-elected to the same board after a two year absence. Ecumenical representatives may be re-elected to the same board after a one year absence. With the exception of the Nominating Committee any person elected to serve on a denominational entity may serve three consecutive terms. Filling an unexpired term counts as one term, thus members of any entity do not always serve nine years before completing eligibility on a board/agency.

The members of the various Ministry Teams are no longer elected by the General Assembly, but are to be appointed by the Ministry Council.

*Ecumenical Representative   +Cumberland Presbyterian Church in America

The Committee submits the following list of nominees:

I. THE BOARD OF DIRECTORS OF THE GENERAL ASSEMBLY CORPORATION

(Members whose terms expire in 2020)

(2) REV. JOHN BUTLER, Cumberland Presbytery, to succeed himself for a three-year term.
(2) MS. BETTY JACOB, McGee Chapel Church, Choctaw Presbytery, to succeed herself for a three-year term.

II. MINISTRY COUNCIL

(Members whose terms expire in 2020)

(3) REV. DONNY ACTON, 1413 Oakridge Drive, Birmingham, AL 35242, to succeed himself for a three-year term.
(1) MR. DAVID CORREA, Calle 76 #87-14, Medellin, COLOMBIA, LaRosa Congregation, Mission Synod, Emaus Presbytery, for a three-year term.
(3) REV. LANNY JOHNSON, 120 S Mill Street, Morrison, TN 37357, to succeed himself for a three-year term.
(1) MS. SAMANTHA HASSELL, 510 N Main Street, Sturgis, KY 42459, Sturgis Congregation, Synod of the Midwest, Covenant Presbytery for a three-year term.
(1) MS CHARELLE WEBB, 3507 Pickering Lane, Pearland, TX 77584, Houston First Congregation, Mission Synod, Trinity Presbytery for a three-year term.

(Members whose terms expire in 2018)

(1) REV. KENNY BUTCHER, 4608 Cather Court, Nashville, TN 37214, Brush Hill Congregation, Tennessee Synod, Nashville Presbytery, to fill a one-year unexpired term

YOUTH ADVISORY MEMBERS
(shall be between the ages of 15 and 17 years of age, elected for a one year term and is eligible for an additional one term)

(2) MR. CAMERON ALDERSON, 122 E Cherry Street, Chandler, IN 47610, to succeed himself for a one-year term.
(1) MS. LEIGHANNE MORGAN, 1468 Williams Cove Road, Winchester, TN 37398, Goshen Congregation, Tennessee Synod, Murfreesboro Presbytery, for a one-year term.
(2) MS. CHARLI UHLRICH, 250 County Road 1950 N, Bethany, IL 61914, to succeed herself for a one-year term.

III. TRUSTEES OF HISTORICAL FOUNDATION

(Members whose terms expire in 2020)

(3) MR. MICHAEL FARE, 401 E Deanna Lane, Nixa, MO 65714, to succeed himself for a three-year term.

IV. TRUSTEES OF MEMPHIS THEOLOGICAL SEMINARY OF THE CUMBERLAND PRESBYTERIAN CHURCH

(Members whose terms expire in 2020)

(2) *REV. NANCY COLE, 3346 Arcadia Drive, Tuscaloosa, AL 35404, to succeed herself for a three-year term.
(2) REV. ANNE HAMES, 118 Paris Street, McKenzie, TN 38201, to succeed herself for a three-year term.
(1) *REV. JIMMY JONATHAN MOSBY, PO Box 45843, Little Rock, AR 72214, for a three-year term.
(3) REV. JENNIFER NEWELL, 2322 Marco Circle, Chattanooga, TN 37421, to succeed herself for a three-year term.
(2) REV. SUSAN PARKER, 655 York Drive, Rogersville, AR 35652, to succeed herself for a three-year term.
(1) REV. KIP RUSH, 516 Franklin Road, Brentwood, TN 37027, Brenthaven Congregation, Tennessee Synod, Nashville Presbytery, for a three-year term.
(1) +MR. CRAIG WHITE, 134 McEntire Lane SW A36, Decatur, AL 35603, for a three-year term.
(1) *MR. REGINALD PORTER JR., 4458 Whitepine Cove, Memphis, TN 38109, for a three-year term.

(Members whose terms expire in 2019)

(1) *MR. LARRY HILLIARD, 206 E Bankhead Street, New Albany, MS 38652, to fill an expired two-year term.

V. STEWARDSHIP, FOUNDATION AND BENEFITS

(Members whose terms expire in 2020)

(2) MR. RANDY DAVIDSON, PO Box 880, Ada, OK 74821, to succeed himself for a three-year term.
(1) REV. DWAYNE TYUS, 426 W Old Hickory Boulevard, Madison, TN 37115, St Luke Congregation, Tennessee Synod, Nashville Presbytery, for a three-year term
(1) REV. MARK HESTER, 763 Finn Long Road, Friendsville, TN 37737, Synod of Southeast, Presbytery of East Tennessee, for a three-year term
(1) REV. GARY TUBB, 103 Forest Drive, Mountain Home, AR 72653, Fellowship Congregation, Great Rivers Synod, Arkansas Presbytery, for a three-year term

GENERAL ASSEMBLY COMMISSIONS:

VI. MILITARY CHAPLAINS AND PERSONNEL

(Members whose terms expire in 2020)

(1) REV. CHARLES McCASKEY, 679 Canter Lane, Cookeville, TN 38501, Cookeville Congregation, Tennessee Synod, Murfreesboro Presbytery, for a three-year term.

GENERAL ASSEMBLY COMMITTEES

VII. JUDICIARY

(Members whose terms expire in 2020)

(2) REV. HARRY CHAPMAN, 49008 El Picador Court SE, Rio Rancho, NM, 87124, to succeed himself for a three-year term.
(1) REV. GEOFFREY KNIGHT, 2119 Avalon Place, Houston, TX 77019, Houston First Congregation, Trinity Presbytery, Mission Synod, for a three-year term
(1) MS. PAMELA BROWN, 6400 North Grove Avenue, Warr Acres, OK, 73012, Stonegate Congregation, Mission Synod, Red River Presbytery, for a three-year term.

VIII. NOMINATING

(Members whose terms expire in 2020)

(1) REV. BRIAN HAYES, 69 Cactus Drive, Benton, KY 42025, Covenant Presbytery, Midwest Synod, for a three year term.
(1) REV. TOM SPENCE, PO Box 802, Burns Flat, OK 73624, Red River Presbytery, Mission Synod, for a three-year term.
(1) MS. JENANN LESLIE, 300 Henley Perry Drive, Marshall, TX 75670, Trinity Presbytery, Mission Synod, for a three-year term
(1) MR. LEE HOLDER, 6589 County Road 747, Hope Presbytery, Synod of the Southeast, for a three-year term

IX. OUR UNITED OUTREACH COMMITTEE

(Members whose terms expire in 2020)

(1) MR. MIKEL DAVIS, 102 Willow Wood Lane, Ovilla, TX 75154, Shiloh Congregation, Red River Presbytery, Mission Synod; for a three-year term.
(1) MS. MARY ANNE COLE, 1726 Karen Circle, Bowling Green, KY 42104, Bowling Green Congregation, Cumberland Presbytery, Synod of the Midwest, for a three-year term.

X. UNIFIED COMMITTEE ON THEOLOGY AND SOCIAL CONCERNS

(Members whose terms expire in 2020)

(1) REV. LISA SCOTT, (address on file in GA office), North Central Presbytery, Synod of the Midwest, for a three-year term.
(1) REV. RICHARD MORGAN, 1468 Williams Cove Road, Winchester, TN 37398, Murfreesboro Presbytery, Tennessee Synod, for a three-year term.

XI. OTHER DENOMINATIONAL PERSONNEL

REPRESENTATIVE TO Caribbean and North American Area Council, World Communion of Reformed Churches:

(Member whose terms expire in 2020)

(1) Ms Sherry Poteet, PO Box 313, Gilmer, TX 75644, Elmira Chapel Congregation, Trinity Presbytery, Mission Synod, for a three -year term.

THE REPORT OF THE
PLACE OF MEETING COMMITTEE

The Place of Meeting Committee consists of the Moderator, a representative of the Cumberland Presbyterian Women's Ministry, and the Stated Clerk who serves as the chairperson. The representative of the Cumberland Presbyterian Women's Ministry is the Convention Coordinator.

The 165th General Assembly, "authorized the committee to select meeting places up to five years in the future and that preference be given that keeps, insofar as possible, the General Assembly and the Convention of Cumberland Presbyterian Women's Ministry, and guest rooms in one facility. It is recognized that these places are hard to find and may cost some additional monies. The place of meeting committee will use its best judgment." The 173rd General Assembly approved exploring the use of college campuses and very large conference centers in addition to hotels/convention centers. When the Office of the General Assembly receives an invitation from a congregation or a presbytery, the Stated Clerk makes a site visit. If adequate facilities are discovered, a follow up visit is made by the Stated Clerk, the Assistant to the Stated Clerk, and the Convention Coordinator of the Cumberland Presbyterian Women's Ministry.

Unless the General Assembly sets aside Bylaw 14.02 Standing Rules 1 to allow for a different meeting time, the annual meeting is the third or the fourth week of June.

Commissioners, delegates to Conventions, and visitors are encouraged to stay at the General Assembly/Convention hotel, to assure meeting the contracted room block. Hotel contracts also include a commitment on food and beverages, thus it is important for boards/agencies to continue to sponsor special meal functions. The luncheons/dinners provide opportunities for the sponsoring agencies/boards to keep the church informed about their respective programs, thus enhancing support.

I. INFORMATION ABOUT FUTURE GENERAL ASSEMBLIES

Continued discussions with the leadership of the Cumberland Presbyterian Church in America regarding joint meetings of the General Assemblies in 2019 and 2020 may impact future meeting locations.

It is helpful to continue scheduling a few years in advance of the meeting to assure that adequate hotel/convention space is available and to negotiate a good rate. If a congregation or a presbytery is interested in hosting the General Assembly/Convention, the Office of the General Assembly will provide information on hosting responsibilities. Hosting the General Assembly/Convention is a service to the Church, allowing the Church to celebrate the good ministries occurring within a particular presbytery, and provides persons within a presbytery the opportunity to participate more fully in the annual meeting.

In the event that no invitation is received in a particular year or a situation arises requiring a change of venue for a particular year, the Corporate Board will be responsible for selecting a place of meeting.

II. SCHEDULE OF FUTURE GENERAL ASSEMBLIES

188th   Norman, Oklahoma (near Oklahoma City)   June 17-21, 2018
(co-hosted by Choctaw Presbytery and the Oklahoma Churches of Red River Presbytery

IV. SCHEDULE OF MEETINGS BY PRESBYTERIES

The following schedule shows the annual meetings and the year that the General Assembly last met in the bounds of a particular presbytery.

Nashville	2016	Red River	2004
Cauca Valley & Andes	2015	East Tennessee	2003
TN/GA	2014	Covenant	2002
Murfreesboro	2013	del Cristo	2001
Hope & Robert Donnell	2012	Cumberland	2000
Missouri	2011	Tennessee-Georgia	1998
Nashville	2010	Robert Donnell	1996
West Tennessee	2009	Nashville	1995
Japan	2008	North Central	1980
Arkansas	2007	Trinity	1969
Grace	2006	Hope	1961
Columbia	2005	Murfreesboro	1956

Respectfully submitted,
Michael G. Sharpe
Pam Phillips Burk
Dwayne Tyus

THE REPORT OF THE UNIFIED COMMITTEE ON THEOLOGY AND SOCIAL CONCERNS

I. MEETING AND OFFICERS

The Unified Committee on Theology and Social Concerns (UCTSC) met in Huntsville, Alabama October 14-15, 2016 and by teleconference February 18, 2017. The following officers were elected during the fall meeting: Reverend Shelia O'Mara (CPC) and Reverend Edmund Cox (CPCA) Co-Chairs; and Reverend Nancy Fuqua (CPCA), Secretary.

II. EXPIRATION OF TERMS

The Committee notes that the terms of service for Elder Sharon Combs, Reverend Edmund Cox, Doctor Nancy Fuqua, and Reverend Robert Thomas all expire in 2017. Each member is eligible to be reelected.

In addition, Reverend LaRuth Jefferson submitted her resignation for the October 2016 meeting. Her term expires in 2017.

The UCTSC was saddened by the deaths of two committee members whose terms expire in 2017: Reverend Randy Jacob and Doctor Phillip Redrick. We commend their faithful service to the church and continue to pray for their families.

III. GENERAL ASSEMBLY REPRESENTATIVE

The Committee elected Doctor Nancy Fuqua to serve as the representative to the meeting of the CPC/CPCA General Assembles in Tampa, Florida.

IV. GENERAL ASSEMBLY REFERRAL

The 186th General Assembly directed "that the Resolution from Japan Presbytery be accepted as information and be referred to the Permanent Committee on Theology and Social Concerns for study and clarification."

RECOMMENDATION 1: That the General Assembly of the Cumberland Presbyterian Church commend Japan Presbytery for their diligent theological work in response to the social concerns that face them on a daily basis.

RECOMMENDATION 2: That this paper be distributed to all presbyteries as a study document and that General Assembly direct presbyteries to use the resolution as a model for the work of presbytery committees on theological and social concerns in order that presbyteries might begin to use their declarative authority and speak theologically to the social issues that confront the Church.

V. STUDY PAPERS

The Committee presents the following papers for consideration by the General Assemblies: *"A Question of Hermeneutics"* (Dr. George Estes) and *"Identifying and Addressing Elder Abuse –A Social Response"* (Elder Sharon Combs).

RECOMMENDATION 3: That the General Assemblies accept the papers, *"A Question of Hermeneutics"* and *"Identifying and Addressing Elder Abuse-A Social Response"* as study papers and that they be used to initiate thought and discussion within the Cumberland Presbyterian Church and the Cumberland Presbyterian Church in America.

RECOMMENDATION 4: That the Office of the General Assembly of both denominations makes these papers available to churches through the stated clerks of the presbyteries.

The Committee had explored writing a paper on racism/racial profiling in the USA. In lieu of a paper on the topic, the Committee is recommending a book for study. The book is available in book or audio format and has a study guide written for it.

RECOMMENDATION 5: That the General Assemblies recommend to presbyteries the book *"America's Original Sin"* by Jim Wallis as a resource on addressing racism in America.

VI. WORKS IN PROGRESS

The UCTSC has struggled with how to respond in a timely way to theological and social concerns that may be affecting Cumberland Presbyterians as we seek to be faithful in the world today. The Committee is developing guidelines for a theological/social concerns panel made up of representatives of the CPC/CPCA to address emerging issues. A select group of persons has been invited to serve on a panel that could be asked to respond to issues in a more timely way. It is not assumed that such responses would have the official sanction of the CPC or CPCA, but that they could provide useful reflections for persons in our two churches. Details are still being worked out and the Committee hopes to activate the panel during 2017.

Respectfully Submitted,
Unified Committee on Theology and Social Concerns

A Question of Hermeneutics

The Christian community today is divided over many issues, despite persistent claims of "unity in Christ." Apart from the obvious doctrinal distinctions between denominations and traditions, a basic rift historically has been between "liberals' and "conservatives," with all sorts of gradations in between. The differences are theological, ecclesiastical, political and social. Yet the lines of demarcation are more fluid than is often realized, changing in relation to the topics under consideration. For example, though many conservative Protestants hardly regard the Catholic Church as Christian (and vice versa), the two might come together on attitudes about Roe v. Wade, or the ordination of women. Though liberal Protestants generally differ with the Catholic Church's official position on abortion and birth control, many applauded Pope Francis' comments on immigration, advocacy for the poor, and climate change in his recent visit to the United States. Liberal Christians, typically open to advocating for justice in the public sector, are suspicious of right wing Christians who display a political agenda. Yet both sides claim to believe in the separation of church and state, rejecting any notion that the state should have a regulatory role in church's life. Practically all Christian groups proclaim the Bible to be the Word of God. However, they diverge significantly when it comes to the interpretation and application of that sacred text. It is the thesis of this essay that attitudes toward Scripture are at the root of many divisions in the Christian community.

How is the Bible the Word of God? And then, how should it be determinative for contemporary life? These are questions of hermeneutics, a term used so speak of the principles of interpretation of Scripture, as well as other ancient literature. Hermeneutics is like a "lens" through which Scripture is viewed. Inevitably the Bible reader is confronted with the challenge of bridging from the original sense and cultural context of the biblical text to our contemporary life, with application of biblical truth to today's culture and circumstances. Some scholars refer to the "three worlds of the text," meaning (a) the world behind the text, its background; (b) the world of the text, its situation in history and geography, along with its literary characteristics, such as poetry or narrative; and (c) the world before or in front of the text, that is, the contemporary situation of today's readers. Because we affirm the Bible as the Word of God, we consider not only what is said to the original hearers but also what the text is saying to us. Though our attention often is directed at interpreting Scripture, the issue also is how Scripture interprets us! Sermons, Bible studies, presentations of Christian teaching and doctrine are exercises in hermeneutics. The serious Bible student engages in what might be called "creative listening" to the text, that is, seeking to discern the sort of material a particular passage is (such as poetry, prophecy, parable, history, narrative, exhortation, instruction, etc.) and what it may have meant to its original audience, then asking how God is speaking through that passage to our situation today.

There are those who adhere to a dogma of "the verbal plenary inerrancy of Scripture," by which they mean every word of the Bible is absolutely true and unassailable, with the caveat that this is the case in the original texts – none of which are extant today. The principle of inerrancy affirms that God is speaking through the Bible, but it scarcely takes note of the fact that it was written by human hands over many centuries. Further, Scripture has been copied, translated and published innumerable times, always involving human agency.

On the other end of the theological spectrum there are those who regard the Bible as little more than "helpful hints" for living. Scripture, they feel, is ancient and therefore has practically no bearing on contemporary life. They may appreciate the Golden Rule or some other biblical dictum that fits their own personal perspective, but to regard Scripture as determinative for their attitudes and decisions seems absurd. They adhere to the oft-repeated belief that 'you can justify almost anything on the basis of Scripture' as a means of dismissing the authority of the Bible. They note that the Crusades, the Inquisition, pogroms, slavery, racial and gender discrimination, papal infallibility, paternalism, divine right of kings and antagonism toward scientific discovery have all been supported by appeals to Scripture.

Somewhere in between these two extremes reside most of us. As part of the Presbyterian and Reformed family of Churches that traditionally takes a high view of Scripture, Cumberland Presbyterians revere the Bible as the Word of God. Nevertheless, we do not always look first to Scripture for guidance on matters of politics, business or life choices. Our worship services typically include multiple presentations and references to Scripture. Calls to worship, offertory sentences, responsive readings and benedictions are scriptural, and a sermon without biblical foundation is no sermon at all, we believe. Further, many congregations offer small group Bible studies, Sunday school lessons based on Scripture, seasonal biblical curricula for the Christian Year, and more. Our members and ministers utilize the wide range of Bible translations available today, along with study helps, commentaries and devotional literature. Even so, devout church folks too often neglect the study of Scripture and may express a sense of inadequacy and unfamiliarity with the content of the Bible.

The *Confession of Faith for Cumberland Presbyterians* affirms Scripture to be "the infallible rule of faith and practice, the authoritative guide for Christian living," [COF 1.05]. The first question posed for the ordination of ministers, elders and deacons is: "Do you believe the scriptures of the Old and New Testaments to be the inspired word of God, the authority for faith and practice?" [Constitution 2.92, 6.36] The Directory for Worship suggests a form for public profession of faith and church covenant which includes a similar question of the new member: "Do you believe the scriptures of the Old and New Testaments to be the inspired word of God, the source of authority for faith and practice, and *will you read and study them for guidance in living the Christian life?*" [DFW, emphasis added] The *Confession* also offers comments about the proper interpretation of Scripture, a hermeneutic. "In order to understand God's word spoken through the scriptures, persons must have the illumination of God's own Spirit. Moreover, they should study the writings of the Bible in their historical settings, compare scripture with scripture, listen to the witness of the church throughout the centuries, and share insights with others in the covenant community." [COF 1.07] We do not have an 'anything goes' hermeneutic! Our *Confession*, firmly based on the Bible, is our standard of doctrine and interpretation. Note what this statement does not affirm: that God wrote or dictated the scriptures; that the scriptures are viewed as "inerrant," rather as "infallible" in matters of faith and practice. Instead of a rigid "bibliolatry," the scriptures are considered to be the "authoritative guide." It may seem to be splitting hairs to differentiate between "infallible" and "inerrant," but there is in fact an important distinction between the two. The latter case often comes across as God literally dictating the Scripture – much like the views of adherents to the Koran or the Book of Mormon. But our *Confession* understands the matter differently. God speaks through the Bible, but does so by using the language, customs, culture, and (yes) weaknesses of human beings. Further, the doctrine of inspiration of the Holy Spirit we espouse includes not only the centuries-long process of writing the Scriptures, but also the canonization process, and the continuing work of interpretation and application of biblical truth from generation to generation. In this connection we can allow for a reasonable distinction between the 'letter' and the 'spirit' of many Scripture texts, taking seriously the original context of the writing *and* today's situation in mission and service.

While it is unlikely that differences between denominations in approach to Scripture will be overcome, perhaps it is not quite as unrealistic to work toward a common understanding of biblical interpretation within our own Churches. This has practical implications for our attitudes toward one another in small group Bible discussions, Sunday school classes, responses to messages from the pulpit and so on. At a time when unification between our two sister denominations is under prayerful consideration, let us make the conscious effort to remove any impediment to our unity that has biblical interpretation as a basis. We acknowledge that within both Cumberland Presbyterian denominations there is a wide range of biblical understanding and interpretation. With that said, we should resolve – first and foremost – to love one another, and as an expression of that love to listen to each other, affirming the even greater common ground we enjoy and embrace as Cumberland Presbyterians. Our goal need not be one hundred percent agreement on biblical interpretation, but rather a mature awareness and consideration of the diversity of theological perspectives that a global and multi-ethnic denomination manifests.

We believe Scripture to be the *written* Word of God. At the same time we affirm that Jesus Christ, God's only Son, is the Word of God *Incarnate*, so that Scripture *"should be understood in light of the birth, life, death and resurrection of Jesus of Nazareth."* [COF 1.06]. This suggests our reading of Scripture is Christocentric. Yet we readily understand that, for example, passages such as the Suffering Servant prophecies in Isaiah had an original meaning and impact that was not focused on Jesus Christ, though we in our reading and proclamation of those texts find him there. We believe further that God's Word is also *spoken* – through creation, through prophets and apostles, and the proclamation and witness of the church. It is remembered that much of Scripture existed as oral tradition before being written. The conviction of inspiration by the Holy Spirit, necessary for understanding of Scripture, is an important component of our hermeneutic, so that the role of the individual believer as well as the corporate community of faith is taken seriously. In other words, we believe the Word of God is still speaking today!

What if we added a "*missional*" calibration to our hermeneutic lens? The word "missional" has come to mean the recognition that God's mission, revealed in Scripture and supremely in Jesus Christ, is the only legitimate purpose of the church in the world. In fact the church is God's strategy for mission in the world. We are a "sent" people -- sent to proclaim and demonstrate, teach and learn, the gospel of Christ in a world of spiritual, physical, emotional, economic, political need. It is sometimes not recognized that the Bible is a book about mission from beginning to end, that it was written by missionaries for missionaries [Kirk, p. 20]! This is a way of saying that Scripture points God's faithful people outward to share (and seek to live out) God's gracious Good News in a world overburdened with bad news. Scripture was written from faith for faith, indeed to inspire others to faith. It was written from within a specific culture and history, yet it has trans-cultural and timeless implications as God's Word for all. Our Church's forbearers were missional in their desire to spread the gospel across a vast frontier. The frontier of the 21st century beckons us to a reading, proclaiming and demonstrating of the biblical message that is missional for the time in which God has granted us to serve.

One of the strengths of the Cumberland Presbyterian Churches, again, is the wide latitude with regard to biblical understanding, worship style, approaches to ministry and mission. What needs greater cultivation, perhaps, is an appreciation of varying opinions. It would be helpful to lay aside the labels intended to diminish the faithfulness and motives of our brothers and sisters in Christ – conservative and liberal, evangelical and traditional, right and left wing, along with the "isms" and "phobias" in currency today. If we agree that our calling is to serve God's mission in the world, then a healthy dialog about strategies, ideologies, and emphases is more attainable, and genuine unity in Christ can grow.

Works Cited

Confession of Faith for Cumberland Presbyterians. Cordova, Tennessee: Office of the General Assembly, 2014, print.
Kirk, J. Andrew. *What Is Mission? Theological Explorations*. Minneapolis: Fortress Press, 2000, print.

For Reflection

1. What governing principles should characterize our use of Scripture?
2. Many Christians take some portions of Scripture literally, but not all. How is this difference in determination made?
3. Study Bibles and commentaries are helpful tools for biblical understanding. Does our church library include some of these?
    Suggested Resources:
    Bible Dictionary
    Harper Study Bible
    Interpreter's Bible Commentary Series
    Interpretation Bible Commentary Series
4. If a small group were to devise a "Bill of Rights" for biblical discussion and attitudes toward differing viewpoints, what would that look like?
5. What role does prayer play in the ongoing work of biblical interpretation?

Identifying and Addressing "Elder Abuse" - (A Social Response)

What is Elder Abuse?

The Administration on Aging (AoA) has reported that each year hundreds of thousands of older persons are abused, neglected, and exploited. Many victims are people who are older, frail, and vulnerable and cannot help themselves. They depend on others to meet their most basic needs. Abusers of older adults are both women and men, and may be family members, friends, or "trusted others."

In general, elder abuse is a term referring to any knowing, intentional, or negligent act by a caregiver or any other person that causes harm or a serious risk of harm to a vulnerable adult. Abuse can come in many forms: ***Physical Abuse, Sexual Abuse, Neglect, Exploitation, Emotional Abuse, Abandonment,*** and ***Self-neglect.***

Physical Abuse: hitting punching, slapping, burning, kicking, restraining, false imprisonment, giving excessive or improper medication;

Sexual Abuse: forcing a person to take part in any sexual conduct without consent, including making them participate in sexual conversation, forced to watch pornography; may also include cases where elder is no longer able to give consent (dementia);

Neglect: Depriving a person of food, heat, clothing, comfort or essential medication and needed services; deprivation –may be *intentional - considered (active neglect)*; or, it could happen out of *lack of knowledge or resources which is then considered (passive neglect);*

Exploitation: *warning signs* -Significant withdrawals from the elder's banking accounts; sudden changes in the elder's financial condition; items or cash missing from the senior's household; suspicious changes in wills, power of attorney, titles, and policies; addition of names to the senior's signature card; unpaid bills or lack of medical care, although the elder has enough money to pay for them; financial activity the senior could not have done, such as an ATM withdrawal when the account holder is bedridden;

Emotional Abuse: This is a verbal or nonverbal act that inflicts emotional pain, anguish, or distress on an older adult. Emotional elder abuse is almost always accompanied by another form of abuse, such as physical abuse. Emotional abuse of the elderly can range *from a simple verbal insult* to *an extreme form of verbal punishment;*

Abandonment: - Deserting a dependent elderly person with the intent to abandon them or leave them unattended at a place for even a while which is likely to endanger their health or welfare;

Self-neglect: warning signs-unusual weight loss, malnutrition, dehydration, unsanitary living conditions: dirt, bugs, soiled bedding and clothes, dirty or unbathed, unsuitable clothing or covering for the weather, unsafe living conditions (no heat or running water; faulty electrical wiring, other fire hazards).
Addressing Elderly in the Home

All seniors are reluctant to leave their homes, as you and I would be; for no one wants to give up their independence. Seniors are the last to admit to no longer being self-sufficient or able to take care of themselves properly.

The line between capable and dependent is often blurred, and it is often difficult to notice the signs when a senior is no longer capable of living alone. The fact is, while most independent seniors are perfectly capable of caring for themselves, others may not be aware of their declining faculties, such as weight loss (forgetting to eat); messy finances (stacks of unpaid bills); suspicious new friends who hang around. While this can be a harmless and a beneficial relationship, it can also indicate the beginnings of a confidence scam.

Addressing Pastoral Peace to the Family

Pastoral peace can be provided if pastors and leaders are more educated on the topic of Elder Abuse. This would help to properly address issues with families where an elderly person might reside; or, how or what signs to look for in single elderly households.

2.63 of the Confession of Faith addresses the responsibilities for the pastors. The current responsibilities (g) and (j) below would work in conjunction with proper understanding of the subject title whereas it could be incorporated into discussion.

2.63(g) states: visit the people, especially the poor, the sick, the dying, and those with other critical needs. (Elderly is a stage of people. Because the word elderly is not categorically mentioned in the list, it would be difficult to recognize the need for attention in this areas).

2.63(j) states: counsel with people, in light of the scriptures, about their personal needs and problems... (one would need more understanding of the subject to incorporate it into discussion).

2.72 states: elders should inform the pastor of any concerns that need his or her attention. (This concern must be recognized first whereas it can be shared with the pastor).

Under **Introduction to the 1984 Confession of Faith, Page XV, Paragraph 3** states: The ancient truth which guides this confession of faith is of two sources: (1) the scriptures; and (2) the previous confessions of both Cumberland Presbyterian churches and the previous confessions of the church in its universal expression. All testimony to Jesus Christ must be tested by the scriptures which are the only unfailing and authoritative word for Christian faith, growth, and practice. All testimony to Jesus Christ is made within the context of the church universal and therefore must not be made in a narrow, sectarian manner or spirit.

The paragraph above attests to the fact that Confession of faith is more than a personal affirmation of faith; it is a scripturally driven testimony based on action through faith.

1 Timothy 5:8 says *"But if anyone does not provide for his own, and especially for those of his household, he has denied the faith and is worse than an unbeliever."*

Our Confession of Faith affirms that the Cumberland Presbyterians are believers of the scripture; therefore, scripturally it would deem the Church as unbelievers if it failed not to at least try to help this stage of people who are considered as part of the church household.

We know it was not the intention that this fragile topic be excluded years ago; for "elderly abuse", in any form, was unthought of due to honor bestowed upon those of old. It appears however that today, the elderly have become "the forgotten ones" of God's children.

Reiterating and giving reference to **paragraph 4, on Page XV under the Introduction to the 1984 Confession of Faith**, we are indeed greatly indebted to the *Confession of Faith of 1883*, the *Confession of Faith of 1814*, and the *Westminster Confession of Faith* out of which the other two arose.

Let this now be the time that we, the Cumberland Presbyterian Church, not only embrace the youth who are the future of our denomination, but "vigilantly" be there for our elderly who yet represent the spirit of the cornerstone upon which our denominational heritage stands.

Psalms 71:9 says *"Cast me not off in the time of old age; forsake me not when my strength faileth."* There is little that you can find in the scriptures on the Christian or Church's responsibility regarding elderly abuse.

Question: Should the Cumberland Presbyterian Church speak out?
Does it go against our belief? Is it deemed meddling to discuss or report suspected elder abuse?

Scripturally, this could fall somewhere close to Genius 4:9 *"Am I my brother's keeper?"* According to Matthew Henry, "When a person is unconcerned in the affairs of others and takes no care when they have opportunity to prevent hurt--especially in their souls, -- that person in effect speaks Cain's language."

Question: How can we, the Cumberland Presbyterian Church, show more concern in preventing harm or hurt on behalf of our elderly and more importantly, prevent the loss of souls?
2 Corinthians 1:3-4 says -*Blessed be God, even the Father of our Lord Jesus Christ, the Father of mercies, and the God of all comfort; who comforted us in all our tribulation, that we may be able to comfort them which are in any trouble, by the comfort wherewith we ourselves are comforted of God.*

Question: How can we as Cumberland Presbyterians assist in comforting the community of elderly who are recognizably in trouble?
In conclusion, the Cumberland Presbyterian Church, who looks to the *"Confession of Faith"* for guidance and direction, and seeks to be the voice of Jesus through his love, also seek to encourage our denomination of Christians to be that witness to the world who says, "We care about our Elderly and as Christians, we will be careful to stay vigilant in upholding God's word by not casting the elderly off in their time of old age; but be more attentive to that which appears to be but is not, and to recognize the unrecognizable cry for help beyond the eyes of dignity which often prevents that cry."

STUDY QUESTIONS – Elder Abuse

1. How can one recognize the warning signs of elder abuse?
    Answer: Changes in personality or behavior

2. What good works am I (or my church) doing for the elderly in my community?

3. What can I or my church do to help make a difference?
    a. Assess the targeted community needs of the elderly.
    b. Educate the church on recognizing the warning signs of Elder Abuse.
    c. Incorporate elderly home visit programs in the church.
    d. Periodically inquire about medications they're taking; example -do they run out often?
    e. Watch for possible financial abuse…no money for food or necessities.
    f. Call and visit as often as you can. Help them to consider you trustworthy.
    g. Allocate a church group which occasionally donates relief time for the caregiver
    h. Cautiously intervene when abuse is suspected; contact local government officials.

4. Share examples of what you, your church or community is doing or has done to help offset, bring awareness to or help prevent suspected elder abuse, keeping in mind it can come in several forms including self-neglect. Below is an example of an increasing problem with aging:

Example: When dad will not give up the keys to his vehicle, the family will be the last ones he will listen to. This is when you bring in outside friends of the family or acquaintances who can assist you by being a witness to the concern of his driving. If the family is that concerned, neighbors, even towns' people (if smaller town), will be concerned for his safety, not to mention possibly harming someone else. Also, ask a non-family member (he respects) to gently talk with him on a personal level and speak the possibility of community concern for his well-being. Then, re-address the issue. (If in a larger city, a patrolman will volunteer to speak to your father out of concern to help the family address the situation.)

If all else fails, you have one or two options: 1) Have their doctor write a letter to declare them incompetent to drive, therefore restricting their driver license; or 2) unnoticeably disable part of the cable from the battery whereas it will disable the vehicle. Depending on their mental awareness, this could resolve the problem.

No situation is addressed the same; however, their safety and protection is what matters.

5. Finally, if we as church members individually chose not to position ourselves personally to help, then donate money to the cause and sole purpose of educating and bringing awareness to the people about the realism of elder abuse…Who knows, you could possibly be protecting your own life down the line.

Your input and thoughts are encouraged. Please send to any member of the Unified Committee for Theology and Social Concerns. Member names and contact info can be found on the USTSC webpage.

Works Cited
Dept. of HHS Administration on Aging (Elder Abuse) Last Modified 7/22/16

Confession of Faith 1984; Confession of Faith of 1883; Confession of Faith of 1814

Westminster Confession of Faith; Matthew Henry Bible Commentary

THE REPORT OF THE UNIFICATION TASK FORCE

I. MEETING AND OFFICERS

The Unification Task Force (UTF) of the Cumberland Presbyterian Church in America (CPCA) and the Cumberland Presbyterian Church (CPC) has met twice since the 2016 meetings of the General Assemblies: November 17-18, 2016 and April 6-7, 2017. Both meetings were held in Nashville, Tennessee. Officers elected at the November 2016 meeting were: Co-chairs Perryn Rice and Robert Rush, Co-secretaries Jay Earheart-Brown and Craig White.

Other members of the UTF from the CPCA include Leon Cole, Elton Hall, Lynne Herring, William Robinson, and Mitchell Walker. Other members from the CPC include Gloria Villa-Diaz, Steve Mosley, Pam Phillips-Burk, Mike Sharpe, and Joy Warren.

William Robinson and Joy Warren were elected to represent the UTF at the 2017 meetings of the General Assemblies in Tampa, Florida.

II. PROPOSED PLAN FOR UNION

The 2014 General Assemblies, in concurrent session at Chattanooga, Tennessee, approved for study a Proposed Plan of Union. That plan has been distributed widely across both denominations, and has generated a great deal of discussion and feedback. For two years, the plan was studied in both churches, generating many responses from individuals and church sessions. We are grateful for all the responses received, both positive and negative.

The 2016 General Assemblies, in concurrent session at Nashville, Tennessee received a revised draft of the Proposed Plan for Union which incorporated many of the suggestions we had heard from across the two churches. We are not proposing any changes to last year's Proposed Plan for Union at the 2017 General Assembly meetings, but reprint it here with the prayer that it will continue to be studied for the next two years, which we are proposing to be a time of continuing relationship building between our two churches at every level. Both Assemblies are planning concurrent meetings for 2017 (Tampa, Florida) and 2018 (Norman, Oklahoma), and we encourage all who participate in those gatherings to be intentional about building and deepening relationships with persons from the other denomination.

Proposed Plan for Union of the
Cumberland Presbyterian Church and the Cumberland Presbyterian Church in America

"There is one, holy, universal, apostolic church. She is the body of Christ, who is her Head and Lord" (*Confession of Faith* 5.01). "The church is one because her head and Lord is one, Jesus Christ. Her oneness under her Lord is manifested in the one ministry of word and sacrament, not in any uniformity of covenantal expression, organization, or system of doctrine" (5.02). "The church, as the covenant community of believers who are redeemed, includes all people in all ages, past, present, and future, who respond in faith to God's covenant of grace, and all who are unable to respond, for reasons known to God, but who are saved by his grace" (5.06). It is on this belief that the Unification Task Force recommends the union of the Cumberland Presbyterian Church in America (CPCA) and the Cumberland Presbyterian Church (CPC). We are one in Christ by the grace of God and the power of the Holy Spirit! We believe that becoming one will strengthen our witness as Christian believers in the world, and that together we will be able to accomplish more for the glory of God. United together in Christ by faith, we are united to one another in love. In this communion we share the grace of Christ with one another, bear one another's burdens, and reach out to all other persons (*Confession of Faith* 5.10).

1.00 Mission Statement for the New Church

The Cumberland Presbyterian Church United affirms the great commission of Christ: "Go, therefore, and make disciples of all nations, baptizing them in the name of the Father, and of the Son, and of the Holy Spirit, and teaching them to obey everything that I have commanded you. And remember I am with you until the end of the age"(Matthew 28:19-20). We celebrate our oneness in faith. As disciples, we seek through worship, global witness, and service to be the hands and feet of Christ and to live out the love of Jesus Christ to the glory of God.

2.00 The Confession of Faith and Government

The Cumberland Presbyterian Church United will use the *Confession of Faith and Government* of the Cumberland Presbyterian Church and the Cumberland Presbyterian Church in America, approved by both General Assemblies of the former denominations in 1984 as its system of faith and government.

NOTE: It should be noted that in the Constitution (4.6, 5.6p) the CPC allows for a session to request permission from Presbytery for a designated elder to be trained and granted permission to serve communion for a one year period of time. This is an exception, NOT A RULE for general practice, for those presbyteries that have difficulty supplying each church with an ordained minister. The responsibility lies with presbytery for proper training and oversight of the designated elder. Again, is this an EXCEPTION. No presbytery is required to apply this exception.

2.01 The Cumberland Presbyterian Church United will use the *Catechism for Cumberland Presbyterians* (2008) for instruction in the faith and will include it in an updated edition of the *Confession of Faith and Government of the Cumberland Presbyterian Church United*.

2.02 The CP *Digest* (CPC) and Summaries of Actions (for both denominations) will continue to serve as resource tools. A new *Digest* will begin with the formation of the Cumberland Presbyterian Church United.

3.00 The Presbyteries and Synods

3.01 In an effort to make union something more than just an idea on paper, and to engage the grassroots in creating the new church, we recommend a restructure of the synod boundaries to create eight synods for the new church, with the following presbyteries in each –

Synod A*	Synod B*	Synod C	Synod D
Brazos River	Angelina	Covenant	Cleveland, Ohio
Del Christo	Arkansas	Missouri	Cumberland
Red River	Choctaw	New Hopewell	North Central
Hong Kong	East Texas	Purchase	Ohio Valley
Japan	Trinity	West Tennessee	
	Andes		
	Cauca Valley		

Synod E	Synod F	Synod G	Synod H
Columbia	East Tennessee	Florence	Birmingham
Elk River	Hiawassee	Hope	Grace
Murfreesboro	Tennessee-Georgia	Huntsville	South Alabama
Nashville	East Coast Korean	Robert Donnell	Tuscaloosa
		Tennessee Valley	

For relationship building during the first six years, all synods will be encouraged to hold an annual general meeting (*Constitution* 8.2) as opposed to a delegated meeting. Synods may petition General Assembly at any point for a change in boundaries.

* *NOTE: There are plans for organizing a new presbytery in Central and/or South America in the near future, as well as dreams for organizing a third presbytery in Asia. As soon as it is practical to do so, whether before or after union, two additional synods should be constituted. Synod I would include Andes, Cauca Valley, and any other presbyteries organized in Latin America. Synod J would include Hong Kong, Japan, and any other presbyteries organized in Asia.*

3.02 Presbyteries will remain as they are constituted at the time of union. During the first six years of the new church's life, synods will be encouraged to study the most beneficial presbyterial boundaries within their jurisdictionto fulfill of the mission of the church. Presbyteries may petition their synod at any time for a change in boundaries.

4.00 Commissioners and Youth Advisory Delegates to the General Assembly

4.01 Commissioners to the General Assembly
Each Presbytery will be entitled to send 2 minister commissioners and 2 elder commissioners to the General Assembly.

NOTE: If presbytery boundaries remain as currently constituted at the time of unification, this will allow for a total possible membership in the General Assembly of 152 commissioners. Of these potential commissioners, 60 would come from former presbyteries of the CPCA, and 92 would come from the former CPC.

4.02 Youth Advisory Delegates
Each presbytery will be entitled to send up to two Youth Advisory delegates to the General Assembly.

5.00 Moderator and Vice Moderator of General Assembly

5.01 The moderator/vice moderator will be elected each year during the first six years with the two offices alternating between persons from the two former denominations.

5.02 The moderator and vice moderator of the Cumberland Presbyterian Church United will reflect its diverse nature, to include international representatives. The church expects the moderator and vice moderator to travel within the denomination, sharing and gathering information among its local churches. Expenses and particular duties will be detailed in the Standing Rules of the Cumberland Presbyterian Church United.

6.00 Stated Clerk and Associate Stated Clerk of the General Assembly

6.01 The new church shall employ a Stated Clerk and an Associate Stated Clerk. Both positions will be full-time jobs. During the first six years of the Cumberland Presbyterian Church United, the Stated Clerk will serve six years and the Associate Stated Clerk will serve four years, after which each would be elected for a four-year period. One position will be filled by a former CPCA and the other position filled by a former CPC during their first terms. The subsequent election of each position will allow for continuity during transitions. Particular duties and responsibilities of the Stated Clerk and Associate Stated Clerk will be detailed in the Standing Rules of the Cumberland Presbyterian Church United.

7.00 Boards and Agencies of the General Assembly

7.01 Each church has programs in various stages of planning and implementation that are the result of commitment to ministry through the church. Insofar as possible, these plans and programs will be continued without interruption for a period of three years. The Cumberland Presbyterian Church has covenantal relationships with the Cumberland Presbyterian Children's Home in Denton, Texas and Bethel University in McKenzie, Tennessee. These covenantal relationships will remain in effect as they exist at the time of Unification, to be renewed every four years. The Cumberland Presbyterian Church United will continue ecumenical partnerships, such as with the World Communion of Reformed Churches.

7.02 Institutional Boards
The General Assembly shall have the following institutional boards: Trustees of Memphis Theological Seminary to include the Program of Alternate Studies and School of Continuing Education Committee, and Trustees of the Historical Foundation. Representation on each Board of Trustees will remain as they are constituted at the time of union.

7.03 Administrative Boards
The General Assembly shall have the following administrative Boards: The Board of Stewardship, Foundation and Benefits and The Board of Directors of the General Assembly Corporation. During the transition period, each of these boards will have equal number of members from each of the former denominations.

7.04 Commission
The General Assembly shall have the following commission: Chaplains and Military Personnel. Representation on the commission will be merged as they are constituted at the time of union until natural rotation occurs.

7.05 Standing Committees

The General Assembly shall have the following standing committees: Theology and Social Concerns, Judiciary, Our United Outreach, Nominating, and Multi-Cultural Ministry.

Committee representation on the Theology and Social Concerns Committee will remain as constituted at the time of union until natural rotations occurs.

Judiciary and Nominating committees in both denominations will each be merged at the time of union.

Committee representation for Our United Outreach will be expanded to include two elected representatives from each new synod (one voting representative from each of the former denominations until natural rotation occurs).

The Committee on Multi-Cultural Ministry is a new committee that will reflect the diversity of the Cumberland Presbyterian Church United. This committee will be comprised of eight (8) elected persons that will reflect the celebrative understanding of humanity in the areas of culture, language, heritage, and experience in the Cumberland Presbyterian Church United. Believing that all have been created in God's image, this committee works to answer the question of our sameness in God's image lived out in diverse ways.

7.06 The Cumberland Presbyterian Church United will have a Mission Programming Agency to provide coordination and oversight for those ministries formally planned and implemented by the two former denominations. After the three-year period, the new programming and denominational structure will consist of the following ministries and entities –

Christian Education & Nurture (Youth Convention & National Sunday School Convention

Missions (Evangelism, Missionary Auxiliary, Women's Ministry)

Clergy Care & Development

Communications (Cumberland Flag, Cumberland Presbyterian Magazine, Missionary Messenger, website)

Composition of each ministry entity will include equal number of persons from each of the former denominations in the new church at the time of union. Composition of the new Mission Programming Agency will include one staff person and one elected member from each ministry entity, along with one elected member representing each of the synods. The elected members will be equally representative of the two former denominations for the first six years. A Ministry Coordinator would provide executive leadership for the Mission Programming Agency.

8. Denominational Staff & Personnel

Currently, the CPCA employs two full time staff members; the CPC employs twenty-five staff members.

8.01 The new organizational structure will discontinue the positions of Administrative Director (CPCA) and the Director of Ministries (CPC) and will create the positions of Associate Stated Clerk and Ministry Coordinator. The duties and parameters of each position and corresponding selection processes will be determined during the Implementation Phase and detailed in the Standing Rules.

8.02 Staffing for the Cumberland Presbyterian Church United will reflect the diversity of the new church. As new staff positions become available, equal opportunity employment practices will prevail.

8.03 Denominational Offices –During the first six years, steps are to be taken to assure that regional sites be located in a minimum of three and a maximum of five locations. Thus, neither the Center in Huntsville nor the Center in Memphis will be designated as "the denominational center." By placing regional sites in a variety of locations this will assure that all areas of the church will be served equally. These regional sites can make use of offices in existing churches, or in homes of regional staff persons. Possible regional locations could be Memphis, Huntsville, Louisville, Texas, South America, Asia, etc.

8.04 Global Staff

There will be endorsed missionaries and partner missionaries in the new church. The new church will continue to support current and future missionaries and global work. Current missionaries include – CP Missionaries: Boyce and Beth Wallace (Colombia, South America), Patrick and Jessica Wilkerson (Colombia, South America), Carlos and Luz Dary Rivera (Mexico), Anay Ortega (Guatemala), Fhanor and Socorro Pejendino (Guatemala), Jacob and Lindsey Sims (Brazil), Daniel and Kay Jang (Philippines), John and Joy Park (Philippines), DSL (Cambodia-Laos). CP Missionaries working with non-denominational missions: Kenneth and Delight Hopson (Uganda),TTG (Kyrgyzstan). Global Work, there are CP Churches in: Australia, Brazil, Cambodia, Colombia, Guatemala, Haiti, Hong Kong, Japan, Laos, Mexico, Philippines, South Korea, and the USA.

9.00 Stewardship and Finance

9.01 Legal control of assets of both churches will be transferred to the Cumberland Presbyterian Church United through appropriate legal transaction. The intent of all designated gifts and endowments will be honored.

9.02 The Cumberland Presbyterian Church United will develop an approach to the financing of the programs of the church that reflects the stewardship understanding of the new constituency. Such a unitary approach will be developed as soon as possible after formation and no later than the end of the first six years.

10.00 Recognition of Ordination
All ordinations, both clergy and lay (elders and deacons), of both denominations will be recognized by the Cumberland Presbyterian Church United. All future ordinations will be governed by the conditions specified in the Constitution. Persons who are recognized by their respective presbyteries as candidates and licentiates at the time the new church is formed will fulfill the requirements as specified by presbytery at the time they became probationers.

11.00 The Name of the New Denomination
The name of the denomination shall be the Cumberland Presbyterian Church United.

12.00 The Logo of the New Church
A new logo will be fashioned by the new church.

RECOMMENDATION 1: That the General Assemblies encourage pastors, elders, sessions, churches, presbyteries and synods to continue their study and discussion of the Proposed Plan of Union, and that responses be directed to the UTF through the Office of the Stated Clerk of the CPC or Office of the Executive Director of the CPCA.

III. REVISED TIMELINE

As we have engaged this work over the past five years, the last couple of years have been particularly challenging due to increased tensions in American society. The publicity surrounding incidents of violence by and against police officers, the Black Lives Matter movement, and those who critique it with the slogan All Lives Matter, increasing incidents like the shooting and killing of church members at Mother Emmanuel AME Church in Charleston, South Carolina by a troubled young white man; all of these and more have made the work of racial reconciliation more difficult in our time. Such incidents, we are convinced, also make the work we are doing to try to heal our denominational divide as Cumberland Presbyterians more urgent and hopeful than ever.

In our Spring 2017 meeting, the UTF wrestled with the urgency of moving forward, and the realities that our two churches still have not learned to trust each other fully yet. Torn between our desire to move ahead in faith, and our fears of pushing unification before its time, the UTF proposed the following tentative timeline toward the organic union of our two churches, which the General Assemblies asked us to seek in 2012.

2017 – 2019	Two years devoted to intentional relationship building and trust development.
June 2019	A Plan for Union with any additional revisions is presented to the two General Assemblies for approval.
2019 – 2020	The Plan is submitted to the Presbyteries of the CPC and the CPCA for ratification.
June 2020	The CPC and CPCA General Assemblies meet concurrently to celebrate the adoption of the plan and begin a new church together, walking into God's future with 20-20 vision.

IV. UNIFICATION SUNDAY

We proposed to the 2016 General Assemblies that a day be set aside in the church calendars of both denominations to pray for and educate our people about the Unification of our churches. The date we proposed in February was not acceptable, and the two assemblies approved the idea, but set the date at a time that we think will not gain much attention in the life of our congregations (fourth Sunday in December). In trying to think about a better solution to this issue, we discussed the possibility of celebrating Unification Sunday just after the GA meetings, since that should be a time when we have been together in worship and work for a week. In light of these considerations, we make the following:

RECOMMENDATION 2: That the fourth Sunday in June be set aside in the church calendars as Unification Sunday beginning in 2018.

V. REFERRAL

The 2016 General Assembly of the CPC adopted a recommendation "That the Unification Task Force meet with representatives of Memphis Theological Seminary, the Program of Alternate Studies, and the School of Continuing Education and Certification to discuss the pathways of education for clergy." In its fall meeting, the UTF tasked members Mitchell Walker, Lynne Herring (both of whom have significant leadership roles with the CPCA's School of Continuing Education), and Jay Earheart-Brown (President of MTS) to meet with Michael Qualls, Director of the Program of Alternate Studies in response to this directive.

In our spring meeting, we heard from the four persons delegated this responsibility about a significant meeting in Huntsville, Alabama at the CPCA Denominational Center on April 3, 2017. Leaders from the two certificate programs shared information about the two programs, and ways that both programs could work together to provide alternate education for clergy for our two denominations. Further relationship building steps are being taken including:

1) Open a position on the advisory board of each program to the Director of the sister program.
2) Pursue reciprocal agreements that allow students in one program to receive credit for approved courses in the sister program and pay the tuition to their original certifying program.
3) Initiate sharing and standardizing forms and certification procedures.
4) Investigate strengthening relationship between MTS and the School of Continuing Education, with the hopes that SCE could have a similar relationship to MTS as PAS does.

Plans for a course to be held at the PAS Summer Extension School in McKenzie, Tennessee were shared. Mitchell Walker and Michael Qualls will co-teach this course that will focus on the relationship between the CPC and CPCA and past and current efforts toward unity between the two.

While there is much work to be done on these fronts, leaders from both programs are deeply committed to the effort to bring the two programs into closer alignment as we move toward Unification.

IV. PLAN FOR OUR WORK AS A TASK FORCE

We voted to organize the larger task force into two subcommittees for the next two-year period. One of the subcommittees would focus on educating, supporting, and equipping unification advocates who have volunteered their time and energy toward helping to bring our churches together. This sub-committee, the Relationship Building and Advocate Support Team, is made up of the following persons: Pam Phillips-Burk, Mitchell Walker, Gloria Villa-Diaz, William Robinson, Perryn Rice, Elton Hall, Lynne Herring, and Mike Sharpe.

The second sub-committee will focus its efforts on legal matters related to the By-laws and Standing Rules that will need to be revised to begin implementation of Unification. The By-laws and Standing Rules Team will focus its efforts on assessing the cost of Unification and doing all that it can to answer outstanding concerns about how implementation may affect current programs in both churches. This Team will be made up of the following persons: Jay Earheart-Brown, Craig White, Robert Rush, Leon Cole, Joy Warren, Steve Mosley, Lynne Herring, and Mike Sharpe.

Our plan is that the full UTF will not meet in the fall of 2017 so that the two working Teams can meet (electronically or by conference call) to plan their work. The full UTF will come together in the spring of 2018 to assess the effectiveness of both groups and prepare a report to the next General Assemblies.

We are working to plan the program for a major presentation to a joint session on Tuesday evening during this year's General Assembly. This program will focus on current relationships between CPC's and CPCA's at every level of our life together. Presenters will share news of the experiences they have had in the past few years building closer ties with brothers and sisters from the other denomination. The evening's program will close with a time for Unification Advocates to hear from leaders of the UTF about concrete steps they can take in the coming months.

Respectfully submitted,
The Unification Task Force of the CPCA and CPC
Perryn Rice and Robert Rush, co-chairs

THE REPORT OF BOARD OF TRUSTEES OF BETHEL UNIVERSITY

As the 2016 school year at Bethel University got underway, a total of 5,367 students took part in one of 26 programs of study that will lead to associate, bachelor's and master's degrees. Around 80 percent of those 26 programs have projected 10-year job growth rates of around 10 percent with some fields having as much as a 17 percent growth rate promising many job possibilities for graduates. Salary projections were also favorable for these programs with an average starting salary being anywhere between $34,000 and $60,000 across most fields.

Our work continues to be far reaching as we have served a student population this year that represents 43 states and 25 foreign countries. This diverse population brings many world traditions together, and students learn a great deal from this exposure.

Continuing with our tradition of helping our students grow spiritually, Bethel University offered both a weekly chapel service and a weekly communion service during the Fall 2016 and Spring 2017 semesters. Worship was led by a number of denominational worship leaders who exposed students to a broad range of Christian doctrines and styles. During the 2016 school year, Bethel's student group, the Cumberland Presbyterian Ministry, has also actively fellowshipped keeping a firm focus on the Cumberland Presbyterian ideals upon which Bethel is built. In fact, Bethel has a number of student organizations that are centered around Christian ideals. There is the Wesley Foundation, the Baptist Collegiate Ministry and Fellowship of Christian Athletes.

A number of local and global opportunities for mission work were also offered to students with local work being covered by Greek and other student organizations and by students who are part of the Student Engagement Scholarship program. Students have visited nursing homes, collected needed materials for local organizations, conducted cleanup projects and worked with students in an after school at risk program. Global mission work offered through Bethel's Program of Global Studies was also an opportunity for students this year with trips to Cuba, Peru and Belize and with an upcoming summer opportunity planned for Colombia, South America.

Bethel University has also earned a number of high level recognitions during the past year. Its May 2016 nursing graduates achieved a 100 percent pass rate on the NCLEX – the licensure examination that determines nurse readiness. This is the third time in the last four years that a Bethel nursing class has achieved the perfect pass rate. Additionally, students from Bethel's Physician Assistant program won the state Medical Challenge Bowl allowing them to compete at the national level in April 2017. Bethel was also named the top accredited online school in Tennessee by Accreditedschoolsonline.org. Similarly, Bethel's College of Professional Studies was recognized as the top university in Tennessee for its support of careers in criminal justice and corrections, according to rankings published by CorrectionalOfficer.org. Bethel University's Criminal Justice program was also ranked 7th in the nation by Affordable Colleges Online. This ranking was based on academic quality, accommodation, guidance and affordability.

Bethel's traditional undergraduate programs are also continually adding value to the classroom experience with various learning enrichment projects. A Steinway piano was purchased, and Odom Lecture Hall stage was renovated for recitals. Additionally, a music department faculty recital was held. The art department hosted an exhibit and lecture by a visiting artist – Al Shull, a professor of art at Lincoln Land Community College in Springfield, Illinois. Furthermore, graduating art majors exhibited their senior work and presented a lecture defending their approaches to art, and the annual Humanities Art Exhibit showcased the talent of approximately 150 students. There was also a symposium on Postmodernism organized by four Bethel faculty members and a 12 Film Lecture Series that gave students the chance to look at history from different perspectives. Other things included Bethel hosting the Kentucky Lake Section of the American Chemical Society Meeting, Bethel's Student Government Association hosting a West Tennessee Summit for SGA teams at area colleges and a trip by some Bethel students to Washington University in St. Louis that also included the opportunity to hear retired U.S. Supreme Court Justice John Paul Stevens speak and to sit in on a criminal law class taught by a Washington University law professor.

In athletics, Bethel's women's basketball team and shooting teams have taken part in National Tournament play this year, and our Bass Fishing Team won the Bassmaster College Bracket Series with Bethel Angler John Garrett moving forward from that event to serve as the only collegiate competitor in the 2017 Bass Masters Classic. Showing character along with physical dominance, Bethel's athletic program was also recognized as one of only 19 NAIA schools to reach Gold Level status for its commitment to the Champions of Character five core values of integrity, respect, responsibility, sportsmanship and servant leadership.

Bethel's performing arts focus continues to be strong too with the Renaissance Performing Arts Scholarship drawing a large number of students to Bethel studies. This year, 280 students have participated in Renaissance. An Emmy picked up by Renaissance Technical Director Daniel Howell for recording, mixing and production shows Bethel's commitment to bringing in teachers and mentors who are committed to their craft and who can share their expertise with students. Also recognized was Renaissance Bluegrass Director Stephen Mougin who was chosen as Mentor of the Year by the International Bluegrass Music Association primarily for his work with Renaissance. Renaissance students continue to have the opportunity to travel across the country to perform and to be exposed to music industry professionals. A new and recent trip was an invitation to the Bethel Marching Band to march in Chicago's annual St. Patrick's Day parade.

Finally, Bethel University is scheduled for the decennial review by the Southern Association of College and Schools Commission on Colleges. According to President Walter Butler, "the ten-year report is due on September 11, 2017."

THE REPORT OF THE BOARD OF TRUSTEES OF THE CUMBERLAND PRESBYTERIAN CHILDREN'S HOME

Thank you for reviewing our report giving you a balance between heart and head.

We strive to be good stewards of your gifts and donations to us. Many of you come to our campus to visit and work. Most of you send money to pay for the expensive work of ending the cycle of abuse and neglect by bringing healing and hope to children and families. All of you support our mission with your prayers and your commitment of time and energy to support the work. Thank you and God bless you.

I. OVERVIEW

Our 113th year of ministry at the Children's Home serves children and families in different ways:

- **Children's Residential Care,**
- **Children's Emergency Shelter Care,**
- **Single Parent Family Services, and**
- **Cumberland Family Services Counseling.**

In the 21st Century, we focus our ministry on ending the maltreatment of children. Child abuse and neglect not only injure children, but impact the lives and families of adults who were once abused. We must stop the cycle of harm, a harm that can be measured in many ways. Foremost, I believe we are called to this redemptive ministry by God. God has called us to feed, clothe, teach, and love the little, the last, the lost and the least.

The harm also creates a toll in human tragedy correlated with crime, addiction, unemployment, incarceration, broken relationships, mental and emotional dysfunction, ill health, violence and self destructive actions. The cost to society is numbing.

So Cumberland provides a safe, nurturing and loving residence where children and families can live and grow. It also provides tools for healing and health through counseling and parenting training. And most importantly, the Children's Home enacts Christ's command to serve in His name. Here are some numbers to give you a flavor of the scope of our ministry.

Cumberland helps children and families in residential and non-residential programs during 2016. In its residential programs, Cumberland served 134 children and 20 single parents. Over 1,191 additional children and families were served through intake and referral services, counseling sessions, or classes in our non-residential programs. Cumberland held over 1,635 separate counseling sessions. More than 2,450 hours of service were performed by volunteers. In all, 1,345 lives were touched with healing and hope by the Cumberland Presbyterian Children's Home during 2016.

Mission
*In response to Christ's love and example,
we serve children and families
by providing healing and hope.*

Campus

Cumberland's 17-acre campus in Denton, Texas, includes three residential cottages for children and teens and 9 apartments for single parent families. Other features include the Parr Family Resource Building, which houses the Library and Technology Center, therapy rooms, meeting facilities and staff offices. The campus is also home to the Gilbert-Parr Activities Building, which houses Cumberland's recreational facilities and a chapel, the 250-seat Lela Stricklen Hall.

Corporate entity and governance

Cumberland is a non-profit corporation incorporated under the laws of the state of Texas. Cumberland is tax-exempt under IRS Code section 501(c)(3). Cumberland is governed by a board of 18 Trustees. The Cumberland Board of Trustees hired the President, CEO & General Counsel to manage the agency.

Trustees: There are currently 18 trustees: ten Cumberland Presbyterians and eight ecumenical partners.

Ecumenical Partners: Patricia Long, Caroline Booth, Cameron Morone, Charles Harris, Knight Miller and Kay Goodman

Cumberland Presbyterians: Mamie Hall, Reverend Melissa Knight, Doctor Robin Henson, Reverend Joyce Merritt, Reverend Don Tabor, Richard Dean, Jay Thomas, Carolyn Harmon, and Reverend Duane Dougherty

Officers: Chair—Richard Dean; Vice-Chair—Patricia Long; Secretary—Caroline Booth.

Leadership

President, CEO & General Counsel: Reverend Richard A. Brown, Esq., LCCA
Vice President, Programs: Doctor Jennifer Livings, LPC-S
Interim Chaplain: Reverend Katie Klein

Organizational Structure

Because our mission calls us to a ministry of service, we have adopted the following "Pyramid of Care©" as an organizational structure. Rather than organizing from the top down, we wish to follow in Christ's example of servant leadership. We place the people we serve, both in residential care and in non-residential care, at the top of the pyramid.

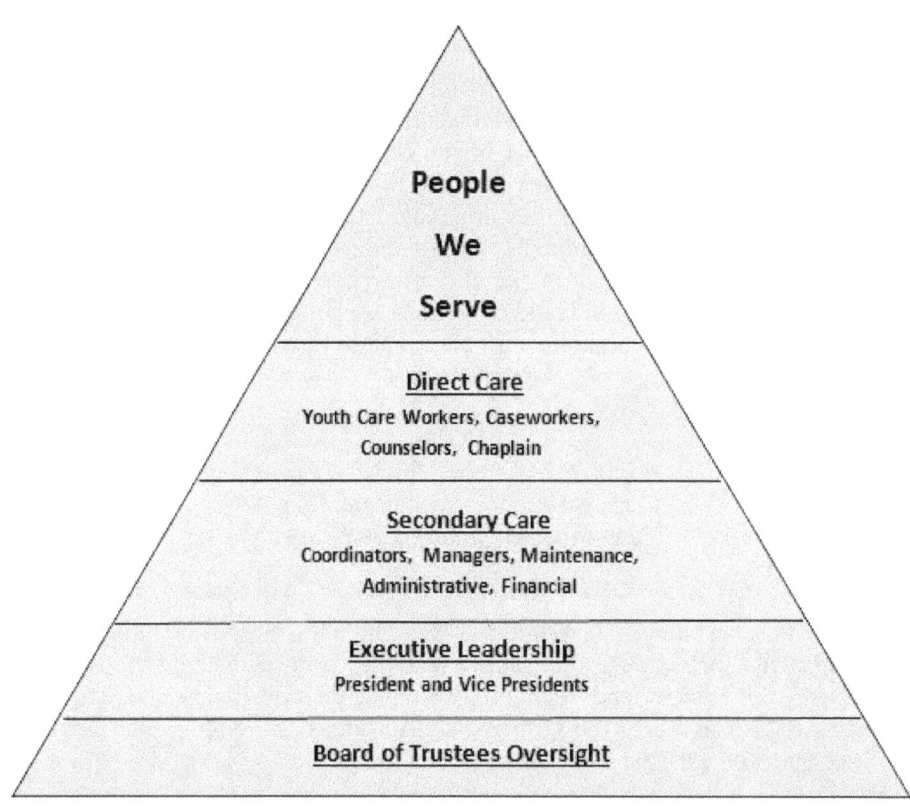

II. OUTCOMES

Memorandum

To: The Board of Trustees
From: Dr. Jennifer Livings, LPC-S
Date: 2-17-2017
Re: Vice President Report

Growing together has been our recent theme in programming since we last met in September. All of our programs are growing and expanding to new horizons to meet our future and current goals. 2016 and 2017 are our years for growth and expansion that have come with challenges and successes. Our continued goal is to increase revenue and serve more clients while maintaining the high quality of care that we have come to expect and provide.

Cumberland Family Services hired a new therapist, Carley Shannon LPC-S. Carley specializes in play therapy and has a background with youths in foster care and those who have experienced trauma. We are on track to soon take various types of Medicaid to expand our revenue possibilities. The addition of our new Intake Specialist, Lizbeth Moreno, has proven to be a wonderful compliment to our already established programming team. Our therapists are ready to take on new challenges in 2017 by expanding caseloads and billing potential. Our CFS program had some challenges and we were not at full capacity in 2016. We have a wonderful team of interns who help serve our SPF families and our community. As always, our therapists are trained and designed to treat trauma and we are eager to have a fully staffed therapy program again for 2017. We are also pleased to report that Robert Mood, our Clinical Coordinator, will be taking a lead role in redesigning and tracking our outcome measures as he has the skill level to take us to new heights with a more focused look at the impact our programs has on individuals lives.

The **General Residential Operation** team has been doing a great job of preparing the emergency cottage for expansion. Our staff were on board with our decision and were more than willing to adjust to accommodate changes. Our GRO team is a huge compliment to our success.

With some of our renovations being completed at the beginning of February we are on target to serve more children and increase revenue. We see our children responding well to these changes and we have had our kids making space and prepare for living with more children. We had a wonderful Christmas and holiday season with fluid communication of needs from programming with fulfillment from our wonderful development team. Our donations this year where better than ever and no child or family went without both needs and wants for Christmas. Our GRO program continues to be a research site. Currently, Dr. Jacquelyn Vickery and her team are conducting a focus group with our youth to understanding how children in foster care respond to current media portrayals of foster care youth.

Single Parent Family program is reaching new heights. We discovered an additional revenue source for SPF. With a few remodeling additions to an already existing building, we added another unit to our program taking us to 9 units total. We will be partnering with Dallas Housing Authority. Regardless that these families are coming from another referral source, our SPF service model continues to be the framework for working with clients. Our SPF Coordinator, Christine Snow, has been busy taking financial trainings and learning about services in our communities to build relationships and serve our families. Since Christine is back at Cumberland we again have the potential to train social work interns that is not otherwise possible as many of the advanced social work programs require a LCSW to be supervising. In community news, UNT and TWU recently announced they will be partnering to great a Master's Social Work program. This is amazing news for Cumberland and our community.

Our **Chaplain**, Pastor Katie Klein, has been very busy this holiday season and is an integral part of the Cumberland family and has brought a wonderful sense of fellowship and relationship building to our campus. The Spiritual Enrichment program is growing and we are working on a model for life skills, spiritual enrichment, and volunteering as a systemic model to be delivered across campus. Katie has been working well with our other coordinators to provide what our children and families need regarding life skills, fellowship, and volunteers. We have seen a great sense of consistency and reliability in our current volunteer base. We are also working on partnering with other agencies to provider life skills training for our community. Finally, Katie is overseeing our ReNew Center as it will a fresh new look due to the dedication of volunteers overseeing this service.

Our **Executive Assistant**, Melanee Fabbri, has done a wonderful job taking on duties in HR, billing, and benefits. Melanee has been instrumental in helping Cumberland get organized. Melanee has taken on duties of reporting payroll and providing reports to our accounting firm, Merki and Associates. In addition, to those duties she continues to teach Love and Logic Parenting classes and frequently goes on speaking engagements to share her story and the work she does at Cumberland.

Facilities continues to offer successes and challenges. Our maintenance team has been working hard to keep our campus looking great. All of our roofs and gutters were replaced in 2016. Of course, our team continues to work hard to meet the growing needs of our campus and take on the various renovations that are necessary for our expansion. Our kitchen in Stricklen Hall is complete offering a wonderful space for our staff and residents to fellowship together. A fresh look at revenue potential for Stricklen Hall continues to be on the horizon. The completion of the kitchen, supported by a grant, was a step in the right direction for this goal.

Programming and Development. Our programming team is working hard on communication with development to fulfill our pyramid of support by driving what is being asked by what is needed by those we serve. With the creation of Debbie Garrett's listing of needs and grant proposal documentation, programming has a way to communicate what is needed in various areas. Our other integral member of the team, Mary Dickerman is working on putting programming needs first and foremost when creating PR communication with our donors and community. Mary's diligence to organize and catalog deposits and donations makes managing our financials much easier.

III. GIVING

Cumberland Presbyterian Children's Home exists today because of the commitment Cumberland Presbyterian individuals and congregations have made in giving every year and through planned gifts. In her will, Miss Victoria Jackson of Bowling Green, Kentucky, created a home for widows and orphans. Her final act of generosity has allowed thousands of lives to be touched by this ministry. For the past 111 years, many faithful and forward thinking people have blessed the children's home, including the increasingly needed family services, with annually recurring and estate gifts.

We are grateful that more than half of CP churches made direct gifts to the children's home this last year. Through these reliable annual gifts and the endowment built from planned giving, Cumberland Presbyterian Children's Home can keep the church's promise to do more than house, clothe and feed our children. The opportunities for spiritual growth and practical life skills for children and families would not exist without the continued prayers and support from the women and men of Cumberland Presbyterian Churches.

We promise to be good stewards of what you give. When you do your own kitchen table bookkeeping, you know that costs for basic goods increase. We never take the sacrifice you are making for granted. Thank you for helping us keep up with the high cost of providing the one on one relationship building that true change requires, especially when we are focused upon vulnerable and traumatized children and families.

We strive to fulfill the mission to which we believe we have been called. The Cumberland Presbyterian Children's Home does not warehouse residents. We seek to enrich the lives of children, teens and families who have been trapped in the cycle of abuse and neglect like so many children and families in our community and yours. Through your donations, we provide direct care to vulnerable children and families.

We also strive to create a model for care that can be duplicated in homes and campuses anywhere. How can we not take care of the need in front of us? But how can we limit our reach to just the need in front of us? We partner with you to become Christ's tender and caring touch to His traumatized children in whatever place and circumstance. Thank you for your generous giving.

IV. FINANCIAL

Expenses

Based on the unaudited 2016 Financial Statements, Cumberland spent just over $3 million bringing healing and hope to children and families. About 87% of our costs provided care to our residents and clients

Income

Again based on the unaudited 2016 Financial Statements, Cumberland derived operational income from the following sources:

Contributions	47.7%
Service Compensation	41.8%
Investment Income	8.2%
Other	2.3%
Total	100.0%

NOTE: The fee for service we receive in Service Compensation covers only a fraction of what it takes to enrich the lives of our cottage residents. Your gifts and contributions make it possible for traumatized youth to make a new beginning.

V. STRATEGIC PLAN

Strategic Vision

1. *Define, implement and celebrate the Cumberland Model*
2. *Engage, educate and energize the Cumberland Community*
3. *Achieve financial viability*

3-Year Strategic Objectives

1. **Define, implement and celebrate the "Cumberland Model"**
   - Protect, prevent, educate and lead
   - End abuse and neglect by stopping the cycle of violence
   - Provide trauma informed care to children and families
   - Equip families with tools to be happy and successful through counseling, case management and parenting training
   - Increase client success and staff satisfaction by driving programs with evidence based results
   - Research and publish about the Cumberland Model in sufficient detail for other service providers to use it as a pattern
   - Brand the "Cumberland Model" and promote it
   - Increase Cumberland's profile among State, Federal and private child and family social service providers

2. **Engage, educate and energize the Cumberland Community.**
   - Engage
     - Inform and educate the Board at least monthly regarding service and finances
     - Expand the Volunteer Program for more direct involvement opportunities
     - Develop an on going board curriculum and training program about trauma informed care and Board governance
     - Implement effective communication among stakeholders
     - Create a plan for continuously identifying, vetting, recruiting and orienting new board members
     - Use Board committees as well as the full board for effective long and short term impact (e.g., add a Building and Grounds Committee and use ad hoc committees for projects)
     - Plan and practice board led donor identification and recruiting
     - Recruit new board members strategically to fill gaps in expertise and financial capacity

   - Educate
     - Provide accurate, consistent and timely financial reports to Board and staff
     - Develop Board new member orientation as well as continuing education
     - Become the primary child and family social service resource for the Cumberland Presbyterian Church and other faith based communities

- Energize
    - Promote the CPCH brand locally with the Denton, faith, business, denominational, legal and nonprofit communities
    - Initiate an annual six figure signature fundraising event
    - Consider the most effective name for the agency

3. **Achieve financial viability.**
    - Balance the annual budget
    - Revenue
        - Add a fourth leg on the revenue stool by creating and implementing a social enterprise plan
        - Initiate a Planned Giving Program
        - Plan and execute a Capital Campaign to revitalize infrastructure and grow the annual fund
        - Transform our Denton real estate into a long term sustainable revenue stream
        - Apply for no fewer than 12 grants per year
    - Stewardship
        - Prepare a contingent plan responsive to exigent circumstances by moving from direct care to case management staffing (e.g., Single Parent Family rather than Foster Care, Supervised Independent Living program rather than Foster Care, or add a Child Placing Agency)
        - Continue to improve the management of the agency by rewarding cooperation, communication and collaboration among the programs and administration
        - Manage Agency budget at the direct care, program administration, executive and board levels by improving cooperation, communication and collaboration

VI. PRESIDENT'S MESSAGE

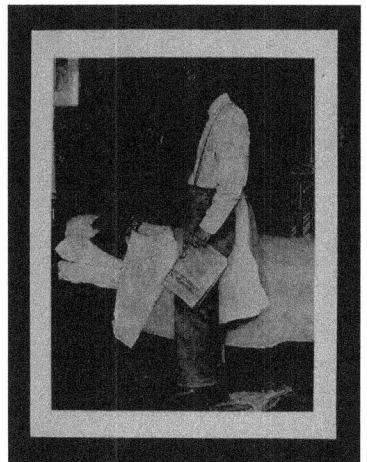

Norman Rockwell "Freedom From Fear"

We are not the first to live in challenging times. Will lessons from the past inform and inspire?

A few monthw ago I attended the third of four funerals during January that touched our Cumberland community. Dr. Livings' grandfather, Donald Fielding, died at the age of 94. Mr. Fielding survived the depression, served in the Army Air Corp during WWII, became a successful small businessman in Highland Park, Dallas (at a time when what is now North Park Mall was farmland "far north" of downtown Dallas) and spent a lifetime serving the powerless. He truly represented the greatest generation.

Mr. Fielding received the Boy Scout's Silver Beaver Award for his distinguished service, in large part for the work he did in the poorest of poor neighborhoods of west Dallas to bring Scouting to kids who got few breaks and had fewer resources. He became an early proponent of school desegregation and fair representation for minorities on the Dallas City Council. His legacy of compassion and protection for the weak, forgotten and young survives through the generations in the work his granddaughter, Dr. Jennifer Livings, tirelessly provides to the Children's Home today.

We are faced with numerous and overwhelming challenges at the Children's Home. I wonder what Don Fielding would say to us? What might Victoria Jackson, Reverend J. L. Elliott, Doctor James Gilbert, Doctor. Judy Keith or Doctor Kevin Henson say to encourage and inspire us? Our almost 113 year history has included many moments of great stress and uncertainty. Yet we have continued to serve children and families despite dark challenges. We do what our foremothers and forefathers have always done: we pay attention to what is going on around us, our hearts be broken with compassion and we roll up our sleeves.

It would be easy to succumb to a paralyzing fear that saps our strength and blunts our reason. I confess that moments during the last year have seemed more than I personally could bear. But as I sat reflectively at Mr. Fielding's funeral service, thinking I was there to represent Cumberland and support a colleague, I began to receive far more than I could give. We have hope. We have strength as a committed body of the community of faith. We act in love, whose power casts out fear. Reading news headlines about the death of children in foster care and listening to legislators jockey for power on the backs of society's most vulnerable populations sometimes seems like we are battling with principalities and powers. At Cumberland we lift up a vision of God's care for the little children and God's nurture of the families in which the children live.

Let FDR's speech and Norman Rockwell's image focus our attention. Let us seek freedom from fear. Our residents are safe. Our clients are learning to withstand threats. The political and economic forces that threaten our future cannot overwhelm the vision God has given us to take care of children and families. God has truly shined in the darkness--for almost 113 year at the Cumberland Presbyterian Children's Home--and the darkness couldn't put it out. May we be faithful to God's vision as we discern it, may we be courageous to act and may we humbly seek God's blessing as we try to follow God's leading.

So now we roll up our sleeves.

2016 Recap

1. Programs
- We served children and families. Our outputs remained stable or increased in the General Residential Operation and Single Parent Family programs, with an increase in the number of people we served. Cumberland Family Services provided higher outcomes for the clients served but operated much of the year with fewer counselors so fewer clients were served compared to 2015.
- We have seen a dramatic increase in the number of engaged volunteers and interns under Debbie Garrett's, Katie Klein's and Christine Snow's leadership. This is a cost effective way to help accomplish our mission.
- We are learning to play smarter and measure our results better. Leadership has taken advantage of an anonymous donation and a scholarship to attend training on measuring outcomes and obtaining more grants.

2. Development
- We focused efforts on identifying donors and asking them for money.
- We vastly improved communication with stakeholders through media and personal visits.
- We have received wisdom and guidance from the Advisory Committee.
- We increased Social Media presence through the work of Debbie Garrett who coordinated with the Program staff.
- Saw gains in PR, media penetration and external exposure in the faith based and local community through Mary Dickerman's efforts.
- Previous Board and Executive leadership increased engagement and support.

3. Finance
- Our 2016 fee for service revenue exceeded our budget projection.
- Several Building & Grounds expenses exceeded our budget: roofing hail damage, Parr HVAC heat handlers, Stricklen kitchen renovation, replacement of phone system and Shelter expansion.
- Our largest cost center, our payroll, was under our budget estimate for 2016.
- We had an increase in Property and Casualty insurance premium.
- We vetted and adopted a 2017 budget sustaining our current service delivery model.
- Spent 2016 learning a new accounting process with our external accounting service.
- Began the discussion about alternative revenue sources beyond our current endowment, fee for service and contributions.

4. Administration
- We successfully updated the Strategic Vision and Strategic Goals
- Cumberland's reputation among foster care peers and stakeholders continued to expand.
- We focused on engaging long time friends of the agency with efforts like the Advisory Committee, reconstituted Ambassador program and creation of the Board Alumni Association.

2017 Plan

1. Monitor Shelter expansion to see if CPS continues to need it, to see if it can give effective service, and if the agency can be sustained fiscally.
2. Increase our share of Section 8 SPF revenue by serving qualified families.
3. Continue the conversation and effort and effort we've begun to maximize our revenue by using our natural resources, social enterprise opportunity, endowment and planned giving.
4. Continue to monitor the foster care industry trends, especially as they relate to our service delivery model.
5. Consider the cost, benefit and alternatives to our service delivery model.

Conclusion: Tough Choices and Hard Work but no Spirit of Fear

2016 did not end as well as we had hoped. The challenges continue. 2017 may bring economic increase. But we must focus on the means under our control to eliminate the deficit. I believe if we faithfully act to serve the children and families, we will be sustained, as we have for almost 113 years.

2 Timothy 1:7 King James Version
⁷ For God hath not given us the spirit of fear; but of power, and of love, and of a sound mind.

Respectfully Submitted,
Reverend Richard A. Brown, Esq., LCCA
President, CEO & General Counsel

THE REPORT OF THE
JOINT COMMITTEE ON AMENDMENTS

The Joint Committee on Amendments met February 24, 2017, in Huntsville, Alabama. Representing the CPCA were Willie Cowan and Vanessa Midgett. Representing the CPC were Harry Chapman and Robert Rush. Also present were Craig White (Stated Clerk, CPCA), Mike Sharpe (Stated clerk, CPC), Jaime Jordan (legal counsel, CPC), and Andy McClung (secretary).

I. RULES OF ORDER

Currently, our Rules of Order 12.5 reads, "No member should vote on a question in which the member has a direct personal or pecuniary interest not common to other members of the judicatory. This does not mean that members are prevented from voting for themselves for an office or other position to which members generally are eligible (see Robert's Rules of Order, Section 44)."

This rule helps judicatory members maintain personal integrity by saying no member of a judicatory should vote on a question in which he or she has a conflict of interest, be it personal, financial, or other. It does not, however, prohibit such a member from voting or participating in discussion. This leaves open the possibility and temptation for a member with a conflict of interest to unduly influence the discussion and vote during a judicatory meeting. Therefore, to help preserve personal integrity of members and to prevent biased and undue influence in such discussion and votes, the Joint Committee on Amendments recommends to the 187th general Assembly of the CPC and the 142nd General Assembly of the CPCA the following amendment to our shared Rules of Order:

RECOMMENDATION 1: That Rules of Order 12.5 be amended to read *"No member of a judicatory shall participate in debate or vote on a matter in which the member has a pecuniary interest, a personal interest, or other conflict of interest not common to other members of the judicatory. A member of a judicatory has such a conflict of interest when the member also belongs to a lower judicatory whose action is the subject of an appeal to or review by the higher judicatory. In such a case, the member may participate as a representative of the lower judicatory but may not participate as a member of the higher judicatory. Members are not prevented from voting for themselves for an office or other position to which members generally are eligible (see Robert's Rules of Order, Section 45)."*

Note that revisions to Robert's Rules of Order necessitate the change from "Section 44" to "Section 45."

II. CONSTITUTION

The exciting and robust mission efforts of the CPC in developing new churches, elders, and ministers outside of the United States have been fruitful. They have also revealed the need to do some portions of such ministry slightly different than how we do things within the U.S. The CPC's Missions Ministry Team and Permanent Judiciary Committee have developed a solution. In order to maintain constitutional integrity while continuing this expansion of the Church, the Joint Committee on Amendments recommends to the 187th general Assembly of the CPC and the 142nd General Assembly of the CPCA the following amendment to our shared Constitution:

RECOMMENDATION 2: That Constitution 9.5 be renumbered as 9.6 and a new 9.5 be inserted, reading as follows: *"9.5 The General Assembly, in order to promote the mission work of the Church and the development of new churches outside the United States, may authorize a synod or its missions entity (utilizing ordained personnel) to act in place of a presbytery with respect to persons, ministers, and churches outside the United States and outside the bounds of any existing presbytery. The missions entity or synod may attach mission work to an existing presbytery, with the presbytery's approval. The General Assembly shall provide for the oversight and responsibility of the body's ecclesiastical actions."*

Respectfully,
The Joint Committee on Amendments

THE REPORT OF THE JOINT COMMITTEE ON THE COVENANT RELATIONSHIP BETWEEN THE GENERAL ASSEMBLY CORPORATION AND BETHEL UNIVERSITY

A special committee to review the covenant relationship between Bethel University and the General Assembly Corporation of the Cumberland Presbyterian Church met on the campus of Bethel University. Sandra Boaz, Lisa Oliver, Tony Janner and Steve Delashmit, representing the General Assembly Corporation, met with the Bethel Board of Trustees Committee members Board Chairman Ben Cantrell, Dewanna Latimer, Nancy McSpadden and Bill Dobbins. Stated Clerk of the General Assembly, Mike Sharpe and Bethel University President, Walter Butler, were in attendance. Naomi Orr of the General Assembly Committee and Ken Quinton of the Bethel Board of Trustees were unable to attend.

Stated Clerk Mike Sharpe discussed the history of the covenant between the church and the university. The closeness of the two had remained intact with this covenant. Walter Butler stressed the importance of being connected to the Cumberland Presbyterian Church and told of some things that are happening at Bethel in its 175th year of existence. The Board members and its president commented of their commitment to always being the Cumberland Presbyterian University and adhere to its values. They will continue to report to the General Assembly Corporation. The support of the Cumberland Presbyterian Church and its membership towards Bethel was noted and greatly appreciated. The university continues to serve Cumberland Presbyterian students, host Cumberland Presbyterian events and support the Memphis Theological Seminary.

The only change in the document was changes made by the Bethel Board of Trustees in its mode of delivery in the mission statement. This reflects Bethel's large online enrollment.

RECOMMENDATION 1: The Joint Committee on the Covenant Relationship Recommends the Adoption of the Following Document:

THE COVENANT BETWEEN BETHEL UNIVERSITY AND CUMBERLAND PRESBYTERIAN CHURCH

I. HISTORICAL RELATIONSHIP BETWEEN BETHEL UNIVERSITY AND THE CUMBERLAND PRESBYTERIAN CHURCH

Bethel University was established in McLemoresville, Tennessee in 1842 as a Cumberland Presbyterian School, under the auspices of the Synod of West Tennessee. The initial purpose was the education and training of ministers, but the school was open to anyone who wanted an education in a moral and religious environment. The school was chartered under the laws of the State of Tennessee in 1847. Bethel College came into being in 1850 under a new state charter granting the college all the rights and privileges of a full collegiate institution.

The Civil War brought hard times to Bethel College and McLemoresville. The area was equally divided between Union and Confederate forces and the college was occasionally occupied by each army. The structures and equipment were damaged, but the greater loss was, the student body who served on both sides of the conflict. Bethel College was re-organized at McLemoresville after the Civil War and in 1872 it was relocated to McKenzie, Tennessee, to take advantage of the crossroads between North Carolina and St. Louis and the L&N Railways. J.M. McKenzie deeded the land for Bethel to the Bethel Board of Trustees on February 2, 1872.

The Synod of West Tennessee ceded Bethel College to the General Assembly of the Cumberland Presbyterian Church in 1919. McKenzie, Tennessee was voted as the permanent location for the college at the General Assembly of 1922 in Greenville, Tennessee.

Bethel College was thoroughly re-organized and standardized in 1923. Bethel College became a four-year Liberal Arts college, chartered by the State of Tennessee and accredited by the Commission on Colleges of Southern Association of Colleges and Schools. In light of Bethel's growth, complexity and impact, the Board of Trustees recognized the need for Bethel College to become Bethel University which occurred in 2009. The University is chartered by the State of Tennessee and accredited by the Commission on Colleges of Southern Association of Colleges and Schools.

II. NATURE AND PURPOSE OF THE COVENANT RELATIONSHIP

The relationship that exists between Bethel University and the Cumberland Presbyterian Church is defined and characterized by the word "covenant." The term "covenant" is rooted in biblical and theological understanding and has found its highest expression among God's people. Thus, covenant within the family of God implies the deepest level of trust between covenanting parties and of commitment to one another. A Christian covenant is a living agreement that offers both parties opportunities for creative adaptation to meet the ever-changing conditions of our world. This covenant, moreover, frees each party from being controlled or ultimately responsible for or to each other, but unites the two parties through their common vision and missions. It seeks to honor the legal independence of each party while retaining and ongoing, mutual moral responsibility.

This covenant relationship does not preclude the university from forming other covenant relationships with other Church bodies.

III. THE ONGOING MISSION OF EACH COVENANT PARTY

A. THE MISSION OF BETHEL UNIVERSITY

Bethel University's mission is to create opportunities for members of the learning community to develop in a Christian environment their highest intellectual, spiritual and social potential. This includes synchronous and asynchronous modes of education.

B. THE MISSION OF THE GENERAL ASSEMBLY CORPORATION
Vision of Ministry of the Cumberland Presbyterian Church

> Biblically based and Christ-centered
> Born out of specific sense of mission,
> The Cumberland Presbyterian Church strives to be true to its heritage:
> > To be open to God's reforming Spirit,
> > To work cooperatively with the larger Body of Christ,
> > and to nurture the connectional bonds that make us one,

The Cumberland Presbyterian Church seeks to be the hands and feet of Christ in witness and service to the world and above all the Cumberland Presbyterian Church lives out the love of God to the glory of Jesus Christ.

IV. THE CORPORATE INTEGRITY OF EACH COVENANT PARTY

A. Bethel University and the Cumberland Presbyterian Church are separate, legally independent and individually responsible entities.

B. Bethel University will be governed by a self-perpetuating Board of Trustees, with no less than a majority of its total membership as active members of the Cumberland Presbyterian Church.

C. Neither the General Assembly Corporation nor any of the General Assembly's councils, boards, agents, officers, or employees shall be liable for any of the debts of Bethel University. In similar fashion, Bethel University is not liable for any of the debts of the Cumberland Presbyterian Church or its agencies, nor does it have a claim on any of the assets of the Cumberland Presbyterian Church or its agencies.

V. COMMITMENT OF EACH PARTY TO THE COVENANT

Both Bethel University and the General Assembly Corporation will demonstrate mutual concern and support for one another. The primary expression of mutual concern and support will involve relationships between the two parties that provide services for each other.

A. THE COMMITMENTS OF BETHEL UNIVERSITY

Bethel University will be a resource to the Cumberland Presbyterian Church and its constituencies for educational purposes related to the Church's mission.

Bethel University is free to solicit funds for both capital and operating expenses from individual and Cumberland Presbyterian and other persons, congregations, presbyteries, trustees, foundations, estates, and any other sources. Any major capital campaign initiated by Bethel University with targets primarily Presbyteries, Synods, and Congregations of the Cumberland Presbyterian Church will be scheduled by mutual consent of Bethel University and the General Assembly Corporation through the Office of the Stated Clerk.

B. The General Assembly Corporation will provide financial support for the university by regular benevolent giving in accordance with an objective funding formula developed by the General Assembly Corporation.

The General Assembly Corporation will encourage support of Bethel University by Synods, Presbyteries, sessions and individual Cumberland Presbyterians through planned giving programs.

The General Assembly Corporation pledges programmatic support to the university by encouraging use of personnel and facilities of the university for denominational events, emphasizing the opportunities afforded by church-related higher education in its youth ministry programs, and providing the specialized services of the denominational Board of Stewardship, Foundation and Benefits.

VI. REVIEW AND REAFFIRMATION OF THE COVENANTAL RELATIONSHIP

There will be a review, and if necessary, revision of the covenant relationship every five years. The General Assembly Corporation and the Board of Trustees of Bethel University will see that such a review is accomplished through appropriate committees. These committees will be appointed by the respective entities.

The review process will be initiated by the administration of the university and the review/reaffirmation process shall consist of an in-depth review of all aspects of the university. The review process will be designed by the administration of the university and a review committee elected by the General Assembly Corporation. The review shall include consideration of changes and/or amendments to the Covenant relationship, as well as any suggestions to the university and the General Assembly resulting from the review. The administration of the university and the General Assembly Corporation committee shall produce a joint written report of the review process to be signed by the General Assembly Corporation Committee and the President of the university and submitted to both the Bethel Board of Trustees and the General Assembly Corporation.

Responsibility for approval of any change in the covenant resides with the Board of Trustees of Bethel University and the General Assembly Corporation. This agreement may be modified or altered prior to the reaffirmation process only with the consent of both parties.

VII. COMMUNICATION BETWEEN COVENANT PARTNERS

Bethel University and the Church will communicate concerning the affairs of the university and the strength of the relationship at least every five years during the reaffirmation and renewal of the covenant. However, Bethel University is encouraged to submit information-only reports through the Stated Clerk to any meeting of the General Assembly Corporation.

VIII. APPROVAL OF THE COVENANT

This document establishes and contains the terms of the covenant relationship between the Cumberland Presbyterian Church and Bethel University. By formal action, the Board of Trustees of Bethel University and the General Assembly Corporation adopt this Covenant and pledge themselves to carry out its provisions.

Approved by the Board of Trustees Bethel University

_____
President, Bethel University
Board of Trustees

_____
President, Bethel University

Approved by the 187th General Assembly Of the Cumberland Presbyterian

_____
General Assembly Stated Clerk

_____
Date

Respectfully Submitted,
The Bethel University Covenant Review Committee

THE REPORT OF THE JOINT COMMITTEE ON THE COVENANT RELATIONSHIP BETWEEN THE GENERAL ASSEMBLY CORPORATION AND THE CUMBERLAND PRESBYTERIAN CHILDREN'S HOME

Consistent with Article VI of the Covenant Between the Cumberland Presbyterian Children's Home and the Cumberland Presbyterian Church General Assembly Corporation ("Covenant"), representatives from the Cumberland Presbyterian Children's Home ("Children's Home" or "CPCH") Board of Trustees and the Cumberland Presbyterian Church General Assembly Corporation ("General Assembly" or "GA") representatives, a Covenant Review Committee ("Committee") met on the grounds of the Children's Home on 21 April 2017 to review the Covenant. The Committee fully and without reservation embraced the intent and purpose of the Covenant and recommends renewal and affirmation of the Covenant (see Appendix A) with the following revisions.

The revisions are offered in the form of Addendum Number One which preserves the language of the original Covenant while reflecting an update via additions and supplements to the original terms.

RECOMMENDATION 1: The Joint Committee on the Covenant Relationship Recommends the Adoption of the Following Document:

The Addendum Number One
22 April 2017

I. HISTORICAL RELATIONSHIP BETWEEN THE CUMBERLAND PRESBYTERIAN CHILDREN'S HOME AND THE CUMBERLAND PRESBYTERIAN CHURCH

The Mission Statement of the Cumberland Presbyterian Children's Home has been revised to read. "In response to Christ's love and example, we serve children and families by providing healing and hope."
The Children's Home is in its 113th year of operation as a ministry of the General Assembly.
As the Children's Home entered the 21st Century, it maintained its core values while updating its delivery of services to fulfill its ministry. Today, CPCH is one ministry with four interrelated programs -- Long Term Residential Foster Care, Emergency Residential Foster Care, Single Parent Family residential and service program and Cumberland Family Services counseling.

II. . . . .

III. . . . .

IV. THE LEGAL RELATIONSHIP AND THE CORPORATE INTEGRITY OF EACH COVENANT PARTY

Separate Legal Entities.
    a. Governance of CPCH. CPCH's Certificate of Formation and By-Laws provide that it shall be managed by a Board of Trustees, of which at least 10 of the 18 Trustees must be members of a local Cumberland Presbyterian Church or Presbytery.

VII. APPROVAL OF THE COVENANT

This document and subsequent Addendums establishes and contains the terms of the Covenant relationship between the Board of Trustees of the Cumberland Presbyterian Children's Home and the Cumberland Presbyterian Church General Assembly Corporation.

This Addendum Number One is signed on the _____ day of _____ 2017.

Cumberland Presbyterian Church
General Assembly Corporation

Board of Trustees of the
Cumberland Presbyterian Children's Home

_____
The Rev. Michael Sharpe
Stated Clerk

_____
The Rev. Dr. Richard A. Brown
President, CEO & General Counsel

Respectfully,
The Joint Committee on the Covenant Between the Cumberland Presbyterian Children's Home and the General Assembly Corporation

APPENDIX A

THE COVENANT BETWEEN
THE CUMBERLAND PRESBYTERIAN CHILDREN'S HOME
AND
THE CUMBERLAND PRESBYTERIAN CHURCH
GENERAL ASSEMBLY CORPORATION

I. HISTORICAL RELATIONSHIP BETWEEN THE CUMBERLAND PRESBYTERIAN CHILDREN'S HOME AND THE CUMBERLAND PRESBYTERIAN CHURCH

The mission statement of the Cumberland Presbyterian Children's Home reminds all that CPCH is and always has been a ministry of the Cumberland Presbyterian Church. The mission statement reads: "As an ecumenical ministry of the Cumberland Presbyterian Church in response to Christ's love and example, the Cumberland Presbyterian Children's Home exists to provide a safe and wholesome environment for the development of children and to bring healing and hope to children and their families."

CPCH has a proud 107-year history of bringing healing and hope to vulnerable children, teens and families. Founded in 1904 in Bowling Green, Kentucky, CPCH was created by the gift of a home to be used to house widows and orphans of Cumberland Presbyterian ministers. In 1932, at the request of what was then called the Texas Synod of the Cumberland Presbyterian Church (CPC), CPCH moved to Denton, Texas, and occupied a home on the corner of Avenue A and Greenlee streets. Subsequently, acreage was acquired at the corner of Bernard and Greenlee streets, and CPCH moved to that location in 1939 upon completion of the construction of the Old Main building.

For 94 years, CPCH specialized solely in caring for children and teens in Residential Care. After careful consideration of society's needs at the time and with the goals of preserving families and reducing the need for its residential care services, CPCH launched a transitional housing program for adult single parents in 1999.

In 2007, after further examination of the needs of the community and how CPCH might be able to positively affect the lives of children and families not living on its campus, CPCH began the Family Outfitters Program. The Family Outfitters Program offers parenting and pre-marital education and individual, marital and family counseling on a sliding fee scale.

Today, CPCH is one ministry with three interrelated programs – Residential Care, Single Parent Family, and Family Outfitters – that help children and families find healing and hope through identifying their strengths and finding solutions to the challenges in their lives.

II. NATURE AND PURPOSE OF THE COVENANT RELATIONSHIP

A. COVENANT RELATIONSHIPS IN GENERAL

The relationship that exists between CPCH and the CPC is defined and characterized by the word "covenant." The term "covenant" is rooted in biblical and theological understanding and has found its highest expression among God's people. Thus, covenant within the family of God implies the deepest level of trust between covenanting parties and of commitment to one another. A Christian covenant is a living agreement that offers both parties opportunities for creative adaptation to meet the ever-changing conditions of our world. This covenant, moreover, frees each party from being controlled or ultimately responsible for or to each other, but unites the two parties through their common vision and missions. It seeks to honor the legal independence of each party while retaining an ongoing, mutual moral responsibility.

B. CONFIRMATION OF THE COVENANT RELATIONSHIP

CPCH and CPC hereby confirm their covenant relationship recognizing that the life and work of each is enriched and made more dynamic through this relationship and also recognizing that each party has its own role that can be strengthened through the mutual exchange of ideas, resources, and support for the mission of the other. This covenant does not restrict either party from entering into a covenant relationship with other parties.

a. Purpose of this Document

This document is a current statement of the covenant relationship between CPCH and the CPC. It is intended that this covenant reflect the spiritual bond between the parties and that the governing documents of each party not be inconsistent with this covenant.

III. THE ONGOING MISSION OF EACH COVENANT PARTY

A. THE MISSION OF CPCH

As an ecumenical ministry fostered by the Cumberland Presbyterian Church in response to Christ's love and example, the Cumberland Presbyterian Children's Home exists to provide a safe and wholesome environment for the development of children and to bring healing and hope to children and their families.

B. THE MISSION OF THE CUMBERLAND PRESBYTERIAN CHURCH

The Cumberland Presbyterian church holds the following Vision of Ministry: Biblically based and Christ-centered, born out of a specific sense of mission, the Cumberland Presbyterian Church strives to be true to its heritage: to be open to God's reforming Spirit, to work cooperatively with the larger Body of Christ, and to nurture the connectional bonds that make us one. The Cumberland Presbyterian Church seeks to be the hands and feet of Christ in witness and service to the world and above all, the Cumberland Presbyterian Church lives out of the love of God to the glory of Jesus Christ.

IV. THE LEGAL RELATIONSHIP AND THE CORPORATE INTEGRITY OF EACH COVENANT PARTY

A. SEPARATE LEGAL ENTITIES

The Cumberland Presbyterian Church conducts ministry through its corporate body, Cumberland Presbyterian Church General Assembly Corporation (GA Corporation). CPCH and GA Corporation are separate legal entities.

B. GOVERNANCE OF CPCH

CPCH's Articles of Incorporation provide that it shall be managed by a Board of Trustees at least nine of the 15 Trustees must be members of a local Cumberland Presbyterian Church or Presbytery.

C. DISTRIBUTION OF ASSETS UPON CPCH DISSOLUTION

Upon the dissolution of CPCH and pursuant to a plan of dissolution adopted according to Texas law, assets shall be distributed to GA Corporation.

V. THE COMMITMENT OF EACH PARTY TO THE COVENANT

A. THE COMMITMENT OF BOTH PARTIES

i. Mutual Concern and Support

Both CPCH and the GA Corporation shall at all times demonstrate mutual concern and support for one another and for their respective missions. The primary expression of mutual concern and support shall involve program relationships between CPCH and GA Corporation.

ii. Governing Boards and Communication

In fulfilling the responsibilities of this covenant, CPCH normally acts through its Board of Trustees and GA Corporation through its General Assembly. Continuing communication between CPCH and the CPC should be affirmed and maintained.

B. THE COMMITMENT OF CPCH

CPCH will be a resource to GA Corporation and its constituencies for social service ministry and education related to the Church's mission. CPCH is free to solicit funds for both capital and operating expenses from individual Cumberland Presbyterian and other persons, congregations, presbyteries, trustees, foundations, estates and any other source. Any major capital campaign initiated by CPCH which targets primarily presbyteries, synods, and congregations of the Cumberland Presbyterian Church will be scheduled by mutual consent of CPCH and GA Corporation through the office of the Stated Clerk.

C. THE COMMITMENT OF GENERAL ASSEMBLY CORPORATION

GA Corporation will annually consider providing financial support for CPCH through GA Corporation's annual budget process and the funding formula developed by GA Corporation's OUO Committee. GA Corporation will encourage synods, presbyteries, sessions, and individual Cumberland Presbyterians to support the mission work of CPCH through planned giving programs.

VI. REVIEW AND REAFFIRMATION OF THE COVENANTAL RELATIONSHIP

CPCH and GA Corporation enter into this Covenant with the hope and expectation that it will be reviewed, refined, and affirmed at least every five years.

VII. APPROVAL OF THE COVENANT

This document establishes and contains the terms of the covenant relationship between the Board of Trustees of the Cumberland Presbyterian Children's Home and the Cumberland Presbyterian Church General Assembly Corporation.

MEMORIAL

I. MEMORIAL FROM ANDES PRESBYTERY REGARDING GENDER DIVERSITY

On April 10, 2017, in a duly convened called meeting, Andes Presbytery approved this Memorial to be submitted for consideration by the 187th General Assembly of the Cumberland Presbyterian Church.

WHEREAS the church in Colombia has been pressured by [the politics of] gender ideology that in our context involves promoting a diversity of genders that is openly contrary to the Bible;

WHEREAS our source of authority is from the Bible, and the Bible teaches:
That in Genesis 1:26 God created humankind as man and woman.
That according to Leviticus 18:22 homosexuality is an aberration before God.
"Do not lie with a man as one lies with a woman; that is detestable." (NIV)
That according to Romans 1:26-27 homosexuality is contrary to God's original design.
"Because of this, God gave them over to shameful lusts. Even their women exchanged natural relations for unnatural ones. In the same way the men also abandoned natural relations with women and were inflamed with lust for one another. Men committed indecent acts with other men, and received in themselves the due penalty for their perversion." (NIV)
That according to 1 Corinthians 6:9-10, practicing homosexuals will not enter into the Kingdom of Heaven.
"Do you not know that the wicked will not inherit the kingdom of God? Do not be deceived: Neither the sexually immoral nor idolaters nor adulterers nor male prostitutes nor homosexual offenders nor thieves nor the greedy nor drunkards nor slanders nor swindlers will inherit the kingdom of God." (NIV);

WHEREAS we are Cumberland Presbyterians and take our doctrinal and practical framework from biblical principles;

WHEREAS we note with concern influences from other denominations and groups that are contrary to our doctrine and historical practice;

WHEREAS some of those influences, especially with reference to the Youth Triennium, have already negatively impacted some of our youth;

WHEREAS we wish to prevent those same influences from permeating our educational material and the development and experiential practice of the church's ministries;

BE IT RESOLVES, that Andes Presbytery requests the General Assembly to closely review and monitor programs and institutions that may unduly influence the doctrine and work of the Cumberland Presbyterian Church and thus prevent an infiltration of concepts that are foreign to our doctrine and practice, with special reference to any ideology that promotes a multiplicity of genders [besides man and woman].

I certify that this copy is true to the Memorial approved by Andes Presbytery on April 10, 2017.

Respectfully,
Rev. Diana Maria Valdez

Spanish version

El 10 de abril de 2017, en reunión extraordinaria debidamente convocada, el Presbiterio de los aprobó este Memorial para ser sometido para la consideración de la Asamblea General de la Iglesia Presbiteriana Cumberland en su reunión ordinaria en 2017.

MEMORIAL DEL PRESBITERIO DE LOS ANDES PARA LA ASAMBLEA GENERAL #187 DE 2017

Por cuanto la iglesia en Colombia ha sufrido influencias de la ideología de género. Que en nuestro contexto implica promover una diversidad de géneros que es abiertamente contraria a la Biblia,
Por cuanto nuestra única fuente de autoridad es la Biblia.
La Biblia enseña:

Que Dios creó un hombre y una mujer, en Génesis 1:26

Que la homosexualidad es una aberración delante de Dios:Lv.. 18:22
"No te acostarás con varón como los que se acuestan con mujer; es una abominación."

Que la homosexualidad quebranta el diseño original de Dios: Ro 1:26,27
"^{26} Por esta razón Dios los entregó a pasiones degradantes; porque sus mujeres cambiaron la función natural por la que es contra la naturaleza; ^{27} y de la misma manera también los hombres, abandonando el uso natural de la mujer, se encendieron en su lujuria unos con otros, cometiendo hechos vergonzosos hombres con hombres, y recibiendo en sí mismos el castigo correspondiente a su extravío."

Que los homosexuales practicantes no entrarán en el Reino de los Cielos: 1Co 6:9,10
"^{9} ¿O no sabéis que los injustos no heredarán el reino de Dios? No os dejéis engañar: ni los inmorales, ni los idólatras, ni los adúlteros, ni los afeminados, ni los homosexuales, ^{10} ni los ladrones, ni los avaros, ni los borrachos, ni los difamadores, ni los estafadores heredarán el reino de Dios."

Por cuanto somos Presbiterianos Cumberland y tomamos nuestro marco doctrinal y de práctica de los principios bíblicos.
Por cuanto percibimos con preocupación influencias de otras denominaciones y grupos que son contrarias a nuestra doctrina y práctica histórica.
Por cuanto algunas de esas influencias, especialmente en el trienio juvenil, ya han causado impacto negativo en algunos de nuestros jóvenes.
Por cuanto quisiéramos prevenir que esas mismas influencias llegaran a permear nuestro material educativo y el desarrollo y práctica vivencial de los ministerios

Entonces el Presbiterio de los Andes, solicita a la Asamblea General que revise y vigile muy de cerca los programas e instituciones que puedan influir en el pensamiento doctrina y trabajo de la Iglesia Presbiteriana Cumberland, y así impedir infiltraciones de pensamientos ajenos a nuestra doctrina y práctica, especialmente con referencia a la ideología de género.

Certifico que es copia fiel del Memorial aprobado por el Presbiterio de los Andes el 10 de abril de 2017.

Respetuosamente,
Rev. Diana María Valdez
Secretaria, Presbiterio de los Andes

GENERAL ASSEMBLY AGENCIES

I. OFFICE OF THE GENERAL ASSEMBLY

A. GENERAL ASSEMBLY OFFICE

	Revised 2017	Proposed 2018
INCOME		
Our United Outreach	$212,836	$211,836
Endowments/Interest	20,000	20,000
Interest on Cash Funds Management	2,500	2,500
Sales of yearbook/digest	2,000	2,000
TOTAL INCOME	**$237,336**	**$236,336**
EXPENSE		
ECUMENICAL RELATIONS		
World Communion of Reformed Churches	$ 6,000	$ 6,000
CANAAC	2,000	2,000
Ecumenical Travel	1,000	1,000
Sub-Total	$ 9,000	$ 9,000
LIAISON WITH CHURCH		
General Assembly Meeting	$ 10,000	$ 10,000
Preliminary Minutes	5,000	5,000
GA Minutes/Mailing	500	500
Yearbook/Mailing	2,500	2,500
Travel/Moderator	8,500	8,500
Travel/Stated Clerk & Staff	8,500	8,500
Sub-Total	$ 35,000	$ 35,000
OFFICE		
Computer Supplies	$ 2,000	$ 2,000
Equipment/Supplies	2,500	2,500
Postage	2,000	2,000
Sub-Total	$ 6,500	$ 6,500
PERSONNEL		
Salaries/Housing	$139,420	$139,420
FICA (Asst to Stated Clerk)	4,300	4,300
Retirement	6,800	6,800
Health Insurance	30,000	30,000
Disability Insurance/Worker's Compensation	800	800
Sub-Total	$181,320	$181,320
STATED CLERK'S CONFERENCE/BOARD EXPENSE		
Legal Fees / Clerk's Conference	$ 1,963	$ 1,963
Corporate Board Expense	2,000	2,000
Sub-Total	$ 3,963	$ 3,963
TOTAL EXPENSE	**$235,783**	**$235,783**
From Reserves	$ 1,553	$ 553

B. GENERAL ASSEMBLY COMMISSIONS AND COMMITTEES

	Revised 2017	Proposed 2018
INCOME		
Contingency	$ 14,000	$ 13,240
Nominating Committee	2,981	2,966
Commission on Chaplains	10,296	10,247
Judiciary Committee	9,710	9,965
Theology and Social Concerns Committee	3,618	3,601
Our United Outreach Committee	92,044	92,044
TOTAL INCOME	**$132,649**	**$132,065**

	Revised 2017	Proposed 2018
EXPENSE		
Contingency	$ 14,000	$ 13,240
Nominating Committee	2,981	2,966
Commission on Chaplains	10,296	10,247
Judiciary Committee	9,710	9,965
Theology and Social Concerns Committee	3,618	3,601
Our United Outreach Committee	92,044	92,044
TOTAL EXPENSE	**$132,649**	**$132,065**

II. MINISTRY COUNCIL

	Revised 2017	Proposed 2018
INCOME		
Endowments		
Grants	$ 0	$ 0
ILP Transfers		
MMT Budget Reserve Fund: out ILP	821,992	728,797
DMT Contingency Fund: in Wells Fargo	114,380	21,832
DMT Contingency Fund: in ILP (reimburse)	(37,484)	(39,457)
DMT Leader Development: out ILP	2,002	7,344
CMT: out ILP	1,308	0
Contributions/Gifts		
Teacher of the Year	0	0
Patron Membership (DMT)	0	0
Christian Education Season Offering	0	0
DMT - General	2,900	500
MC - General	5,900	5,900
CMT - General	0	0
Our United Outreach		
OUO Income	992,386	1,002,915
In lieu of Our United Outreach	6,720	6,720
Birthplace Shrine Chaplaincy	3,750	3,750
Children's Fest	6,874	10,100
Clergy Crisis	6,000	6,000
CP Magazine Subscriptions	30,000	30,000
Cumberland Presbyterians Resources	80,112	80,112
CPWM		
Convention	10,000	10,000
Convention Offering	250	250
General	1,000	1,000
Sales Merchandise	700	700
CPYC	66,132	86,707
Discipleship Blueprints	2,400	2,400
Encounter	105,224	105,224
Faith Out Loud	9,000	0

	Revised 2017	Proposed 2018
Faith in 3D	$ 5,000	$ 0
Family Week: Brochure Fees	1,500	300
Global Missions Interns and Consultants: out ILP	20,000	36,000
Intersections	2,380	0
Ministers Conference	10,000	10,000
Missionary Setup	124,000	0
Missionary Support	327,601	333,078
New Church Development (NCD) Subsidies	213,646	213,646
New Exploration Iniative - NCD	12,000	12,000
NPI: Children's CP Curriculum	600	0
NPI: Learning Circles	0	0
Presbyterian Youth Triennium	0	6,500
Program Planning Calendar - Sales	920	920
Stir	5,000	5,000
The Forum	9,992	0
Young Adult Ministry	2,500	1,168
Youth Evangelism Conference	36,000	0
Youth Ministry Planning Council	648	648
TOTAL INCOME	**$2,903,333**	**$2,684,334**

EXPENSES

Ministry Council Administration Salaries

Salaries	$ 805,041	$ 754,985
Clergy Housing Allowance	167,216	163,108
Health Insurance	133,248	133,248
Retirement	37,537	43,092
FICA	34,774	32,468
Tax Sheltered Annuity	6,287	6,287
Insurance/Disability	3,168	4,096

Ministry Council Administration General Expenses

Annual Credit Card Fees	$ 3,678	$ 3,678
Computer Equipment	0	0
Computer Software (Wufoo, Adobe, BaseCamp)	10,000	10,000
CPCA Partnership	0	0
Educational Publications for Distribution	3,000	3,000
Employee Events	2,500	2,500

	Revised 2017	Proposed 2018
Employee Recognition	3,450	3,450
Foundation Direcory Online	500	500
Government Fees (annual reports)	40	40
Legal	2,000	2,000
MC Supplemental Report	5,000	0
P & C Insurance	17,162	19,090
Staff Resource Materials	1,997	1,997
Subscriptions/Membership	2,558	2,246
Telephone/Internet	624	624
Temporary Help	29,150	29,150
MC/Elected Team Member Recognition	1,040	1,040
Office Supplies	12,000	12,000
Postage	1,800	1,800
Professional Development	0	0
Beth-El Farmworker	$ 40,500	$ 40,500
Birthplace Shrine Chaplaincy: Chaplain's Stipend	3,750	3,750
Children's Fest	7,154	10,100
Clergy Crisis Support: Distribution	6,000	6,000
Coalition of Applachian Ministry	12,700	12,700
Congregational Expenses	3,000	3,000
CP Magazine	54,033	54,033
Cumberland Presbyterian Resources	67,628	67,628
CPWM		
General	7,100	7,100
Sales Merchandise	5,300	2,000
Convention	11,950	11,950
Offering	250	250
CPYC	65,550	86,050
Cross-Culture Immigrant Leadership Training	4,000	4,000
Discipleship Blueprints	2,400	2,400
Ecumenical Stewardship Center	4,500	4,500
Ecumenical Youth Ministry Staff Team Partnership	500	0
Encounter	38,012	38,012
Faith in 3D - Partnership	5,000	0
Faith Out Loud	9,000	0
Family Week	$ 1,500	$ 300

	Revised 2017	Proposed 2018
General Assembly	32,800	32,750
General Consultants	34,800	36,000
Global Mission Interns and Consultants	20,000	7,200
Intersections	6,270	0
Kaleo	5,000	0
Leadership Referral Services	2,100	2,100
Leader Development	0	5,492
Ministers		
Conference	16,000	16,000
Encouragement & Recognition	3,818	3,818
Retreat	1,000	1,000
Missionary Messenger	78,348	75,144
Missionary Setup	124,000	0
Missionary Support	372,601	388,078
National Farm Worker	3,500	3,500
National Youth Workers Conference	2,000	0
New Church Development (NCD) Subsidies	215,996	215,996
New Exploration Initiative	12,000	12,000
New Program Iniatives		
Children's Curriculum	600	200
CPWM Girls and Young Women Council	10,200	9,800
CP Learning Circles	6,000	6,000
DMT	12,000	12,000
PREP Staff Expenses	996	996
Presbyterial Expenses	3,000	3,000
Presbyterian Youth Triennium	10,000	5,000
Presbyteries/Councils	141,220	130,120
Program Planning Calendar	5,150	5,150
Project Vida	8,500	8,500
Prostestant Church Owned Pub Assoc (DMT)	200	200
Stir	5,000	5,000
Support Ministries	1,000	1,000
The Forum	300	0
Third Age Ministry	500	500
Travel (includes elected member travel)	85,210	78,410
Web Development/Maintenance	$ 1,200	$ 2,000

	Revised 2017	Proposed 2018
Young Adult Conference	18,500	0
Young Adult Ministry	2,500	8,000
Young Adult Volunteers	5,000	5,000
Youth Evangelism Conference	10,000	10,000
Youth Ministry Planning Council - UBCD	2,500	2,500
TOTAL EXPENSES	**$2,901,405**	**$ 2,682,126**
Surplus/(Deficit)	$ 1,927	$ 2,208

III. BOARD OF STEWARDSHIP

INCOME

	Revised 2017	Proposed 2018
Contributions		
Contributions/Gifts	$ 26,000	$ 26,000
ILP Contributions	2,000	2,000
Endowment Contributions	400	1,000
Total Contributions	**28,400**	**29,000**
Our United Outreach	136,000	136,000
Investment Earnings		
Endowment Earnings	92,000	98,000
ILP Earnings	14,000	16,000
Endowment WF Income	18,000	19,000
Total Investment Earnings	**124,000**	**133,000**
Realized Gain/Loss - Endowment	20,000	22,000
Unrealized Gain/Loss - Endowment	94,000	99,500
Total Investment Gains/Losses	**114,000**	**121,500**
Service Fees		
Management Fees - Acct Coordinator	1,600	1,600
Management Fees	51,000	55,000
Total Service Fees	**52,600**	**56,600**
TOTAL INCOME	**$455,000**	**$ 476,100**

EXPENSE

	Revised 2017	Proposed 2018
Salaries		
Salaries	$214,277	$ 220,159
Housing Allowance	21,000	21,000
Total Salaries	**235,277**	**241,159**
Benefits		
Health Insurance	64,000	70,000
Retirement	10,746	10,746
FICA	9,630	9,630
Insurance/Disability	800	800
Total Benefits	**85,176**	**91,176**
Events		
Conference/Events	500	500
Tax Guide for Ministers	3,700	3,700
Total Events	**4,200**	**4,200**
Board Expense		
Board/Agency Travel	12,000	15,000
Board/Agency Recognition	$ 600	$ 600
Total Board Expense	**12,600**	**15,600**

	Revised 2017	Proposed 2018
Resource Purchases		
Subscriptions	100	100
Total Resources Purchases	**100**	**100**
Contracted Services		
Legal	500	500
Temporary Help	1,000	1,000
Total Contracted Services	**1,500**	**1,500**
Insurance		
Insurance/Liability	4,000	4,000
	4,000	4,000
Professional Development		
Subscriptions & Membership	500	500
Total Professional Development	**500**	**500**
Payment/Subsidies		
ESC Stewardship Expense	3,500	3,500
ILP Withdrawal	2,500	2,500
Endowment Distribution	92,000	98,000
Total Payments/Subsidies	**98,000**	**104,000**
Equipment		
Office Equipment	800	800
Computer Equipment	2,000	2,000
Computer Maintenance	150	150
Computer Software	$ 500	$ 500
Total Equipment	**3,450**	**3,450**
Supplies		
Computer Supplies	500	500
Office Supplies	2,500	2,500
Total Supplies	**3,000**	**3,000**
Postage/Shipping		
Postage	1,000	1,000
Shipping	167	167
Total Postage/Shipping	**1,167**	**1,167**
Employee Recognition		
Employee Recognition	1,000	1,000
Total Employee Recognition	**1,000**	**1,000**
Travel		
Staff Travel	4,500	4,500
Total Travel	**4,500**	**4,500**
Miscellaneous		
Miscellaneous	430	648
Total Miscellaneous	**430**	**647**
Organization		
Organizational Expense	100	100
Total Organization	**100**	**100**
TOTAL EXPENSE	**$455,000**	**$ 476,100**

IV. HISTORICAL FOUNDATION

INCOME		
Our United Outreach	$ 79,439	$ 79,439
Endowments	55,000	55,000
Gifts	11,000	11,000
ILP Earnings	6,550	7,550
Denomination Day Offering	5,000	5,000
TOTAL INCOME	**$ 156,989**	**$ 157,989**

	Revised 2017	Proposed 2018
EXPENSE		
Salaries	$ 93,141	$ 95,088
FICA / Retirement	14,053	14,404
Insurance	10,034	10,034
Board Travel	5,000	5,000
Legal Fees	200	200
Continuing Education	1,000	1,000
Subscriptions/Memberships	2,000	2,000
Archival Equipment	2,000	2,000
Computer Supplies	500	500
Office Supplies	2,000	2,000
Postage	300	300
Acquisitions	8,000	8,000
Birthplace Shrine	4,000	4,000
Employee Recognition	600	600
Staff Travel	7,000	7,000
Denomination Day Project	5,000	5,000
TOTAL EXPENSE	**$ 154,828**	**$ 157,126**

V. MEMPHIS THEOLOGICAL SEMINARY

	Revised 2017	Proposed 2018
REVENUE		
Student Tuition Fees	$2,591,335	$ 2,420,370
Investment	306,608	306,608
Gifts and Grants	1,671,667	1,731,945
Other Revenues	129,682	128,700
TOTAL REVENUES	**$4,699,292**	**$ 4,587,623**
EXPENSES		
Business Office	$ 333,191	$ 340,464
Dean's Office	150,325	156,616
Chapel	42,689	44,316
Formation For Ministry	110,840	92,605
Financial Leadership Ministry	82,123	93,435
Educational Development Committee	15,500	15,500
Advancement Office	341,718	389,775
Doctor of Ministry	74,400	60,200
Facilities	568,778	567,204
Faculty	1,063,461	940,017
Summer Classes	37,600	37,600
January Classes	11,000	11,000
Financial Aid	63,616	64,084
Information Technology	156,765	142,426
Library	264,658	255,496
President's Office	263,612	261,823
Admissions	163,224	158,603
Student Services	84,540	84,943
Registrar & Institutional Research	129,347	134,161
Annual Fund/Alumni Affairs	0	100,779
Communications	49,588	49,825
Student Housing	97,810	91,642
Certificate & Continuing Education	25,938	16,950
Methodist House of Studies	0	37,037
Student Government	2,775	2,775
Theology & Arts	43,216	37,359
Scholarships	407,972	423,208
Program of Alternate Studies	130,177	130,801
Depreciation	214,658	185,891
TOTAL EXPENSES	**$5,071,360**	**$4,926,535**
Increase (decrease) in net assets	(372,058)	(338,912)

VI. SHARED SERVICES

	Revised 2017	Proposed 2018
REVENUE		
Our United Outreach	$ 341,066	343,420
TOTAL REVENUES	**$ 341,066**	**$ 343,420**
EXPENSES		
Salaries	$ 51,011	$ 52,286
Health Insurance	27,651	30,441
Retirement	2,488	2,614
FICA	3,807	4,000
Accounting Coordinator	1,600	1,600
Audit	21,000	21,000
Payroll Service	6,500	6,900
Bank Charges	17,500	17,500
Technology System Consultants - EMS	18,000	18,000
Software Maintenance Agreement - Blackbaud	14,500	15,700
Building & Maintenance	45,845	45,845
Pest Control	840	840
Lawn & Ground Maintenance	18,500	18,500
Lawn Treatment	1,500	1,500
Utilities - Building 1	23,490	24,650
Utilities - Building 2	18,106	18,500
Janitorial Service	8,100	8,100
Security System Monitoring	1,100	1,100
Trash Collection	1,850	1,850
Telephone/Internet	9,400	9,400
Heating & AC Maintenance Agreement	10,000	10,000
Insurance/Liability	11,844	11,844
Office Equipment Maintenance	14,000	14,000
Computer Maintenance	500	500
Computer Software	2,500	2,500
Office Supplies	2,500	2,500
Postage	750	750
Employee Events	1,000	1,000
TOTAL EXPENSE	$ 335,282	$ 343,420
Surplus/Deficit	$ 5,784	$ 0

The Proceedings of the

ONE HUNDRED EIGHTY-SEVENTH GENERAL ASSEMBLY

of the

CUMBERLAND PRESBYTERIAN CHURCH

session held in

PALM HARBOR, FLORIDA
June 18 - 23, 2017

At Palm Harbor, Florida and within the facilities of the Innisbrook Resort, there the eighteenth day of June in the year of our Lord, two thousand seventeen, at the appointed hour of seven o'clock in the evening, Minister and Elder Commissioners from the various presbyteries, youth advisory delegates and visitors assembled for Concurrent meetings of the General Assemblies of the Cumberland Presbyterian Church and the Cumberland Presbyterian Church in America.

FIRST DAY – SUNDAY – JUNE 18, 2017

OPENING WORSHIP

In the Inverness Ballroom of the Innisbrook Resort, the one hundred eighty-seventh General Assembly of the Cumberland Presbyterian Church, the one hundred forty-second General Assembly of the Cumberland Presbyterian Church in America, the Convention of Cumberland Presbyterian Women's Ministry, and visitors gathered for worship at 7:00 p.m. Liturgists for the service were Ms. Yvonne Frierson, National Missionary Society President (CPCA), Reverend Jennifer Newell, Worship Director, Tennessee-Georgia Presbytery CPC) and Ms. Jamie Kay Berkley, Women's Ministry Convention President (CPC). The music director was Reverend Chris Warren, Murfreesboro Presbytery (CPC). The special music was sung by Elder John Rainey, Cleveland Ohio Presbytery (CPCA). The pianist was Reverend Michael Sharpe, Stated Clerk (CPC). Ushers were Reverend Chuck Reed, Reverend Eddie Jenkins, Tom Beckmeyer, Lisa Beckmeyer, Max White, Ginger White, Spiro Cachia, Donna Cachia, and Carol Felicia.

The Reverend Michael Jones, Vice Moderator, Tennessee Valley Presbytery (CPCA) presented the sermon, *"The Evidence of Love,"* taken from Luke 10:29-37. The Sacrament of Holy Communion was led by Co-Celebrants Reverend Dwayne Tyus, Moderator, Nashville Presbytery (CPC) and Reverend Ann Williams Pierre, Hiwassee Presbytery (CPCA). Reverend Kay Ward Creer, Ms. Jerlene Rather, Mr. Moses Chein, Ms. Joy Wallace, Mr. Glee Thompson, Mr. Thomas Ward, Reverend Stan Wood and Mr. Glenn Strain (all from the CPCA) assisted with Communion. Also the following CPC Elders assisted with Communion: Bill Dobbins, Tom Longmire, Lorna Light, Elder Jimmie Moore, Elder Judith Steffen-Drake, Karen Lock, and Linda Scott; and Reverend Roger Reid.

FIRST DAY – MONDAY – JUNE 19, 2017

MORNING DEVOTIONAL

The morning began at 8:30 a.m. with a Devotional. The service was led by liturgist, Reverend Jennifer Newell, Tennessee-Georgia Presbytery and music leader, Reverend Chris Warren, Nashville Presbytery. The devotion was presented by Retiring Moderator, Reverend Dwayne Tyus. His message was taken from Colossians 1:15 – 20.

THE ASSEMBLY IS CONSTITUTED

The Moderator, the Reverend Dwayne Tyus, called the assembly to order at 8:50 a.m.
The Constituting Prayer was offered by Reverend Rickey Page, Nashville Presbytery.

WELCOME

Moderator Tyus introduced Pastor Host, Reverend Eddie Jenkins, Grace Presbytery, who welcomed the General Assembly to Florida. Reverend Jenkins introduced Ms. Kelli Snow, Board of Directors of the Palm Harbor Chamber of Commerce, Marketing Director for Chick-fil-A, and co-pastor of World Wide Word of Faith Church. Ms. Snow brought greetings to the body on behalf of the Palm Harbor area and introduced Ms. Kim Adams, Honorary Mayor of Palm Harbor, who also brought greetings to the body.

ADOPTION OF AGENDA

After thanking the pastor host and the host committee for their hard work, Moderator Tyus asked for a motion that the agenda be adopted. On Motion, the agenda was adopted.

CREDENTIALS REPORT

Elder Christy Miller, Tennessee-Georgia Presbytery presented the Report of the Credentials Committee. There were forty-two (42) ministers, thirty-five (35) elders, for a total of seventy-seven (77) commissioners present at 8:30 a.m. There were twenty-one (21) Youth Advisory Delegates present. On motion, the report of the Credentials Committee was received, marked Appendix "A" and filed.

VOTE FOR MODERATOR

Moderator Tyus declared the floor open for nominations for the Office of Moderator of the one hundred eighty-seventh General Assembly.
Reverend Tony Janner, West Tennessee Presbytery, nominated Reverend David Lancaster, West Tennessee Presbytery to be Moderator of the 187th General Assembly of the Cumberland Presbyterian Church. There being no other nominations, a motion was made that nominations cease and we move to elect by acclamation. Motion passed. By vote, Reverend David Lancaster was elected Moderator of the 187th General Assembly of the Cumberland Presbyterian Church. Moderator Lancaster was escorted to the podium by Reverend Janner. Former Moderator Tyus presented the Moderator's Cross, gavel and stole to newly elected Moderator Lancaster. A prayer for Moderator Lancaster was offered by Reverend Janner.
Moderator Lancaster assumed the podium and addressed the body, thanking the body for the honor to serve. The Moderator spoke with humility of his walk in faith in the Cumberland Presbyterian Church.

VOTE FOR VICE-MODERATOR

Moderator Lancaster opened the floor for nominations for Vice-Moderator. Elder Roy Shanks, North Central Presbytery, nominated Reverend Lisa Scott, North Central Presbytery, to be Vice-Moderator of the 187th General Assembly of the Cumberland Presbyterian Church. There being no other nominations, a motion was made that nominations cease and we move to elect by acclamation. Motion passed. By vote, Reverend Lisa Scott was elected Vice-Moderator of the of the 187th General Assembly of the Cumberland Presbyterian Church.
Elder Shanks escorted Reverend Scott to the podium and introduced her to the body. Vice-Moderator Scott addressed the body thanking the body for the humbling honor of serving the church as Vice Moderator.

PRESENTATION BY THE STATED CLERK

The Stated Clerk, Reverend Michael Sharpe, invited retiring Moderator, Dwayne Tyus and his wife, Guin, to the podium. The Stated Clerk thanked the Tyus' for their service to the 186th General Assembly with Guin Tyus serving as "Official Chauffer." The Stated Clerk presented the former Moderator with replicas of the Moderator's cross and gavel, representing the ones used by the 186th General Assembly of the Cumberland Presbyterian Church.

COMMUNICATIONS

The Stated Clerk announced that there were no official communications. An invitation was given for the presentation of resolutions or memorials. There were none.

CORRECTIONS TO THE PRELIMINARY MINUTES

The Stated Clerk reported that a copy of all corrections to the preliminary minutes were handed out to all commissioners during orientation and would be reflected in the final printing of the minutes.

COMMITTEE APPOINTMENTS AND REFERRALS

The Stated Clerk reported that all referrals to the committees will be printed in the minutes as presented in the preliminary minutes with the changes handed out during orientation.

INTRODUCTION OF BOARD/AGENCY REPRESENTATIVES

The Stated Clerk introduced the following Board/Agency Representatives:

Bethel University	Walter Butler
Commission on Military Chaplains	Cassandra Thomas
Children's Home	Duane Dougherty
Historical Foundation	Robin McCaskey Hughes/Lisa Oliver
Judiciary	Andy McClung
Memphis Theological Seminary	Linda Howell
Ministry Council	Tom Sanders/Lanny Johnson
Our United Outreach	Cliff Hudson
Stewardship	Boyd Day
Theology & Social Concerns	Nancy Fuqua
Unification Task Force	Joy Warren (CPC)
	William Robinson (CPCA)

RECESS

Moderator Tyus declared the General Assembly of the Cumberland Presbyterian Church in recess. The committees will reconvene on Tuesday at 9:00 am.

FIELD TRIP TO BETH-EL FARMWORKER MINISTRY

The opportunity was made available for all who desired to travel by chartered bus to Beth-El Farmworker Ministry. While there, participants enjoyed a reception for the Moderators and Vice-Moderators of the Cumberland Presbyterian Church and the Cumberland Presbyterian Church in America, Moderator Reverend David Lancaster (CPC), Vice-Moderator Elder L. Leon Cole, (CPCA), Reverend Lisa Scott (CPC); the Immediate Moderator, Reverend Dwayne Tyus (CPC); the Cumberland Presbyterian Women's Ministry President, Ms. Jamie Kay Berkley; the Cumberland Presbyterian Women's Ministry President- Elect, Faith Parra; National Missionary Society President (CPCA), Ms. Yvonne Frierson. Beth-El Farmworker Ministry provided walking and bus tours of their facilities as well as finger foods and a Mariachi band. This was a very enjoyable outing for General Assembly commissioners and visitors.

SECOND DAY – TUESDAY – JUNE 20, 2017

The General Assembly began their day with committees meeting at 9:00 a.m. While some committees held a devotional in their meeting rooms, Joint Devotions were led by the National Missionary Society of the Cumberland Presbyterian Church in America. Participants in the Joint Devotions were worship leader, Elder Justina Johnson (CPCA), Reverend Pam Phillips-Burk (CPC) – invocation, Sister Mamie Hall (CPCA) – scripture reading, The Missionary Choir (CPCA) – special music, Sister Ann Buchanan (CPCA) – offertory, Sister Edna Sheridan (CPCA) – introduction of speaker, Elder Yvonne Frierson (CPCA) – President's Moments, and Moderator Leon Cole (CPCA) – benediction.

The speaker was Reverend Endia Scruggs, pastor of Madkins Chapel CPCA. Reverend Scruggs presented a moving devotional taken from Luke 10:29-39 which conveyed the message that we are all neighbors.

The day was devoted to committee work until 5:00 p.m. Attendance for the day: forty-five (45) minister commissioners, thirty-seven (37) elder commissioners for a total of eighty-two (82) commissioners and twenty-one (21) Youth Advisory Delegates.

EVENING PROGRAM

At 7:30 p.m. in Inverness Hall, commissioners and visitors participated in a Joint Worship Service led by the Unification Task Force. Worship leadership included liturgists, Reverend William Robinson (CPCA) and Reverend Joy Warren (CPC); music director, Melody Dieking (CPCA); accompanist Patti Needham (CPC) and special music, Reverend Chris Warren (Cumberland Presbyterian Church). The message, presented by Reverend Stan Wood, entitled *"The Blending of Two Sticks,"* based upon Ezekiel 37:16-18, 21-22. Reverend Wood presented a moving sermon calling upon the Cumberland Presbyterian Church in America and the Cumberland Presbyterian Church to join together as one. Reverend Joy Warren led the congregation in two activities: *"Responding To The Message"* and *"Connecting With Our Neighbor."*

At 8:30 p.m. the annual reception honoring women in ministry was held at Toscana Clubhouse. Attendees enjoyed rich fellowship and refreshments as they celebrated women in ministry.

THIRD DAY – WEDNESDAY – JUNE 22, 2016

The General Assembly and visitors began the day with a Joint Devotional at 8:30 a.m. Moderator Elder L. Leon Cole, (CPCA), welcomed the congregation and introduced Dr. Walter Butler, President of Bethel University. Dr. Butler spoke about Bethel University and introduced the video presentation celebrating Bethel's 175 years of educational excellence.

Captain Lawrence P. Greenslit, Presbyterian Council for Chaplains and Military Personnel was introduced. Captain Greenslit spoke of the partnership that the Cumberland Presbyterian Church and Cumberland Presbyterian Church in America has with other presbyterian bodies endorsing chaplains for the military, the Veterans Administration and federal prisons. Following his presentation, Reverend Michael Walker and Reverend Cassandra Thomas presented Captain Greenslit with awards in honor of his service to the PCCMP and the Cumberland Presbyterian Church and Cumberland Presbyterian Church in America upon his upcoming retirement.

The session was closed by Moderator Reverend David Lancaster.

The committees used the remainder of the day in meetings, preparing and reviewing reports and collecting signatures. Attendance for the day: thirty-five (35) minister commissioners, thirty-six (36) elder commissioners and seventeen (17) youth advisory delegates.

At 7:00 p.m., the 187th General Assembly and visitors gathered for worship. The worship was led by liturgist, Reverend Jennifer Newell, Tennessee-Georgia Presbytery with music by Loida Garcia and Nacion Santa Internacional Group. The guest speaker was Reverend Kathy Dain (PCUSA), Director at Beth-El Farmworker Ministry. Her message, *"Your NeighborHood"* taken from Luke 8:26-39.

An offering of $2,219 was received and given to Beth-El Farmworker Ministry.

FOURTH DAY – THURSDAY – JUNE 23, 2016

At 8:30 a.m., the General Assembly and visitors began the day with joyful singing and a devotional led by youth advisory delegate, Ms. Shelby Stover, Presbytery of East Tennessee. Her devotional was taken from Luke 10:29-37. Liturgist was Reverend Jennifer Newel – Tennessee-Georgia Presbytery; music director was Reverend Chris Warren, Murfreesboro Presbytery; pianist was Ms. Robin McCaskey Hughes, Red River Presbytery.

CALL TO ORDER

The Moderator, Reverend Doctor David Lancaster, called the assembly to order at 9:10 a.m.

There were forty-four (44) ministers, thirty-one (31) elders for a total of seventy-five (75) commissioners, and eighteen (18) youth advisory delegates present as of 9:10 a.m. The opening prayer was given by Reverend Daniel Barkley, Grace Presbytery.

PARLIMENTARIAN APPOINTED

The Moderator appointed the Reverend Andy McClung, West Tennessee Presbytery, as Parliamentarian.

GREETINGS AND PRESENTATIONS

Reverend Susan Parker, Hope Presbytery brought greetings from Haitian Council of Church. Reverend Parker expressed thanks for support from the Cumberland Presbyterian Church on behalf of the churches and clergy in training.

The body received a presentation from Ms. Jodie Rush, Discipleship Ministry Team, who reported that the Connect @ GA children had reached out to Commissioners and the Innisbrook staff. She charged all to challenge churches to allow children to be a part of the local churches' service ministry.

Reverend Milton Ortiz presented the inspirational Stott Wallace Video featuring our newest missionaries: the Sims (Brazil) and the Wilkersons (Colombia). Reverend Ortiz introduced Reverend Lynn Thomas who introduced Reverend Patrick Wilkerson (Presbytery of East Tennessee) and wife, Jessica and family. Reverend Thomas also asked Reverend Josue Guerrero, Emaus Presbytery, to come forward. Reverend Thomas conducted a commissioning service for Reverend Patrick Wilkerson and his wife, Jessica, as they prepare to leave for the mission field in Colombia. Reverend Josue Guerrero offered a prayer to the Wilkersons. Reverend Wilkerson then addressed the body, thanking the Cumberland Presbyterian Church for their support and speaking about future plans for the mission field and encouraging continued support for all missions and missionaries. Reverend Thomas offered a prayer for the Wilkersons, commissioning them for their future work. Reverend Ortiz pronounced the benediction and charge. The body joined in singing, *"Here I Am, Lord."*

Moderator Lancaster took a moment of personal privilege to speak to the commissioning of the Wilkersons and the importance of the work the Cumberland Presbyterian Church is doing as a denomination in the mission field.

Greetings were extended on behalf of the Cumberland Presbyterian Church in America from Elder L. Leon Cole, Moderator (CPCA). Moderator Cole spoke of the work that we have done together this week, looking forward to our march together both at the General Assembly level as well as out in the world.

ANNOUNCEMENTS

The Stated Clerk gave the following announcements and instructions:
- Reminded commissioners and YADs to sit in front tables.
- Please turn in attendance cards.
- Instructed Commissioners/YAD's wishing to address the Assembly to approach the aisle microphone, introduce themselves by name and the presbytery they represent.
- Anyone making a motion should write out the motion and give a copy to the Engrossing Clerk before returning to their seat.
- Committees will be seated in the front together during the presentation of the committee's report.

ASSEMBLY BUSINESS

Moderator Cole presented a *Resolution of Forgiveness, Unity, and Resolve* issued to the Cumberland Presbyterian Church General Assembly by the Cumberland Presbyterian Church in America General Assembly. Moderator Cole asked the Cumberland Presbyterian Church General Assembly to receive the resolution.

A motion was made to receive the resolution. The resolution was received by a vote of Halleluiah! The Moderator declared that the resolution was received unanimously. Resolution Marked "B" and filed.

NOMINATING COMMITTEE

The Report of the Nominating Committee was presented in the preliminary minutes. A motion was made to accept the report. The Moderator opened the floor for further nominations. There being no further nominations, by vote, all persons nominated were elected.

THE REPORT OF THE COMMITTEE ON JUDICIARY

The Report of the Committee on Judiciary was presented by Reverend Dwayne Tyus (Nashville Presbytery). The report was read by YADs Brenna Truitt (Murfreesboro Presbytery), Shelby Stover (Presbytery of East Tennessee), Carly Bell (Cumberland Presbytery), and Austin Womack (Nashville Presbytery).

A motion was made by Elder Mollie Williams (West Tennessee Presbytery) that the report be concurred in and the recommendations be adopted. Motion passed by the necessary 2/3rd majority. The report was marked "C" and filed.

THE REPORT OF THE COMMITTEE ON CHILDREN'S HOME/HIGHER EDUCATION

The Report of the Committee on Children's Home/Higher Education was presented by Reverend Thomas Sweet (Presbytery of East Tennessee). The report was read by youth advisory delegates, Lydia Cook (Robert Donnell Presbytery), Macie Clark (North Central Presbytery), and David Whalen (West Tennessee Presbytery). A motion was made by Reverend Sweet that the report be concurred in and the recommendations be adopted. Motion passed. The report was marked "D" and filed.

THE REPORT OF THE COMMITTEE ON THEOLOGY AND SOCIAL CONCERNS/ UNIFICATION TASKFORCE

The Report of the Committee on Theology and Social Concerns was presented and read by Reverend Lisa Scott (North Central Presbytery) and Reverend Tommy Clark (Columbia Presbytery). A motion was made to concur in the report and adopt its recommendations by Reverend Scott with an editorial change. The motion passed. Report marked "E" and filed.

VICE MODERATOR TAKES THE PODIUM

Moderator Lancaster asked Vice-Moderator Lisa Scott to moderate the meeting.

REPORT OF THE COMMITTEE ON MINISTRY COUNCIL/ COMMUNICATION/DISCIPLESHIP

The Report of the Ministry Council/Communications/Discipleship Committee was presented by Reverend Lisa Oliver (Murfreesboro Presbytery). Reverend Oliver made the motion that the report be concurred in and the recommendations be adopted. Motion passed. The report was marked "F" and filed.

MODERATOR RESUMES THE PODIUM

Moderator Lancaster returned to the podium.

RECESS

The Moderator declared a 15 minute recess at 11:06 a.m.

CALL TO ORDER

The Moderator called the meeting back to order at 11:30 a.m.

VICE MODERATOR TAKES THE PODIUM

The Moderator asked the Vice-Moderator to moderate the meeting.

Dr. Barry Anderson, Executive Director of Student Service - Memphis Theological Seminary, announced that the winner of the Clergy Stole was Reverend Emily Trapp (West Tennessee Presbytery).

Reverend Rickey Page (Nashville Presbytery) made a motion to excuse YAD Calee Copely (Hope Presbytery) and Steve Kaneaster (Red River Presbytery) from the remainder of the meeting. Motion passed.

THE REPORT OF THE COMMITTEE ON MISSIONS/PASTORAL DEVELOPMENT

The Report of the Committee on Missions/Pastoral Development was presented by Reverend Rickey Page (Nashville Presbytery). The report was read by youth advisory delegate, Duncan Shelton (Presbytery of East Tennessee). A motion was made by Reverend Rhonda McGowan (Tennessee-Georgia Presbytery) that the report be concurred in and the recommendations be adopted. Motion passed. The report was marked "G" and filed.

THE REPORT OF THE COMMITTEE ON CHAPLAINS/HISTORICAL FOUNDATION

The Report of the Committee on Chaplains/Historical Foundation was presented by Reverend Theresa Martin (Tennessee-Georgia Presbytery). The report was read youth advisory delegates, Audrey Adams (West Tennessee Presbytery), Skylar Birch (North Central Presbytery) and Mary Cook (Robert Donnell Presbytery). A motion was made by Reverend Duane Dougherty (Trinity Presbytery) that the report be concurred in and the recommendations be adopted. Motion passed. The report was marked "H" and filed.

CPWM GREETINGS

Greetings were brought from the Cumberland Presbyterian Women's Ministry President, Mrs. Faith Parra, who invited the body to next year's General Assembly sponsored by Choctaw and Red River Presbyteries.

ASSEMBLY BUSINESS

Reverend Tony Janner made a motion to excuse Elder Hedemarrie Dussan (Grace Presbytery) whose husband was taken to the hospital on Wednesday evening. Motion passed. Reverend Janner offered a prayer for the family.

THE REPORT OF THE COMMITTEE ON STEWARDSHIP/ELECTED OFFICERS

The Report of the Committee Stewardship/Elected Officers was presented by Reverend Tony Janner (West Tennessee Presbytery). The report was read by youth advisory delegates, Elizabeth Mahoney (Murfreesboro Presbytery), Katelyn Bayless (Arkansas Presbytery), and Alina Ferraz (Grace Presbytery). A motion was made by Reverend Janner that the report be concurred in and the recommendations be adopted. The motion passed. The report was marked "I" and filed.

MODERATOR RESUMES THE PODIUM

Moderator Lancaster returned to the podium.

RESOLUTION OF GRATITUDE

A Resolution of Gratitude was presented by the Reverend Susan Parker (Hope Presbytery). A motion was made to adopt the resolution. Motion passed.

Thank You Resolution for General Assembly

The 187th General Assembly of the Cumberland Presbyterian Church is grateful first to Almighty God for the opportunity to meet together to worship and serve. We are humbled and awed by the presence of the Holy Spirit in this meeting in our worship, meetings and interactions with our brothers and sisters.

The 187th General Assembly wishes to thank Reverend Eddie Jenkins, from Hope CP church, Grace Presbytery, for his leadership as pastor host. We also wish to thank the members of the committee and all who were involved in planning and preparing this meeting.

We are grateful for the leadership in our moving and inspiring worship services. We were blessed to have heard the Holy Spirit speak through Reverend India Scruggs, Reverend Stan Wood, Reverend Kathy Dain, youth advisory delegate, Shelby Stover, and Reverend Jennifer Newell.

This General Assembly was blessed to have Reverend Jennifer Newell also as worship leader and Reverend Chris Warren as music director. They were assisted by other music leaders, numerous musicians, singers, choirs, and other musically talented individuals who blessed us with wonderful songs and music.

The Cumberland Presbyterian Church has benefited and is thankful to our current moderator, Reverend David Lancaster and vice-moderator, Reverend Lisa Scott as well as former moderator, Reverend Dwayne Tyson. We wish to express gratitude to our leader, Reverend Michael Sharpe for his diligent work at General Assembly and throughout the year. And we recognize this work would not be accomplished without his able assistant, Mrs. Elizabeth Vaughn and all the staff who work so hard to accomplish so many tasks.

We also give thanks for each committee chairperson, for each commissioner and youth delegate who has participated in the deliberations of the Assembly.

This General Assembly has been particularly blessed to be able to share many activities with our brother and sisters from the Cumberland Presbyterian Church of America. Our candid discussions and loving exchanges have blessed us all and hopefully inspire us all to return to our homes and explore more options for opportunities to worship with our CPCA brothers and sisters.

We also thank the wonderful staff at Innisbrook Resort for their competence and friendliness and we thank the Good Lord for the beautiful surroundings provided for our enjoyment.

As we go forward, may our wonderful, omnipotent and awesome God help us to lead and guide the Cumberland Presbyterian Church as it carries out the recommendations adopted by this body. May God be with us, sustain us and inspire us for the future and give us safe journeys home.

READING OF THE MINUTES

A motion was made to approve the minutes of Sunday – Wednesday as printed in the packet with one editorial change. Motion passed.

A motion was made to not break for lunch. Motion passed by necessary 2/3rd vote.

The minutes for Wednesday and Thursday were read by the Engrossing Clerk. On motion, the minutes were approved as corrected.

RECESS

The Moderator announced a short recess to prepare for closing worship.

CLOSING WORSHIP

The closing worship was led by Reverend Jennifer Newell (Tennessee-Georgia Presbytery), and pianist, Reverend Mike Sharpe, Stated Clerk. Reverend Newell's devotional was based on Mathew 9: 9-13. A memorial roll of ministers, who died during the past year, was read during worship. The list was printed in the Preliminary Minutes on page 23.

ADJOURNMENT

A motion was made to adjourn the Meeting of the 187th General Assembly of the Cumberland Presbyterian Church to meet June 17-21, 2018 at Embassy Suites Hotel & Conference Center (Norman, Oklahoma), near Oklahoma City. Motion passed. The closing prayer was offered by Moderator Lancaster at 1:01 p.m.

AUDITED FINANCIAL STATEMENTS OF

THE AGENCIES OF
THE CUMBERLAND PRESBYTERIAN
CHURCH CENTER

DECEMBER 31, 2016

THE AGENCIES OF THE CUMBERLAND PRESBYTERIAN CHURCH CENTER

TABLE OF CONTENTS
DECEMBER 31, 2016

	PAGE
Independent Auditor's Report	1
Combined Statement of Financial Position	2
Combined Statement of Activity	3
Combined Statement of Cash Flows	4
Individual Statements of Financial Position	
Our United Outreach	5
General Assembly Corporation	6
Ministry Council	7
Shared Services	8
Historical Foundation	9
Board of Stewardship, Foundation, and Benefits	10
Small Church Loan Program	11
Insurance Program	12
Ministerial Aid	13
Investment Loan Program	14
Retirement Fund	15
Endowment Program	16
Individual Statements of Activity	
Our United Outreach	17
General Assembly Corporation	18
Ministry Council	19
Shared Services	20
Historical Foundation	21
Board of Stewardship, Foundation, and Benefits	22
Small Church Loan Program	23
Insurance Program	24
Ministerial Aid	25
Investment Loan Program	26
Retirement Fund	27
Endowment Program	28
Notes to Financial Statements	29 - 43

To the General Assembly Corporation
The Agencies of The Cumberland Presbyterian Church Center
Memphis, Tennessee

INDEPENDENT AUDITOR'S REPORT

We have audited the accompanying combined financial statements of The Agencies of The Cumberland Presbyterian Church Center, which comprise the combined statement of financial position as of December 31, 2016, and the related combined statements of activities and cash flows for the year then ended, and the related notes to the combined financial statements.

Management's Responsibility for the Financial Statements

Management is responsible for the preparation and fair presentation of these financial statements in accordance with accounting principles generally accepted in the United States of America; this includes the design, implementation, and maintenance of internal control relevant to the preparation and fair presentation of financial statements that are free from material misstatement, whether due to fraud or error.

Auditor's Responsibility

Our responsibility is to express an opinion on these combined financial statements based on our audit. We conducted our audit in accordance with auditing standards generally accepted in the United States of America. Those standards require that we plan and perform the audit to obtain reasonable assurance about whether the financial statements are free from material misstatement.

An audit involves performing procedures to obtain audit evidence about the amounts and disclosures in the combined financial statements. The procedures selected depend on the auditor's judgment, including the assessment of the risks of material misstatement of the combined financial statements, whether due to fraud or error. In making those risk assessments, the auditor considers internal control relevant to the entity's preparation and fair presentation of the combined financial statements in order to design audit procedures that are appropriate in the circumstances, but not for the purpose of expressing an opinion on the effectiveness of the entity's internal control. Accordingly, we express no such opinion. An audit also includes evaluating the appropriateness of accounting policies used and the reasonableness of significant accounting estimates made by management, as well as evaluating the overall presentation of the combined financial statements.

We believe that the audit evidence we have obtained is sufficient and appropriate to provide a basis for our audit opinion.

Opinion

In our opinion, the combined financial statements referred to above present fairly, in all material respects, the financial position of The Agencies of The Cumberland Presbyterian Church Center as of December 31, 2016, and the changes in their net assets and their cash flows for the year then ended in accordance with accounting principles generally accepted in the United States of America.

FOUTS & MORGAN
Certified Public Accountants

Memphis, Tennessee
May 15, 2017

THE AGENCIES OF
THE CUMBERLAND PRESBYTERIAN CHURCH CENTER

COMBINED STATEMENT OF FINANCIAL POSITION
DECEMBER 31, 2016

ASSETS

Cash	$ 618,382
Due from other agencies, boards, and divisions	6,154,184
Accounts receivable	2,313
Interest and dividends receivable, net of allowance for uncollectible interest	110,963
Health insurance tax credit receivable	2,311
Securities and investments	
Cash equivalents	3,989,248
Mortgage backed securities	12,072,303
Equity mutual funds	4,320,718
Real estate investment trusts	5,665,886
Private investment entities	68,197,599
Real estate	90,573
Inventory - at lower of cost or market	686
Prepaid expenses	140,996
Loans receivable, net of allowance for loan losses	9,544,756
Buildings and land	2,760,412
Furniture and equipment	156,745
Less: Accumulated depreciation	(744,350)
Total Assets	$ 113,083,725

LIABILITIES AND NET ASSETS

Liabilities:	
Accounts payable	$ 68,961
Notes payable to individual investors	2,388,752
Unearned subscriptions	7,984
Due to other agencies, boards, and divisions	6,418,239
Funds held in trust for others	33,418
Depository accounts held for church organizations	14,117,998
Total liabilities	23,035,352
Net Assets:	
Unrestricted	8,566,800
Temporarily restricted	1,700,773
Permanently restricted	56,583,193
Net assets available for benefits, at fair value	23,197,607
Total net assets	90,048,373
Total Liabilities and Net Assets	$ 113,083,725

See accompanying notes.

THE AGENCIES OF
THE CUMBERLAND PRESBYTERIAN CHURCH CENTER

COMBINED STATEMENT OF ACTIVITY
FOR THE YEAR ENDED DECEMBER 31, 2016

	Unrestricted	Temporarily Restricted	Permanently Restricted	Net Assets Available for Benefits	Totals
Revenues, gains, and other support:					
Contributions and gifts	$ 4,977,257	$ 1,182,351	$ 1,294,280	$ -	$ 7,453,888
Insurance program premium revenue	1,600,183	-	-	-	1,600,183
Endowment earnings	-	-	395,778	-	395,778
Interest and dividend income	291,571	47,309	15,706	119,950	474,536
Management service fees	52,683	-	-	(16,410)	36,273
Registration fees	15,731	-	-	-	15,731
Sales and subscription income	197,344	-	-	-	197,344
Net realized and unrealized gain on investments	71,753	-	3,089,740	1,256,898	4,418,391
Other income	3,009	-	-	-	3,009
Participant retirement contributions	-	-	-	686,942	686,942
Net assets released from restriction	1,614,457	(844,463)	(544,505)	-	225,489
Total revenues, gains, and other support	8,823,988	385,197	4,250,999	2,047,380	15,507,564
Net revenues, gains, and other support - after provision for loan losses	8,823,988	385,197	4,250,999	2,047,380	15,507,564
Expenses:					
Our United Outreach	497,322	-	-	-	497,322
General Assembly Corporation	427,997	-	-	-	427,997
Ministry Council	4,668,123	-	-	-	4,668,123
Shared Services	414,105	-	-	-	414,105
Historical Foundation	204,065	-	-	-	204,065
Board of Stewardship, Foundation and Benefits	342,321	-	-	-	342,321
Small Church Loan Program	51,635	-	-	-	51,635
Insurance Program	1,843,750	-	-	-	1,843,750
Ministerial Aid	64,266	-	-	-	64,266
Investment Loan Program	84,165	-	-	-	84,165
Retirement Fund	-	-	-	1,578,924	1,578,924
Endowment Program	-	-	4,519,864	-	4,519,864
Total expenses	8,597,749	-	4,519,864	1,578,924	14,696,537
Change in net assets	226,239	385,197	(268,865)	468,456	811,027
Net assets at beginning of year	8,340,561	1,315,576	56,852,058	22,729,151	89,237,346
Net assets at end of year	$ 8,566,800	$ 1,700,773	$ 56,583,193	$ 23,197,607	$ 90,048,373

See accompanying notes.

THE AGENCIES OF
THE CUMBERLAND PRESBYTERIAN CHURCH CENTER

COMBINED STATEMENT OF CASH FLOWS
FOR THE YEAR ENDED DECEMBER 31, 2016

Cash flows from operating activities	
Combined change in net assets	$ 811,027
Adjustments to reconcile combined change in net assets to net cash used in operating activities:	
Depreciation	65,289
Net realized/unrealized (gain) loss on investments - Investment Loan Program	27,745
Net realized/unrealized (gain) loss on investments - Retirement Fund	(255,117)
Net realized/unrealized (gain) loss on investments - Endowment Program	(2,052,412)
(Increase) decrease in operating assets:	
Due from other agencies, boards, and divisions	(517,220)
Accounts receivable	5,091
Interest and dividends receivable	(23,942)
Health insurance tax credit receivable	7,395
Prepaid assets	(27,751)
Increase (decrease) in operating liabilities:	
Accounts payable	39,545
Accrued expenses	(17)
Unearned subscriptions	(1,718)
Due to other agencies, boards, and divisions	509,572
Funds held in trust for others	2,072
Notes payable to individual investors	510,171
Depository accounts held for church organizations	4,335,894
Net cash provided by (used in) operating activities	3,435,624
Cash flows from investing activities	
Proceeds from sale of investments:	
Endowment Program	8,439,178
Retirement Fund	4,599,568
Investment Loan Program	10,599,503
Purchase of investments:	
Endowment Program	(6,347,502)
Retirement Fund	(4,813,435)
Investment Loan Program	(16,169,328)
Loan principal payments received	606,496
Loan principal disbursed	(265,076)
Net cash provided by (used in) investing activities	(3,350,596)
Net increase in cash	85,028
Cash at the beginning of the year	533,354
Cash at the end of the year	$ 618,382

See accompanying notes.

THE AGENCIES OF
THE CUMBERLAND PRESBYTERIAN CHURCH CENTER
OUR UNITED OUTREACH
STATEMENT OF FINANCIAL POSITION
DECEMBER 31, 2016

ASSETS

Endowment earnings receivable	$ 31,984
Due from other agencies, boards, and divisions	8,000
Endowments - held by Endowment Program	2,591,320
Total Assets	$ 2,631,304

LIABILITIES AND NET ASSETS

Liabilities:	
Cash borrowed from other agencies, boards, and divisions	$ 15,542
Due to outside church organizations	42,270
Total liabilities	57,812
Net Assets:	
Unrestricted	(17,828)
Permanently restricted	2,591,320
Total net assets	2,573,492
Total Liabilities and Net Assets	$ 2,631,304

See accompanying notes.

THE AGENCIES OF
THE CUMBERLAND PRESBYTERIAN CHURCH CENTER
GENERAL ASSEMBLY CORPORATION
STATEMENT OF FINANCIAL POSITION
DECEMBER 31, 2016

ASSETS

Endowment earnings receivable	$ 5,657
Health insurance tax credit receivable	1,432
Inventory	686
Due from other agencies, boards, and divisions	375,526
	383,301
Endowments - held by Endowment Program	435,755
Total Assets	$ 819,056

LIABILITIES AND NET ASSETS

Liabilities:	
Accounts payable	$ 444
Cash borrowed from other agencies, boards, and divisions	195,553
Due to other agencies, boards, and divisions	12,937
Funds held in trusts for others	33,418
Total liabilities	242,352
Net Assets:	
Unrestricted	140,952
Permanently restricted	435,752
Total net assets	576,704
Total Liabilities and Net Assets	$ 819,056

See accompanying notes.

THE AGENCIES OF
THE CUMBERLAND PRESBYTERIAN CHURCH CENTER
MINISTRY COUNCIL
STATEMENT OF FINANCIAL POSITION
DECEMBER 31, 2016

ASSETS

Cash	$ 227,911
Accounts receivable	1,972
Endowment earnings receivable	168,111
Health insurance tax credit receivable	879
Due from other agencies, boards, and divisions	2,366,124
Securities and investments	
Real estate	51,818
	2,816,815
Endowments - held by Endowment Program	15,861,602
Total Assets	$ 18,678,417

LIABILITIES AND NET ASSETS

Liabilities:	
Accounts payable	$ 23,527
Unearned subscriptions	7,984
Total liabilities	31,511
Net Assets:	
Unrestricted	1,268,290
Temporarily restricted	1,517,011
Permanently restricted	15,861,605
Total net assets	18,646,906
Total Liabilities and Net Assets	$ 18,678,417

See accompanying notes.

THE AGENCIES OF
THE CUMBERLAND PRESBYTERIAN CHURCH CENTER
SHARED SERVICES
STATEMENT OF FINANCIAL POSITION
DECEMBER 31, 2016

ASSETS

Cash	$ 172,151
Accounts receivable	341
Buildings and land	2,760,412
Less: Accumulated depreciation	(587,605)
Furniture and equipment	156,745
Less: Accumulated depreciation	(156,745)
Total Assets	$ 2,345,299

LIABILITIES AND NET ASSETS

Liabilities:	
Accounts payable	$ 1,500
Net Assets:	
Unrestricted	2,343,799
Total Liabilities and Net Assets	$ 2,345,299

See accompanying notes.

THE AGENCIES OF
THE CUMBERLAND PRESBYTERIAN CHURCH CENTER
HISTORICAL FOUNDATION
STATEMENT OF FINANCIAL POSITION
DECEMBER 31, 2016

ASSETS

Cash	$	54,943
Endowment earnings receivable		17,941
Due from other agencies, boards, and divisions		178,109
Securities and investments		
Real estate		38,755
		289,748
Endowments - held by Endowment Program		1,490,760
Total Assets	$	1,780,508

LIABILITIES AND NET ASSETS

Net Assets:		
Unrestricted	$	66,976
Temporarily restricted		183,762
Permanently restricted		1,529,770
Total net assets		1,780,508
Total Liabilities and Net Assets	$	1,780,508

See accompanying notes.

THE AGENCIES OF
THE CUMBERLAND PRESBYTERIAN CHURCH CENTER
BOARD OF STEWARDSHIP, FOUNDATION, AND BENEFITS
STATEMENT OF FINANCIAL POSITION
DECEMBER 31, 2016

ASSETS

Cash	$	696
Endowment earnings receivable		23,952
Due from other agencies, boards, and divisions		407,711
		432,359
Endowments - held by Endowment Program		1,919,029
Total Assets	$	2,351,388

LIABILITIES AND NET ASSETS

Liabilities:		
Cash borrowed from other agencies, boards, and divisions	$	17,463
Net Assets:		
Unrestricted		414,899
Permanently restricted		1,919,026
Total net assets		2,333,925
Total Liabilities and Net Assets	$	2,351,388

See accompanying notes.

THE AGENCIES OF
THE CUMBERLAND PRESBYTERIAN CHURCH CENTER
SMALL CHURCH LOAN PROGRAM
STATEMENT OF FINANCIAL POSITION
DECEMBER 31, 2016

ASSETS

Interest receivable, net of allowance for uncollectible interest	$	1,814
Loans receivable, net of allowance for loan losses		174,240
Due from other agencies, boards, and divisions		274,202
Total Assets	$	450,256

LIABILITIES AND NET ASSETS

Net Assets:		
Permanently restricted	$	450,256
Total Liabilities and Net Assets	$	450,256

See accompanying notes.

THE AGENCIES OF
THE CUMBERLAND PRESBYTERIAN CHURCH CENTER
INSURANCE PROGRAM
STATEMENT OF FINANCIAL POSITION
DECEMBER 31, 2016

ASSETS

Cash	$ 21,210
Prepaid expenses	140,996
Due from other agencies, boards, and divisions	1,966,456
Total Assets	$ 2,128,662

LIABILITIES AND NET ASSETS

Liabilities:	
Accounts payable	$ 43,490
Net Assets:	
Unrestricted	2,085,172
Total Liabilities and Net Assets	$ 2,128,662

See accompanying notes.

THE AGENCIES OF
THE CUMBERLAND PRESBYTERIAN CHURCH CENTER
MINISTERIAL AID
STATEMENT OF FINANCIAL POSITION
DECEMBER 31, 2016

ASSETS

Cash	$	39,153
Endowment earnings receivable		9,978
Due from other agencies, boards, and divisions		312,433
		361,564
Endowment Funds - held by Endowment Program		3,116,905
Total Assets	$	3,478,469

LIABILITIES AND NET ASSETS

Net Assets:		
Unrestricted	$	361,564
Permanently restricted		3,116,905
Total net assets		3,478,469
Total Liabilities and Net Assets	$	3,478,469

See accompanying notes.

THE AGENCIES OF
THE CUMBERLAND PRESBYTERIAN CHURCH CENTER
INVESTMENT LOAN PROGRAM
STATEMENT OF FINANCIAL POSITION
DECEMBER 31, 2016

ASSETS

Endowment earnings receivable	$ 8,000
Interest and dividends receivable, net of allowance for uncollectible interest	64,165
Securities and investments	
Cash equivalents	3,111,410
Bonds and mortgage backed securities	12,072,303
Loans receivable, net of allowance for loan losses	7,136,619
Total Assets	$ 22,392,497

LIABILITIES AND NET ASSETS

Liabilities:	
Notes payable to individual investors	$ 2,388,752
Due to other agencies, boards, and divisions	3,982,771
Depository accounts held for church organizations	14,117,998
Total liabilities	20,489,521
Net Assets:	
Unrestricted	1,902,976
Total Liabilities and Net Assets	$ 22,392,497

See accompanying notes.

THE AGENCIES OF
THE CUMBERLAND PRESBYTERIAN CHURCH CENTER
RETIREMENT FUND
STATEMENT OF FINANCIAL POSITION
DECEMBER 31, 2016

ASSETS

Interest and dividends receivable, net of allowance for uncollectible interest	$ 12,064
Securities and investments	
Cash equivalents	316,860
Equity mutual funds	1,274,831
Real estate investment trusts	1,405,704
Private investment entities	20,188,148
Total Assets	$ 23,197,607

LIABILITIES AND NET ASSETS

Net Assets:	
Net assets available for benefits, at fair value	$ 23,197,607
Total Liabilities and Net Assets	$ 23,197,607

See accompanying notes.

THE AGENCIES OF
THE CUMBERLAND PRESBYTERIAN CHURCH CENTER
ENDOWMENT PROGRAM
STATEMENT OF FINANCIAL POSITION
DECEMBER 31, 2016

ASSETS

Cash	$ 330,876
Interest and dividends receivable, net of allowance for uncollectible interest	32,920
Securities and investments	
Cash equivalents	560,978
Equity mutual funds	3,045,887
Real estate investment trusts	4,260,182
Private investment entities	48,009,451
Loans receivable, net of allowance for loan losses	2,233,897
	58,474,191
Less: Net endowment assets of The Agencies of The Cumberland Presbyterian Church Center, as reflected on separate statements of financial position	(25,415,371)
Total Assets	$ 33,058,820

LIABILITIES AND NET ASSETS

Liabilities:	
Due to other agencies, boards, and divisions	$ 2,380,261
Net Assets:	
Permanently restricted:	
Cumberland Presbyterian Children's Home	4,957,139
Discipleship Ministry Team	2,036,164
Missions Ministry Team	13,441,191
Memphis Theological Seminary	10,313,096
Board of Stewardship, Foundation, and Benefits	1,919,029
Our United Outreach	2,591,320
General Assembly Corporation	435,755
Communications Ministry Team	121,902
Pastoral Development Ministry Team	262,345
The Historical Foundation	1,490,760
Ministerial Aid	3,116,905
Bethel University	2,914,192
Other designated persons and organizations	12,494,132
Total net assets	56,093,930
Less: Net endowment assets of The Agencies of The Cumberland Presbyterian Church Center, as reflected on separate statements of financial position	(25,415,371)
Total Liabilities and Net Assets	$ 33,058,820

See accompanying notes.

THE AGENCIES OF
THE CUMBERLAND PRESBYTERIAN CHURCH CENTER
OUR UNITED OUTREACH
STATEMENT OF ACTIVITY
FOR THE YEAR ENDED DECEMBER 31, 2016

	Unrestricted	Temporarily Restricted	Permanently Restricted	Totals
Revenues, gains, and other support:				
Contributions	$ 2,394,190	$ -	$ 31,023	$ 2,425,213
Endowment earnings	-	-	15,583	15,583
Income from oil royalties	8,891	-	-	8,891
Net realized and unrealized gain on investments	-	-	138,434	138,434
Net assets released from restriction	130,147	-	(130,147)	-
	2,533,228	-	54,893	2,588,121
Expenses:				
Distribution to other agencies, boards, and divisions of The Cumberland Presbyterian Church:				
Bethel University	119,196	-	-	119,196
Board of Stewardship	143,035	-	-	143,035
Commission on Chaplains	9,226	-	-	9,226
Committee on Theology and Social Concern	3,243	-	-	3,243
Committee on Judiciary	8,701	-	-	8,701
Communications Ministry Team	125,351	-	-	125,351
Contingency Fund	14,000	-	-	14,000
Cumberland Presbyterian Children's Home	71,518	-	-	71,518
Discipleship Ministry Team	6,228	-	-	6,228
Evaluation Committee	3,500	-	-	3,500
General Assembly Council	190,714	-	-	190,714
Historical Foundation	71,518	-	-	71,518
Memphis Theological Seminary	136,837	-	-	136,837
Ministry Council	1,019,400	-	-	1,019,400
Missions Ministry Team	31,640	-	-	31,640
Nominating Committee	2,670	-	-	2,670
Pastoral Development Ministry Team	9,342	-	-	9,342
Program of Alternate Studies	30,037	-	-	30,037
Shared Service (Maintenance/Operations)	405,267	-	-	405,267
Shared Service (OUO Committee)	92,044	-	-	92,044
Unification Task Force	35,000			35,000
Property tax	3,760	-	-	3,760
	2,532,227	-	-	2,532,227
Change in net assets	1,001	-	54,893	55,894
Net assets at beginning of year	(18,829)	-	2,536,427	2,517,598
Net assets at end of year	$ (17,828)	$ -	$ 2,591,320	$ 2,573,492

See accompanying notes.

THE AGENCIES OF
THE CUMBERLAND PRESBYTERIAN CHURCH CENTER
GENERAL ASSEMBLY CORPORATION
STATEMENT OF ACTIVITY
FOR THE YEAR ENDED DECEMBER 31, 2016

	Unrestricted	Temporarily Restricted	Permanently Restricted	Totals
Revenues, gains, and other support:				
Our United Outreach	$ 190,967	$ -	$ -	$ 190,967
Contributions and gifts	270,938	-	-	270,938
Endowment earnings	22,764	-	-	22,764
Interest income	10,600	-	-	10,600
Other income	(5,882)	-	-	(5,882)
Net realized and unrealized gain on investments	-	-	23,385	23,385
Net assets released from restriction	20,121	-	(20,121)	-
	509,508	-	3,264	512,772
Expenses:				
Conferences and events	20,254	-	-	20,254
Employee benefits	28,141	-	-	28,141
Equipment maintenance	2,361	-	-	2,361
Grants made	176,027	-	-	176,027
Insurance	1,964	-	-	1,964
Miscellaneous	450	-	-	450
Office	2,486	-	-	2,486
Payroll taxes	4,416	-	-	4,416
Postage and shipping	393	-	-	393
Printing and publications	1,434	-	-	1,434
Retirement	8,081	-	-	8,081
Salaries	167,783	-	-	167,783
Supplies	721	-	-	721
Travel	13,486	-	-	13,486
Total expenses	427,997	-	-	427,997
Change in net assets	81,511	-	3,264	84,775
Net assets at beginning of year	59,441	-	432,488	491,929
Net assets at end of year	$ 140,952	$ -	$ 435,752	$ 576,704

See accompanying notes.

THE AGENCIES OF
THE CUMBERLAND PRESBYTERIAN CHURCH CENTER
MINISTRY COUNCIL
STATEMENT OF ACTIVITY
FOR THE YEAR ENDED DECEMBER 31, 2016

	Unrestricted	Temporarily Restricted	Permanently Restricted	Totals
Revenues, gains, and other support:				
Our United Outreach	$ 1,224,118	$ -	$ -	$ 1,224,118
Contributions	-	1,144,472	25,120	1,169,592
Endowment earnings	(776,713)	-	96,799	(679,914)
Gifts - designated	2,129,377	-	-	2,129,377
Gifts - undesignated	125,992	-	-	125,992
Interest income	23,153	41,435	-	64,588
Registration fees	15,731	-	-	15,731
Sales of materials, literature, etc.	164,886	-	-	164,886
Subscription income	32,458	-	-	32,458
Net realized and unrealized gain on investments	-	-	857,761	857,761
Net assets released from restrictions	1,916,908	(786,692)	(1,130,216)	-
	4,855,910	399,215	(150,536)	5,104,589
Expenses:				
Computer	7,776	-	-	7,776
Conferences and events	113,820	-	-	113,820
Consulting fees	21,006	-	-	21,006
Contract labor	14,613	-	-	14,613
Dues and subscriptions	1,668	-	-	1,668
Employee benefits	120,888	-	-	120,888
Equipment maintenance	472	-	-	472
Grants made	2,626,146	-	-	2,626,146
Insurance	18,795	-	-	18,795
Legal fees	230	-	-	230
Miscellaneous	15,478	-	-	15,478
Missionary support	323,627	-	-	323,627
Office	76	-	-	76
Payroll taxes	34,161	-	-	34,161
Postage and shipping	51,267	-	-	51,267
Printing and publications	144,311	-	-	144,311
Purchases for resale	32,554	-	-	32,554
Rent	510	-	-	510
Retirement	40,020	-	-	40,020
Salaries	949,686	-	-	949,686
Supplies	15,179	-	-	15,179
Telephone	2,931	-	-	2,931
Training	1,070	-	-	1,070
Travel	131,839	-	-	131,839
Total expenses	4,668,123	-	-	4,668,123
Change in net assets	187,787	399,215	(150,536)	436,466
Net assets at beginning of year	1,080,503	1,117,796	16,012,141	18,210,440
Net assets at end of year	$ 1,268,290	$ 1,517,011	$ 15,861,605	$ 18,646,906

See accompanying notes.

THE AGENCIES OF
THE CUMBERLAND PRESBYTERIAN CHURCH CENTER
SHARED SERVICES
STATEMENT OF ACTIVITY
FOR THE YEAR ENDED DECEMBER 31, 2016

	Unrestricted	Temporarily Restricted	Permanently Restricted	Totals
Revenues, gains, and other support:				
Our United Outreach	$ 405,267	$ -	$ -	$ 405,267
Expenses:				
Accounting fees	21,050	-	-	21,050
Bank fees	14,620	-	-	14,620
Computer	1,759	-	-	1,759
Consulting fees	40,421	-	-	40,421
Contract labor	270	-	-	270
Depreciation	65,289	-	-	65,289
Employee benefits	15,840	-	-	15,840
Equipment maintenance	20,421	-	-	20,421
Insurance	12,162	-	-	12,162
Miscellaneous	75,000	-	-	75,000
Occupancy	78,853	-	-	78,853
Payroll taxes	3,807	-	-	3,807
Postage and shipping	271	-	-	271
Property tax	1,945	-	-	1,945
Retirement	2,488	-	-	2,488
Salaries	49,767	-	-	49,767
Supplies	1,160	-	-	1,160
Telephone	8,982	-	-	8,982
Total expenses	414,105	-	-	414,105
Change in net assets	(8,838)	-	-	(8,838)
Net assets at beginning of year	2,352,637	-	-	2,352,637
Net assets at end of year	$ 2,343,799	$ -	$ -	$ 2,343,799

See accompanying notes.

THE AGENCIES OF
THE CUMBERLAND PRESBYTERIAN CHURCH CENTER
HISTORICAL FOUNDATION
STATEMENT OF ACTIVITY
FOR THE YEAR ENDED DECEMBER 31, 2016

	Unrestricted	Temporarily Restricted	Permanently Restricted	Totals
Revenues, gains, and other support:				
Our United Outreach	$ 71,518	$ -	$ -	$ 71,518
Contributions and gifts	2,833	37,879	26,897	67,609
Endowment earnings	-	-	8,917	8,917
Interest income	-	5,874	-	5,874
Net realized and unrealized gain on investments	-	-	79,393	79,393
Net assets released from restriction	128,842	(57,771)	(71,071)	-
	203,193	(14,018)	44,136	233,311
Expenses:				
Archival acquisitions	34,853	-	-	34,853
Archival equipment	26,347	-	-	26,347
Birthplace shrine	10,246	-	-	10,246
Computer equipment and supplies	840	-	-	840
Contract labor	5,845	-	-	5,845
Dues and subscriptions	1,786	-	-	1,786
Employee benefits	10,271	-	-	10,271
Insurance	3,381	-	-	3,381
Miscellaneous	22	-	-	22
Office	166	-	-	166
Payroll taxes	5,913	-	-	5,913
Postage and shipping	248	-	-	248
Printing and publications	1,552	-	-	1,552
Purchases for resale	1,508	-	-	1,508
Rent	110	-	-	110
Retirement	7,730	-	-	7,730
Salaries	77,302	-	-	77,302
Supplies	1,639	-	-	1,639
Training	6,416	-	-	6,416
Travel	7,890	-	-	7,890
Total expenses	204,065	-	-	204,065
Change in net assets	(872)	(14,018)	44,136	29,246
Net assets at beginning of year	67,848	197,780	1,485,634	1,751,262
Net assets at end of year	$ 66,976	$ 183,762	$ 1,529,770	$ 1,780,508

See accompanying notes.

THE AGENCIES OF
THE CUMBERLAND PRESBYTERIAN CHURCH CENTER
BOARD OF STEWARDSHIP, FOUNDATION AND BENEFITS
STATEMENT OF ACTIVITY
FOR THE YEAR ENDED DECEMBER 31, 2016

	Unrestricted	Temporarily Restricted	Permanently Restricted	Totals
Revenues, gains, and other support:				
Our United Outreach	$ 143,035	$ -	$ -	$ 143,035
Contributions and gifts	27,387	-	200	27,587
Endowment earnings	(3,283)	-	11,621	8,338
Interest income	13,144	-	-	13,144
Management service fees	52,683	-	-	52,683
Net realized and unrealized gain on investments	-	-	102,903	102,903
Net assets released from restriction	95,270	-	(95,270)	-
	328,236	-	19,454	347,690
Expenses:				
Accounting	2,872	-	-	2,872
Computer	1,972	-	-	1,972
Dues and subscriptions	870	-	-	870
Employee benefits	58,599	-	-	58,599
Grants made	42,176	-	-	42,176
Insurance	3,575	-	-	3,575
Legal	16	-	-	16
Payroll taxes	7,472	-	-	7,472
Postage and shipping	974	-	-	974
Printing and publications	4,033	-	-	4,033
Relocation	20	-	-	20
Retirement	9,227	-	-	9,227
Salaries	184,527	-	-	184,527
Stewardship fees	3,500	-	-	3,500
Stewardship materials and events	20	-	-	20
Supplies	2,245	-	-	2,245
Travel and board meetings	20,223	-	-	20,223
Total expenses	342,321	-	-	342,321
Change in net assets	(14,085)	-	19,454	5,369
Net assets at beginning of year	428,984	-	1,899,572	2,328,556
Net assets at end of year	$ 414,899	$ -	$ 1,919,026	$ 2,333,925

See accompanying notes.

THE AGENCIES OF
THE CUMBERLAND PRESBYTERIAN CHURCH CENTER
SMALL CHURCH LOAN PROGRAM
STATEMENT OF ACTIVITY
FOR THE YEAR ENDED DECEMBER 31, 2016

	Unrestricted	Temporarily Restricted	Permanently Restricted	Totals
Revenues, gains, and other support:				
Contributions	$ -	$ -	$ 51,635	$ 51,635
Interest income	-	-	15,706	15,706
Net assets released from restriction	51,635	-	(51,635)	-
	51,635	-	15,706	67,341
Expenses:				
Distribution to other agencies, boards, and divisions of The Cumberland Presbyterian Church:				
Investment Loan Program	51,635	-	-	51,635
Change in net assets	-	-	15,706	15,706
Net assets at beginning of year	-	-	434,550	434,550
Net assets at end of year	$ -	$ -	$ 450,256	$ 450,256

See accompanying notes.

THE AGENCIES OF
THE CUMBERLAND PRESBYTERIAN CHURCH CENTER
INSURANCE PROGRAM
STATEMENT OF ACTIVITY
FOR THE YEAR ENDED DECEMBER 31, 2016

	Unrestricted	Temporarily Restricted	Permanently Restricted	Totals
Revenues, gains, and other support:				
Premium revenue	$ 1,600,183	$ -	$ -	$ 1,600,183
Contributions	26,540	-	-	26,540
Interest income	13,810	-	-	13,810
Net realized gain on investments	10,687	-	-	10,687
Net unrealized gain on investments	88,810	-	-	88,810
	1,740,030	-	-	1,740,030
Expenses:				
Consulting fees	733	-	-	733
Dues and subscriptions	763	-	-	763
Employee benefits	4,825	-	-	4,825
Insurance premiums	1,806,713	-	-	1,806,713
Miscellaneous	2,040	-	-	2,040
Payroll taxes	1,923	-	-	1,923
Postage and shipping	364	-	-	364
Retirement	1,256	-	-	1,256
Salaries	25,133	-	-	25,133
Total expenses	1,843,750	-	-	1,843,750
Change in net assets	(103,720)	-	-	(103,720)
Net assets at beginning of year	2,188,892	-	-	2,188,892
Net assets at end of year	$ 2,085,172	$ -	$ -	$ 2,085,172

See accompanying notes.

THE AGENCIES OF
THE CUMBERLAND PRESBYTERIAN CHURCH CENTER
MINISTERIAL AID
STATEMENT OF ACTIVITY
FOR THE YEAR ENDED DECEMBER 31, 2016

	Unrestricted	Temporarily Restricted	Permanently Restricted	Totals
Revenues, gains, and other support:				
Contributions	$ -	$ -	$ 3,851	$ 3,851
Endowment earnings	(11,139)	-	18,442	7,303
Interest income	8,424	-	-	8,424
Net realized and unrealized gain on investments	-	-	164,671	164,671
Net assets released from restriction	39,905	-	(39,905)	-
	37,190	-	147,059	184,249
Expenses:				
Ministerial aid	64,266	-	-	64,266
Change in net assets	(27,076)	-	147,059	119,983
Net assets at beginning of year	388,640	-	2,969,846	3,358,486
Net assets at end of year	$ 361,564	$ -	$ 3,116,905	$ 3,478,469

See accompanying notes.

THE AGENCIES OF
THE CUMBERLAND PRESBYTERIAN CHURCH CENTER
INVESTMENT LOAN PROGRAM
STATEMENT OF ACTIVITY
FOR THE YEAR ENDED DECEMBER 31, 2016

	Unrestricted	Temporarily Restricted	Permanently Restricted	Totals
Revenues, gains, and other support:				
Interest income	$ 727,363	$ -	$ -	$ 727,363
Interest expense	(504,923)	-	-	(504,923)
Net interest income	222,440	-	-	222,440
Net gain (loss) on investments	(27,744)	-	-	(27,744)
	194,696	-	-	194,696
Expenses:				
Accounting fees	5,225	-	-	5,225
Legal fees	13,282	-	-	13,282
Management fee	51,000	-	-	51,000
Miscellaneous	11,252	-	-	11,252
Office	2,327	-	-	2,327
Postage and shipping	693	-	-	693
Supplies	386	-	-	386
Total expenses	84,165	-	-	84,165
Change in net assets	110,531	-	-	110,531
Net assets at beginning of year	1,792,445	-	-	1,792,445
Net assets at end of year	$ 1,902,976	$ -	$ -	$ 1,902,976

See accompanying notes.

THE AGENCIES OF
THE CUMBERLAND PRESBYTERIAN CHURCH CENTER
RETIREMENT FUND
STATEMENT OF ACTIVITY
FOR THE YEAR ENDED DECEMBER 31, 2016

	Net Assets Available for Benefits
Additions to Net Assets attributed to:	
Investment income:	
Interest and dividend income	$ 119,950
Management service fees	(16,410)
Net realized gain on investments	158,981
Net unrealized gain on investments	1,097,917
Net investment income	1,360,438
Contributions:	
Contributions by participants	686,942
	2,047,380
Deductions from Net Assets attributed to:	
Disbursements to participants	1,578,924
Change in plan assets available for benefits	468,456
Net assets available for benefits at beginning of year	22,729,151
Net assets available for benefits at end of year	$ 23,197,607

See accompanying notes.

THE AGENCIES OF
THE CUMBERLAND PRESBYTERIAN CHURCH CENTER
ENDOWMENT PROGRAM
STATEMENT OF ACTIVITY
FOR THE YEAR ENDED DECEMBER 31, 2016

	Unrestricted	Temporarily Restricted	Permanently Restricted	Totals
Changes in Permanently Restricted Net Assets:				
Revenues, gains, and other support:				
Contributions	$ -	$ -	$ 1,294,280	$ 1,294,280
Interest and dividend income	-	-	394,314	394,314
Net realized gain on investments	-	-	319,515	319,515
Net unrealized gain on investments	-	-	2,770,264	2,770,264
	-	-	4,778,373	4,778,373
Expenses:				
Distribution for designated purposes	-	-	3,062,313	3,062,313
Distribution of earnings	-	-	1,966,488	1,966,488
Other expenses	-	-	34,109	34,109
	-	-	5,062,910	5,062,910
Change in net assets	-	-	(284,537)	(284,537)
Net assets at beginning of year	-	-	56,378,467	56,378,467
Net assets at end of year	$ -	$ -	$ 56,093,930	$ 56,093,930
Represented by funds held in trust for others:				
Bethel University	$ -	$ -	$ 2,914,192	$ 2,914,192
Cumberland Presbyterian Children's Home	-	-	4,957,139	4,957,139
Memphis Theological Seminary	-	-	10,313,096	10,313,096
Other designated persons and organizations	-	-	12,494,132	12,494,132
	-	-	30,678,559	30,678,559
Represented by funds held for The Agencies of The Cumberland Presbyterian Church Center:				
Discipleship Ministry Team	-	-	2,036,164	2,036,164
Missions Ministry Team	-	-	13,441,191	13,441,191
Board of Stewardship, Foundation, and Benefits	-	-	1,919,029	1,919,029
Our United Outreach	-	-	2,591,320	2,591,320
General Assembly Corporation	-	-	435,755	435,755
Communications Ministry Team	-	-	121,902	121,902
Pastoral Development Ministry Team	-	-	262,345	262,345
The Historical Foundation	-	-	1,490,760	1,490,760
Ministerial Aid	-	-	3,116,905	3,116,905
	-	-	25,415,371	25,415,371
Net assets at end of year	$ -	$ -	$ 56,093,930	$ 56,093,930

See accompanying notes.

THE AGENCIES OF
THE CUMBERLAND PRESBYTERIAN CHURCH CENTER

NOTES TO FINANCIAL STATEMENTS
DECEMBER 31, 2016

Note A - Nature of Activities and Significant Accounting Policies

Nature of Activities - By the covenant of Abraham and his descendants according to faith, God has established the church in the world through His Son Jesus Christ. This household of faith, the universal church, consists of all those persons in every nation and every age who confess Jesus Christ as Lord and Savior and who respond to His call for discipleship. The church in the world never exists for herself alone, but to glorify God and work for reconciliation through Christ. Christ claims the church and gives her the word and sacraments in order to bring God's grace and judgment to persons.

The General Assembly is the highest judicatory of this church and represents in one body all the particular churches thereof. It bears the title of the General Assembly of the Cumberland Presbyterian Church and constitutes the bond of union, peace, correspondence, and mutual confidence among all its churches and judicatories. The Agencies of The Cumberland Presbyterian Church Center have been established by the General Assembly and in 2000 it caused the Cumberland Presbyterian Church General Assembly Corporation to be formed. The Agencies consist of the following entities:

Cumberland Presbyterian Church General Assembly Corporation
Ministry Council of the Cumberland Presbyterian Church, Inc.
Board of Stewardship, Foundation, and Benefits of the Cumberland Presbyterian Church, Inc.
Historical Foundation of the Cumberland Presbyterian Church and the Cumberland Presbyterian Church in America

Contributions - Contributions received are recorded as unrestricted, temporarily restricted, or permanently restricted, depending on the existence and/or nature of any donor restrictions.

Support that is restricted by the donor is reported as an increase in unrestricted net assets if the restriction expires in the reporting period in which the support is recognized. All other donor restricted support is reported as an increase in temporarily or permanently restricted net assets depending on the nature of the restriction. When a restriction expires, temporarily restricted net assets are reclassified to unrestricted net assets.

Donated Equipment and Services - Donated equipment is reflected as contributions in the accompanying financial statements at their estimated values at the date of receipt. No equipment was donated to the Center during the year ended December 31, 2016. No amounts have been reflected in the statements for donated services because they did not meet the criteria for recognition under FASB ASC 958-605-25.

Use of Estimates - The preparation of financial statements in conformity with generally accepted accounting principles requires management to make estimates and assumptions that affect the reported amounts of assets and liabilities and disclosure of contingent assets and liabilities at the date of the financial statements and the reported amounts of revenues and expenses during the reporting period. Actual results could differ from these estimates.

NOTES CONTINUED

Note A - Nature of Activities and Significant Accounting Policies - Continued

The Cumberland Presbyterian Church Investment Loan Program, Inc.'s notes receivable consist of loans made to congregations, governing bodies, church organizations, and other qualifying related entities. The ability of each borrower to repay its loan generally depends upon the contributions received from its members. The number of members of each congregation and its revenue is likely to fluctuate.

The Program must rely on the borrower's or guarantor's continued financial viability for repayment of loans. If a borrower or guarantor experiences a decrease in contributions or revenues, payments on that loan may be adversely affected. Even though the loans are collateralized by real estate, realization of the appraised value upon default is not assured and is dependent upon the local economic conditions of the borrower. Therefore, the determination of the adequacy of the allowance for notes receivable losses is based on estimates that are particularly susceptible to significant changes in the economic environment and market conditions for the geographic areas where the borrowers are located.

While management uses available information to recognize losses on notes receivable, further reductions in the carrying amounts of notes receivable may be necessary based on changes in the economic conditions for the geographic area of the borrowers. It is therefore reasonably possible that the estimated losses on notes receivable may change materially in the near term. However, the amount of the change that is reasonably possible cannot be estimated.

Promises to Give - Unconditional promises to give are recognized as revenue or gains in the period received and as assets or decreases of liabilities depending on the form of the benefits received. Conditional promises to give are recognized when the conditions on which they depend are substantially met. The Center has no promises to give at December 31, 2016.

Inventory - Inventories are stated at the lower of cost or market. Cost is determined using the average cost method.

Depreciation - In years past, Shared Services has recorded property and equipment as assets and depreciated them. Depreciation of property and equipment was computed using the straight-line method over the estimated useful lives of the assets. Purchases of equipment after 1996 are not capitalized, but expensed when purchased; therefore, no depreciation expense has been recorded for items acquired in 1997 and thereafter. The difference between the cost of fixed assets expensed and depreciation expense that would be recorded is immaterial. In 2008, the Center purchased land and two incomplete office buildings. The cost of these plus the construction costs necessary to complete the new Center were capitalized and are being depreciated over an estimated useful life of 39 years. In 2009, the Shared Services agency purchased a large amount of computer equipment and capitalized these costs. The computer equipment purchased is being depreciated over an estimated useful life of four years.

Property and Equipment - Property and equipment is recorded at historical cost. Donated property and equipment is recorded at fair market value at the date of donation. Such donations are reported as unrestricted support unless the donor has restricted the donated asset to a specific purpose. Assets donated with explicit restrictions regarding their use and contributions of cash that must be used to acquire property and equipment are reported as restricted support. Absent donor stipulations regarding how long those donated assets must be maintained, the Center reports expirations of donor restrictions when the donated or acquired assets are placed in service as instructed by the donor. The Center re-classes temporarily restricted net assets to unrestricted net assets at that time.

NOTES CONTINUED

Note A - Nature of Activities and Significant Accounting Policies - Continued

Investments - Investments are stated at fair value. Investments in private investment entities are valued based on the Center's proportional share of the net asset valuations reported by the general partners of the underlying entities. The reported values of all other investments (with the exception of notes receivable) are measured by quoted prices in active markets. Realized and unrealized gains and losses are reflected in the statement of activities. (See Note L)

The Center's investments include various types of securities in various companies within various markets. Investment securities are exposed to several risks, such as interest rate, market and credit risks. Due to the risks associated with certain investment securities, it is at least reasonably possible that changes in the values of investment securities will occur in the near term and those changes could materially affect the amounts reported in the Center's combined financial statements.

Fair Value Measurements - Fair value under accounting principles generally accepted in the United States of America is defined as the price that would be received to sell an asset or paid to transfer a liability in an orderly transaction between market participants at the measurement date. Generally accepted accounting principles establishes a three-tier fair value hierarchy that prioritizes the inputs used to measure fair value. These tiers include: Level 1, defined as observable inputs such as quoted prices available in active markets for identical assets or liabilities; Level 2, defined as pricing inputs other than quoted prices in active markets that are either directly or indirectly observable; and Level 3, defined as unobservable inputs about which little or no market data exists, therefore requiring an entity to develop its own assessment about the assumptions the market participants would use in pricing an asset or liability.

Income Tax Status - The Center is a not-for-profit organization exempt from federal income taxes under Internal Revenue Code (IRC) Section 501(c)(3). Thus, no provision for federal income taxes has been made. The Center has a defined contribution retirement plan which is qualified under Internal Revenue Code Section 403(b); no provision for income taxes has been included in the Plan's financial statements.

Cash and Cash Equivalents - For purposes of the statement of cash flows, all highly liquid investments with a maturity of three months or less are considered to be cash equivalents. However, cash and cash equivalents reported as securities and investments by the Endowment Program, Investment Loan Program and Retirement Fund are considered investments for purposes of the statement of cash flows.

Loans Receivable and Allowance for Losses - Loans receivable are stated at unpaid principal balances, less the allowance for notes receivable losses. Inter-agency loans are shown as due to/from other agencies, boards, and divisions.

The allowance for loans receivable is maintained at a level which, in management's judgment, is adequate to absorb credit losses inherent in the loans receivable portfolio. The amount of the allowance is based on management's evaluation of the collectability of the portfolio, including the nature of the portfolio, credit concentrations, trends in historical loss experience, economic conditions, and other risks inherent in the portfolio. Although management uses available information to recognize losses on notes receivable, because of uncertainties associated with the various local economic conditions of the borrowers and collateral values, it is reasonably possible that a material change could occur in the allowance for notes receivable in the near term. However, the amount of the change that is reasonably possible cannot be estimated. When considered necessary, the allowance is increased by a charge to expense and reduced by actual charge-offs, net of recoveries.

NOTES CONTINUED

Note B - Retirement Plan

General - The Cumberland Presbyterian Church Retirement Plan Number Two is available to certain employees of the Church and its agencies. All agencies, boards, and divisions match each employee's contribution up to five percent of the employee's salary. The total retirement contribution expense for The Agencies of The Cumberland Presbyterian Church Center for 2016 was $67,546.

The Plan obtained its latest determination letter on January 31, 1972, in which the Internal Revenue Service stated that the Plan, as then designed, was in compliance with the applicable requirements of the Internal Revenue Code. The Plan has been amended since receiving the determination letter. However, the Plan administrator and the Plan's tax counsel believe that the plan is currently designed and being operated in compliance with the applicable requirements of the Internal Revenue Code. The Plan is a "church plan" and is, therefore, not subject to ERISA.

Eligibility - Employees who are 18 years of age are immediately eligible to participate in the plan.

Vesting - Participants are immediately 100% vested in their accounts.

Investments - The Plan's investments are held by a bank-administered trust fund. The trust is the funding vehicle for the Plan, and all contributions are made to the trust. The cost and market value of the Plan's investments at December 31, 2016, are as follows:

	Cost	Market Value
Total	$ 17,869,881	$ 23,197,607

Note C - Endowment Program

The Endowment Program includes assets of The Agencies of The Cumberland Presbyterian Church Center and the assets of other agencies, boards, and divisions.

The Program's investments, other than notes receivable, real estate, and certificates of deposit, are held by a bank-administered trust fund. The costs and market value of the Program's investments held in trust at December 31, 2016, are as follows:

	Cost	Market Value
Total	$ 43,882,470	$ 55,903,392

The Center has interpreted the Uniform Prudent Management of Institutional Funds Act ("UPMIFA") requiring a portion of a donor restricted endowment of perpetual duration be classified as permanently restricted assets. The amount of the endowment that must be retained permanently is in accordance with explicit donor stipulations as outlined in their respective trust agreements.

NOTES CONTINUED

Note C - Endowment Program - Continued

The primary objective of these endowments is to provide a balance between capital appreciation, preservation of capital, and current income. This is a long-term goal designed to maximize returns without undue risk. The Board of Stewardship has set distribution rates with certain beneficiaries of the Endowment Program.

Unless otherwise stated in the donor agreement, the Board of Stewardship shall select the investment portfolio where the endowments will be invested as described in the Investment Policy of the Center. The Investment Policy of the Center outlines the asset allocations, permissible investments, and objectives of the portfolios.

Endowment Net Asset Composition by Type of Fund as of December 31, 2016:

	Permanently Restricted	Total
Donor-restricted endowment funds	$ 56,093,930	$ 56,093,930
Total funds	$ 56,093,930	$ 56,093,930

Changes in Endowment Net Assets for the year ended December 31, 2016:

	Permanently Restricted	Total
Endowment net assets, beginning of year	$ 56,378,467	$ 56,378,467
Investment return	3,547,858	3,547,858
Contributions	1,294,280	1,294,280
Appropriation of endowment assets for expenditures	(5,126,675)	(5,126,675)
Endowment net assets, end of year	$ 56,093,930	$ 56,093,930

Description of Amount Classified as Permanently Restricted Net Assets (Endowment Only):

Permanently Restricted Net Assets -

The portion of perpetual endowment funds that is required to be retained permanently either by explicit donor stipulation or by UPMIFA	$ 56,093,930
Total endowment funds classified as permanently restricted net assets	$ 56,093,930

NOTES CONTINUED

Note D - Investment Loan Program

Nature of Activities - On March 19, 1999, the State of Tennessee approved the charter for the Cumberland Presbyterian Church Investment Loan Program, Inc., a subsidiary corporation of the Board of Stewardship, Foundation and Benefits of the Cumberland Presbyterian Church, Inc. The Program is designed to allow participants to help provide the loans needed to finance the growth of Cumberland Presbyterian congregations in the 21st century.

1. It provides building loans secured by first mortgages to congregations, presbyteries, and church agencies.

2. It allows congregations, presbyteries, church agencies, and individual members of the Cumberland Presbyterian Church to invest their funds in interest bearing accounts from which withdrawals can be made "on demand" replacing the function of the Cash Funds Management Program.

3. All participants have the opportunity to invest funds for specific terms (such as three years or five years) in order to receive a higher rate of interest. A prospectus outlines the added investment options offered.

Securities and Investments - The cost and market values of Investment Loan Program investments at December 31, 2016, are as follows:

	Cost	Market Value
Total	$ 15,795,731	$ 15,183,713

Notes Payable to Individual Investors - Notes payable to individual investors are made through a general offering in the states of Kentucky, New Mexico, Tennessee, and Texas to eligible individual investors and must be purchased in minimum face amounts of $500. All notes payable to individual investors shown in these financial statements are Adjustable Rate Ready Access Notes. Adjustable Rate Ready Access Notes are payable on demand and pay an adjustable interest rate that may be adjusted each month. Additions of principal may be made to Adjustable Rate Ready Access Notes at any time. Withdrawals from Adjustable Rate Ready Access Notes may be made at any time and are payable upon written request of the investor; however, the Program reserves the right to require the investor to provide up to thirty (30) days written notice of any intended withdrawal before such withdrawal is made. Both additions to and withdrawals from Adjustable Rate Ready Access Notes must be made in minimum amounts of $250. The Program may review certain factors, such as investment gap analysis, loan demand, cash flow needs, and the current policy of the Federal Reserve, before establishing each month's rate of interest.

The notes are non-negotiable and may be assigned only upon the Program's written consent. The notes are unsecured and of equal priority with all other current indebtedness of the Program.

NOTES CONTINUED

Note D - Investment Loan Program - Continued

Depository Accounts Held for Church Organizations - The Cumberland Presbyterian Church Investment Loan Program, Inc. accepts depository accounts in which church organizations may place funds with the Program, in minimum amounts of $500. All depository accounts shown in these financial statements are Adjustable Rate Ready Access accounts. Like the Program's notes, depository accounts are general obligations of the Program, are unsecured and not insured, and are of equal priority with all other current indebtedness of the Program including notes. The interest rate on the depository accounts is adjusted pursuant to the policies of the Cumberland Presbyterian Church Investment Loan Program, Inc. as they may be adopted from time to time by its Board of Directors. The Cumberland Presbyterian Church Investment Loan Program, Inc. may terminate any depository account upon sixty (60) days written notice to the church organization.

Loans Receivable - Amounts that have been loaned are included on the Statement of Financial Position as loans receivable. There are 26 loans outstanding at December 31, 2016.

Loans receivable are collectible primarily through monthly payments based on up to a twenty-five year amortization period. Interest rates, as determined by the board, are based on the Prime Interest Rate as reported in the Wall Street Journal plus 2.5% per annum. On loans originated for $500,000 or less, the interest rate will be adjusted triennially. On loans originated for more than $500,000, the interest rate will be adjusted annually for the term of the loan.

The composition of loans is as follows:

Loans receivable (secured by real estate)	$ 8,145,619
Less: allowance for loan losses	(1,009,000)
	$ 7,136,619

A summary of changes in the allowance for loan losses is as follows:

Balance at beginning of year	$ 1,009,000
Recovery of provision charged to operations	-
Balance at end of year	$ 1,009,000

Estimated receipts of principal payments for the five years subsequent to 2016 are:

Year ending December 31,	Amount
2017	$ 424,799
2018	426,647
2019	447,402
2020	469,104
2021	1,273,255
Thereafter	4,095,412
	$ 7,136,619

NOTES CONTINUED

Note E - Funds Held in Trust

The Discipleship Ministry Team leader of the Ministry Council is responsible for certain funds held in trust for outside groups. Funds invested by the executive director in Investment Loan Program amounted to the following as of December 31, 2016:

P.R.E.M. $ 208,017

The General Assembly Corporation is responsible for funds held in trust for certain committees and commissions. These funds are shown as liabilities in the Statement of Financial Position of the General Assembly Corporation. Activity in these funds for the year ended December 31, 2016, is as follows:

	Nominating Committee	Committee on Judiciary	Non-USA Moderator Travel Fund
Balance January 1, 2016	$ 5,473	$ 2,951	$ -
Our United Outreach	2,670	7,847	-
Contributions	103	-	-
Disbursements	(1,786)	(7,748)	-
Balance December 31, 2016	$ 6,460	$ 3,050	$ -

	Committee on Theology and Social Concerns	Commission on Chaplains
Balance January 1, 2016	$ 14,168	$ 8,753
Our United Outreach	-	128
Contributions	1,491	-
Disbursements	(632)	-
Balance December 31, 2016	$ 15,027	$ 8,881

Note F - Insurance Program

The Cumberland Presbyterian Group Health and Life Insurance Program is a fully insured, experience-rated plan with a policy year ending on the last day of February. Any excess of premium over medical claims and other plan expenses is retained by the insurer; excess losses are no longer carried forward as a charge against the experience for subsequent policy years, as in the past, but must be absorbed by the insurer. The plan is the responsibility of the Board of Stewardship, Foundation, and Benefits.

The plan has one Investment Loan Program account and one account in the Endowment Program. Both are used as a stabilization reserve to provide some protection against unexpected medical claims volatility. The balance at December 31, 2016 of the Investment Loan Program account is $87,907. The balance at December 31, 2016 of the Endowment Program account is $1,878,549.

NOTES CONTINUED

Note G - Concentrations of Credit Risk Arising from Cash Deposits in Excess of Insured Limits

The Center maintains its cash balances in a financial institution located in Memphis, Tennessee. The balances are insured by the Federal Deposit Insurance Corporation up to $250,000 as of December 31, 2016. At various times there were balances that exceeded these FDIC limits. Cash and cash equivalents classified as securities and investments are items held in equities backed by the Federal Government. These equities, while backed by the Federal Government, are not insured by the Federal Deposit Insurance Corporation. At December 31, 2016, a total of $233,310 exceeded the FDIC limits.

Note H - Real Estate

Real estate assets of both the Ministry Council and the Historical Foundation are held for investment and are therefore not depreciated. These assets amounted to the following at December 31, 2016:

Property Location	Ministry Council	Historical Foundation	Total
San Francisco, California	$ 51,818	$ -	$ 51,818
Birthplace Shrine Chapel, Dickson County, Tennessee	-	21,500	21,500
McAdow Home, Dickson County, Tennessee	-	17,255	17,255
Total	$ 51,818	$ 38,755	$ 90,573

Note I - Leases

The Ministry Council leases three copiers and two postage machines for use in its offices. Lease payments for the year ended December 31, 2016, totaled $12,208. The leases expire during 2017 and the minimum lease payments for the next year amount to $11,199.

NOTES CONTINUED

Note J - Combined Statement of Activities Expenses

The total expenses of various Agencies are included in the Combined Statement of Activities as follows:

Expense Description	Agencies
Our United Outreach	Our United Outreach
General Assembly Corporation	General Assembly Corporation
Ministry Council	Ministry Council
Shared Services	Shared Services
Historical Foundation	Historical Foundation
Board of Stewardship, Foundation, and Benefits	Board of Stewardship, Foundation, and Benefits
Small Church Loan Program	Small Church Loan Program
Insurance Program	Insurance Program
Ministerial Aid	Ministerial Aid
Investment Loan Program	Investment Loan Program
Retirement Fund	Retirement Fund
Endowment Program	Endowment Program

Costs originating from Shared Services (formerly Central Services - made up of Building and Maintenance, Computer Services Division, and Central Accounting Division) are now funded by Our United Outreach appropriations instead of being charged to the various applicable agencies based on usage.

Inter-agency revenue and expense items for Our United Outreach and endowment earnings have been eliminated on the combined statement of activity.

Note K - Fair Value Measurements

Prices for closed-end bond funds and equity mutual funds are readily available in the active markets in which those securities are traded, and the resulting fair values are categorized as level 1.

Prices for mortgage backed securities, bond mutual funds, and real estate investment trusts are determined on a recurring basis based upon inputs that are readily available in public markets or can be derived from information available in publicly quoted markets and are categorized as level 2.

NOTES CONTINUED

Note K - Fair Value Measurements - Continued

There is limited or no observable data for the prices of private investment entities that are held by the Center and the resulting fair values of these securities are categorized as level 3.

Fair values of assets measured on a recurring basis at December 31, 2016 are as follows:

		Fair Value Measurements at Reporting Date Using		
	Fair Value	Quoted Prices In Active Market for Identical Assets (Level 1)	Significant Other Observable Inputs (Level 2)	Significant Unobservable Inputs (Level 3)
December 31, 2016				
Mortgage backed securities	$ 12,072,303	$ -	$ 12,072,303	$ -
Equity mutual funds	4,320,718	4,320,718	-	-
Real estate investment trusts	5,665,886	-	5,665,886	-
Private investment entities	68,197,599	-	-	68,197,599
Total	$ 90,256,506	$ 4,320,718	$ 17,738,189	$ 68,197,599

Because of the multiple number and complexity of the calculations necessary, management does not believe it is practicable to estimate fair value of loans receivable, net of allowance for loan losses. Therefore, no adjustment has been made to the net carrying value of $9,544,756 listed on the Combined Statement of Financial Position.

NOTES CONTINUED

Note K - Fair Value Measurements - Continued

The following table provides information related to the previously mentioned investments that are valued based primarily on net asset value at December 31, 2016:

	Fair Value	Unfunded Commitments	Redemption Frequency (If Currently Eligible)	Redemption Notice Period
Private Investment Entities				
GT Emerging Markets (QP), L.P.	$ 5,761,140	None	Annual	90 Days
GT Offshore Fund, Ltd. (Class A)	8,470,688	None	Annual	90 Days
GT Offshore Fund, Ltd. (Class B)	10,229,421	None	Annual	90 Days
GT Institutional Fixed Income Fund LP	11,061,030	None	Annual	90 Days
GT ERISA Fund, Ltd. (Class A)	3,646,878	None	Annual	90 Days
GT ERISA Fund, Ltd. (Class B)	3,917,334	None	Annual	90 Days
GT Real Assets, L.P.	1,361,420	None	Annual	90 Days
GT Real Assets II, L.P.	260,649	None	Annual	91 Days
GT Special Opportunities III, L.P.	2,087,653	None	see note	see note
Palladian Partners VIII L.P.	435,322	None	Annual	90 Days
Midland Intl Equity QP Fund, L.P.	9,521,549	None	Quarterly	60 Days
Midland U.S. QP Fund, L.P.	11,444,515	None	Quarterly	60 Days
	$ 68,197,599			

The GT Special Opportunities III, L.P. provides for an annual redemption upon 90 days notice after an initial lock-up period of eighteen months.

NOTES CONTINUED

Note K - **Fair Value Measurements** - Continued

The following table summarizes fair value by fund for investments in private investment entities that are valued based primarily on net asset value at December 31, 2016:

Private Investment Entities	Retirement Fund	Endowment Program	Total Fair Value
GT Emerging Markets (QP), L.P.	$ 1,751,950	$ 4,009,190	$ 5,761,140
GT Offshore Fund, Ltd. (Class A)	-	8,470,688	8,470,688
GT Institutional Fixed Income Fund LP	3,239,585	7,821,445	11,061,030
GT Offshore Fund, Ltd. (Class B)	-	10,229,421	10,229,421
GT ERISA Fund, Ltd. (Class A)	3,646,878	-	3,646,878
GT ERISA Fund, Ltd. (Class B)	3,917,334	-	3,917,334
GT Real Assets, L.P.	422,510	938,910	1,361,420
GT Real Assets II, L.P.	74,471	186,178	260,649
GT Special Opportunities III, L.P.	625,237	1,462,416	2,087,653
Palladian Partners VIII LP.	118,724	316,598	435,322
Midland Intl Equity QP Fund, L.P.	2,876,644	6,644,905	9,521,549
Midland U.S. QP Fund, L.P.	3,515,085	7,929,430	11,444,515
	$ 20,188,418	$ 48,009,181	$ 68,197,599

NOTES CONTINUED

Note K - Fair Value Measurements - Continued

Assets measured at fair value on a recurring basis using significant unobservable inputs (Level 3):

Fair value at beginning of year	$ 67,163,648
Investments and distributions, net	677,685
Realized/unrealized gains (losses)	356,266
Fair value at end of year	$ 68,197,599

Gains and losses (realized and unrealized) for Level 3 assets included in net assets for the year are reported as follows:

On the Combined Statement of Activity, under Revenues, gains, and other support:

Permanently restricted net assets:	
Endowment program	$ 86,958
Net assets available for benefits:	
Retirement fund	269,308
Total net assets	$ 356,266

These investments without readily determinable values comprise approximately 60.31% of total assets at December 31, 2016.

All assets have been valued using a market approach.

A description of the Private Investment Entities and the investment objectives is as follows:

<u>GT Emerging Markets (QP), L.P.</u> - This fund is organized as a "fund of funds" which seek to achieve long-term capital appreciation through investments in limited partnerships, off-shore corporations, open-end mutual funds, closed-end mutual funds, commingled trust funds, and separately managed accounts that invest primarily in "emerging markets." Investments may also be made in industrialized nations such as the United States and Japan.

<u>GT Offshore Fund, Ltd. / GT ERISA Fund, Ltd.</u> - These are open-ended "umbrella" funds, incorporated as exempted companies in the Cayman Islands with multiple classes of Shares. Each class of share is separately valued and pursues its own clearly defined investment objective(s) and strategy(ies). These funds overall investment objectives are as follows:

Class A is broadly diversified among multiple investment managers and multiple investment strategies. The strategies employed may include multi-strategy arbitrage, capital structure arbitrage, distressed debt, long/short equity or niche financing.

Class B seeks to achieve a superior rate of return exceeding that of the MSCI World Index with less volatility while minimizing market risk through a hedged approach. The primary investment strategy will be a long/short equity strategy. This class is broadly diversified among multiple investment managers and multiple long/short equity strategies.

NOTES CONTINUED

Note K - Fair Value Measurements - Continued

GT Real Assets, L.P. - This fund is organized as a "fund of funds" investment vehicle that will pool and invest funds, generally through "Managed Investment Vehicles," for the purpose of generating attractive risk-adjusted returns by opportunistically investing in a broad spectrum of resources, real assets, and other investment strategies.

GT Special Opportunities, III, L.P. - This fund is organized as a "fund of funds" investment vehicle that will pool and invest funds, generally through "Managed Investment Vehicles," for the purpose of achieving a superior rate of return. The fund focuses on a very limited number of investment strategies that are considered to be opportunistic based upon prevailing market conditions. At times, the fund may only invest in one strategy and do so in a non-diversified manner, perhaps with only a single manager. The strategies sought by the fund will often be niche-focused. Accordingly, the risk level for the fund is anticipated to be extremely high.

Midland International Equity QP Fund, L.P. - This is an international equity fund which seeks to identify listed companies selling at a discount to intrinsic net worth on liquid stock exchanges of non-U.S. countries. The focus of this fund is long-term capital appreciation. This fund seeks to outperform the MSCI EAFE Index, net of fees and taxes, over a full market cycle.

Midland U.S. QP Fund, L.P. - This fund's objective is to outperform the broad U.S. equity market, defined as the Russell 3000 Index, net of fees and taxes over a full market cycle. The fund seeks to compound capital at attractive rates through direct and indirect long-term ownership of publicly traded businesses domiciled in the United States.

Note L - Securities and Investments

Securities and investments at December 31, 2016 are as follows:

	Ministry Council	Historical Foundation	Investment Loan Program	Retirement Fund	Endowment Program	Total
Cash and cash equivalents	$ -	$ -	$ 3,111,410	$ 316,860	$ 560,978	$ 3,989,248
Mortgage backed securities	-	-	12,072,303	-	-	12,072,303
Equity mutual funds	-	-	-	1,274,831	3,045,887	4,320,718
Real estate investment trusts	-	-	-	1,405,704	4,260,182	5,665,886
Private investment entities	-	-	-	20,188,148	48,009,451	68,197,599
Real estate	51,818	38,755	-	-	-	90,573
	$ 51,818	$ 38,755	$ 15,183,713	$ 23,185,543	$ 55,876,498	$ 94,336,327

Note M - Subsequent Events

Subsequent events were evaluated through May 15, 2017, which is the date the financial statements were available to be issued.

BETHEL UNIVERSITY

FINANCIAL STATEMENTS
AND OTHER INFORMATION

JULY 31, 2016 AND 2015

BETHEL UNIVERSITY

Table of Contents

	Page
INDEPENDENT AUDITOR'S REPORT	1 - 3
FINANCIAL STATEMENTS	
Statements of Financial Position	4
Statements of Activities	5 - 6
Statements of Cash Flows	7 - 8
Notes to Financial Statements	9 - 31
SUPPLEMENTARY INFORMATION	
Financial Responsibility Composite Score	32 - 33
University Key Financial Ratios	34 - 36
Unrestricted Net Assets Exclusive of Plant, Property, Equipment, and Related Debt and Obligation Under Financing Arrangement	37
OTHER INFORMATION	
Schedule of Expenditures of Federal Awards	38
Notes to Schedule of Expenditures of Federal Awards	39
INDEPENDENT AUDITOR'S REPORT ON INTERNAL CONTROL OVER FINANCIAL REPORTING AND ON COMPLIANCE AND OTHER MATTERS BASED ON AN AUDIT OF FINANCIAL STATEMENTS PERFORMED IN ACCORDANCE WITH *GOVERNMENT AUDITING STANDARDS*	40 - 41
INDEPENDENT AUDITOR'S REPORT ON COMPLIANCE FOR EACH MAJOR PROGRAM AND ON INTERNAL CONTROL OVER COMPLIANCE REQUIRED BY UNIFORM GUIDANCE	42 - 44
SCHEDULE OF FINDINGS AND QUESTIONED COSTS	45 - 46
SCHEDULE OF PRIOR YEAR FINDINGS AND QUESTIONED COSTS	47

Independent Auditor's Report

The Board of Trustees
Bethel University
McKenzie, Tennessee

Report on the Financial Statements

We have audited the accompanying financial statements of Bethel University (the "University"), which comprise the statements of financial position as of July 31, 2016 and 2015, and the related statements of activities and cash flows for the years then ended, and the related notes to the financial statements.

Management's Responsibility for the Financial Statements

Management is responsible for the preparation and fair presentation of these financial statements in accordance with accounting principles generally accepted in the United States of America; this includes the design, implementation, and maintenance of internal control relevant to the preparation and fair presentation of financial statements that are free from material misstatement, whether due to fraud or error.

Auditor's Responsibility

Our responsibility is to express an opinion on these financial statements based on our audits. We conducted our audits in accordance with auditing standards generally accepted in the United States of America and the standards applicable to financial audits contained in *Government Auditing Standards*, issued by the Comptroller General of the United States. Those standards require that we plan and perform the audit to obtain reasonable assurance about whether the financial statements are free from material misstatement.

An audit involves performing procedures to obtain audit evidence about the amounts and disclosures in the financial statements. The procedures selected depend on the auditor's judgment, including the assessment of the risks of material misstatement of the financial statements, whether due to fraud or error. In making those risk assessments, the auditor considers internal control relevant to the entity's preparation and fair presentation of the financial statements in order to design audit procedures that are appropriate in the circumstances, but not for the purpose of expressing an opinion on the effectiveness of the entity's internal control. Accordingly, we express no such opinion. An audit also includes evaluating the appropriateness of accounting policies used and the reasonableness of significant accounting estimates made by management, as well as evaluating the overall presentation of the financial statements.

 Bethel University

We believe that the audit evidence we have obtained is sufficient and appropriate to provide a basis for our audit opinion.

Opinion

In our opinion, the financial statements referred to above present fairly, in all material respects, the financial position of Bethel University as of July 31, 2016 and 2015, and the changes in its net assets and its cash flows for the years then ended in accordance with accounting principles generally accepted in the United States of America.

Other Matters

Other Information

Our audits were conducted for the purpose of forming an opinion on the financial statements as a whole. The accompanying schedule of expenditures of federal awards, as required by Title 2 U.S. *Code of Federal Regulations* (CFR) Part 200, *Uniform Administrative Requirements, Cost Principles, and Audit Requirements for Federal Awards* (Uniform Guidance), is presented for purposes of additional analysis and is not a required part of the financial statements. Such information is the responsibility of management and was derived from and relates directly to the underlying accounting and other records used to prepare the financial statements. The information has been subjected to the auditing procedures applied in the audit of the financial statements and certain additional procedures, including comparing and reconciling such information directly to the underlying accounting and other records used to prepare the financial statements or to the financial statements themselves, and other additional procedures in accordance with auditing standards generally accepted in the United States of America. In our opinion, the information is fairly stated, in all material respects, in relation to the financial statements as a whole.

Disclaimer of Opinion on Supplementary Information

Our audits were conducted for the purpose of forming an opinion on the financial statements as a whole. The Schedules of Financial Responsibility Composite Score, University Key Financial Ratios, and Unrestricted Net Assets Exclusive of Property, Buildings, Equipment, Related Debt and Obligation Under Financing Arrangement, which are the responsibility of management, are presented for purposes of additional analysis and are not a required part of the financial statements. Such information has not been subjected to the auditing procedures applied in the audit of the financial statements and, accordingly, we do not express an opinion or provide any assurance on it.

 Bethel University

Other Reporting Required by Government Auditing Standards

In accordance with *Government Auditing Standards*, we have also issued our report dated November 11, 2016, on our consideration of the University's internal control over financial reporting and on our tests of its compliance with certain provisions of laws, regulations, contracts, and grant agreements and other matters. The purpose of that report is to describe the scope of our testing of internal control over financial reporting and compliance and the results of that testing, and not to provide an opinion on internal control over financial reporting or on compliance. That report is an integral part of an audit performed in accordance with *Government Auditing Standards* in considering the University's internal control over financial reporting and compliance.

Crosslin, PLLC

Nashville, Tennessee
November 11, 2016

BETHEL UNIVERSITY
STATEMENTS OF FINANCIAL POSITION

ASSETS

	July 31, 2016	July 31, 2015
Cash and cash equivalents	$ 1,494,925	$ 1,629,656
Perkins loan cash	78,214	121,257
Receivables:		
Contributions, net (Note B)	12,113,005	3,095,957
Students, net of allowances of $1,422,292 and $1,642,713 respectively	1,333,506	1,894,824
Perkins loans, net of allowances of $237,841 and $227,246, respectively	188,367	229,462
Other	918,376	303,045
Note receivable	-	7,792,839
Inventories	260,658	236,476
Prepaid expenses, deposits, and other assets (Note F)	1,145,071	171,460
Investments (Note C)	3,556,561	6,415,396
Beneficial interest in assets held by others (Note D)	3,552,714	3,660,425
Property, buildings, and equipment:		
Land	260,851	461,570
Buildings and improvements	85,468,815	64,058,325
Equipment, furniture and automobiles	8,566,821	8,172,402
Library books	1,284,514	1,284,514
Property held under capital leases (Note F)	-	405,440
Construction in progress	274,289	2,249,390
	95,855,290	76,631,641
Less: Accumulated depreciation	(21,691,537)	(19,347,823)
Total property and equipment, net	74,163,753	57,283,818
Total assets	$ 98,805,150	$ 82,834,615

LIABILITIES AND NET ASSETS

	2016	2015
Liabilities:		
Accounts payable and accrued liabilities	$ 6,438,104	$ 6,689,778
Accrued payroll and benefits	443,545	758,835
Deferred tuition revenue	2,793,384	4,373,119
Annuities payable	385	-
Debt (Note E)	5,547,696	45,625,243
Obligation under financing arrangement, net (Note F)	47,951,755	-
Obligations under capital leases (Note F)	-	61,048
Advances from the federal government	346,924	411,781
Total liabilities	63,521,793	57,919,804
Net Assets:		
Unrestricted	22,874,163	12,074,952
Temporarily restricted (Notes G and H)	2,074,644	2,252,644
Permanently restricted (Notes G and H)	10,334,550	10,587,215
Total net assets	35,283,357	24,914,811
Total liabilities and net assets	$ 98,805,150	$ 82,834,615

See accompanying notes to financial statements.

BETHEL UNIVERSITY
STATEMENTS OF ACTIVITIES

	Year Ended July 31, 2016			
	Unrestricted	Temporarily Restricted	Permanently Restricted	Total
Revenue, gains and other support:				
Regular tuition and fees	$ 51,512,171	$ -	$ -	$ 51,512,171
Degree completion tuition	7,480,380	-	-	7,480,380
Institutional scholarships and grants	(13,071,993)	-	-	(13,071,993)
Net tuition and fees	45,920,558	-	-	45,920,558
Bookstore income	1,324,252	-	-	1,324,252
Private gifts and contracts	10,461,052	612,551	12,975	11,086,578
Investment loss	(15,480)	(12,262)	-	(27,742)
Unrealized loss on beneficial interests in assets held by others	-	-	(107,711)	(107,711)
Auxiliary fund revenues	7,264,067	-	-	7,264,067
Government grants	2,163,269			2,163,269
Other income	1,648,420	-	-	1,648,420
Net assets released from restrictions	776,627	(776,627)	-	-
Reclassification	159,591	(1,662)	(157,929)	-
Total revenue, gains and other support	69,702,356	(178,000)	(252,665)	69,271,691
Expenses:				
Education and general:				
Instruction	27,466,606	-	-	27,466,606
Academic support	10,325,896	-	-	10,325,896
Student services	10,008,562	-	-	10,008,562
Institutional support	6,493,886	-	-	6,493,886
Auxiliary enterprises	4,608,195	-	-	4,608,195
Total expenses	58,903,145	-	-	58,903,145
Net increase (decrease) in net assets	10,799,211	(178,000)	(252,665)	10,368,546
Net assets, beginning of year	12,074,952	2,252,644	10,587,215	24,914,811
Net assets, end of year	$ 22,874,163	$ 2,074,644	$ 10,334,550	$ 35,283,357

	Year Ended July 31, 2015			
	Unrestricted	Temporarily Restricted	Permanently Restricted	Total
	$ 54,803,497	$ -	$ -	$ 54,803,497
	9,969,474	-	-	9,969,474
	(13,489,677)	-	-	(13,489,677)
	51,283,294	-	-	51,283,294
	1,603,502	-	-	1,603,502
	2,453,030	336,809	32,990	2,822,829
	40,153	40,006	-	80,159
	-	-	(32,133)	(32,133)
	7,012,353	-	-	7,012,353
	1,143,928			1,143,928
	1,538,379	-	-	1,538,379
	1,825,176	(1,825,176)	-	-
	(479,780)	-	479,780	-
	66,420,035	(1,448,361)	480,637	65,452,311
	36,237,140	-	-	36,237,140
	9,762,945	-	-	9,762,945
	7,191,508	-	-	7,191,508
	6,169,543	-	-	6,169,543
	4,166,901	-	-	4,166,901
	63,528,037	-	-	63,528,037
	2,891,998	(1,448,361)	480,637	1,924,274
	9,182,954	3,701,005	10,106,578	22,990,537
	$ 12,074,952	$ 2,252,644	$ 10,587,215	$ 24,914,811

See accompanying notes to financial statements.

BETHEL UNIVERSITY
STATEMENTS OF CASH FLOWS

	Year ended July 31,	
	2016	2015
CASH FLOWS FROM OPERATING ACTIVITIES:		
Increase in net assets	$ 10,368,546	$ 1,924,274
Adjustments to reconcile increase in net assets to net cash provided by operating activities		
Non-cash:		
Allowance for doubtful student accounts, contributions and Perkins loans receivable	(207,322)	99,331
Gain on disposal of property and equipment	(28,168)	-
Unrealized (gain) loss on investments and beneficial interests in assets held by others	(218,454)	(107,868)
Non-cash contributions	(45,000)	(171,180)
Gain on the change in fair value of interest rate swap	-	(245,586)
Depreciation and amortization	2,588,126	2,918,820
(Increase) decrease in:		
Perkins loan cash	43,043	(44,613)
Contributions receivable	(9,017,048)	(343,451)
Student accounts receivable	781,739	(627,463)
Perkins loans receivable	30,500	47,249
Other receivables	(615,331)	(219,321)
Inventories	(24,182)	37,360
Prepaid expenses, deposits, and other assets	(986,996)	(18,014)
Increase (decrease) in:		
Accounts payable and student account deposits	(251,674)	1,804,845
Accrued payroll and benefits	(315,290)	235,699
Deferred tuition revenue	(1,579,735)	(2,335,519)
Contributions restricted for long-term investments	(12,975)	(32,990)
Total adjustments	(9,858,767)	997,299
Net cash provided by operating activities	509,779	2,921,573
CASH FLOWS FROM INVESTING ACTIVITIES:		
Withdrawal of investments, net	-	143,012
Payments received on note receivable	7,792,839	205,615
Payment of accounts payable for property, buildings and equipment	(1,602,512)	(1,598,218)
Purchases of property, buildings and equipment	(14,628,089)	(1,886,348)
Proceeds from disposal of property and equipment	31,589	-
Net cash used in investing activities	(8,406,173)	(3,135,939)
CASH FLOWS FROM FINANCING ACTIVITIES:		
Increase in annuity obligations	385	-
Proceeds from notes payable and line-of-credit	8,378,862	11,512,988
Proceeds from financing arrangement, net	48,300,000	-
Payments on notes payable and line-of-credit	(48,456,409)	(10,357,854)
Repayments of financing arrangement and capital lease obligations	(409,293)	(403,092)
Contributions restricted for long-term investments	12,975	32,990
Changes in advances from the federal government	(64,857)	-
Net cash provided by in investing activities	7,761,663	785,032

See accompanying notes to financial statements.

BETHEL UNIVERSITY
STATEMENTS OF CASH FLOWS - Continued

	Year ended July 31,	
	2016	2015
Net (decrease) increase in cash and cash equivalents	(134,731)	570,666
Cash and cash equivalents at beginning of year	1,629,656	1,058,990
Cash and cash equivalents at end of year	$ 1,494,925	$ 1,629,656
Supplemental disclosures of cash flow information:		
Interest paid	$ 2,416,773	$ 2,722,774
Non-cash financing and investing activities:		
Purchases of property and equipment	16,593,084	2,057,628
Amount financed through capital leases, accounts payable, debt, or received through donations	(1,964,995)	(171,280)
Total paid for property and equipment	$ 14,628,089	$ 1,886,348

Property held for investment of $3,185,000 was placed in service during fiscal 2016 and transferred to property and equipment.

See accompanying notes to financial statements.

BETHEL UNIVERSITY
NOTES TO FINANCIAL STATEMENTS
JULY 31, 2016 AND 2015

A. SUMMARY OF SIGNIFICANT ACCOUNTING POLICIES

   Organization and Business Purpose

   Bethel University (the "University") is a private, residential, coeducational University affiliated with the Cumberland Presbyterian Church, dedicated primarily to educating students in the liberal arts and science while also offering select pre-professional programs, a graduate teacher education program, a master of business administration program, a master of criminal justice program, and a master of physician's assistant program. In addition to its traditional academic programs, the University also offers a degree-completion program. The University is accredited by the Southern Association of Colleges and Schools, Commission on Colleges, and its education emphasizes academic excellence, high achievement, intellectual and personal integrity, and participation in community life. Its Christian heritage finds expression in commitment to the values of personal growth, justice, community, and service.

   Accrual Basis and Financial Statement Presentation

   The financial statements of the University have been prepared on the accrual basis of accounting.

   The University classifies its revenues, expenses, gains, and losses into three classes of net assets based on the existence or absence of donor-imposed restrictions. Net assets of the University and changes therein are as follows:

   > Unrestricted net assets - Net assets that are not subject to donor-imposed stipulations and net assets where donor-imposed stipulations have been met within the reporting period.

   > Temporarily restricted net assets - Net assets subject to donor-imposed stipulations that may or will be met by actions of the University.

   > Permanently restricted net assets - Net assets subject to donor-imposed stipulations that the University is required to maintain permanently. Generally, the donors of these assets permit the University to use all or a part of the income earned on related investments for general or specific purposes.

   The amount of each of these classes of net assets is displayed in the statements of financial position and the amount of change in each class of net assets is displayed in the statements of activities.

BETHEL UNIVERSITY
NOTES TO FINANCIAL STATEMENTS
JULY 31, 2016 AND 2015

A. SUMMARY OF SIGNIFICANT ACCOUNTING POLICES - Continued

Use of Estimates in the Preparation of Financial Statements

The preparation of financial statements in conformity with accounting principles generally accepted in the United States of America requires management to make assumptions that affect the reported amounts of assets and liabilities, disclosure of contingent assets and liabilities at the date of the financial statements, and the reported amounts of revenues and expenses during the reporting period. The more significant areas include the recovery period for property and equipment, the allocation of certain operating expenses to functional categories, the collection of contributions receivable, and the adequacy of the allowance for doubtful student receivables. Management believes that such estimates have been based on reasonable assumptions and that such estimates are adequate. Actual results could differ from those estimates.

Contributions

The University reports gifts of cash and other assets as restricted support if received with donor-imposed stipulations that limit the use of the donated assets. When a donor-imposed restriction expires, *i.e.,* when the purpose of the restriction is accomplished, temporarily restricted net assets are reclassified to unrestricted net assets and reported in the statement of activities as net assets released from restrictions. The University has elected to report contributions received with donor-imposed restrictions as an increase to unrestricted net assets if the restrictions are met in the same fiscal year that the contributions are received.

The University reports gifts of land, equipment, and other assets as unrestricted support unless explicit donor-imposed stipulations specify how the donated assets must be used. Gifts of long-lived assets with explicit restrictions that specify how the assets are to be used and gifts of cash or other assets that must be used to acquire long-lived assets are reported as restricted support. Absent explicit donor-imposed stipulations regarding how long the long-lived assets must be maintained, the University reports expirations of donor-imposed restrictions when the donated or acquired long-lived assets are placed in service.

Contribution of services are recognized if the services received (a) create or enhance non-financial assets or (b) require specialized skills, provided by individuals possessing those skills and would typically need to be purchased if not provided by donation.

In the event a donor makes changes to the nature of a restricted gift, which affects its classification among the net asset categories, such amounts are reflected as reclassifications in the statements of activities.

BETHEL UNIVERSITY
NOTES TO FINANCIAL STATEMENTS
JULY 31, 2016 AND 2015

A. SUMMARY OF SIGNIFICANT ACCOUNTING POLICIES - Continued

Perkins Loan - Cash

As required by federal regulations, cash related to the Federal Perkins Loan Program is maintained in a separate bank account.

Student Accounts Receivable

The University records accounts receivable at their estimated net realizable value. An allowance for doubtful accounts is recorded based upon management's estimate of uncollectible accounts determined by analysis of specific student balances and a general reserve based upon agings of outstanding balances. Past due balances and delinquent receivables are charged against the allowance when they are determined to be uncollectible by management.

Notes Receivable - Students

Notes receivable from students at July 31, 2016 and 2015, totaled $188,367 and $229,462, respectively, net of allowances of $237,841 and $227,246, respectively. Student loans are granted by the University under the federally funded Perkins loan program. These funds are disbursed based upon the demonstration of financial need on the Perkins loan, at which time the loan will also begin accruing interest. Perkins loan amounts are then repaid through a third party billing service. Student loans are considered past due when payment has not been received within 30 days. At July 31, 2016 and 2015, student loans represented 0.19% and 0.28%, respectively, of total assets.

The allowance for doubtful accounts is established based on prior collection experience and current economic factors which, in management's judgment, could influence the ability of loan recipients to repay the amounts per the loan terms. Loan balances are written off only when they are deemed to be permanently uncollectible.

Contributions Receivable

Contributions receivable are recorded at their estimated fair value using a discount rate commensurate with the rate on U.S. Government Securities whose maturities correspond to the maturities of the contributions. Contributions receivable are considered to be either conditional or unconditional promises to give. A conditional contribution is one which depends on the occurrence of a specified uncertain future event to become binding on the donor. Conditional contributions are not recorded as revenue until the condition is met, at which time they become unconditional. Unconditional contributions are recorded as revenue at the time verifiable evidence of the promise to give is received.

BETHEL UNIVERSITY
NOTES TO FINANCIAL STATEMENTS
JULY 31, 2016 AND 2015

A. SUMMARY OF SIGNIFICANT ACCOUNTING POLICIES - Continued

Inventories

Inventories consist primarily of books and supplies and are stated at the lower of cost (market. Cost is determined using the average cost method.

Investments

Investments in marketable equity securities with readily determinable fair values ar investments in debt securities are stated at their fair values in the statements of financi position. Fair value of investments is determined based on quoted market prices or usir Level 2 or 3 inputs as described in Note I. All gains and losses (both realized ar unrealized) and other investment income are reported in the statements of activities.

Property and Equipment

Property and equipment are recorded at cost at the date of acquisition or fair value at tl date of donation in the case of gifts. Depreciation on property and equipment calculated on the straight-line method over estimated useful lives of 20 - 40 years f(buildings and improvements, 5 – 7 years for equipment and furniture, 5 years f(automobiles, and 20 years for other property. Property held under capital leases a1 depreciated on the straight-line method based on the shorter of the estimated useful li: of the property to the University or the life of the capital lease. Library books ar repairs/renovations to buildings and equipment that do not add value or extend the usefi life of the assets are expensed as incurred. Depreciation, operation, and maintenanc charges are allocated to appropriate functional expense categories.

The estimate to complete construction in progress is $2,925,711 as of July 31, 2016.

Deferred Revenue

Deferred revenue consists primarily of charges and cash receipts collected prior to yea end for services rendered after year-end. These receipts pertain to upcoming tuition ar fees.

Advances from the Federal Government for Student Loans

The Perkins Loan Program is a campus-based program providing revolving loan func for financial assistance to eligible postsecondary school students based on financi need. The Department of Education provides funds along with the University, which a1 used to make loans to eligible students at low interest rates. Refundable governmei advances for Perkins at July 31, 2016 and 2015 was $346,924 and $411,78

BETHEL UNIVERSITY
NOTES TO FINANCIAL STATEMENTS
JULY 31, 2016 AND 2015

A. SUMMARY OF SIGNIFICANT ACCOUNTING POLICIES - Continued

Advertising Costs

Advertising costs are expensed as incurred and totaled approximately $1,294,097 and $1,373,849 for the years ended July 31, 2016 and 2015, respectively.

Tax Status

The University is exempt from Federal income taxes under §501(a) of the Internal Revenue Code ("IRC") as an organization described in IRC §501(c)(3). Accordingly, no provision for income taxes has been made in the accompanying financial statements. The University is not classified as a private foundation.

The University accounts for the effect of any uncertain tax positions based on a more likely than not threshold to the recognition of the tax positions being sustained based on the technical merits of the position under examination by the applicable taxing authority. If a tax position or positions are deemed to result in uncertainties of those positions, the unrecognized tax benefit is estimated based on a cumulative probability assessment that aggregates the estimated tax liability for all uncertain tax positions. Tax positions for the University include, but are not limited to, the tax-exempt status and determination of whether certain income is subject to unrelated business income tax; however, the University has determined that such tax positions do not result in an uncertainty requiring recognition.

Fair Value Measurements

Assets and liabilities recorded at fair value in the statements of financial position are categorized based on the level of judgment associated with the inputs used to measure their fair value. Related disclosures are included in Note I. Level inputs, as defined by Financial Accounting Standards Board Accounting Standards Codification ("ASC") 820, *Fair Value Measurements and Disclosures,* are as follows:

Level 1 - Values are unadjusted quoted prices for identical assets and liabilities in active markets accessible at the measurement date.

Level 2 - Inputs include quoted prices for similar assets or liabilities in active markets, quoted prices from those willing to trade in markets that are not active, or other inputs that are observable or can be corroborated by market data for the term of the instrument. Such inputs include market interest rates and volatilities, spreads and yield curves.

Level 3 - Certain inputs are unobservable (supported by little or no market activity) and significant to the fair value measurement. Unobservable inputs reflect the University's best estimate of what hypothetical market participants would use to determine a transaction price for the asset or liability at the reporting date.

BETHEL UNIVERSITY
NOTES TO FINANCIAL STATEMENTS
JULY 31, 2016 AND 2015

A. SUMMARY OF SIGNIFICANT ACCOUNTING POLICIES - Continued

Classification of Expenses

Expenses are classified functionally as a measure of service efforts and accomplishments. Direct expenses incurred for a single function are allocated entirely to that function. Joint expenses applicable to more than one function are allocated on the basis of objectively summarized information or management estimates.

Reclassifications

Certain reclassifications have been made to the 2015 financial statements in order for them to conform to the 2016 presentation.

B. CONTRIBUTIONS RECEIVABLE

Contributions receivable at July 31, 2016 and 2015 consist of the following:

	2016	2015
Contributions receivable (present value)	$ 12,283,098	$ 3,263,547
Less: allowance for doubtful contributions	(170,093)	(167,590)
	$ 12,113,005	$ 3,095,957

Expected maturities of contributions receivable at July 31, 2016 are as follows:

Fiscal Year Ending July 31,	Amount
2017	$ 2,467,440
2018	1,731,076
2019	1,575,785
2020	1,475,577
2021	1,477,886
Thereafter	3,979,270
Total expected contributions	12,707,034
Less: allowance for net present value using a weighted average discount rate of 1.00%	(423,936)
Present value of contributions receivable	$ 12,283,098

BETHEL UNIVERSITY
NOTES TO FINANCIAL STATEMENTS
JULY 31, 2016 AND 2015

C. INVESTMENTS

The investments of the University are principally administered by the University or by the Board of Stewardship of the Cumberland Presbyterian Church, Inc. (the "Board"). The funds administered by the Board are co-mingled with funds of other agencies of the Church. The University's portion represents approximately 5.2% and 5.3% of the funds administered by the Board at July 31, 2016 and 2015, respectively. The investments of the University, including investment property with a book value of $472,810 and $3,185,000 as of July 31, 2016 and 2015, respectively, are invested as follows:

	2016	2015
Administered by the Board:		
Marketable equity and debt securities	$2,880,910	$3,039,801
Administered by the University:		
Marketable equity and debt securities	6,948	12,669
Certificates of deposits	100,292	100,092
Investment Property and Other	568,411	3,262,834
	$3,556,561	$6,415,396

D. BENEFICIAL INTEREST IN ASSETS HELD BY OTHERS

Beneficial interest in assets held by others represents arrangements in which a donor establishes and funds a perpetual trust administered by an individual or organization other than the University. The fair value of perpetually held trusts in which the University had a beneficial interest as of July 31, 2016 and 2015, was $3,552,714 and $3,660,425, respectively. The University records these trusts at estimated fair value. Income distributed to the University from the beneficial interest assets is temporarily restricted for scholarships.

BETHEL UNIVERSITY
NOTES TO FINANCIAL STATEMENTS
JULY 31, 2016 AND 2015

E. DEBT

The University has the following debt obligations at July 31, 2016 and 2015:

	2016	2015
Note payable to Kubota Credit Corporation, U.S.A., 0% interest, collateralized by specified equipment.	$ 185	$ 2,411
Note payable to Regions Bank, payable in monthly installments of $180,180 including interest of 5.25% through June 20, 2018, with a final payment of $15,593,640 due July 20, 2018; collateralized by substantially all real property. Paid in full December 31, 2015.	-	19,219,554
Note payable to Farmers and Merchants Bank, bearing interest at 6% with the full principal payment due on February 28, 2017; collateralized by accounts receivable. Paid in full December 31, 2015.	-	720,450
Note payable to Farmers and Merchants Bank, bearing interest at 6% with the full principal payment due on July 29, 2015; collateralized by accounts receivable; paid in full August 18, 2015.	-	400,592
Note payable to Farmers and Merchants Bank, bearing interest at 6% with the full principal payment due on August 25, 2015; collateralized by accounts receivable; maturity extended to February 23, 2016. Paid in full January 19, 2016.	-	400,590
Line-of-credit totaling $2,000,000 with Centennial Bank; bearing variable interest calculated as Prime Rate as published by The Wall Street Journal plus 1.00 % with a floor of 5%; line-of-credit matures and full payment due February 1, 2018; collateralized by accounts receivable, equipment, and inventory.	2,000,000	-

BETHEL UNIVERSITY
NOTES TO FINANCIAL STATEMENTS
JULY 31, 2016 AND 2015

E. DEBT - Continued

	2016	2015
Construction line-of-credit totaling $607,800 (maximum) with Centennial Bank, bearing interest at 5% with the principal draws due in full on January 31, 2017; collateralized by future grant payments.	184,998	-
Note payable to City of Paris, bearing interest at 0%, with monthly principal payments of $8,663 due beginning on September 30, 2014, through final maturity on August 31, 2022.	632,363	736,313
Line-of-credit totaling $500,000 with First Bank, bearing interest at 4.5%, maturing on August 1, 2015; collateralized by real property; paid in full on August 24, 2015.	-	13,610
Note payable at First Bank, bearing interest at 5%, maturing on August 23, 2015; collateralized by real property; paid in full on August 21, 2015.	-	400,000
Note payable to Carroll Bank & Trust, bearing interest at 5.0%, with the full principal balance maturing June 11, 2016; collateralized by certain real property. Paid in full December 31, 2015	-	1,965,573
Note payable to Carroll Bank & Trust, bearing interest at 5.0%, with the full principal balance maturing October 8, 2015; collateralized by certain real property; maturity extended and paid in full December 31, 2015.	-	500,150
Note payable to Carroll Bank & Trust, bearing interest at 5.25%, with the full principal balance maturing February 17, 2017; collateralized by certain real property.	2,000,150	-

BETHEL UNIVERSITY
NOTES TO FINANCIAL STATEMENTS
JULY 31, 2016 AND 2015

E. DEBT - Continued

	2016	2015
Note payable to Renasant Bank, payable in monthly installments of $13,609 including interest of 4.50% through June 12, 2018, with a final payment of $469,356 due July 12, 2018; collateralized by an agreement not to transfer or encumber certain real property.	730,000	-
Note payable to a related party private company totaling $16,666,000, bearing interest at one year LIBOR plus 7%, payable in monthly installments of interest only. Starting on August 1, 2016, and continuing until August 1, 2018, principal payments due in monthly installments of $126,258, with the remaining balance due at final maturity on August 31, 2018. Balance paid in full December 31, 2015. (See Note R).	-	16,666,000
Line-of-credit with a related party private company totaling $5,000,000, bearing interest at one year LIBOR plus 9%, payable in monthly installments of interest only starting on August 31, 2013, and continuing until August 31, 2018; at which time the outstanding balance is due. Paid in full December 31, 2015.	-	4,600,000
	$5,547,696	$45,625,243

The anticipated maturities of the University's notes payable are as follows:

Fiscal Year Ending July 31,	Amount
2017	$2,422,471
2018	2,700,762
2019	103,950
2020	103,950
2021	103,950
Thereafter	112,613
	$5,547,696

BETHEL UNIVERSITY
NOTES TO FINANCIAL STATEMENTS
JULY 31, 2016 AND 2015

E. DEBT - Continued

Interest Expense

For the years ending July 31, 2016 and 2015, Bethel University incurred interest expense of $2,416,773 and $2,722,774, respectively.

Compliance with Covenants

The Renasant Bank loan agreement contains a debt service coverage ratio that requires the University to maintain a debt coverage ratio of 1.25x, tested annually by the bank. Based on the University's calculations as of July 31, 2016, the University was in compliance with this covenant and ratio.

F. OBLIGATIONS UNDER CAPITAL LEASES AND FINANCING ARRANGEMENT

The University entered into capital lease agreements primarily for computer equipment relating to the University's notebook computer program and a phone system. The agreements expired at various dates through March 2016. The equipment at July 31, 2016 and 2015, totaled $405,440, net of accumulated depreciation of $391,833 and $385,204, respectively.

Interest rates on capitalized leases for computer equipment ranged from 4.26% to 4.37% and were imputed based on the lessor's implicit rate of return.

On December 28, 2015, the United States Department of Agriculture (USDA) funded a Campus Facility Acquisition through a Rural Development Communities Facilities Loan with NCCD - Bethel Properties LLC, a separate legal entity independent of the University. The loan to NCCD - Bethel Properties LLC totaled $48,300,000, bearing a fixed interest of 3.25% with a repayment term of 40 years. NCCD - Bethel Properties LLC utilized the proceeds of the loan to lease certain University buildings, in which the University leased back from NCCD - Bethel Properties LLC. The University remits the lease payments to NCCD - Bethel Properties LLC, who in turn repays USDA. The monthly lease payments equal the monthly note payment. The agreement expires December 28, 2055. Due to easement and right of way concerns, substantially all of the McKenzie campus is incorporated into the lease, lease-back transaction ("financing arrangement"). Buildings held under the capital lease at July 31, 2016 totaled $57,998,848, net of accumulated depreciation of $6,062,642.

BETHEL UNIVERSITY
NOTES TO FINANCIAL STATEMENTS
JULY 31, 2016 AND 2015

F. OBLIGATIONS UNDER CAPITAL LEASES AND FINANCING ARRANGEMENT - Continued

In compliance with U.S. generally accepted accounting principles, the University elected to capitalize certain debt-refinancing costs and amortize these costs over the life of the capitalized lease. The original amount of the debt-refinancing costs capitalized was $914,837 and have been reflected in the statement of financial position under the caption, prepaid expenses, deposits and other assets. Accumulated amortization and amortization expense as of and for the fiscal year ended July 31, 2016 was $13,385. Annually, the University will incur amortization expense of $22,871, until the lease expires December 28, 2055.

Minimum future lease payments under capital leases as of July 31, 2016, are as follows:

Fiscal Year Ending July 31,	Amount
2017	$ 2,161,908
2018	2,161,908
2019	2,161,908
2020	2,161,908
2021	2,161,908
Thereafter	74,187,905
	84,997,445
Less: Amount representing interest	(37,045,690)
Present value of net minimum lease payments	$ 47,951,755

- 20 -

BETHEL UNIVERSITY
NOTES TO FINANCIAL STATEMENTS
JULY 31, 2016 AND 2015

G. TEMPORARILY AND PERMANENTLY RESTRICTED NET ASSETS

At July 31, 2016 and 2015, temporarily restricted net assets are available for the following purposes:

	2016	2015
Scholarships	$ 457,896	$ 108,963
Time restrictions and other	1,616,748	2,143,681
	$2,074,644	$2,252,644

At July 31, 2016 and 2015, permanently restricted net assets are as follows:

	2016	2015
Beneficial interest in assets held by others	$ 3,552,714	$ 3,660,425
Endowments	6,781,836	6,926,790
	$10,334,550	$10,587,215

The endowments represent nonexpendable funds that are subject to restrictions requiring the principal to be invested and only the income used as specified by the donors.

Net assets were released from donor restrictions by incurring expenses satisfying the restricted purposes. The following is a summary of the assets released from restrictions for the years ended July 31, 2016 and 2015:

	2016	2015
Institutional support expenditures	$373,745	$ 443,222
Scholarship and grant expenditures	402,882	353,854
Other	-	1,028,100
	$776,627	$1,825,176

BETHEL UNIVERSITY
NOTES TO FINANCIAL STATEMENTS
JULY 31, 2016 AND 2015

H. ENDOWMENT

The University's endowment consists of individual donor-restricted funds established for a variety of purposes. As required by U.S. generally accepted accounting principles, net assets associated with endowment funds are classified and reported based on the existence or absence of donor-imposed restrictions.

Interpretation of Relevant Law

The Board of Trustees of the University has interpreted the applicable state laws as requiring the preservation of the original gift as of the gift date of the donor-restricted endowment funds absent explicit donor stipulations to the contrary. As a result of this interpretation, the University classified as permanently restricted net assets (a) the original value of gifts donated to the permanent endowment, (b) the original value of subsequent gifts to the permanent endowment, and (c) accumulations to the permanent endowment made in accordance with the direction of the applicable donor gift instrument at the time the accumulation is added to the fund. The remaining portion of the donor-restricted endowment fund that is not classified in permanently restricted net assets is classified as temporarily restricted net assets until those amounts are appropriated for expenditure by the University in a manner consistent with the standard of prudence prescribed by applicable state laws. In accordance with applicable state laws, the University considers the following factors in making a determination to appropriate or accumulate donor-restricted endowment funds:

- The duration and preservation of the fund
- The purposes of the University and the donor-restricted endowment fund
- General economic conditions
- The possible effect of inflation and deflation
- The expected total return from income and the appreciation of investments
- Other resources of the University
- The investment policies of the University

BETHEL UNIVERSITY
NOTES TO FINANCIAL STATEMENTS
JULY 31, 2016 AND 2015

H. ENDOWMENT - Continued

Changes in Endowment Net Assets

	Temporarily Restricted	Permanently Restricted	Total
Endowment net assets, August 1, 2014	$ -	$ 10,106,578	$ 10,106,578
Reclassification	619,998	479,780	1,099,778
Investment return:			
Investment income	40,006	-	40,006
Net depreciation (realized and unrealized)	-	(32,133)	(32,133)
Total investment return	40,006	(32,133)	7,873
Contributions	-	32,990	32,990
Appropriation of endowment assets for expenditure (scholarships)	-	-	-
Endowment net assets, July 31, 2015	660,004	10,587,215	11,247,219
Reclassification	(1,662)	(157,929)	(159,591)
Investment return:			
Investment income	(12,262)	-	(12,262)
Net depreciation (realized and unrealized)	-	(107,711)	(107,711)
Total investment return	(12,262)	(107,711)	(119,973)
Contributions	-	12,975	12,975
Appropriation of endowment assets for expenditure (scholarships)	-	-	-
Endowment net assets, July 31, 2016	$ 646,080	$ 10,334,550	$ 10,980,630

BETHEL UNIVERSITY
NOTES TO FINANCIAL STATEMENTS
JULY 31, 2016 AND 2015

H. ENDOWMENT - Continued

Return Objectives and Risk Parameters

The University has adopted investment and spending policies for endowment assets that attempt to provide a predictable stream of funding to programs supported by its endowment while seeking to maintain the purchasing power of the endowment assets. Endowment assets include those assets of donor-restricted funds that the University must hold in perpetuity or for a donor-specified period(s). Under this policy, as approved by the Board of Trustees, the endowment assets are invested with an overall total return objective as established for each time horizon: 1) Short Term, 2) Intermediate, and 3) Long Term according to the funding needs of the University. The returns will be compared with the generally accepted indices, i.e., the S&P 500, certain Bond Indices, and MSCI EAFE stock indices, and an index of U.S. Treasury Bills depending on the time horizon in place. At July 31, 2016 and 2015, the endowment assets consist of investments in certificates of deposit, marketable debt and equity securities, and beneficial interests in assets held by others.

Strategies Employed for Achieving Objectives

To satisfy its rate-of-return objectives, the University relies on a total return strategy in which investment returns are achieved through both capital appreciation (realized and unrealized) and current yield (interest and dividends). The University targets an investment allocation based on the three time horizons described above and that places emphasis on diversification of assets within prudent risk constraints.

Spending Policy and How the Investment Objectives Relate to Spending Policy

During fiscal year 2009, the University's Board of Trustees adopted a spending policy, which is based on the "Total Return" concept of determining the amount available for distribution. Total Return takes into consideration all of the elements of long-term investment return. The appropriate spending amount is based on the projected long-term Total Return of the funds, less an estimate of future inflation. The goal of the Total Return approach is to provide for a level of current income that protects the future purchasing power of the fund, thereby providing for increasing amounts of future income. The University anticipates that this percentage will be in the range of 3 to 5% of market value based on historical measurements of Total Return and Inflation. The market value of the fund will be noted each year on a specific date and a three-year rolling average market value will be established. The rolling three-year market value will be multiplied by the approved spending percentage which will be set annually.

BETHEL UNIVERSITY
NOTES TO FINANCIAL STATEMENTS
JULY 31, 2016 AND 2015

I. FAIR VALUES OF FINANCIAL INSTRUMENTS

Required disclosures concerning the estimated fair values of financial instruments are presented below. The estimated fair value amounts have been determined based on the University's assessment of available market information and appropriate valuation methodologies. The following table summarizes required fair value disclosures under ASC 825, *Financial Instruments*, and measurements at July 31, 2016 and 2015 for the assets and liabilities measured at fair value on a recurring basis under ASC 820, *Fair Value Measurements and Disclosures*:

	Carrying Amount	Estimated Fair Value	Measured at Fair Value	Fair Value Measurements Using		
				Level 1	Level 2	Level 3
July 31, 2016						
Assets:						
Investments:						
Cash and cash equivalents	$ 223,019	$ 223,019	$ 223,019	$223,019	$ -	$ -
Certificates of deposits	100,292	100,292	100,292	100,292	-	-
Equity funds:						
U.S. Equities	130,212	130,212	130,212	130,212	-	-
Venture Capital	2,630,228	2,630,228	2,630,228	-	-	2,630,228
Investment Property	472,810	472,810	472,810	-	-	472,810
Total Investments	$3,556,561	$3,556,561	$3,556,561	$453,523	$ -	$3,103,038
Beneficial interests in trusts	3,552,714	3,552,714	3,552,714	-	3,552,714	-
Liabilities:						
Debt and financing arrangement	$53,499,451	$59,493,600	-	-	-	-

- 25 -

BETHEL UNIVERSITY
NOTES TO FINANCIAL STATEMENTS
JULY 31, 2016 AND 2015

I. FAIR VALUES OF FINANCIAL INSTRUMENTS - Continued

	Carrying Amount	Estimated Fair Value	Measured at Fair Value	Fair Value Measurements Using		
				Level 1	Level 2	Level 3
July 31, 2015						
Assets:						
Investments:						
Cash and cash equivalents	$ 251,867	$ 251,867	$ 251,867	$251,867	$ -	$ -
Certificates of deposits	100,092	100,092	100,092	100,092	-	-
Equity funds:						
Mutual Funds	102,626	102,626	102,626	102,626	-	-
U.S. Equities	421,017	421,017	421,017	421,017	-	-
Total Equity Funds	523,643	523,643	523,643	523,643	-	-
Venture Capital	2,354,794	2,354,794	2,354,794	-	-	2,354,794
Investment Property	3,185,000	3,185,000	3,185,000	-	-	3,185,000
Total Investments	$6,415,396	$6,415,396	$6,415,396	$875,602	$ -	$5,539,794
Beneficial interests in trusts	3,660,425	3,660,425	3,660,425	-	3,660,425	-
Liabilities:						
Notes payable and long-term obligation	45,686,291	50,805,043	-	-	-	-

BETHEL UNIVERSITY
NOTES TO FINANCIAL STATEMENTS
JULY 31, 2016 AND 2015

I. FAIR VALUES OF FINANCIAL INSTRUMENTS - Continued

Changes in Level 3 assets are as follows:

	Fair Value Measurements Using Significant Unobservable Inputs (Level 3)	
	2016	2015
Beginning Balance	$ 5,539,794	$ 5,711,244
Purchases and sales, net	(2,436,756)	(171,450)
Ending Balance	$ 3,103,038	$ 5,539,794

The following methods and assumptions were used to estimate the fair value of each class of financial instruments:

<u>Cash equivalents, receivables, accounts payable and accrued payroll and benefits, deferred revenue and advances from the Federal government for student loans</u>

The carrying values of these items approximate their fair values due to the short maturities of these instruments.

<u>Investments</u>

Fair values are based on quoted market prices, where available, and Level 2 and 3 inputs. The carrying amounts and the fair values of the University's investments are presented in Note C.

<u>Notes payable and obligations under financing arrangement and capital leases</u>

For fixed rate debt, fair value was estimated using discounted cash flow analyses based on the University's current incremental borrowing rates for similar types of borrowing arrangements.

J. FUND RAISING ACTIVITIES

The University conducts fundraising activities each year. The total cost of these activities for fiscal years 2016 and 2015, was $896,376 and $1,030,307, respectively.

BETHEL UNIVERSITY
NOTES TO FINANCIAL STATEMENTS
JULY 31, 2016 AND 2015

K. RETIREMENT PLAN

The University's full-time employees may participate in either a retirement plan administered by the Cumberland Presbyterian Board of Finance or the TIAA/CREF Plan, which is a national pension plan. The University makes payments to the plans by withholding an employee-elected percentage from the employee's salary with the University matching the employee's deduction up to five percent (5%). Total matching contributions were made by the University for fiscal years 2016 and 2015, of $449,299 and $454,206, respectively.

L. CONCENTRATION OF RISKS

Concentration of Risk

The University generates revenue predominantly from tuition and fees, investment income, gifts, auxiliary enterprises and contributions. In planning and budgeting during a fiscal year, significant reliance is placed on meeting tuition, gift, auxiliary, investment earnings and contribution goals in order for the University to sustain successful operations. In the event that enrollment or gifts and contributions significantly decrease in any one year, operations could be adversely affected.

Financial instruments that potentially subject the University to concentrations of credit risk and market risk consist principally of cash equivalents, investments, and student receivables.

The University, in connection with its activities, grants credit to students that involves, to varying degrees, elements of credit risk. The maximum accounting loss from credit risk is limited to the amounts that are recognized in the accompanying statements of financial position as student accounts receivable at July 31, 2016 and 2015.

The University also has two bank deposits in excess of those insured under regulatory insurance limits.

BETHEL UNIVERSITY
NOTES TO FINANCIAL STATEMENTS
JULY 31, 2016 AND 2015

M. **OPERATING LEASES**

The University leases office and classroom space for satellite campuses for programs offered through its College of Professional Studies, office space for University services, and an activities space for a University athletic program. These leases expire at various dates through fiscal year 2023. Minimum future rental payments under non-cancelable operating leases as of July 31, 2016 are as follows:

Fiscal Year Ending July 31,	Amount
2017	$1,333,573
2018	1,264,059
2019	1,152,870
2020	247,112
2021	96,000
Thereafter	106,800
	$4,200,414

Operating lease payments under the non-cancelable leases totaled $2,078,036 and $2,906,508 for the years ended July 31, 2016 and 2015, respectively.

On July 31, 2013, the University entered into a sale-leaseback agreement with a related party for a building in Paris, Tennessee. The purchasor entered into a note receivable with the University for $8,200,000, which approximated the carrying value of the building, and therefore, no gain or loss was recognized. The purchasor was paying the note receivable over 30 years at an interest rate of 2%. The University was leasing the building for six years with monthly payments of $120,275. The note receivable totaled $7,792,839 at July 31, 2015.

On December 31, 2015, the University purchased the building in Paris, Tennessee back from the related party with proceeds from USDA that were provided within the lease, leaseback transaction with NCCD Bethel Properties LLC, as discussed in Note F. The sales price of $14,246,061 approximated the original sales price to the related party plus the remaining lease payments.

On August 10, 2011, the University entered into a ten (10) year lease, which expires August 31, 2021, with a related party. The building leased provides office space for University services to students. Operating lease payments under the non-cancelable lease totaled $50,400 for each of the years ended July 31, 2016 and 2015, respectively.

BETHEL UNIVERSITY
NOTES TO FINANCIAL STATEMENTS
JULY 31, 2016 AND 2015

N. FUNCTIONAL ALLOCATION OF EXPENSES

During the years ended July 31, 2016 and 2015, the University allocated the cost of certain professional fees and the operation and maintenance of physical plant, including depreciation and amortization expense of $2,574,741 and $2,918,920 respectively, over the cost of providing instruction, academic support, student services, institutional support, and auxiliary enterprises as follows:

	2016	2015
Instruction	$ 4,690,617	$6,113,190
Academic support	1,763,408	224,105
Student services	1,709,215	990,753
Institutional support	1,108,995	849,960
Auxiliary enterprises	786,965	574,061
Total operation and maintenance of physical plant	$10,059,200	$8,752,069

O. LITIGATION AND CONTINGENCIES

The University is a defendant in legal actions from time to time in the normal course of operations. It is not currently possible to state the ultimate liability, if any, in these matters. In the opinion of management, any resulting liability from these actions will not have a material adverse effect on the financial position of the activities of the University.

P. RELATED PARTY TRANSACTIONS

During fiscal years 2016 and 2015, the University had an agreement with a company owned by a member of the University's faculty. Under the agreement, the company developed and is maintaining the following online programs of study for the University:

    Master of Business Administration
    Master of Arts in Education
    Master of Science in Criminal Justice
    Bachelor of Science in Organizational Leadership
    Bachelor of Science in Criminal Justice
    Bachelor of Science in Emergency Services Management
    Associates of Arts
    Associates of Science
    Dual Enrollment

BETHEL UNIVERSITY
NOTES TO FINANCIAL STATEMENTS
JULY 31, 2016 AND 2015

P. RELATED PARTY TRANSACTIONS - Continued

Specifically, the company is responsible for developing course work, producing lectures and graphic presentations, and maintaining student records. Fees under the agreement range from $149 to $319 per student, per course. The most recent agreement was executed effective April 1, 2015 for twelve (12) months, and automatically renews for an additional term of twelve (12) months unless terminated in accordance with the agreement. Total fees incurred during fiscal years 2016 and 2015 were $6,473,190 and $7,096,337, respectively.

During fiscal years 2016 and 2015, the University entered into an agreement with a company co-founded by a member of the Board of Trustees. Under the agreement, the company was granted rights as the University's exclusive technology supplier for the Registered Nurse to Bachelor of Science in Nursing (RN to BSN) online program of study. The company has developed a learning management system (LMS) that is used as a platform for online curriculum delivery for the Colleges of Arts and Sciences and Health Sciences. The curriculum is developed by and remains the property of the University. Additionally, the company provides online support for students and faculty and has developed a process within the LMS to obtain other analytical data. Fees under the agreement are $50 per user per class for licensing rights to the product, including all enhancements, modifications, and new releases or modules. The agreement was executed March 9, 2015 and shall continue for five (5) years, which will automatically extend for an additional two (2) years unless terminated in accordance with the agreement. Total fees incurred during fiscal years 2016 and 2015 were $419,750 and $0, respectively.

The University entered into a note payable and a line-of-credit with a private company owned by a member of the Board of Trustees. On December 31, 2015, the University paid the note payable and line-of-credit in full with proceeds from USDA that were provided within the lease, leaseback transaction with NCCD Bethel Properties LLC. Total outstanding balances during fiscal year 2016 and 2015 were $-0- and $21,266,000 respectively (See Note E).

At various times throughout the fiscal year, the University transacts business with a related party as part of the normal business operations of the University.

The University entered into leasing arrangements with related parties as described in Note M.

Q. SUBSEQUENT EVENTS

The University has evaluated subsequent events through November 11, 2016, the issuance date of the University's financial statements, and has determined that there are no subsequent events requiring disclosure.

SUPPLEMENTARY INFORMATION

BETHEL UNIVERSITY
SUPPLEMENTARY INFORMATION
YEAR ENDED JULY 31, 2016

FINANCIAL RESPONSIBILITY COMPOSITE SCORE

As explained on the United States Department of Education's website (https://studentaid.ed.gov/sa/about/data-center/school/composite-scores),

> Section 498(c) of the Higher Education Act of 1965, as amended, requires for-profit and non-profit institutions to annually submit audited financial statements to the Department to demonstrate they are maintaining the standards of financial responsibility necessary to participate in the Title IV programs. One of many standards, which the Department utilizes to gauge the financial responsibility of an institution, is a composite of three ratios derived from an institution's audited financial statements. The three ratios are a primary reserve ratio, an equity ratio, and a net income ratio. These ratios gauge the fundamental elements of the financial health of an institution, not the educational quality of an institution.
>
> The composite score reflects the overall relative financial health of institutions along a scale from negative 1.0 to positive 3.0. A score greater than or equal to 1.5 indicates the institution is considered financially responsible.
>
> Schools with scores of less than 1.5 but greater than or equal to 1.0 are considered financially responsible, but require additional oversight. These schools are subject to cash monitoring and other participation requirements.

For the fiscal years ended July 31, 2014, 2015, and 2016, management calculated the University's financial responsibility composite scores as follows:

BETHEL UNIVERSITY
SUPPLEMENTARY INFORMATION
YEAR ENDED JULY 31, 2016

FINANCIAL RESPONSIBILITY COMPOSITE SCORE - Continued

Ratios:	2014		2015		2016	
Primary Reserve Ratio:	0.0102		0.0207		0.0017	
Expendable Net Assets		$ 700,412		$ 1,312,554		$ 99,357
Total Expense		$ 68,701,441		$ 63,528,037		$ 58,903,145
Equity Ratio:	0.2794		0.3008		0.3571	
Modified Net Assets		$ 22,990,537		$ 24,914,811		$ 35,283,357
Modified Assets		$ 82,297,078		$ 82,834,615		$ 98,805,150
Net Income Ratio:	0.0597		0.0435		0.1549	
Change in Unrestricted Net Assets		$ 4,362,204		$ 2,891,998		$ 10,799,211
Total Unrestricted Revenue		$ 73,063,645		$ 66,420,035		$ 69,702,356
Strength Factor Scores:						
Primary Reserve strength factor score	0.1020		0.2066		0.0169	
Equity strength factor score	1.6762		1.8047		2.1426	
Net Income strength factor score	3.0000		3.0000		3.0000	
Composite Score:						
Primary Reserve Weighted Score	0.0408		0.0826		0.0067	
Equity Weighted Score	0.6705		0.7219		0.8570	
Net Income Weighted Score	0.6000		0.6000		0.6000	
Total Composite Score (Rounded):	1.3		1.4		1.5	

UNIVERSITY KEY FINANCIAL RATIOS

The financial health of the University can be evaluated through the use of ratios. The following ratios are customarily utilized by higher education institutions to measure financial condition. There are four fundamental financial questions addressed by analysis of four core ratios.

- Are resources sufficient and flexible enough to support the mission? - Primary Reserve Ratio
- Do operating results indicate the institution is living within available resources? - Net Operating Revenues Ratio
- Does asset performance and management support the strategic direction? - Return on Net Assets
- Are financial resources, including debt, managed strategically to advance the mission? - Viability Ratio

When combined, these four ratios deliver a single measure of the University's overall financial health, referred to as the Composite Financial Index. The following charts analyze the aforementioned ratios for the fiscal year ended July 31, 2014, 2015, and 2016:

BETHEL UNIVERSITY
SUPPLEMENTARY INFORMATION
YEAR ENDED JULY 31, 2016

UNIVERSITY KEY FINANCIAL RATIOS - Continued

Composite Financial Index

The Composite Financial Index (CFI) is calculated based upon the values of its four component ratios: 1) Primary Reserve, 2) Net Operating Revenue, 3) Return on Net Assets, and 4) Viability Ratio. Once each of the four ratios is calculated, further weighting is conducted to measure the relative strength of the score and its importance in the composite score. The CFI combines the four core ratios identified below into a single score. The combination, using a prescribed weighting plan, allows a weakness or strength in one ratio to be offset by another ratio result. The CFI reflects a picture of the financial health of the institution at a point in time.

COMPOSITE FINANCIAL INDEX (CFI)

FY14	FY15	FY16
2.2	1.1	3.0

Primary Reserve Ratio

The Primary Reserve Ratio is intended to address the question of sufficiency and flexibility for support of the mission. The ratio measures the financial strength of the University by comparing expendable net assets, which includes those assets the University can access and spend quickly to meet obligations, to total expenses at the end of every fiscal year. This ratio identifies the University's financial strength and flexibility by identifying how long the University can function by using reserves without the generation of any new net assets. A primary reserve ratio of .40 or 40% is advisable, implying that the university has the ability to cover over 4 ½ months of expenses. Key items that can impact this ratio include principal payments on debt, using net assets to fund capital construction projects, endowment returns, and total operating expenses. Although not reaching the benchmark, the University's ratio is trending in a positive direction.

PRIMARY RESERVE RATIO   **EXPLANATION**

FY14	FY15	FY16	
$ 9,182,954	$12,074,952	$22,874,163	+ unrestricted net assets EOY
$ 3,701,005	$ 2,252,644	$ 2,074,644	+ temporarily restricted net assets EOY
$58,145,110	$57,283,818	$74,163,753	-- land, building, and equipment, net of depreciation EOY
$44,715,695	$42,019,386	$49,314,303	+ long-term debt EOY
$68,701,441	$63,528,037	$58,903,145	total expenses
-0.01	-0.01	0.00	Ratio
-0.09	-0.11	0.01	strength factor
0.0	0.0	0.0	weighted value

BETHEL UNIVERSITY
SUPPLEMENTARY INFORMATION
YEAR ENDED JULY 31, 2016

UNIVERSITY KEY FINANCIAL RATIOS - Continued

Net Operating Revenues Ratio

The Net Operating Revenues Ratio is intended to indicate if the University is living within its available resources. The University needs to generate some level of surplus over long periods of time because operations are one source for reinvestment in future initiatives. Short-term deficits may occur as a result of strategic decisions. It is when deficits are unplanned or unmanaged and occurring as a result of core operations that evaluation of operations is necessitated. A positive ratio indicates the University is in good financial condition. An organization should establish a target percentage, and establishing a benchmark should be in line with operating growth. A ratio of 2 to 4 percent indicates the University operated within its means and should be maintained over time; however, fluctuations from year to year are normal. A large ratio identifies an operating surplus and a stronger financial position. While a negative ratio indicates an operating loss for the year, universities need to be careful about too large of a positive ratio, indicating under spending on mission critical initiatives.

NET OPERATING REVENUES RATIO (%):
Using Change in Unrestricted Net Assets

FY14	FY15	FY16	EXPLANATION
$ 4,362,204	$ 2,891,998	$10,799,211	change in unrestricted net assets
$73,063,645	$66,420,035	$69,702,356	total unrestricted revenue
6.0	4.4	15.5	ratio
4.59	3.35	10.00	strength factor
0.5	0.3	1.0	weighted value

Return on Net Assets Ratio

The Return on Net Assets Ratio is intended to assess if the asset performance and management support the strategic direction. The ratio measures whether the University is financially better off than in the previous year by measuring total economic return or the level of change in total net assets. This ratio is the most comprehensive measure of growth or decline in wealth over time. There is not a specific threshold; however, 3 to 4 percent is a generally acceptable real rate of return. An improving trend in this ratio indicates the university is increasing its net assets and is likely to be in a position to set aside financial resources to strengthen its future financial flexibility. Key items that may impact this ratio include changes in the net operating revenue ratio, endowment returns, capital gifts and grants, capital transfers, and endowment gifts. This indicator can be greatly impacted when borrowing money for a capital project and when the capital item is added to Net Assets. Looking at the trend will even out the anomalies.

BETHEL UNIVERSITY
SUPPLEMENTARY INFORMATION
YEAR ENDED JULY 31, 2016

UNIVERSITY KEY FINANCIAL RATIOS - Continued

Return on Net Assets Ratio - Continued

RETURN ON NET ASSETS RATIO (%)   **EXPLANATION**

FY14	FY15	FY16	
$ 3,440,711	$ 1,924,274	$10,368,546	change in net assets
$19,549,826	$22,990,537	$24,914,811	total net assets BOY
17.6	8.4	41.6	ratio
8.80	4.18	10.00	strength factor
1.8	0.8	2.0	weighted value

Viability Ratio

The Viability Ratio is intended to address the question of whether financial resources are being strategically managed to advance the mission of the University. It measures availability of expendable net assets for coverage of debt should the University be required to settle its obligations as of the date on the balance sheet. A 1:1 ratio is desired, indicating adequate net assets to meet obligations. This ratio is one of the most basic determinants of clear financial health and is regarded as governing the University's ability to assume new debt. A ratio of 1.25 or greater indicates a strong creditworthy University with sufficient resources to satisfy debt obligations; however, each university should identify the ratio that is right for its mission specific needs. A viability ratio that falls below 1:1 hinders the university's ability to respond to adverse condition, to secure external capital, and to have flexibility to fund new objectives. Key items that may impact this ratio include principal payments on debt, using net assets for capital construction projects, issuance of new debt, and endowment returns. Although not reaching the benchmark, the University's ratio is trending in a positive direction.

VIABILITY RATIO   **EXPLANATION**

FY14	FY15	FY16	
$ 9,182,954	$12,074,952	$22,874,163	+ unrestricted net assets EOY
$ 3,701,005	$ 2,252,644	$ 2,074,644	+ temporarily restricted net assets EOY
$58,145,110	$57,283,818	$74,163,753	-- land, building, and equipment, net of depreciation EOY
$44,479,635	$42,019,386	$49,314,303	+ long-term debt EOY
$44,479,635	$42,019,386	$49,314,303	long-term debt EOY
-0.02	-0.02	0.00	ratio
-0.04	0.05	0.00	strength factor
0.0	0.0	0.0	weighted value

BETHEL UNIVERSITY
SUPPLEMENTARY INFORMATION
YEAR ENDED JULY 31, 2016

UNRESTRICTED NET ASSETS EXCLUSIVE OF PLANT, PROPERTY, EQUIPMENT, RELATED DEBT AND OBLIGATION UNDER FINANCING ARRANGEMENT

The Southern Association of School and Colleges, Commission on Colleges (SACSCOC), has various core requirements for meeting standards. One such standard is core requirement 2.11.1 requiring, among other things, the University to present a statement of financial position of unrestricted net assets, exclusive of plant assets and plant-related debt, which represents the change in unrestricted net assets attributable to operations. The chart below is provided to meet this SACSCOC requirement. Although the University's net unrestricted assets, excluding plant, property, equipment, and related debt is negative, the trend over the past three fiscal years is positive, indicating the University has taken measures to strengthen its financial stability.

**Statements of Financial Position of
Unrestricted Net Assets, Exclusive of Plant
Assets and Plant-Related Debt**

	July 31,		
	2016	2015	2014
Restatement of Net Assets without plant and plant-related debt			
Unrestricted Net Assets	*$ 22,874,163*	*$ 12,074,952*	*$ 9,182,954*
Less: property, plant, and equipment, net	(74,163,753)	(57,283,818)	(58,145,110)
Add: plant-related debt	49,499,301	36,624,268	38,989,174
URNA not including plant and debt	**$ (1,790,289)**	**$ (8,584,598)**	**$(9,972,982)**

OTHER INFORMATION

BETHEL UNIVERSITY
SCHEDULE OF EXPENDITURES OF FEDERAL AWARDS
YEAR ENDED JULY 31, 2016

Federal Grantor/Pass-through Grantor/ Program or Cluster Title	Federal CFDA Number	Federal Expenditures
U.S. Department of Education - Direct Awards		
Student Financial Assistance - Cluster: (1)		
Federal Direct Student Loans Program (Note C)	84.268	$55,601,116
Federal Perkins Loan Program (Note B)	84.038	664,049
Federal Work-Study Program (Note D)	84.033	145,293
Federal Supplemental Educational		
Opportunity Grants Program (Note D)	84.007	334,921
Federal Pell Grant Program	84.063	12,745,014
Teacher Education Assistance for University and		
Higher Education Grant	84.379	143,198
Total Student Financial Assistance - Cluster		69,633,591
U.S. Department of Education - Pass-through		
Program from:		
Special Education: Grants to States		
Tennessee Teachers Assistants Grant	84.027A	7,106
Total U.S. Department of Education		69,640,697
U.S. Department of Homeland Security – Pass-through		
Program from:		
State Department of Military:		
Hazard Mitigation Grant (1) (Note D)	97.039	1,997,498
Total Expenditures of Federal Awards		$71,638,195

(1) Tested as a major program

See independent auditor's report.

BETHEL UNIVERSITY
NOTES TO SCHEDULE OF EXPENDITURES OF FEDERAL AWARDS
YEAR ENDED JULY 31, 2016

A. BASIS OF PRESENTATION

The accompanying schedule of expenditures of federal awards is presented in accordance with the requirements by Title 2 U.S. *Code of Federal* Regulations (CFR) Part 200, *Uniform Administrative Requirements, Cost Principles, and Audit Requirements for Federal Awards* (Uniform Guidance), on the accrual basis of accounting consistent with the basis of accounting used by the University in the preparation of its financial statements.

The University has elected not to use the 10-percent due minimis indirect cost rate allowed under the Uniform Guidance.

B. FEDERAL PERKINS LOAN PROGRAM - CFDA #84.038

The outstanding loan balance for the Federal Perkins Loan Program at July 31, 2016 was $426,208, net of the allowance for uncollectible loans of $237,841. Total loan disbursements for the program for the year ended July 31, 2016, were $22,000. Other disbursements include an expenditure for repayment of fund capital in the amount of $64,857.

C. FEDERAL DIRECT LOANS PROGRAM - CFDA #84.268

During the fiscal year ending July 31, 2016, the University processed $55,601,116 of new loans under the Federal Direct Loans program (which includes subsidized and unsubsidized Stafford Loans, Parents' for Undergraduate Students, and Supplemental Loans for Students)

D. MATCHING FUNDS

The University provided matching funds of $111,641 for the Federal Supplemental Educational Opportunity Grants program and $48,431 for the Federal Work Study program during the fiscal year ended July 31, 2016.

The University provided matching funds, the majority of which were in-kind, of $161,823 for the Hazard Mitigation Grant, while the State of Tennessee, Department of Military also provided matching funds of $161,823.

Independent Auditor's Report on Internal Control Over
Financial Reporting and on Compliance and Other Matters
Based on an Audit of Financial Statements Performed in
Accordance with *Government Auditing Standards*

The Board of Trustees
Bethel University
McKenzie, Tennessee

We have audited, in accordance with the auditing standards generally accepted in the United States of America and the standards applicable to financial audits contained in *Government Auditing Standards* issued by the Comptroller General of the United States, the financial statements of Bethel University (the "University"), which comprise the statements of financial position as of July 31, 2016, and the related statements of activities and cash flows for the year then ended, and the related notes to the financial statements, and have issued our report thereon dated November 11, 2016.

Internal Control Over Financial Reporting

In planning and performing our audit of the financial statements, we considered the University's internal control over financial reporting (internal control) to determine the audit procedures that are appropriate in the circumstances for the purpose of expressing our opinion on the financial statements, but not for the purpose of expressing an opinion on the effectiveness of the University's internal control. Accordingly, we do not express an opinion on the effectiveness of the University's internal control.

A *deficiency in internal control* exists when the design or operation of a control does not allow management or employees, in the normal course of performing their assigned functions, to prevent, or detect and correct misstatements on a timely basis. A *material weakness* is a deficiency, or a combination of deficiencies, in internal control such that there is a reasonable possibility that a material misstatement of the entity's financial statements will not be prevented, or detected and corrected on a timely basis. A *significant deficiency* is a deficiency, or a combination of deficiencies, in internal control that is less severe than a material weakness, yet important enough to merit attention by those charged with governance.

The Board of Trustees
Bethel University

Our consideration of the internal control was for the limited purpose described in the first paragraph of this section and was not designed to identify all deficiencies in internal control that might be material weaknesses or significant deficiencies. Given these limitations, during our audit we did not identify any deficiencies in internal control that we consider to be material weaknesses. However, material weaknesses may exist that have not been identified.

Compliance and Other Matters

As part of obtaining reasonable assurance about whether the University's financial statements are free from material misstatement, we performed tests of its compliance with certain provisions of laws, regulations, contracts, and grant agreements, noncompliance with which could have a direct and material effect on the determination of financial statement amounts. However, providing an opinion on compliance with those provisions was not an objective of our audit, and accordingly, we do not express such an opinion. The results of our tests disclosed no instances of noncompliance or other matters that are required to be reported under *Government Auditing Standards*.

Purpose of this Report

The purpose of this report is solely to describe the scope of our testing of internal control and compliance and the results of that testing, and not to provide an opinion on the effectiveness of the University's internal control or on compliance. This report is an integral part of an audit performed in accordance with *Government Auditing Standards* in considering the University's internal control and compliance. Accordingly, this communication is not suitable for any other purpose.

Crosslin, PLLC

Nashville, Tennessee
November 11, 2016

Independent Auditor's Report on Compliance For Each Major
Programs and on Internal Control Over Compliance
Required by Uniform Guidance

The Board of Trustees
Bethel University
McKenzie, Tennessee

Report on Compliance for Each Major Federal Program

We have audited Bethel University's (the "University") compliance with the types of compliance requirements described in the *OMB Compliance Supplement* that could have a direct and material effect on the University's major federal programs for the year ended July 31, 2016. The University's major federal programs are identified in the summary of auditor's results section of the accompanying schedule of findings and questioned costs.

Management's Responsibility

Management is responsible for compliance with federal statutes, regulations, and the terms and conditions of its federal awards applicable to its federal programs.

Auditor's Responsibility

Our responsibility is to express an opinion on compliance for each of the University's major federal programs based on our audit of the types of compliance requirements referred to above. We conducted our audit of compliance in accordance with auditing standards generally accepted in the United States of America; the standards applicable to financial audits contained in *Government Auditing Standards*, issued by the Comptroller General of the United States; and the audit requirements of Title 2 U.S. *Code of Federal Regulations* (CFR) Part 200, *Uniform Administrative Requirements, Cost Principles, and Audit Requirements for Federal Awards* (Uniform Guidance). Those standards and the Uniform Guidance require that we plan and perform the audit to obtain reasonable assurance about whether noncompliance with the types of compliance requirements referred to above that could have a direct and material effect on a major federal program occurred. An audit includes examining, on a test basis, evidence about the University's compliance with those requirements and performing such other procedures as we considered necessary in the circumstances.

We believe that our audit provides a reasonable basis for our opinion on compliance for each major federal program. However, our audit does not provide a legal determination of the University's compliance.

The Board of Trustees
Bethel University

Opinion on Each Major Federal Program

In our opinion, the University complied, in all material respects, with the types of compliance requirements referred to above that could have a direct and material effect on each major federal program for the year ended July 31, 2016.

Report on Internal Control Over Compliance

Management of the University is responsible for establishing and maintaining effective internal control over compliance with the types of compliance requirements referred to above. In planning and performing our audit of compliance, we considered the University's internal control over compliance with the types of requirements that could have a direct and material effect on each major federal program to determine the auditing procedures that are appropriate in the circumstances for the purpose of expressing an opinion on compliance for each major federal program and to test and report on internal control over compliance in accordance with the Uniform Guidance, but not for the purpose of expressing an opinion on the effectiveness of internal control over compliance. Accordingly, we do not express an opinion on the effectiveness of the University's internal control over compliance.

A *deficiency in internal control over compliance* exists when the design or operation of a control over compliance does not allow management or employees, in the normal course of performing their assigned functions, to prevent, or detect and correct, noncompliance with a type of compliance requirement of a federal program on a timely basis. A *material weakness in internal control over compliance* is a deficiency, or combination of deficiencies, in internal control over compliance, such that there is a reasonable possibility that material noncompliance with a type of compliance requirement of a federal program will not be prevented, or detected and corrected, on a timely basis. A *significant deficiency in internal control over compliance* is a deficiency, or a combination of deficiencies, in internal control over compliance with a type of compliance requirement of a federal program that is less severe than a material weakness in internal control over compliance, yet important enough to merit attention by those charged with governance.

Our consideration of internal control over compliance was for the limited purpose described in the first paragraph of this section and was not designed to identify all deficiencies in internal control over compliance that might be material weaknesses or significant deficiencies. We did not identify any deficiencies in internal control over compliance that we consider to be material weaknesses. However, material weaknesses may exist that have not been identified.

The Board of Trustees
Bethel University

The purpose of this report on internal control over compliance is solely to describe the scope of our testing of internal control over compliance and the results of that testing based on the requirements of the Uniform Guidance. Accordingly, this report is not suitable for any other purpose.

Crosslin, PLLC

Nashville, Tennessee
November 11, 2016

BETHEL UNIVERSITY
SCHEDULE OF FINDINGS AND QUESTIONED COSTS
YEAR ENDED JULY 31, 2016

I. SUMMARY OF INDEPENDENT AUDITOR'S RESULTS

Financial Statements

Type of auditor's report issued: <u>Unmodified</u>

Internal control over financial reporting:

- Material weakness(es) identified? ___Yes _X_ No
- Significant deficiency(ies) identified? ___Yes _X_ None Reported

Noncompliance material to financial statements noted? ___Yes _X_ No

Federal Awards

Internal control over major program:

- Material weakness(es) identified? ___Yes _X_ No
- Significant deficiency(ies) identified? ___Yes _X_ None Noted

Type of auditor's report issued on compliance for major program: <u>Unmodified</u>

Any audit findings disclosed that are required to be reported in accordance with 2 CFR 200.516(a)? ___Yes _X_ No

BETHEL UNIVERSITY
SCHEDULE OF FINDINGS AND QUESTIONED COSTS
YEAR ENDED JULY 31, 2016

I. SUMMARY OF INDEPENDENT AUDITOR'S RESULTS - Continued

Major Programs:

CFDA Number	Name of Federal Program	Amount Expended
SFA Cluster:		
84.063	Federal Pell Grant Program	$12,745,014
84.268	Federal Direct Student Loans Program	55,601,116
84.038	Federal Perkins Loan Program	664,049
84.007	Federal Supplemental Educational Opportunity Grants Program	334,921
84.033	Federal Work-Study Program	145,293
84.038	Perkins Loans ($426,208 outstanding balance of loans)	-
84.379	TEACHER Education Assistance for College and Higher Education Grant	143,198
97.039	Hazard Mitigation Grant	$1,997,498

Dollar threshold used to distinguish between type A
and type B programs $750,000

Auditee qualified as low-risk auditee   _X_ Yes ___ No

II. FINANCIAL STATEMENT FINDINGS

   A. Material Weakness in Internal Control

      None Reported.

   B. Compliance Findings

      None Reported.

III. FINDINGS AND QUESTIONED COSTS FOR FEDERAL AWARDS

   None Reported.

BETHEL UNIVERSITY
SCHEDULE OF PRIOR YEAR FINDINGS AND QUESTIONED COSTS
YEAR ENDED JULY 31, 2016

The University had no prior audit findings related to the testing of its federal award programs.

**CUMBERLAND PRESBYTERIAN
CHILDREN'S HOME**

FINANCIAL STATEMENTS
AND
AUDITORS' REPORT

DECEMBER 31, 2016

CUMBERLAND PRESBYTERIAN CHILDREN'S HOME

TABLE OF CONTENTS

	Page
Independent Auditors' Report	1
Statement of Financial Position	3
Statement of Activities	4
Statement of Cash Flows	5
Statement of Functional Expenses	6-7
Notes to the Financial Statements	8-14
Supplemental Information	
Schedule of Board of Stewardship Endowments	16-17

Members:
AMERICAN INSTITUTE OF
CERTIFIED PUBLIC
ACCOUNTANTS
TEXAS SOCIETY OF CERTIFIED
PUBLIC ACCOUNTANTS

HANKINS, EASTUP, DEATON, TONN & SEAY
A PROFESSIONAL CORPORATION
CERTIFIED PUBLIC ACCOUNTANTS

902 NORTH LOCUST
P.O. BOX 977
DENTON, TX 76202-0977

TEL. (940) 387-8563
FAX (940) 383-4746

Independent Auditors' Report

Cumberland Presbyterian Children's Home
Denton, Texas

We have audited the accompanying financial statements of Cumberland Presbyterian Children's Home (a nonprofit organization), which comprise the statement of financial position as of December 31, 2016 and the related statements of activities and cash flows for the year then ended, and the related notes to the financial statements.

Management's Responsibility for the Financial Statements

Management is responsible for the preparation and fair presentation of these financial statements in accordance with accounting principles generally accepted in the United States of America; this includes the design, implementation, and maintenance of internal control relevant to the preparation and fair presentation of financial statements that are free from material misstatement, whether due to fraud or error.

Auditor's Responsibility

Our responsibility is to express an opinion on these financial statements based on our audit. We conducted our audit in accordance with auditing standards generally accepted in the United States of America. Those standards require that we plan and perform the audit to obtain reasonable assurance about whether the financial statements are free of material misstatement.

An audit involves performing procedures to obtain audit evidence about the amounts and disclosures in the financial statements. The procedures selected depend on the auditor's judgment, including the assessment of the risks of material misstatement of the financial statements, whether due to fraud or error. In making those risk assessments, the auditor considers internal control relevant to the entity's preparation and fair presentation of the financial statements in order to design audit procedures that are appropriate in the circumstances, but not for the purpose of expressing an opinion on the effectiveness of the entity's internal control. Accordingly, we express no such opinion. An audit also includes evaluating the appropriateness of accounting policies used and the reasonableness of significant accounting estimates made by management, as well as evaluating the overall presentation of the financial statements. We believe that the audit evidence we have obtained is sufficient and appropriate to provide a basis for our audit opinion.

Opinion

In our opinion, the financial statements referred to above present fairly, in all material respects, the financial position of Cumberland Presbyterian Children's Home as of December 31, 2016, and the changes in its net assets and its cash flows for the year then ended in accordance with accounting principles generally accepted in the United States of America.

Hankins, Eastup, Deaton, Tonn & Seay
Denton, Texas
June 19, 2017

Page left blank intentionally

CUMBERLAND PRESBYTERIAN CHILDREN'S HOME

STATEMENT OF FINANCIAL POSITION
DECEMBER 31, 2016

ASSETS:

Cash and cash equivalents	$ 245,239
Due from Board of Stewardship	79,441
Other receivables	81,650
Prepaid expenses	3,717
Land, buildings and equipment, net	3,714,904
Other long-term investments	9,217,916
TOTAL ASSETS	**$13,342,867**

LIABILITIES AND NET ASSETS:

Liabilities:	
Accounts payable	$ 90,754
Accrued liabilities	78,775
Total Liabilities	169,529
Net Assets:	
Unrestricted	7,304,842
Temporarily restricted	28,434
Permanently restricted	5,840,062
Total Net Assets	13,173,338
TOTAL LIABILITIES AND NET ASSETS	**$13,342,867**

See Accompanying Notes to the Financial Statements.

CUMBERLAND PRESBYTERIAN CHILDREN'S HOME

STATEMENT OF ACTIVITIES
FOR THE YEAR ENDED DECEMBER 31, 2016

	Unrestricted	Temporarily Restricted	Permanently Restricted	Total
Revenues, Gains and Other Support:				
Contributions and grants	$ 636,876	$ -	$ 1,089	$ 637,965
CPS revenue	613,193	-	-	613,193
Other program fees	31,649	-	-	31,649
Denominational support	70,123	-	-	70,123
Income on long-term investments	94,906	-	34,593	129,499
Unrealized gains on investments	88,590	2,156	287,966	378,712
Oil and gas royalties	4,303	-	-	4,303
Special events	677	-	-	677
Rents	35,591	-	-	35,591
Insurance proceeds	242,817	-	-	242,817
Subtotal	1,818,725	2,156	323,648	2,144,529
Net assets released from Restrictions	1,971,320	(11,768)	(1,959,552)	-
Total Revenue, Gains and Other Support	3,790,045	(9,612)	(1,635,904)	2,144,529
Expenses:				
Program services:				
Children's residential program	1,211,471	-	-	1,211,471
Emergency shelter program	861,485	-	-	861,485
Single parent family program	211,492	-	-	211,492
Cumberland family services	246,135	-	-	246,135
Management and general	211,027	-	-	211,027
Fundraising	177,168	-	-	177,168
Total Expenses	2,918,778	-	-	2,918,778
Change in net assets	871,267	(9,612)	(1,635,904)	(774,249)
Net assets at beginning of year	6,433,575	38,046	7,475,966	13,947,587
Net assets at end of year	$ 7,304,842	$ 28,434	$ 5,840,062	$13,173,338

See Accompanying Notes to the Financial Statements.

CUMBERLAND PRESBYTERIAN CHILDREN'S HOME

STATEMENT OF CASH FLOWS
FOR THE YEAR ENDED DECEMBER 31, 2016

Cash Flows from Operating Activities:	
Change in net assets	$ (774,249)
Adjustments to reconcile change in net assets to net cash provided by operating activities:	
Depreciation	202,150
(Increase) Decrease in receivables	(22,243)
(Increase) Decrease in prepaid expenses	(2,506)
Increase (Decrease) in accounts payable/accrued liabilities	69,625
Unrealized losses (gains) on investments	(378,712)
Contributions restricted for long-term investment	(1,089)
Net Cash Provided (Used) by Operating Activities	(907,024)
Cash Flows from Investing Activities:	
Purchase of fixed assets	(71,230)
Investment withdrawals	771,664
Net Cash Provided by Investing Activities	700,434
Cash Flows from Financing Activities:	
Proceeds from contributions restricted for investment in endowment	1,089
Net Cash Provided by Financing Activities	1,089
Net Increase (Decrease) in Cash and Cash Equivalents	(205,501)
Cash and Cash Equivalents at Beginning of Year	450,740
Cash and Cash Equivalents at End of Year	$ 245,239
Supplemental Data:	
Interest paid during the year	$ 3,554

See Accompanying Notes to the Financial Statements.

CUMBERLAND PRESBYTERIAN CHILDREN'S HOME

STATEMENT OF FUNCTIONAL EXPENSES
FOR THE YEAR ENDED DECEMBER 31, 2016

	Program Services			
	Children's Residential Program	Emergency Shelter Program	Single Parent Family Program	Cumberland Family Services
Salaries and Wages	$ 575,726	$ 435,305	$ 112,337	$ 126,379
Employee Benefits	78,172	59,105	15,253	17,161
Payroll Taxes	44,658	33,765	8,714	9,804
Total Salaries and Related Expenses	698,556	528,175	136,304	153,344
Activities and travel	47,050	21,353	1,811	3,523
Clothing and supplies	13,340	10,151	256	9,261
Food and dining out	80,057	26,216	681	599
Training and education	18,544	7,576	75	1,878
Medical and dental	2,630	2,402	-	-
Other program expenses	-	-	3,820	416
Utilities	60,701	45,896	11,844	13,324
Property, liability insurance	27,722	20,961	5,409	6,084
Repairs and maintenance	143,013	108,131	27,904	31,395
Supplies, postage, printing	11,061	8,363	2,158	2,428
Computer software, maintenance	5,840	4,416	1,140	1,282
Permits and fees	2,138	1,616	417	469
Special events expense	-	-	-	-
Vehicle expenses	2,607	1,972	509	573
General assembly	-	-	-	-
Professional fees	15,330	11,591	2,992	3,365
Public relations/communications	-	-	-	-
Investment management fees	-	-	-	-
Board expense	-	-	-	-
Interest	-	-	-	-
Total Expenses Before Depreciation	1,128,589	798,819	195,320	227,941
Depreciation	82,882	62,666	16,172	18,194
TOTAL EXPENSES	$ 1,211,471	$ 861,485	$ 211,492	$ 246,135

The accompanying notes are an integral part of this statement

	Supporting Services			
Total	Fundraising	Administration	Total	Total Expenses
$ 1,249,747	$ 70,210	$ 84,252	$ 154,462	$ 1,404,209
169,691	9,533	11,439	20,972	190,663
96,941	5,446	6,535	11,981	108,922
1,516,379	85,189	102,226	187,415	1,703,794
73,737	11,217	-	11,217	84,954
33,008	-	-	-	33,008
107,553	825	7,466	8,291	115,844
28,073	-	12,795	12,795	40,868
5,032	-	-	-	5,032
4,236	-	-	-	4,236
131,765	7,403	8,884	16,287	148,052
60,176	3,380	4,057	7,437	67,613
310,443	17,441	20,931	38,372	348,815
24,010	23,651	1,619	25,270	49,280
12,678	712	855	1,567	14,245
4,640	261	313	574	5,214
-	629	-	629	629
5,661	318	381	699	6,360
-	-	1,761	1,761	1,761
33,278	1,871	2,245	4,116	37,394
-	14,164	-	14,164	14,164
-	-	25,356	25,356	25,356
-	-	6,455	6,455	6,455
-	-	3,554	3,554	3,554
2,350,669	167,061	198,898	365,959	2,716,628
179,914	10,107	12,129	22,236	202,150
$ 2,530,583	$ 177,168	$ 211,027	$ 388,195	$ 2,918,778

CUMBERLAND PRESBYTERIAN CHILDREN'S HOME

NOTES TO FINANCIAL STATEMENTS
DECEMBER 31, 2016

NOTE A - SUMMARY OF SIGNIFICANT ACCOUNTING POLICIES

Organization

Cumberland Presbyterian Children's Home (CPCH) is a nonprofit organization originally chartered in Kentucky in 1904 and moved to Denton, Texas in 1932. Its purpose is to provide long-term residential basic child care for children between the ages of 3 and 17. CPCH is licensed to care for up to 40 children. CPCH's primary sources of revenue are income from child care, donations and income from long-term investments.

Basis of Presentation

The accompanying financial statements have been prepared on the accrual basis of accounting in accordance with accounting principles generally accepted in the United States of America. Net assets and revenues, expenses, gains, and losses are classified based on the existence or absence of donor-imposed restrictions. Accordingly, net assets of CPCH and changes therein are classified and reported as follows:

Unrestricted Net Assets – not subject to donor-imposed restrictions. Unrestricted net assets may be designated for specific purposes by action of the Board of Directors.

Temporarily Restricted Net Assets – subject to donor-imposed stipulations that may be fulfilled by actions of CPCH to meet the stipulations or that become unrestricted at the date specified by the donor.

Permanently Restricted Net Assets – subject to donor-imposed stipulations that they be retained and invested permanently by CPCH to use all or part of the investment return on these net assets for specified or unspecified purposes.

Income Taxes

CPCH is exempt from Federal income taxes under Section 501(c)(3) of the Internal Revenue Code. In addition, CPCH has been determined by the Internal Revenue Service not to be a private foundation within the meaning of Section 509(a)(1) and 170 (b)(1)(A)(vi) of the Code.

Fixed Assets

All acquisitions of property and equipment in excess of $5,000 and all expenditures for repairs, maintenance, or improvements that significantly prolong the useful lives of the assets are capitalized. Prior to 1/1/13 CPCH used an acquisition cost threshold of $1,000 but increased the threshold to $5,000 at that date in order to reduce the administrative costs of recording and tracking items of furniture and equipment. Purchases of property and equipment are recorded at cost. Donations of property and equipment are recorded as support at their estimated fair value at the date of gift. Such donations are reported as unrestricted support unless the donor has restricted the donated asset to a specific purpose. Assets donated with explicit restrictions regarding their use and contributions of cash that must be used to acquire property and equipment are reported as restricted support. Absent donor stipulations regarding how long those donated assets must be maintained, CPCH reports expirations of donor restrictions when the donated or acquired assets are placed in service as instructed by the donor. CPCH reclassifies temporarily restricted net assets to unrestricted net assets at that time. Property and equipment are depreciated using the straight-line method over the estimated useful life of assets.

CUMBERLAND PRESBYTERIAN CHILDREN'S HOME

NOTES TO FINANCIAL STATEMENTS
DECEMBER 31, 2016

The class lives of the more significant items within each property classification are as follows:

Vehicles	5 years
Equipment	5 to 10 years
Furniture and fixtures	5 to 10 years
Buildings	20 to 40 years

Investment Securities

Investments in marketable securities with readily determinable fair values and all investments in debt securities are valued at their fair values in the statement of financial position. Unrealized gains and losses are included in the change in net assets.

Estimates

The preparation of financial statements in conformity with generally accepted accounting principles requires management to make estimates and assumptions that affect the reported amounts of assets and liabilities at the date of the financial statements and the reported amounts of revenues and expenses during the reporting period. Accordingly, actual results could differ from those estimates.

FASB 116 and 117

In accordance with Statement of Financial Accounting Standards ("SFAS") No. 116, *Accounting for Contributions Received and Contributions Made*, contributions received are recorded as unrestricted, temporarily restricted, or permanently restricted support depending on the existence and/or nature of donor restrictions. CPCH reports gifts of cash and other assets as restricted support if they are received with donor stipulations that limit the use of the donated assets. When a donor restriction expires, that is, when a stipulated time restriction ends or purpose restriction is accomplished, temporarily restricted net assets are reclassified to unrestricted net assets and reported in the statement of activities as net assets released from restrictions. Contributions that are restricted by the donor are reported as increases in unrestricted net assets if the restrictions expire in the fiscal year in which the contributions are recognized.

Unconditional promises to give are recorded as revenue when received. Unconditional promises to give that are due within one year are recorded at the face amount of the commitment. Unconditional promises to give that are due beyond one year are not reflected at the face amount of the commitment, but when material are discounted to a present value, or net realizable value, using a 3% discount rate. Unconditional promises to give that are determined to be uncollectible are written off as an expense at that time. At December 31, 2016, CPCH had no outstanding unconditional promises to give.

CPCH reports gifts of land, buildings, and equipment as unrestricted support unless explicit donor stipulations specify how the donated assets must be used. Gifts of long-lived assets with explicit restrictions that specify how the assets are to be used and gifts of cash or other assets that must be used to acquire long-lived assets are reported as restricted support. Absent explicit donor stipulations about how long those long-lived assets must be maintained, CPCH reports expirations of donor restrictions when the donated or acquired long-lived assets are placed in service.

CUMBERLAND PRESBYTERIAN CHILDREN'S HOME

NOTES TO FINANCIAL STATEMENTS
DECEMBER 31, 2016

Contributed Services and Materials

In addition to receiving cash contributions, CPCH occasionally receives in-kind contributions from various donors. It is the policy of CPCH to record the estimated fair market value of certain in-kind donations as an asset or expense in its financial statements, and similarly increase donations by a like amount.

A substantial number of volunteers have donated significant amounts of time to CPCH's programs and supporting services. Contributions of donated services that create or enhance non-financial assets or that require specialized skills, are provided by individuals possessing these skills, and would typically need to be purchased if not provided by donation, are recorded at their fair values in the period received. For the year ended December 31, 2016, there were no amounts recorded for contributed services and materials.

Cash and Cash Equivalents

For purposes of the statement of cash flows, CPCH considers all highly liquid investments with a maturity of three months or less to be cash equivalents.

NOTE B – INVESTMENTS

Investments in equity securities with readily determinable fair values and all investments in debt securities are measured at fair value. All non cash contributions are recorded at fair value at the date of receipt. Stock is recorded at the average of the high and low selling price on the date received. Investments sold are recorded at amount received on the trade date.

Investment income and realized gains and losses are reported as increases in unrestricted net assets unless the donor placed restrictions on the income's use. The change in fair value between years along with realized gains or losses are reflected in the statement of activities in the year of the change.

Some investments are held and managed by the Board of Stewardship, Finance and Benefits of the Cumberland Presbyterian Church, while other investments are held in an investment brokerage account in the name of CPCH, and are managed by investment managers of the brokerage firm. No single investment exceeds five percent of CPCH's net assets.

NOTE C – ENDOWMENTS

CPCH's endowments consist of 88 individual donor-restricted funds established by individual donors for a variety of purposes. Net assets associated with endowments are classified and reported based on the existence or absence of donor-imposed restrictions.

A reconciliation of the beginning and ending balances of endowment funds is as follows:

	Permanently Restricted
Balance, 12/31/15	$6,691,470
Contributions	1,089
Earnings	33,493
Investment gains	241,387
Distributions	(1,953,533)
Balance, 12/31/16	$5,013,906

CUMBERLAND PRESBYTERIAN CHILDREN'S HOME

NOTES TO FINANCIAL STATEMENTS
DECEMBER 31, 2016

Funds with Deficiencies

From time to time, the fair value of assets associated with individual donor restricted endowment funds may fall below the level that the donor requires CPCH to retain as a fund of perpetual duration. CPCH did not have any net deficiencies of this nature as of December 31, 2016.

Return Objectives and Risk Parameters

CPCH has adopted investment and spending policies for endowment assets that attempt to provide a predictable stream of funding to programs supported by its endowment while seeking to maintain the purchasing power of the endowment assets. Under this policy, as approved by the board of trustees, the endowment assets are invested in equity securities, fixed-income securities and short-term reserves with asset allocation within defined acceptable ranges, while assuming a moderate level of investment risk. CPCH expects its endowment funds, over time, to provide an average rate of return sufficient to provide operating funds as needed. Actual returns in any given year may vary from this amount.

Strategies Employed for Achieving Objectives

To satisfy its long-term rate-of-return objectives, CPCH relies on a total return strategy in which investment returns are achieved through both capital appreciation (realized and unrealized) and current yield (interest and dividends). CPCH targets a diversified asset allocation that places a greater emphasis on equity-based investments to achieve its long-term return objectives within prudent risk constraints.

Spending Policy and How the Investment Objectives Relate to Spending Policy

CPCH has no written spending policy that commits it to annual distributions from any of the endowment's fund balances. CPCH normally appropriates for distribution each year sufficient earnings needed to fund its operating budget. Accordingly, over the long term, CPCH expects the current spending policy to allow its endowment to continue to grow. This is consistent with CPCH's objective to maintain the purchasing power of the endowment assets held in perpetuity or for a specified term as well as to provide additional real growth through new gifts and investment return.

NOTE D – FAIR VALUE OF FINANCIAL INSTRUMENTS

CPCH's financial instruments, none of which are held for trading purposes, include cash, securities and receivables. CPCH has estimated fair value of financial instruments in accordance with requirements of SFAS No. 157. The estimated fair value amounts have been determined by CPCH, using available market information and appropriate valuation methodologies. However, considerable judgment is necessarily required in interpreting market data to develop the estimates of fair value. Accordingly, the estimates presented herein are not necessarily indicative of the amounts that CPCH could realize in a current market exchange. The use of different market assumptions and estimation methodologies may have a material effect on the estimated fair value amounts. The carrying amount of cash and cash equivalents, and receivables approximated fair market value at December 31, 2016 because of their relatively short maturity and market terms. The fair value of long term investments at December 31, 2016 is determined based on quoted market values for U.S. government securities, fixed income securities and equity securities.

CUMBERLAND PRESBYTERIAN CHILDREN'S HOME

NOTES TO FINANCIAL STATEMENTS
DECEMBER 31, 2016

NOTE D – FAIR VALUE OF FINANCIAL INSTRUMENTS (CONT'D)

Financial instruments are considered Level 1 when their values are determined using quoted prices in active markets for identical assets that the reporting entity has the ability to access at the measurement date. Level 2 inputs are inputs other than quoted prices included within Level 1, such as quoted prices for similar assets in active or inactive markets, inputs other than quoted prices that are observable for the asset, or inputs that are derived principally from or corroborated by observable market data by correlation or other means.

Financial instruments are considered Level 3 when their values are determined using pricing models, discounted cash flow methodologies or similar techniques and at least one significant model assumption or input is unobservable. Level 3 financial instruments also include those for which the determination of fair value requires significant management judgment or estimation.

In accordance with these definitions, the following table represents CPCH's fair value hierarchy for its investments measured at fair value as of December 31, 2016:

	Quoted Prices for Active Markets for Identical Assets (Level 1)	Significant Other Observable Inputs (Level 2)	Total
Equity securities	$7,323,032	$ -	$7,323,032
Fixed income securities	-	1,694,356	1,694,356
Certificate of deposit	-	200,528	200,528
Total	$7,323,032	$1,894,884	$9,217,916

The estimated fair value of investments was determined by CPCH in accordance with its investment policy. Estimated fair value is determined by CPCH based on a number of factors, including: comparable publicly traded securities, the costs of investments to CPCH, as well as the current and projected operating performance. Changes in unrealized appreciation or depreciation of the investments are recognized as unrealized gains and losses in the statement of activities. Because of the inherent uncertainty of these valuations, the estimated values may differ from the actual fair values that may or may not be ultimately realized.

NOTE E - LAND, BUILDINGS AND EQUIPMENT

Land, buildings and equipment at December 31, 2016 consist of the following:

	Cost	Accumulated Depreciation	Book Value
Land	$ 23,477		$ 23,477
Buildings	5,870,217	$2,575,043	3,295,174
Campus infrastructure	583,513	257,634	325,879
Furniture & equipment	346,640	320,070	26,570
Vehicles	171,761	127,957	43,804
Total	$6,995,608	$3,280,704	$3,714,904

CUMBERLAND PRESBYTERIAN CHILDREN'S HOME

NOTES TO FINANCIAL STATEMENTS
DECEMBER 31, 2016

NOTE F - TEMPORARILY RESTRICTED NET ASSETS

Temporarily restricted net assets are available for the following purposes or periods:

Lena Hart Educational Fund	$ 3,934
Humphrey Scholarship Endowment	1,019
Walker Trimble Scholarship Fund	2,043
David Long Memorial Fund	278
Sybil V. Cockerham College Fund	1,239
Eleanor Sargeant Endowment	558
For periods after December 31, 2016 - term endowment to be received in a future year – Naomi Locke Trust	19,363
Total	$ 28,434

NOTE G - OTHER LONG-TERM INVESTMENTS

	Total	Unrestricted	Temporarily Restricted	Permanently Restricted
Endowments held by the Board of Stewardship	$4,957,138	$ -	$ -	$4,957,138
Certificate of deposit – First United Bank	200,528	200,528	-	-
Mutual funds held by First National Bank – Virginia Ekiss Trust	355,847	-	-	355,847
Mutual funds held by Regions Bank – Laura Harpole Trust	102,548	-	-	102,548
Mutual funds held by Fairfield Natl. Bank - Naomi Locke Trust	19,363	-	19,363	-
Funds held at J P Morgan:				
Lena Hart Educational Fund	6,434	-	3,934	2,500
Humphrey Scholarship Endowment	4,500	-	1,019	3,481
Walker Trimble Scholarship Fund	10,323	-	2,043	8,280
David Long Memorial Fund	1,278	-	278	1,000
Sibyl V. Cockerham College Fund	3,239	-	1,239	2,000
Eleanor Sargeant Endowment	3,138	-	558	2,580
Operating Reserve	3,190,978	3,190,978	-	-
Funds held at Charles Schwab: Operating Reserve	1,562	1,562	-	-
4,000 shares Exxon-Mobil held by CPCH - Jessie DiCarlo Endowment	361,040	-	-	361,040
Total	$9,217,916	$3,393,068	$ 28,434	$5,796,414

CUMBERLAND PRESBYTERIAN CHILDREN'S HOME

NOTES TO FINANCIAL STATEMENTS
DECEMBER 31, 2016

NOTE H – PERMANENTLY RESTRICTED NET ASSETS

Permanently restricted net assets are restricted as follows:

Investments in perpetuity, the income from which is expendable to support any activities of CPCH	$5,840,062
Total	$5,840,062

NOTE I – SUBSEQUENT EVENTS

Management evaluates subsequent events through the date of the report, which is the date the financial statements were available to be issued.

NOTE J – COMPONENTS OF INVESTMENT RETURN

Investment return for the year ended December 31, 2016, including interest and dividends on investments and interest earned on cash balances is summarized as follows:

Unrestricted investment return:		
Interest and dividend income:		
JP Morgan investments	$	69,105
Exxon Mobil stock investment		11,920
Other		14,981
Unrealized gains on investments		88,590
Total unrestricted investment return		184,596
Restricted investment return:		
Interest income:		
Board of Stewardship investments		33,493
Unrealized gains on investments		290,122
Total restricted investment return		323,615
Less investment management fees		(25,356)
Total Investment Return	$	482,855

NOTE K – BANK LINE OF CREDIT

From time to time CPCH draws on a $200,000 line of credit established at First United Bank of Texas for working capital purposes. A total of $300,000 was borrowed and repaid on the line of credit during 2016, with no balance owed at the end of the year. Total interest paid during 2016 on the line of credit was $3,554.

SUPPLEMENTAL SCHEDULE

CUMBERLAND PRESBYTERIAN CHILDREN'S HOME

SCHEDULE OF BOARD OF STEWARDSHIP ENDOWMENTS
DECEMBER 31, 2016

Donor-established Endowments:

	Balance
Merlyn & Joann Kitterman Alexander	$ 1,031
W.A. and Elizabeth Bearden Trust	11,743
Grace Johnson Beasley Memorial Endowment	27,341
Bethlehem CPC Memorial Endowment	4,469
Bridges Scholarship Fund	30,758
J.T. and Dorothy Britt Trust	8,268
Children's Home Endowment	238,521
Lavenia Campbell Cole Trust 20%	15,040
Lavenia Campbell Cole Annuity Endowment	61,080
Lavenia Cole Testamentary Trust 25%	470,038
Mrs. A.L. Colvin Memorial Fund	1,120
John W. and Eva Cox Trust Fund	22,892
Steve Curry Trust	401,838
Daniel Class, First Cumberland Presbyterian Church	23,641
Donnie Curry Davis Memorial	138,342
Mary Elberta Davis Memorial	14,762
Fred and Mattie Mae Dwiggins Memorial Trust	59,272
J.S. Eustis Memorial Trust Fund	9,358
Clester H. Evans, Sr., Trust	15,623
John M. Friedel Trust	16,160
Joyce C. Frisby Memorial Endowment	20,815
Vaughn and Mary Elizabeth Fults Trust	14,907
Garner-Miller Memorial Trust	9,197
James C. and Freda M. Gilbert Endowment	85,393
Henry and Jayne Glaspy Memorial Fund	6,101
Rev. W.J. Gregory Memorial	76,679
Glenn Griffin Endowment	32,689
Rev. and Mrs. Henry M. Guynn Memorial	3,397
Chad Harper Endowment	12,418
Newsome and Imogene Harvey Endowment	1,875
Clarence & Lula Herring Endowment	4,463
Kenneth and Clara Holsopple Trust	39,512
George and Lottie M. Hutchins Trust	840,311
Norma K. Johnson Memorial Library	8,433
P.F. Johnson Memorial Endowment	13,999
Robert and Genevie Johnson Endowment	4,029
Mr. and Mrs. Robert L. Johnson	8,821
Violet Louise Jolly Endowment	891
Eulava Joyce Memorial Trust	7,360
Ruth Cypert and Harlie Klugler Memorial Fund	14,822
Blanche R. Lake Endowment	10,682
Wade P. Lane/Maude Dorough Memorial Trust	7,031
Adolphus M. Latta Memorial Trust	37,937
Mr. and Mrs. Robert F. Little Endowment Fund	26,653
Charles E. and Addie Mae Lloyd Endowment Fund	16,710
Tony and Ann Martin Endowment	2,665
Mrs. Lucille (Lucy) Mast Endowment	2,709

CUMBERLAND PRESBYTERIAN CHILDREN'S HOME

SCHEDULE OF BOARD OF STEWARDSHIP ENDOWMENTS (CONT'D)
DECEMBER 31, 2016

Donor-established Endowments:

	Balance
W.B. and Azales McClurkan, Sr. Memorial	$ 14,287
Williams J. McCall Memorial Trust	7,360
McEwen Church Trust	5,655
McKinley and Barnett Families Endowment	617,113
J.C. McKinley Endowment	13,938
Velma McKinley Trust	13,938
Mary McKnight Memorial Trust	8,295
Kenneth and Mae Moore Endowment Fund	5,204
Operational Trust Fund	109,496
Bert and Pat Owen Endowment	1,158
Hamilton & Merion Parks Family Trust #3	13,483
Joe Parr Trust Fund	57,862
Martha Sue Parr Endowment	1,181
Mary M. Poole Endowment Fund	707,914
Jack and Mary Proctor Memorial Trust Fund	47,200
SQ&K Maurine Proctor Trust	4,181
Mary Acena Prewitt Trust Fund	66,726
Rev. and Mrs. Joe Reed Memorial	3,045
Marguerite D. Richards Endowment	18,799
Agnes Durbin Richardson Trust	22,299
Pat N. & Essie H. Roberts Memorial	43,524
Frances Benefield Roberts Trust Fund	1,724
Rev. and Mrs. John A. Russell Memorial	3,365
John Ann and Mary Shimer	11,080
Rev. W.B. and Lydia Snipes Memorial Trust	21,098
Don M. & Nancy Tabor Endowment Trust	25,466
Townsend Trust Fund	28,407
Hattie A. Wheeless Fund	14,613
Whitfield Family Endowment	8,906
Porter and Hattie S. Williamson Memorial Trust	126,746
Helen Wynn Endowment Fund	11,697
Maxie and Will Young Memorial Endowment	15,342
Dixie Campbell Zinn Memorial Trust	4,612
Dr. John P. Austin Endowment	19,628
Total	$ 4,957,138

Memphis Theological Seminary
of the Cumberland Presbyterian Church
Financial Statements
July 31, 2016 and 2015

MEMPHIS THEOLOGICAL SEMINARY OF THE CUMBERLAND PRESBYTERIAN CHURCH

Table of Contents — *July 31, 2016 and 2015*

	Page
Independent Auditor's Report	3
Financial Statements	
Statements of Financial Position	5
Statement of Activities	6
Statement of Functional Expenses	7
Statements of Cash Flows	8
Notes to the Financial Statements	9
Supplementary Information	
Schedule of Expenditures of Federal Awards	20
Non-Financial Section	
Independent Auditor's Report on Internal Control over Financial Reporting and on Compliance and Other Matters Based on an Audit of Financial Statements Performed in Accordance with *Government Auditing Standards*	22
Independent Auditor's Report on Compliance for a Major Program and on Internal Control over Compliance Required by the Uniform Guidance	24
Schedule of Findings and Questioned Costs	26
Summary Schedule of Prior Audit Findings	27

INDEPENDENT AUDITOR'S REPORT

To the Board of Trustees
Memphis Theological Seminary of the Cumberland Presbyterian Church
Memphis, Tennessee

Report on the Financial Statements

We have audited the accompanying financial statements of Memphis Theological Seminary of the Cumberland Presbyterian Church (a nonprofit organization), which comprise the statement of financial position as of July 31, 2016, and the related statements of activities, functional expenses, and cash flows for the year then ended, and the related notes to the financial statements.

Management's Responsibility for the Financial Statements

Management is responsible for the preparation and fair presentation of these financial statements in accordance with accounting principles generally accepted in the United States of America; this includes the design, implementation, and maintenance of internal control relevant to the preparation and fair presentation of financial statements that are free from material misstatement, whether due to fraud or error.

Auditor's Responsibility

Our responsibility is to express an opinion on these financial statements based on our audit. We conducted our audit in accordance with auditing standards generally accepted in the United States of America and the standards applicable to financial audits contained in *Government Auditing Standards*, issued by the Comptroller General of the United States. Those standards require that we plan and perform the audit to obtain reasonable assurance about whether the financial statements are free from material misstatement.

An audit involves performing procedures to obtain audit evidence about the amounts and disclosures in the financial statements. The procedures selected depend on the auditor's judgment, including the assessment of the risks of material misstatement of the financial statements, whether due to fraud or error. In making those risk assessments, the auditor considers internal control relevant to the entity's preparation and fair presentation of the financial statements in order to design audit procedures that are appropriate in the circumstances, but not for the purpose of expressing an opinion on the effectiveness of the entity's internal control. Accordingly, we express no such opinion. An audit also includes evaluating the appropriateness of accounting policies used and the reasonableness of significant accounting estimates made by management, as well as evaluating the overall presentation of the financial statements.

We believe that the audit evidence we have obtained is sufficient and appropriate to provide a basis for our audit opinion.

Opinion

In our opinion, the financial statements referred to above present fairly, in all material respects, the financial position of Memphis Theological Seminary of the Cumberland Presbyterian Church as of July 31, 2016, and the changes in its net assets and its cash flows for the year then ended in accordance with accounting principles generally accepted in the United States of America.

CANNON WRIGHT BLOUNT PLLC   756 RIDGE LAKE BLVD   MEMPHIS TN 38120

PHONE 901.685.7500   FAX 901.685.7569   WWW.CANNONWRIGHTBLOUNT.COM

Other Matters

Other Information

Our audit was conducted for the purpose of forming an opinion on the financial statements as a whole. The accompanying schedule of expenditures of federal awards, as required by Title 2 U.S. *Code of Federal Regulations* (CFR) Part 200, *Uniform Administrative Requirements, Cost Principles*, and *Audit Requirements for Federal Awards*, is presented for purposes of additional analysis and is not a required part of the financial statements. Such information is the responsibility of management and was derived from and relates directly to the underlying accounting and other records used to prepare the financial statements. The information has been subjected to the auditing procedures applied in the audit of the financial statements and certain additional procedures, including comparing and reconciling such information directly to the underlying accounting and other records used to prepare the financial statements or to the financial statements themselves, and other additional procedures in accordance with auditing standards generally accepted in the United States of America. In our opinion, the information is fairly stated, in all material respects, in relation to the financial statements as a whole.

Other Reporting Required by *Government Auditing Standards*

In accordance with *Government Auditing Standards*, we have also issued our report dated November 15, 2016, on our consideration of Memphis Theological Seminary of the Cumberland Presbyterian Church's internal control over financial reporting and on our tests of its compliance with certain provisions of laws, regulations, contracts, and grant agreements and other matters. The purpose of that report is to describe the scope of our testing of internal control over financial reporting and compliance and the results of that testing, and not to provide an opinion on internal control over financial reporting or on compliance. That report is an integral part of an audit performed in accordance with *Government Auditing Standards* in considering Memphis Theological Seminary of the Cumberland Presbyterian Church's internal control over financial reporting and compliance.

Report on Summarized Comparative Information

We have previously audited the Memphis Theological Seminary of the Cumberland Presbyterian Church's 2015 financial statements, and we expressed an unmodified audit opinion on those audited financial statements in our report dated November 20, 2015. In our opinion, the summarized comparative information presented herein as of and for the year ended July 31, 2015, is consistent, in all material respects, with the audited financial statements from which it has been derived.

Cannon Wright Blount PLLC

Memphis, Tennessee
November 15, 2016

MEMPHIS THEOLOGICAL SEMINARY OF THE CUMBERLAND PRESBYTERIAN CHURCH

Statements of Financial Position   *July 31, 2016 and 2015*

ASSETS

	2016	2015
Cash and cash equivalents	$ 417,767	$ 605,352
Investments, at fair value	10,272,557	10,419,542
Tuition and fees receivable, net of allowance of $80,448 in 2016 and $274,323 in 2015	125,517	155,851
Pledges receivable, net of discounts on pledges	715,178	800,740
Other receivables	242,364	103,298
Capital assets, net of accumulated depreciation	3,153,924	3,219,212
Cash value of life insurance	36,692	36,972
Land held for sale	27,448	27,448
Other assets	43,437	78,211
Total assets	$ 15,034,884	$ 15,446,626

LIABILITIES AND NET ASSETS

Liabilities		
Accounts payable and accrued expenses	$ 303,359	$ 286,106
Prepaid revenue	-	123,667
Line of credit	100,000	170,000
Notes payable	1,647,333	1,515,251
Total liabilities	2,050,692	2,095,024
Net Assets		
Unrestricted		
Board designated	74,114	79,437
Other unrestricted	2,965,501	3,391,099
Temporarily restricted	3,247,881	3,419,361
Permanently restricted	6,696,696	6,461,705
Total net assets	12,984,192	13,351,602
Total liabilities and net assets	$ 15,034,884	$ 15,446,626

See independent auditor's report and notes to the financial statements

MEMPHIS THEOLOGICAL SEMINARY OF THE CUMBERLAND PRESBYTERIAN CHURCH

Statement of Activities

For the Year Ended July 31, 2016
(with summarized comparative totals for the year ended July 31, 2015)

	Unrestricted	Temporarily Restricted	Permanently Restricted	2016 Total	2015 Total
Operating Revenues and Support					
Tuition and fees, net of scholarships of $472,805 and $460,331	$ 1,862,835	$ -	$ -	$ 1,862,835	$ 2,150,542
Contributions and grants	1,403,695	455,205	234,991	2,093,891	2,230,759
Other revenue and support	220,307	-	-	220,307	196,002
Net assets released from restrictions	611,317	(611,317)	-	-	-
Total operating revenues and support	4,098,154	(156,112)	234,991	4,177,033	4,577,303
Expenses					
Educational program services					
Instruction	1,771,063	-	-	1,771,063	1,752,064
Library	360,000	-	-	360,000	232,297
Student services	298,726	-	-	298,726	272,384
Financial leadership for ministry	71,546	-	-	71,546	93,390
Program for alternative studies	130,849	-	-	130,849	144,785
Academic support	120,725	-	-	120,725	136,663
Supporting services					
Institutional support	1,191,013	-	-	1,191,013	975,553
Development and fundraising	585,630	-	-	585,630	658,437
Total expenses	4,529,552	-	-	4,529,552	4,265,573
Increase (decrease) in net assets from operations	(431,398)	(156,112)	234,991	(352,519)	311,730
Non-operating revenues and expenses					
Investment income (loss) (Note 3)	477	(15,368)	-	(14,891)	342,572
Change in net assets	(430,921)	(171,480)	234,991	(367,410)	654,302
Net assets, beginning of year	3,470,536	3,419,361	6,461,705	13,351,602	12,697,300
Net assets - end of year	$ 3,039,615	$ 3,247,881	$ 6,696,696	$ 12,984,192	$ 13,351,602

See independent auditor's report and notes to the financial statements

MEMPHIS THEOLOGICAL SEMINARY OF THE CUMBERLAND PRESBYTERIAN CHURCH

Statement of Functional Expenses

For the Year Ended July 31, 2016
(with summarized comparative totals for the year ended July 31, 2015)

	Educational Program Services						Supporting Services					
	Instruction	Library	Student Services	Financial Leadership for Ministry	Program for Alternative Studies	Academic Support	Facilities Operations	Security Services	Institutional Support	Development and Fund Raising	2016 Total	2015 Total
Salaries and Wages	$ 1,115,779	$111,351	$204,766	$ 43,187	$ 71,266	$ 89,795	$ 172,615	$ -	$ 478,096	$ 250,837	$2,537,692	$2,473,723
Benefits	184,781	36,545	31,596	1,416	13,860	18,162	37,640	-	83,719	51,378	459,097	429,134
Professional Development	30,156	-	1,745	-	-	1,670	1,715	-	1,685	3,905	40,876	15,521
Travel/Auto Expense	2,211	235	2,111	1,359	4,631	3,195	1,988	-	5,203	4,670	25,603	23,685
Office Supplies and Expense	13,742	50,701	7,879	1,847	1,907	1,923	7,353	-	49,997	49,774	185,123	148,040
Consultants / Professional	18,672	-	-	2,135	-	-	-	59,661	81,510	-	161,978	133,188
Special Events	29,913	-	6,299	6,063	32,307	-	-	-	29,909	74,570	179,061	133,248
Student / Covenant Groups	40,550	-	-	-	-	-	-	-	-	-	40,550	44,913
Repairs and Maintenance	105	1,200	-	-	-	-	143,358	-	1,760	-	146,560	74,705
Utilities	-	-	-	-	-	-	77,328	-	-	-	77,328	78,981
Insurance Expense	-	-	-	-	-	-	108,704	-	-	-	108,704	99,954
Property Taxes	-	-	-	-	-	-	12,051	-	-	-	12,051	20,368
Other Expense	7,596	793	5,656	6,576	604	154	(2,742)	-	142,435	43,357	204,429	82,181
Interest Expense	-	-	-	-	-	-	70,126	-	-	-	70,126	71,411
Capital Campaign Expense	-	-	-	-	-	-	-	-	-	97,056	97,056	252,573
Depreciation	-	-	-	-	-	-	183,309	-	-	-	183,309	183,948
Allocation of Facilities Operations & Security	327,499	159,089	38,674	8,963	6,274	5,826	(813,445)	(59,661)	316,699	10,082	-	-
	$ 1,771,064	$360,000	$298,726	$ 71,546	$ 130,849	$ 120,725	$ -	$ -	$1,191,013	$ 585,629	$4,529,552	$4,265,573

See independent auditor's report and notes to the financial statements

MEMPHIS THEOLOGICAL SEMINARY OF THE CUMBERLAND PRESBYTERIAN CHURCH

Statements of Cash Flows — *For the Years Ended July 31, 2016 and 2015*

	2016	2015
Cash Flows from Operating Activities		
Change in net assets	$ (367,410)	$ 654,302
Adjustments to reconcile change in net assets to net cash provided by (used in) operating activities:		
Depreciation	183,309	183,948
Capital (gains) losses on investments	89,914	(271,823)
Bad debt expense	100,656	25,656
Discount on pledges	(10,893)	(12,867)
Changes in operating assets and liabilities:		
(Increase) decrease in assets		
Tuition, fees and other receivables	(209,388)	(100,322)
Pledges receivable	96,455	(6,097)
Other assets	34,774	(46,353)
Increase (decrease) in liabilities		
Accounts payable and accrued expenses	17,253	(5,148)
Prepaid revenue	(123,667)	(6,021)
Net cash provided by (used for) operating activities	(188,997)	415,275
Cash Flows from Investing Activities		
Purchases of investments	(190,139)	(448,989)
Reinvestments of investment earnings	(67,542)	(76,233)
Sale of investments	314,752	378,950
(Increase) decrease in cash surrender value of life insurance	280	3,308
Purchases of property and equipment	(118,021)	(91,932)
Net cash flows from (used for) investing activities	(60,670)	(234,896)
Cash Flows from Financing Activities		
Increase (decrease) in line of credit	(70,000)	(100,000)
Proceeds from issuance of notes payable	1,680,262	-
Principal payments on notes payable	(1,548,180)	(92,242)
Net cash flows from (used for) financing activities	62,082	(192,242)
Net increase (decrease) in cash and cash equivalents	(187,585)	(11,863)
Cash and cash equivalents, beginning of year	605,352	617,215
Cash and cash equivalents, end of year	$ 417,767	$ 605,352
Supplemental Disclosure:		
Interest paid during the year	$ 69,059	$ 77,092

See independent auditor's report and notes to the consolidated financial statements

MEMPHIS THEOLOGICAL SEMINARY OF THE CUMBERLAND PRESBYTERIAN CHURCH
Notes to the Financial Statements *July 31, 2016 and 2015*

Note 1 – Organization and Purpose

The Memphis Theological Seminary of the Cumberland Presbyterian Church (the "Seminary") is an ecumenical Protestant seminary serving the mid-south region from its campus in Memphis, Tennessee. Memphis Theological Seminary of the Cumberland Presbyterian Church provides postgraduate theological education to clergy and church leaders of the parent denomination and qualified students from other denominations. Memphis Theological Seminary of the Cumberland Presbyterian Church is governed by a Board of Trustees elected by the General Assembly of the Cumberland Presbyterian Church.

Note 2 – Significant Accounting Policies

Financial Statement Presentation

Memphis Theological Seminary of the Cumberland Presbyterian Church prepares its financial statements in accordance with accounting principles generally accepted in the United States of America, which involves the application of accrual accounting. Under generally accepted accounting principles, Memphis Theological Seminary of the Cumberland Presbyterian Church reports information regarding its financial position and activities according to three classes of net assets as follows:

Unrestricted Net Assets — Net assets that are not subject to donor-imposed stipulations. Unrestricted net assets may be designated for specific purposes by action of the Board of Trustees or may otherwise be limited by contractual agreements with outside parties.

Temporarily Restricted Net Assets — Net assets whose use by the Seminary is subject to donor-imposed stipulations that can be fulfilled by actions of the Seminary pursuant to those stipulations or that expire by the passage of time.

Permanently Restricted Net Assets — Net assets subject to donor-imposed stipulations that they be maintained permanently by the Seminary. Generally, the donors of these assets permit the Seminary to use all or part of the investment return on these assets.

Contributions

Contributions received by Memphis Theological Seminary of the Cumberland Presbyterian Church are recorded as unrestricted, temporarily restricted, or permanently restricted support depending on the existence and/or nature of any donor restrictions. Temporarily restricted net assets are reclassified to unrestricted net assets upon satisfaction of the time or purpose restrictions.

Investment Valuation and Income Recognition

Investments are reported at fair value. Fair value is the price that would be received to sell an asset or paid to transfer a liability in an orderly transaction between market participants at the measurement date. See Notes 3 and 4 for discussion and computation of fair value.

Unrealized holding gains and losses are included in current year revenue and support as a component of investment income. Realized gains and losses are computed using the specific identification method.

Capital Assets

All acquisitions of property and equipment and expenditures for repairs and maintenance that prolong the useful lives of assets in excess of $1,000 are capitalized at cost. Expenditures for normal repair and maintenance are expensed to operations as they occur. Depreciation is provided through the straight-line method over the assets' estimated useful lives which range from three to ten years for equipment, fifteen years for library books and twenty-five to forty years for buildings.

MEMPHIS THEOLOGICAL SEMINARY OF THE CUMBERLAND PRESBYTERIAN CHURCH
Notes to the Financial Statements *July 31, 2016 and 2015*

Note 2 – Significant Accounting Policies (continued)

Cash Equivalents

Cash equivalents are defined as short term, highly liquid investments that are both readily convertible to known amounts of cash and are so near maturity that they present insignificant risk of changes in value because of changes in interest rates.

Use of Estimates in the Preparation of Financial Statements

The preparation of financial statements in conformity with generally accepted accounting principles requires management to make estimates and assumptions that affect the amounts reported in the financial statements and accompanying notes. Actual results could differ from those estimates.

Income Taxes

Memphis Theological Seminary of the Cumberland Presbyterian Church is a not-for-profit organization that is exempt from income taxes under Internal Revenue Code Section 501(c)(3) and is also exempt from state income taxes. The Seminary is generally no longer subject to federal and state audit for tax years prior to the year ended July 31, 2013.

Donated Property, Equipment and Services

Donations of property and use of property are recorded as support at their estimated fair value at the date of donation. Such donations are reported as unrestricted support unless the donor has restricted the donated asset to a specific purpose. The value of donated property was $0 in 2016 and 2015.

Donated services are recognized as contributions if the services (a) create or enhance non-financial assets or (b) require specialized skills, are performed by people with those skills, and would otherwise be purchased by the Organization. There were no contributed services recorded for accounting and consulting in 2016 and 2015.

Functional Allocation of Expenses

The cost of providing the various educational programs and supporting services has been summarized on a functional basis in the statement of functional expenses. Accordingly, certain costs have been allocated among the programs and services benefited.

Reclassification of Prior Year Amounts

Certain amounts in the July 31, 2015, financial statements have been reclassified to conform to the July 31, 2016, presentation.

Subsequent Events

Memphis Theological Seminary of the Cumberland Presbyterian Church evaluated all events or transactions that occurred through November 15, 2016, the date Memphis Theological Seminary of the Cumberland Presbyterian Church approved these financial statements for issuance.

Fair Value Measurement

ASC Subtopic 820-10 *Fair Value Measurements,* (formerly SFAS No. 157), defines fair value as the price that would be received for an asset or paid to transfer a liability in the principal or most [advantageo]us market for the asset or liability in an orderly transaction between market participants at the [measurem]ent date. SFAS No. 157 established a three-level fair value hierarchy that prioritizes the inputs used to [measure fa]ir value. This hierarchy requires entities to maximize the use of observable inputs and minimize the [use of unob]servable inputs.

[The three l]evels of inputs used to measure fair value are as follows:

[Leve]l 1 – Quoted prices in active markets for identical assets or liabilities.

[Leve]l 2 – Observable inputs other than quoted prices included in Level 1, such as quoted prices for similar [asse]ts and liabilities in active markets; quoted prices for identical or similar assets or liabilities in markets [that] are not active; or inputs that are observable or can be corroborated by observable market data.

[Leve]l 3 – Unobservable inputs that are supported by little or no market activity and that are significant to the [fair] value of the assets or liabilities. This includes certain pricing models, discounted cash flow [meth]odologies and similar techniques that use significant unobservable inputs.

[The estima]ted fair value of Memphis Theological Seminary of the Cumberland Presbyterian Church's financial [instruments] has been determined by management using available market information. However, considerable [judgment is] required in interpreting market data to develop the estimates of fair value. Accordingly, the fair values [are not nec]essarily indicative of the amounts that Memphis Theological Seminary of the Cumberland Presbyterian [Church wou]ld realize in a current market exchange. The use of different market assumptions may have a material [effect on th]e estimated fair value amounts.

[The carryin]g amounts of cash and cash equivalents, net receivables, cash value of life insurance, payables, [accrued lia]bilities, and debt are a reasonable estimate of their fair value, due to their short term nature, method of [valuation] and interest rates for current debt.

[Financia]l assets that are measured at fair value on a recurring basis (at least annually) have been segregated [into the mo]st appropriate level within the fair value hierarchy based on the inputs used to determine the fair value [at the mea]surement date.

MEMPHIS THEOLOGICAL SEMINARY OF THE CUMBERLAND PRESBYTERIAN CHURCH
Notes to the Financial Statements *July 31, 2016 and 2015*

Note 3 – Fair Value Measurement (continued)

The following table sets forth by level, within the fair value hierarchy, the Seminary's financial instruments at fair value as of July 31, 2016:

	Total	Level 1	Level 2	Level 3
Investment securities				
Cash/cash equivalents	$ 728,900	$ 728,900	$ -	$ -
Money market funds	10,046	10,046	-	-
Bonds and bond funds	25,434	25,434	-	-
Common and preferred stocks	120,713	120,713	-	-
Real estate investment funds	736,330	-	736,330	-
Mutual funds	214,288	214,288	-	-
Private investment entities	8,436,846	-	-	8,436,846
Total investments	$ 10,272,557	$ 1,099,381	$ 736,330	$ 8,436,846
Land held for sale	$ 27,448	$ -	$ -	$ 27,448

The following table sets forth by level, within the fair value hierarchy, the Seminary's financial instruments at fair value as of July 31, 2015:

	Total	Level 1	Level 2	Level 3
Investment securities				
Cash/cash equivalents	$ 446,350	$ 446,350	$ -	$ -
Money market funds	4,274	4,274	-	-
Bonds and bond funds	1,449,162	10,971	1,438,191	-
Common and preferred stocks	136,617	136,617	-	-
Real estate investment funds	736,910	-	736,910	-
Mutual funds	409,957	409,957	-	-
Private investment entities	7,236,272	-	-	7,236,272
Total investments	$ 10,419,542	$ 1,008,169	$ 2,175,101	$ 7,236,272
Land held for sale	$ 27,448	$ -	$ -	$ 27,448

The private investment entities are investments entered into by the Board of Stewardship to achieve greater rates of return. They include funds whose inputs used to determine fair value are considered unobservable and are therefore Level 3 inputs.

The carrying value of the above land held for sale is based on expected recoverability at the time of sale. Memphis Theological Seminary of the Cumberland Presbyterian Church uses appraised values and other information available to determine the carrying value. The inputs used to determine fair value are considered unobservable and are therefore Level 3 inputs.

MEMPHIS THEOLOGICAL SEMINARY OF THE CUMBERLAND PRESBYTERIAN CHURCH
Notes to the Financial Statements *July 31, 2016 and 2015*

Note 3 – Fair Value Measurement (continued)

Transactions in Level 3 assets for the years ended July 31, 2016 and 2015, were as follows:

	2016	2015
Private investment entities		
Beginning balance	$ 7,236,272	$ 6,967,450
Change in allocation of investments	(250,521)	(168,572)
Reinvestments	1,409,870	37,735
Realized/unrealized gains (losses)	41,225	399,659
Ending balance	$ 8,436,846	$ 7,236,272
Land held for sale		
Beginning balance	$ 27,448	$ 27,448
Ending balance	$ 27,448	$ 27,448

Investment income (loss) was as follows for the years ended July 31, 2016 and 2015:

	2016	2015
Investment income	$ 75,023	$ 70,750
Realized investment gains (losses)	59,487	35,462
Unrealized investment gains (losses)	(149,401)	236,360
Net investment income (loss)	$ (14,891)	$ 342,572

Note 4 – Endowments

Nearly all of Memphis Theological Seminary of the Cumberland Presbyterian Church's investments, which contain endowments, are managed by the Board of Stewardship, Foundation and Benefits of the Cumberland Presbyterian Church, Inc., and maintained in pooled investment accounts with other funds. The investments generally originate from gifts and contributions for which separate identifiable investment accounts are created that indicate the source of the funds and/or the purpose for which the funds are to be used. Many of these accounts are designated for monthly distributions to Memphis Theological Seminary of the Cumberland Presbyterian Church based on one-twelfth of 5% of the rolling average value. The Board of Stewardship, Foundation and Benefits, issues an aggregate amount to Memphis Theological Seminary of the Cumberland Presbyterian Church and charges the applicable accounts for their proportionate share. In addition, Memphis Theological Seminary of the Cumberland Presbyterian Church can request on an as needed basis, additional distributions that will be used for the purpose for which the account was created.

MEMPHIS THEOLOGICAL SEMINARY OF THE CUMBERLAND PRESBYTERIAN CHURCH

Notes to the Financial Statements
July 31, 2016 and 2015

Note 4 – Endowments (continued)

The Seminary has interpreted the Uniform Prudent Management of Institutional Funds Act ("UPMIFA") requiring a portion of a donor restricted endowment of perpetual duration be classified as permanently restricted assets. The amount of the endowment that must be retained permanently is in accordance with explicit donor stipulations as outlined in their respective endowment agreements. The Seminary has other endowment funds that are temporarily restricted by the donor as to purpose and are classified as temporarily restricted until they are expended on their respective purposes. Investment income and net appreciation on these permanently and temporarily restricted endowments is classified as temporarily restricted or permanently restricted if so directed by the donor in the respective endowment agreements or as unrestricted in the absence of donor instructions. The Seminary has other donated funds and board designated funds that are included in investments and are not restricted as to use. These funds, as well as investment income and net appreciation on these funds are classified as unrestricted. Expenditures (withdrawals) of the temporarily restricted and unrestricted funds are approved by management. The funds held by the Board of Stewardship, Foundation and Benefits of the Cumberland Presbyterian Church, Inc. are invested with the primary objective of providing a balance between capital appreciation, preservation of capital, and current income. This is a long-term goal designed to maximize returns without undue risk. The Board of Stewardship selects the investment portfolio where the endowments will be invested as described in the Investment Policy of The Cumberland Presbyterian Church Center, which outlines the asset allocations, permissible investments, and objectives of the portfolios.

Changes in endowment net assets for the years ended July 31, 2016 and 2015, were as follows:

	Unrestricted Board Designated	Unrestricted Other	Temporarily Restricted	Permanently Restricted	Total
Balance at July 31, 2014	$ 82,263	$ 1,585,815	$ 2,080,907	$ 6,252,462	$ 10,001,447
Investment return:					
Investment income	720	28,871	35,842	-	65,433
Change in market value	2,500	134,328	123,638	11,356	271,822
Total investment return	3,220	163,199	159,480	11,356	337,255
Contributions	-	251,102	-	197,887	448,989
Appropriation of endowment assets for expenditure	(6,046)	(213,403)	(148,700)	-	(368,149)
Reclassifications	-	(5,009)	5,009	-	-
Balance at July 31, 2015	79,437	1,781,704	2,096,696	6,461,705	10,419,542
Investment return:					
Investment income	595	31,864	35,083	-	67,542
Change in market value	3,487	(42,950)	(50,451)	-	(89,914)
Total investment return	4,082	(11,086)	(15,368)	-	(22,372)
Contributions	-	105,148	-	84,991	190,139
Appropriation of endowment assets for expenditure	(4,945)	(179,699)	(130,108)	-	(314,752)
Balance at July 31, 2016	$ 78,574	$ 1,696,067	$ 1,951,220	$ 6,546,696	$ 10,272,557

MEMPHIS THEOLOGICAL SEMINARY OF THE CUMBERLAND PRESBYTERIAN CHURCH
Notes to the Financial Statements *July 31, 2016 and 2015*

Note 5 – Capital Assets

Capital assets are as follows at July 31, 2016 and 2015:

	2016	2015
Building and improvements	$ 4,357,318	$ 4,292,602
Furniture and equipment	892,587	886,529
Library books	1,853,526	1,809,944
Vehicles	44,014	48,514
	7,147,445	7,037,589
Less accumulated depreciation	4,597,189	4,418,380
	2,550,256	2,619,209
Land	208,650	208,650
Construction in progress	395,018	391,353
Capital assets, net	$ 3,153,924	$ 3,219,212

Depreciation expense for the years ended July 31, 2016 and 2015, was $183,309 and $183,948, respectively.

Note 6 – Concentration of Credit Risk

Memphis Theological Seminary of the Cumberland Presbyterian Church has cash equivalents invested by the Board of Stewardship, Foundation and Benefits. At July 31, 2016, these funds total $246,559 and are not insured by the Federal Deposit Insurance Corporation (FDIC).

In addition, Memphis Theological Seminary of the Cumberland Presbyterian Church maintains cash balances in accounts at a well-established financial institution located in Memphis, Tennessee. These balances are insured by the Federal Deposit Insurance Corporation up to certain limits. At July 31, 2016, Memphis Theological Seminary of the Cumberland Presbyterian Church had no uninsured balances.

Memphis Theological Seminary of the Cumberland Presbyterian Church's tuition and fees receivable are from students for which the majority receive some form of financial assistance. Management maintains an allowance for uncollectible based on periodic reviews of each individual student's account.

Note 7 - Pledges Receivable

Pledges receivable primarily represent pledges from numerous donors to be used for a capital campaign which was initiated in a prior year. The campaign has three purposes: 1) to help fund the construction of a new free-standing chapel; 2) to fund construction of a new classroom/office building; and 3) to increase endowments. At the beginning of the current fiscal year, the fund raising campaign was changed from a capital campaign to a comprehensive campaign in which pledges made could still be designated to the capital campaign, but could also be designated to support facilities maintenance, support the annual fund, or be undesignated. Pledges receivable for the capital/comprehensive campaign totaled $604,642 and $651,097 at July 31, 2016 and 2015, respectively. Pledges receivable also include a pledge to offset the cost of a faculty member. Pledges receivable to offset the cost of the faculty member totaled $150,000 and $200,000 as of July 31, 2016 and 2015, respectively. These amounts have been discounted to present value using a rate of 3.07%. Management considers all pledges receivable at July 31, 2016 and 2015, to be fully collectible.

MEMPHIS THEOLOGICAL SEMINARY OF THE CUMBERLAND PRESBYTERIAN CHURCH
Notes to the Financial Statements *July 31, 2016 and 2015*

Note 7 - Pledges Receivable (continued)

The pledges, net of the discount, are due to be received as follows:

	2016	2015
Less than one year	$ 310,345	$ 145,269
One year to five years	444,297	705,828
Gross contributions receivable	754,642	851,097
Less: discount to present value	(39,464)	(50,357)
Contributions receivable, net	$ 715,178	$ 800,740

Note 8 – Line of Credit

Memphis Theological Seminary of the Cumberland Presbyterian Church has a $400,000 revolving line of credit agreement with a local bank that matures September 2017. Borrowings outstanding under the agreement ($100,000 at July 31, 2016 and $170,000 at July 31, 2015) bear interest at the bank's prime rate (3.50 percent at July 31, 2016). The line is guaranteed by the Board of Stewardship, Foundation and Benefits.

Note 9 – Notes Payable

Notes payable consist of the following at July 31, 2016 and 2015:

	2016	2015
Note payable, due in monthly installments of $5,360 at a variable interest (4.75% at July 31, 2015) through January 2031	$ -	$ 718,284
Note payable, due in monthly installments of $5,058 at a variable interest (4.75% at July 31, 2015) through April 2032	-	486,441
Note payable, due in monthly installments of $1,618 at a variable interest (4.75% at July 31, 2015) through April 2033	-	248,051
Note payable, due in monthly installments of $1,436 at a variable interest (4.75% at July 31, 2015) through September 2033	-	62,475
Note payable, due in monthly installments of $10,052 bearing interest at 3.85% through November 2025 and a single balloon payment of the remaining unpaid balance in December 2025	1,647,333	-
Total notes payable	$ 1,647,333	$ 1,515,251

The note payable at July 31, 2016, is secured by property owned by the Seminary and located at 168 East Parkway, Memphis, Tennessee.

MEMPHIS THEOLOGICAL SEMINARY OF THE CUMBERLAND PRESBYTER

Notes to the Financial Statements

Note 9 – Notes Payable (continued)

Scheduled principal payments required for the years ending July 31 are as follows:

	Amount
2017	$ 58,217
2018	60,498
2019	62,869
2020	65,180
2021	67,887
Thereafter	1,332,682
Total notes payable	$ 1,647,333

Note 10 – Retirement Plan

Memphis Theological Seminary of the Cumberland Presbyterian Church sponsors a qualified de retirement plan for eligible employees as defined by the plan under IRC Section 403(b). Employe participate in the plan immediately upon hire and contributions to the plan are vested in participant in the plan may make voluntary contributions to the plan of up to the lesser of twenty annual compensation received by the participant during the plan year, or the maximum allowed Theological Seminary of the Cumberland Presbyterian Church matches participant's contributior of 3.5%. Contributions to the plan by Memphis Theological Seminary of the Cumberland Presby the years ended July 31, 2016 and 2015, were $54,380 and $55,409, respectively.

Note 11 – Related Party

Memphis Theological Seminary of the Cumberland Presbyterian Church and the Board of separate corporations but both are affiliated with the Cumberland Presbyterian Church in that the of the Church elects the members of the Board of Trustees of Memphis Theological Seminary of Presbyterian Church and the Board of Stewardship. There are no common board members be Theological Seminary of the Cumberland Presbyterian Church and the Board of Stewardship. and from the Board of Stewardship as of July 31, 2016 and 2015, are as follows:

	2016	2015
Due the Board of Stewardship from the Seminary:		
Notes Payable	$ -	$ 1,515,
Accrued Interest	$ -	$ 1,
Seminary assets held by the Board of Stewardship:		
Seminary cash held	$ -	$ 239,
Seminary investments held	$ 10,116,325	$ 10,267,
Other Receivables	$ 69,689	$ 90,

MEMPHIS THEOLOGICAL SEMINARY OF THE CUMBERLAND PRESBYTERIAN C

Notes to the Financial Statements — *July 31, 2016*

Note 12 – Temporarily Restricted Net Assets

Temporarily restricted net assets consist of the following at July 31, 2016 and 2015:

	2016	2015
Endowment restrictions	$ 1,951,220	$ 2,096,696
Capital campaign restriction	920,229	1,009,418
Comprehensive campaign restriction	42,142	-
Faculty salary restriction	141,722	188,696
Financial Leadership for Ministries	152,567	110,433
Other restrictions	40,001	14,118
	$ 3,247,881	$ 3,419,361

Note 13 – Concentration of Revenue

In the year ended July 31, 2016, approximately 15% of total operating revenues and support was rec one individual.

Supplementary Information

MEMPHIS THEOLOGICAL SEMINARY OF THE CUMBERLAND PRESBYTERIAN CHURCH

Schedule of Expenditures of Federal Awards *For the Year Ended July 31, 2016*

Federal Grantor/ Pass-Through Grantor/ Program or Cluster Title	CFDA Number	Total Expended
U.S. Department of Education Federal Family Education Loan Program	84.032	$ 2,199,664

Basis of Presentation

The accompanying schedule of expenditures of federal awards (the "Schedule") includes the federal award activity of Memphis Theological Seminary of the Cumberland Presbyterian Church under programs of the federal government for the year ended July 31, 2016. The information in this Schedule is presented in accordance with the requirements of Title 2 CFR U.S. *Code of Federal Regulations* Part 200, *Uniform Administrative Requirements, Cost Principles, and Audit Requirements for Federal Awards* (Uniform Guidance). Because the Schedule presents only a selected portion of the operations of Memphis Theological Seminary of the Cumberland Presbyterian Church, it is not intended to and does not present the financial position, changes in net assets or cash flows of Memphis Theological Seminary of the Cumberland Presbyterian Church.

Summary of Significant Accounting Policies

Expenditures reported on the Schedule are reported on the accrued basis of accounting. Such expenditures are recognized following the cost principles contained in OMB Circular A-21, *Cost Principles for Educational Institutions*, wherein certain types of expenditures are not allowable or are limited as to reimbursement.

Non-Financial Information

INDEPENDENT AUDITOR'S REPORT ON INTERNAL CONTROL OVER FINANCIAL REPORTING AND ON COMPLIANCE AND OTHER MATTERS BASED ON AN AUDIT OF FINANCIAL STATEMENTS PERFORMED IN ACCORDANCE WITH *GOVERNMENT AUDITING STANDARDS*

To the Board of Trustees
Memphis Theological Seminary of the Cumberland Presbyterian Church
Memphis, Tennessee

We have audited, in accordance with the auditing standards generally accepted in the United States of America and the standards applicable to financial audits contained in *Government Auditing Standards* issued by the Comptroller General of the United States, the financial statements of Memphis Theological Seminary of the Cumberland Presbyterian Church (a nonprofit organization), which comprise the statement of financial position as of July 31, 2016, and the related statements of activities, functional expenses, and cash flows for the year then ended, and the related notes to the financial statements, and have issued our report thereon dated November 15, 2016.

Internal Control over Financial Reporting

In planning and performing our audit of the financial statements, we considered Memphis Theological Seminary of the Cumberland Presbyterian Church's internal control over financial reporting (internal control) to determine the audit procedures that are appropriate in the circumstances for the purpose of expressing our opinion on the financial statements, but not for the purpose of expressing an opinion on the effectiveness of Memphis Theological Seminary of the Cumberland Presbyterian Church's internal control. Accordingly, we do not express an opinion on the effectiveness of Memphis Theological Seminary of the Cumberland Presbyterian Church's internal control.

A *deficiency in internal control* exists when the design or operation of a control does not allow management or employees, in the normal course of performing their assigned functions, to prevent, or detect and correct, misstatements on a timely basis. A *material weakness* is a deficiency, or a combination of deficiencies, in internal control, such that there is a reasonable possibility that a material misstatement of the entity's financial statements will not be prevented, or detected and corrected on a timely basis. A *significant deficiency* is a deficiency, or a combination of deficiencies, in internal control that is less severe than a material weakness, yet important enough to merit attention by those charged with governance.

Our consideration of internal control was for the limited purpose described in the first paragraph of this section and was not designed to identify all deficiencies in internal control that might be material weaknesses or significant deficiencies. Given these limitations, during our audit we did not identify any deficiencies in internal control that we consider to be material weaknesses. However, material weaknesses may exist that have not been identified.

Compliance and Other Matters

As part of obtaining reasonable assurance about whether Memphis Theological Seminary of the Cumberland Presbyterian Church's financial statements are free from material misstatement, we performed tests of its compliance with certain provisions of laws, regulations, contracts, and grant agreements, noncompliance with which could have a direct and material effect on the determination of financial statement amounts. However, providing an opinion on compliance with those provisions was not an objective of our audit, and accordingly, we do not express such an opinion. The results of our tests disclosed no instances of noncompliance or other matters that are required to be reported under *Government Auditing Standards*.

CANNON WRIGHT BLOUNT PLLC   756 RIDGE LAKE BLVD   MEMPHIS TN 38120

PHONE 901.685.7500   FAX 901.685.7569   WWW.CANNONWRIGHTBLOUNT.COM

Purpose of this Report

The purpose of this report is solely to describe the scope of our testing of internal control and compliance and the results of that testing, and not to provide an opinion on the effectiveness of the organization's internal control or on compliance. This report is an integral part of an audit performed in accordance with *Government Auditing Standards* in considering the organization's internal control and compliance. Accordingly, this communication is not suitable for any other purpose.

Cannon Wright Blount PLLC

Memphis, Tennessee
November 15, 2016

INDEPENDENT AUDITOR'S REPORT ON COMPLIANCE FOR A MAJOR PROGRAM AND ON INTERNAL CONTROL OVER COMPLIANCE REQUIRED BY THE UNIFORM GUIDANCE

To the Board of Trustees
Memphis Theological Seminary of the Cumberland Presbyterian Church
Memphis, Tennessee

Report on Compliance for a Major Federal Program

We have audited Memphis Theological Seminary of the Cumberland Presbyterian Church's compliance with the types of compliance requirements described in the *OMB Compliance Supplement* that could have a direct and material effect on Memphis Theological Seminary of the Cumberland Presbyterian Church's major federal program for the year ended July 31, 2016. Memphis Theological Seminary of the Cumberland Presbyterian Church's major federal program is identified in the summary of auditor's results section of the accompanying schedule of findings and questioned costs.

Management's Responsibility

Management is responsible for compliance with federal statutes, regulations, and the terms and conditions of its federal awards applicable to its federal program.

Auditor's Responsibility

Our responsibility is to express an opinion on compliance for Memphis Theological Seminary of the Cumberland Presbyterian Church's major federal program based on our audit of the types of compliance requirements referred to above. We conducted our audit of compliance in accordance with auditing standards generally accepted in the United States of America; the standards applicable to financial audits contained in *Government Auditing Standards*, issued by the Comptroller General of the United States; and the audit requirements of Title 2 U.S. *Code of Federal Regulations* Part 200, *Uniform Administrative Requirements, Cost Principles,* and *Audit Requirements for Federal Awards* (Uniform Guidance). Those standards and the Uniform Guidance require that we plan and perform the audit to obtain reasonable assurance about whether noncompliance with the types of compliance requirements referred to above that could have a direct and material effect on a major federal program occurred. An audit includes examining, on a test basis, evidence about Memphis Theological Seminary of the Cumberland Presbyterian Church's compliance with those requirements and performing such other procedures as we considered necessary in the circumstances.

We believe that our audit provides a reasonable basis for our opinion on compliance for the major federal program. However, our audit does not provide a legal determination of Memphis Theological Seminary of the Cumberland Presbyterian Church's compliance.

Opinion on a Major Federal Program

In our opinion, Memphis Theological Seminary of the Cumberland Presbyterian Church complied, in all material respects, with the types of compliance requirements referred to above that could have a direct and material effect on its major federal program for the year ended July 31, 2016.

Report on Internal Control over Compliance

Management of Memphis Theological Seminary of the Cumberland Presbyterian Church is responsible for establishing and maintaining effective internal control over compliance with the types of compliance requirements referred to above. In planning and performing our audit of compliance, we considered Memphis Theological Seminary of the Cumberland Presbyterian Church's internal control over compliance with the types of requirements that could have a direct and material effect on a major federal program to determine the auditing procedures that are appropriate in the circumstances for the purpose of expressing an opinion on compliance for a major federal program and to test and report on internal control over compliance in accordance with the Uniform Guidance, but not for the purpose of expressing an opinion on the effectiveness of internal control over compliance. Accordingly, we do not express an opinion on the effectiveness of Memphis Theological Seminary of the Cumberland Presbyterian Church's internal control over compliance.

A *deficiency in internal control over compliance* exists when the design or operation of a control over compliance does not allow management or employees, in the normal course of performing their assigned functions, to prevent, or detect and correct, noncompliance with a type of compliance requirement of a federal program on a timely basis. A *material weakness in internal control over compliance* is a deficiency, or combination of deficiencies, in internal control over compliance, such that there is a reasonable possibility that material noncompliance with a type of compliance requirement of a federal program will not be prevented, or detected and corrected, on a timely basis. A *significant deficiency in internal control over compliance* is a deficiency, or a combination of deficiencies, in internal control over compliance with a type of compliance requirement of a federal program that is less severe than a material weakness in internal control over compliance, yet important enough to merit attention by those charged with governance.

Our consideration of internal control over compliance was for the limited purpose described in the first paragraph of this section and was not designed to identify all deficiencies in internal control over compliance that might be material weaknesses or significant deficiencies. We did not identify any deficiencies in internal control over compliance that we consider to be material weaknesses. However, material weaknesses may exist that have not been identified.

The purpose of this report on internal control over compliance is solely to describe the scope of our testing of internal control over compliance and the results of that testing based on the requirements of the Uniform Guidance. Accordingly, this report is not suitable for any other purpose.

Cannon Wright Blount PLLC

Memphis, Tennessee
November 15, 2016

MEMPHIS THEOLOGICAL SEMINARY OF THE CUMBERLAND PRESBYTERIAN CHURCH

Schedule of Findings and Questioned Costs   *For the Year Ended July 31, 2016*

SECTION I - SUMMARY OF AUDITOR'S RESULTS

Financial Statements

Type of auditor's report issued:	*Unmodified*
Internal control over financial reporting:	
- Material weakness(es) identified?	_____ yes __X__ no
- Significant deficiencies identified that are not considered to be material weaknesses?	_____ yes __X__ none noted
- Noncompliance material to financial statements noted?	_____ yes __X__ no

Federal Awards:

Internal control over major programs:	
- Material weakness(es) identified?	_____ yes __X__ no
- Significant deficiencies identified that are not considered to be material weaknesses?	_____ yes __X__ none noted
Type of auditor's report issued on compliance for major program:	*Unmodified*
Any audit findings disclosed that are required to be reported in accordance with 2 CFR section 200.516(a)?	_____ yes __X__ no

Identification of major programs:

CFDA 84.032	U.S. Department of Education Federal Family Education Loan Program
Threshold for distinguishing type A and B programs:	*$750,000*
Auditee qualified as low risk auditee:	__X__ yes _____ no

SECTION II - FINANCIAL STATEMENT FINDINGS

There are no financial statement findings for the year ended July 31, 2016.

SECTION III - FEDERAL AWARD FINDINGS AND QUESTIONED COSTS

There are no federal award findings or questioned costs for the year ended July 31, 2016.

MEMPHIS THEOLOGICAL SEMINARY OF THE CUMBERLAND PRESBYTERIAN CHURCH

Summary Schedule of Prior Audit Findings — *For the Year Ended July 31, 2016*

There were no findings or questioned costs for the year ended July 31, 2015.

APPENDICES

REPORT OF THE CREDENTIALS COMMITTEE
(Appendix A)

The Credentials Committee certifies the list of commissioners on pages 5 and 6 of the Preliminary Minutes with the following changes:

On the part of Elder Delegates, Denise Gales, Red River Presbytery, is not present.

On the part of Youth Advisory Delegates, Stephen McKoon, Red River Presbytery, is not present.

Enrollment as of 8:30 a.m. is certified as thirty-one (31) ministers and twenty-eight (28) elders for a total of fifty-nine (59) Commissioners with twenty-one (21) Youth Advisory Delegates.

Respectfully submitted,
Lanny Johnson
Roger Reid
Christy Miller, Chair

RESOLUTION OF FORGIVENESS, UNITY, AND RESOLVE
(Appendix B)

WHEREAS, we Cumberland Presbyterians are considering the call of God as we embrace our 2017 Theme of "Connecting With Our Neighbor" (Luke 10: 29-37) during the 142nd convening of the Cumberland Presbyterian Church in America (CPCA), General Assembly; and

WHEREAS, Jesus commands his followers with specific instructions: go, teach, baptize, forgive and make disciples.(Matthew 28:18-20), and

WHEREAS, the Colored Cumberland Presbyterian Church was formed in May of 1874 as a result of the racism and segregation practices that existed within the Cumberland Presbyterian Church and directed towards its African American membership. Where, in defense of Cumberland Presbyterian institutionalized segregation and resulting unequal representation, African American members petitioned the Cumberland Presbyterian Church for assistance in organizing a separate body for African Americans, allowing the African American membership) to become independent and self-reliant, to develop its own clergy and other leaders, and maintain its own church buildings, all with encouragement and financial support from the parent denomination. The resulting predominately African American (black) church was re-named as the Second Cumberland Presbyterian Church before assuming its current name; and

WHEREAS, we proudly celebrate the faith and conviction of our early CPCA fathers, our committed African American Presbyterians ancestors. We recognize their witness as fellow pilgrims on the journey of faith and as our spiritual ancestors who "earnestly contended for the faith that was once delivered to the saints" (Jude 1:3). We commend them for their vision and proclaim those Church Fathers as our spiritual ancestors who taught us not only to reverence the mystery of God through word, thought, and deed, but also to celebrate the African American heritage of Christianity through witness in the tradition of those few, but brave and faithful men and women of color: and

WHEREAS, we joyfully acknowledge that God is truly the sustainer of us all! We recognize that fact as evident in that the CPCA and CPC entities both are still in existence and are both focused, working to carry out the Great Commission; and, although in many ways working separately in God's vineyard, both CPC and CPCA congregations have a willingness and desire to live in His heavenly will as is evident in their continued partnership; and

WHEREAS, relations between the two Cumberland Presbyterian Churches have for the most part been very cordial, with many of the CPCA ministers having received training at Memphis Theological Seminary. The two denominations continue to share a Confession of Faith and cooperate in many common ministries; and

WHEREAS, in true Christian fashion the 186th General Assembly of the Cumberland Presbyterian

Church does recognize, confess, and condemn and repent of past failures to love brothers and sisters from minority cultures in accordance with what the Gospel requires, as well as failures to lovingly confront their brothers and sisters concerning racial sins and personal bigotry, and failing to "learn to do good, seek justice and correct oppression (Isaiah 1:17);" and

WHEREAS, the 186th General Assembly of the CPC has resolved to apologize to us, their African American brothers and sisters, and seeks our forgiveness, and has further resolved to work to restore the broken relationships their sin has caused. The CPC has resolved to recommit itself to the gospel task of racial reconciliation, diligently seeking effective courses of action to further that goal, with humility, sincerity and zeal, for the glory of God and the furtherance of the Gospel; and

WHEREAS, we also seek the healing of our division as Cumberland Presbyterians. We know, not just in our hearts and minds, but where our faith resides, that the path of forgiveness is the direction we are meant to take. "All of this is from God, who reconciled us to himself through Christ, and has given us the ministry of reconciliation; that is, in Christ, God was reconciling the world to him…and entrusting the message of reconciliation to us." (2 Corinthians 5:18–19); and have therefore hereby

RESOLVED, the Cumberland Presbyterian Church in America in its entirety hopes and prays that the Apology will be words of action and sincerity not only in the sanctuary, but in every facet of our daily lives. In the new spirit this Apology has created, let us unite our hearts and minds in the wholeness of life that God has given us. May God grant us strength and vision for the journey towards right relations and wellbeing and see the possibilities and promise of healing; and be it further

RESOLVED, that the Cumberland Presbyterian Church in America accepts the CPC apology and we extend to you our forgiveness in the name of our lord and savior, Jesus Christ. Ephesians 4: 31-32, says, " let all bitterness and wrath and anger and clamor and evil speaking be put away from you with all malice, and be kind, one to another, tender-hearted, forgiving one another, even as God, for Christ's sake, hath forgiven you"; and be it further

RESOLVED, because of Jesus Christ our Lord and Savior and His great love toward us, we extend that same love, forgiveness, grace and mercy towards you. We pray that the genuineness of your repentance and our forgiveness will be reflected in the attitudes and actions of all. We forgive you, for Christ's sake, Amen.

REPORT OF THE COMMITTEE ON JUDICIARY
(Appendix C)

I. REFERRALS

Referrals to this committee are as follows: The Report of the Permanent Committee on Judiciary, The Report of the Joint Committee on Amendments, and The Memorial from Andes Presbytery Regarding Gender Diversity.

II. PERSONS OF COUNSEL

Reverend Andy McClung, Permanent Judiciary Committee; Reverend Elinor Brown, Discipleship Ministry Team; and Stated Clerk Mike Sharpe appeared before the committee.

III. CONSIDERATION OF REFERRALS

A. REPORT OF THE JOINT COMMITTEE ON AMENDMENTS

Rules of Order 12.5 bars members of a judicatory from voting on matters in which they have a conflict of interest, but it does not limit their ability to participate in debate on those matters. Recognizing that influence can be wielded in debate or discussion which may impact the vote on that issue, the Committee offers the following:

RECOMMENDATION 1: That Recommendation 1 of the Report of the Joint Committee on Amendments, "that Rules of Order 12.5 be amended to read "No member of a judicatory shall participate in debate or vote on a matter in which the member has a pecuniary interest, a personal interest, or other conflict of interest not common to other members of the judicatory. A member of a

judicatory has such a conflict of interest when the member also belongs to a lower judicatory whose action is the subject of an appeal to or review by the higher judicatory. In such a case, the member may participate as a representative of the lower judicatory but may not participate as a member of the higher judicatory. Members are not prevented from voting for themselves for an office or other position to which members generally are eligible (see Robert's Rules of Order, Section 45).",", be adopted.

Note that revisions to Robert's Rules of Order necessitate the change from "Section 44" to "Section 45."

We note with joy the expansion of the Cumberland Presbyterian Church into new mission fields across the globe. While we celebrate this growth, it seems to have out-paced our rules. In order to provide the best possible support to these new churches and their pastors, we offer the following:

RECOMMENDATION 2: That Recommendation 2 of the Report of the Joint Committee on Amendments, "that Constitution 9.5 be renumbered as 9.6 and a new 9.5 be inserted, reading as follows: "9.5 The General Assembly, in order to promote the mission work of the Church and the development of new churches outside the United States, may authorize a synod or its missions entity (utilizing ordained personnel) to act in place of a presbytery with respect to persons, ministers, and churches outside the United States and outside the bounds of any existing presbytery. The missions entity or synod may attach mission work to an existing presbytery, with the presbytery's approval. The General Assembly shall provide for the oversight and responsibility of the body's ecclesiastical actions.",", be adopted.

B. REPORT OF THE PERMANENT COMMITTEE ON JUDICIARY

Should Recommendation 2 be adopted by the General Assembly and ratified by Presbyteries, that change in structure requires a companion change in our Bylaws. We commend the Permanent Judiciary Committee for bringing this to our attention in a timely manner, and offer the following:

RECOMMENDATION 3: That Recommendation 1 of the Report of the Permanent Committee on Judiciary, "that the General Assembly Bylaw 11.05, which refers to the Judiciary Committee, be amended by inserting 11.05.06. "The committee shall have oversight of and responsibility for ecclesiastical decisions made by a body acting in the place of a presbytery with respect to mission work and mission fields. The oversight and responsibility exercised by 4 the committee shall be the same as that exercised by a synod with respect to a presbytery under its care, specifically Constitution 8.5, a, b and c.",", be adopted.

C. THE MEMORIAL FROM ANDES PRESBYTERY REGARDING GENDER DIVERSITY

The Committee discussed the Memorial from Andes Presbytery, and its request that the General Assembly closely review and monitor programs and institutions that may unduly influence the doctrine and work of the Cumberland Presbyterian Church and thus prevent an infiltration of concepts that are foreign to our doctrine and practice."

We heard from Reverends Elinor Brown and Michael Sharpe, and considered past actions and current policies of the General Assembly and its agencies regarding our relationship with outside "programs and institutions." Specifically, we direct your attention to the following:
• Cumberland Presbyterian Digest 9.4n INTERPRETIVE, 1951, which states that "if membership in or affiliation with such organization outside the denomination involves a change in doctrine of the church or the commitment of the church board or agency to some matter of doctrine contrary to our Confession of Faith, prior approval must be had from three-fourths of the presbyteries of the church as well as the prior approval of not less than 75 percent of the full membership of the General Assembly."
• 2015 Minutes of the General Assembly (page 41) "Referrals from General Assembly" to the Ministry Council, Section C.1: Presbyterian Church USA Evaluation: "The Ministry Council and Discipleship Ministry Team in particular have been and will continue to be vigilant to ensure any content or program in association with the PCUSA does not run counter to CP beliefs as articulated in the Confession of Faith."

We are satisfied that our past commitment to "review and monitor" all joint ministry efforts is still being honored.

RECOMMENDATION 4: That the Memorial from Andes Presbytery, "REGARDING GENDER DIVERSITY" which states:

"On April 10, 2017, in a duly convened called meeting, Andes Presbytery approved this Memorial to be submitted for consideration by the 187th General Assembly of the Cumberland Presbyterian Church.

WHEREAS the church in Colombia has been pressured by [the politics of] gender ideology that in our context involves promoting a diversity of genders that is openly contrary to the Bible;
WHEREAS our source of authority is from the Bible, and the Bible teaches:
That in Genesis 1:26 God created humankind as man and woman.
That according to Leviticus 18:22 homosexuality is an aberration before God.
"Do not lie with a man as one lies with a woman; that is detestable." (NIV)
That according to Romans 1:26-27 homosexuality is contrary to God's original design.
"Because of this, God gave them over to shameful lusts. Even their women exchanged natural relations for unnatural ones. In the same way the men also abandoned natural relations with women and were inflamed with lust for one another. Men committed indecent acts with other men, and received in themselves the due penalty for their perversion." (NIV)
That according to 1 Corinthians 6:9-10, practicing homosexuals will not enter into the Kingdom of Heaven.
"Do you not know that the wicked will not inherit the kingdom of God? Do not be deceived: Neither the sexually immoral nor idolaters nor adulterers nor male prostitutes nor homosexual offenders nor thieves nor the greedy nor drunkards nor slanders nor swindlers will inherit the kingdom of God." (NIV);
WHEREAS we are Cumberland Presbyterians and take our doctrinal and practical framework from biblical principles;
WHEREAS we note with concern influences from other denominations and groups that are contrary to our doctrine and historical practice;
WHEREAS some of those influences, especially with reference to the Youth Triennium, have already negatively impacted some of our youth;
WHEREAS we wish to prevent those same influences from permeating our educational material and the development and experiential practice of the church's ministries;
BE IT RESOLVES, that Andes Presbytery requests the General Assembly to closely review and monitor programs and institutions that may unduly influence the doctrine and work of the Cumberland Presbyterian Church and thus prevent an infiltration of concepts that are foreign to our doctrine and practice, with special reference to any ideology that promotes a multiplicity of genders [besides man and woman].

I certify that this copy is true to the Memorial approved by Andes Presbytery on April 10, 2017. Respectfully, Rev. Diana Maria Valdez," be denied.

Spanish version

El 10 de abril de 2017, en reunión extraordinaria debidamente convocada, el Presbiterio de los aprobó este Memorial para ser sometido para la consideración de la Asamblea General de la Iglesia Presbiteriana Cumberland en su reunión ordinaria en 2017.

MEMORIAL DEL PRESBITERIO DE LOS ANDES PARA LA ASAMBLEA GENERAL #187 DE 2017
Por cuanto la iglesia en Colombia ha sufrido influencias de la ideología de género. Que en nuestro contexto implica promover una diversidad de géneros que es abiertamente contraria a la

Biblia,
Por cuanto nuestra única fuente de autoridad es la Biblia.
La Biblia enseña:

Que Dios creó un hombre y una mujer, en Génesis 1:26

Que la homosexualidad es una aberración delante de Dios:Lv.. 18:22
"No te acostarás con varón como los que se acuestan con mujer; es una abominación."

Que la homosexualidad quebranta el diseño original de Dios: Ro 1:26,27
"26 Por esta razón Dios los entregó a pasiones degradantes; porque sus mujeres cambiaron la función natural por la que es contra la naturaleza; 27 y de la misma manera también los hombres, abandonando el uso natural de la mujer, se encendieron en su lujuria unos con otros, cometiendo hechos vergonzosos hombres con hombres, y recibiendo en sí mismos el castigo correspondiente a su extravío."

Que los homosexuales practicantes no entrarán en el Reino de los Cielos: 1Co 6:9,10
"9 ¿O no sabéis que los injustos no heredarán el reino de Dios? No os dejéis engañar: ni los inmorales, ni los idólatras, ni los adúlteros, ni los afeminados, ni los homosexuales, 10 ni los ladrones, ni los avaros, ni los borrachos, ni los difamadores, ni los estafadores heredarán el reino de Dios." Por cuanto somos Presbiterianos Cumberland y tomamos nuestro marco doctrinal y de práctica de los principios bíblicos.
Por cuanto percibimos con preocupación influencias de otras denominaciones y grupos que son contrarias a nuestra doctrina y práctica histórica.
Por cuanto algunas de esas influencias, especialmente en el trienio juvenil, ya han causado impacto negativo en algunos de nuestros jóvenes.
Por cuanto quisiéramos prevenir que esas mismas influencias llegaran a permear nuestro material educativo y el desarrollo y práctica vivencial de los ministerios

Entonces el Presbiterio de los Andes, solicita a la Asamblea General que revise y vigile muy de cerca los programas e instituciones que puedan influir en el pensamiento doctrina y trabajo de la Iglesia Presbiteriana Cumberland, y así impedir infiltraciones de pensamientos ajenos a nuestra doctrina y práctica, especialmente con referencia a la ideología de género.

Certifico que es copia fiel del Memorial aprobado por el Presbiterio de los Andes el 10 de abril de 2017.

Respetuosamente,
Rev. Diana María Valdez, Secretaria, Presbiterio de los Andes," ser negado.

Respectfully submitted,
The Committee on Judiciary

REPORT OF THE COMMITTEE ON
CHILDREN'S HOME AND HIGHER EDUCATION
(Appendix D)

I. REFERRALS

Referrals to this committee are as follows: The Report of the Board of Trustees of Memphis Theological Seminary, The Report of the Board of Trustees of Bethel University, The Report of the Board of Trustees of the Cumberland Presbyterian Children's Home, The Report of the Joint Committee on the Covenant Relationship between the General Assembly Corporation and Bethel University, and The Report of the Joint Committee on the Covenant Relationship between the General Assembly Corporation and Cumberland Presbyterian Children's Home.

II. PERSONS OF COUNSEL

Appearing before this committee were: Reverend Duane Dougherty, member of the Board of Trustees of the Cumberland Presbyterian Children's Home and Jennifer Livings and Debby Garrett also from the Cumberland Presbyterian Children's Home; Reverend Jay Earheart-Brown, President Memphis Theological Seminary; Reverend Linda Howell, member of the Board of Trustees for Memphis Theological Seminary; and Reverend Michael Qualls, Director of Program of Alternate Studies; Dr. Walter Butler, President of Bethel University, and his wife, Jennifer Butler; Nancy McSpadden, Elton Hall, Nancy Bean, and Robert Truitt.

III. THE REPORT OF THE BOARD OF TRUSTEES OF MEMPHIS THEOLOGICAL SEMINARY

For 157 years Memphis Theological Seminary has witnessed to the importance of an educated ministry. MTS continues to minister in an ever changing world. The mission of the seminary is to be kept before the Cumberland Presbyterian Church in thought and prayer and in such tangible ways as Seminary/PAS Sunday on August 20, 2017.

We are grateful for the vital work of Memphis Theological Seminary and especially its trustees who have served with honor.

RECOMMENDATION 1: That Recommendation 1 of the Report of the Board of Trustees of Memphis Theological Seminary, "that the General Assembly express its gratitude to trustees Marble, Ward, Wharton, and Coombs for their faithful service to Memphis Theological Seminary and the Cumberland Presbyterian Church," be adopted.

The Ministry for the Real World campaign is a vital strategy to insure that Memphis Theological Seminary continues to fulfill its calling. Having secured around $14 million in gifts and pledges toward its goal of $25 million, the campaign is moving ahead of schedule and hopes to continue raising needed support and funds. The committee agrees in principle with the Board of Trustees recommendation noting only that the General Assembly's role is to work first through presbyteries who in turn work through churches and other groups.

RECOMMENDATION 2: That Recommendation 2 of the Report of the Board of Trustees of Memphis Theological Seminary, "that the General Assembly encourage individuals, churches, and groups across the Cumberland Presbyterian Church to consider investing in the development of future leaders through the "Ministry for the Real World" campaign," be denied.

RECOMMENDATION 3: That the General Assembly encourage presbyteries who in turn encourage churches, groups, and individuals across the Cumberland Presbyterian Church to consider investing in the development of future leaders through the "Ministry for the Real World" campaign."

The committee notes the retirement of Reverend Stan Wood, D.Min. after long years of diligent service to MTS in a variety of roles, most recently as Vice President of Academic Affairs and Dean.

RECOMMENDATION 4: That the General Assembly express its gratitude to Reverend R. Stan Wood, D.Min. for his faithful service to Memphis Theological Seminary as well as the Cumberland Presbyterian Church/ Cumberland Church in America.

We pray that God will continue to call women and men to the office of ministry, and that they will be well prepared to fulfill their calling. We encourage those God calls to find Memphis Theological Seminary as a priority in their educational journey of faith. The committee agrees in principle with the recommendation of the Board of Trustees noting that presbyterial probationary care committees are central to encouraging probationers to attend MTS.

RECOMMENDATION 5: That Recommendation 3 of the Report of the Board of Trustees of Memphis Theological Seminary, "that the General Assembly urge all probationers to consider Memphis Theological Seminary and the Program of Alternate Studies as their first options for meeting educational requirements for ordained ministry," be denied.

RECOMMENDATION 6: That the General Assembly urge presbyteries through their probationary care committees to guide probationers toward considering Memphis Theological Seminary and the Program of Alternate Studies as their first options for meeting educational requirements for ordained ministry.

The committee agrees in principle with the Board of Trustees recommendation concerning Seminary/PAS Sunday and simply directs encouragement first through the presbytery.

RECOMMENDATION 7: That Recommendation 5 of the Report of the Board of Trustees of Memphis Theological Seminary, "that the third Sunday in August, (August 20, 2017 and August 19, 2018) be included in the General Assembly Calendar as Seminary/PAS Sunday, and that the General Assembly encourage all churches to share information about MTS and PAS and receive a special offering on that day, or on a more convenient day of the session's choosing," be denied.

RECOMMENDATION 8: That the third Sunday in August, (August 20, 2017 and August 19, 2018) be included in the General Assembly Calendar as Seminary/PAS Sunday, and that the General Assembly encourage all presbyteries who in turn encourage churches to share information about MTS and PAS and receive a special offering on that day, or on a more convenient day of the session's choosing.

(Note: August 20, 2017 and August 19, 2018 as the date of Seminary/PAS Sunday are included in the Stated Clerk's Report under Church Calendar 2017-2018)

IV. THE REPORT OF THE BOARD OF TRUSTEES OF BETHEL UNIVERSITY

Bethel University for 175 years has lived out its educational calling. The University continues to grow and reach students in an ever changing world. The mission of Bethel University is to be kept before the Cumberland Presbyterian Church in thought and prayer and in such tangible ways as Bethel University Sunday on November 5, 2017. Every five years Bethel's covenant relationship is reviewed. Only minor changes in wording of the mission relative to the online aspect of education were made from the last review.

V. THE REPORT OF THE JOINT COMMITTEE ON THE COVENANT RELATIONSHIP BETWEEN THE GENERAL ASSEMBLY CORPORATION AND BETHEL UNIVERSITY

RECOMMENDATION 9: That Recommendation 1 of The Joint Committee on the Covenant Relationship Between GAC/Bethel University, "that the Joint Committee on the Covenant Relationship Recommends the Adoption of the Following Document:

THE COVENANT BETWEEN
BETHEL UNIVERSITY AND CUMBERLAND PRESBYTERIAN CHURCH

I. HISTORICAL RELATIONSHIP BETWEEN
BETHEL UNIVERSITY AND THE CUMBERLAND PRESBYTERIAN CHURCH

Bethel University was established in McLemoresville, Tennessee in 1842 as a Cumberland Presbyterian School, under the auspices of the Synod of West Tennessee. The initial purpose was the education and training of ministers, but the school was open to anyone who wanted an education in a moral and religious environment. The school was chartered under the laws of the State of Tennessee in 1847. Bethel College came into being in 1850 under a new state charter granting the college all the rights and privileges of a full collegiate institution.

The Civil War brought hard times to Bethel College and McLemoresville. The area was equally divided between Union and Confederate forces and the college was occasionally occupied by each army. The structures and equipment were damaged, but the greater loss was, the student body who served on both sides of the conflict. Bethel College was re-organized at McLemoresville after the Civil War and in 1872 it was relocated to McKenzie, Tennessee, to take advantage of the crossroads between North Carolina and St. Louis and the L&N Railways. J.M. McKenzie deeded the land for Bethel to the Bethel Board of Trustees on February 2, 1872.

The Synod of West Tennessee ceded Bethel College to the General Assembly of the Cumberland Presbyterian Church in 1919. McKenzie, Tennessee was voted as the permanent location for the college at the General Assembly of 1922 in Greenville, Tennessee. Bethel College was thoroughly re-organized and standardized in 1923. Bethel College became a four-year Liberal Arts college, chartered by the State of Tennessee and accredited by the Commission on Colleges of Southern Association of Colleges and Schools. In light of Bethel's growth, complexity and impact, the Board of Trustees recognized the need for Bethel College to become Bethel University which occurred in 2009. The University is chartered by the State of Tennessee and accredited by the Commission on Colleges of Southern Association of Colleges and Schools.

II. NATURE AND PURPOSE OF THE COVENANT RELATIONSHIP

The relationship that exists between Bethel University and the Cumberland Presbyterian Church is defined and characterized by the word "covenant." The term "covenant" is rooted in biblical and theological understanding and has found its highest expression among God's people. Thus, covenant within the family of God implies the deepest level of trust between covenanting parties and of commitment to one another. A Christian covenant is a living agreement that offers both parties opportunities for creative adaptation to meet the ever-changing conditions of our world. This covenant, moreover, frees each party from being controlled or ultimately responsible for or to each other, but unites the two parties through their common vision and missions. It seeks to honor the legal independence of each party while retaining and ongoing, mutual moral responsibility. This covenant relationship does not preclude the university from forming other covenant relationships with other Church bodies.

III. THE ONGOING MISSION OF EACH COVENANT PARTY

A. THE MISSION OF BETHEL UNIVERSITY

Bethel University's mission is to create opportunities for members of the learning community to develop in a Christian environment their highest intellectual, spiritual and social potential. This includes synchronous and asynchronous modes of education.

B. THE MISSION OF THE GENERAL ASSEMBLY CORPORATION

Vision of Ministry of the Cumberland Presbyterian Church Biblically based and Christ-centered Born out of specific sense of mission, the Cumberland Presbyterian Church strives to be true to its heritage: To be open to God's reforming Spirit, To work cooperatively with the larger Body of Christ, and to nurture the connectional bonds that make us one,

The Cumberland Presbyterian Church seeks to be the hands and feet of Christ in witness and service to the world and above all the Cumberland Presbyterian Church lives out the love of God to the glory of Jesus Christ.

IV. THE CORPORATE INTEGRITY OF EACH COVENANT PARTY

A. Bethel University and the Cumberland Presbyterian Church are separate, legally independent and individually responsible entities.

B. Bethel University will be governed by a self-perpetuating Board of Trustees, with no less than a majority of its total membership as active members of the Cumberland Presbyterian Church.

C. Neither the General Assembly Corporation nor any of the General Assembly's councils, boards, agents, officers, or employees shall be liable for any of the debts of Bethel University. In similar fashion, Bethel University is not liable for any of the debts of the Cumberland Presbyterian Church or its agencies, nor does it have a claim on any of the assets of the Cumberland Presbyterian Church or its agencies.

V. COMMITMENT OF EACH PARTY TO THE COVENANT

Both Bethel University and the General Assembly Corporation will demonstrate mutual concern and support for one another. The primary expression of mutual concern and support will involve relationships between the two parties that provide services for each other.

A. THE COMMITMENTS OF BETHEL UNIVERSITY

Bethel University will be a resource to the Cumberland Presbyterian Church and its constituencies for educational purposes related to the Church's mission. Bethel University is free to solicit funds for both capital and operating expenses from individual and Cumberland Presbyterian and other persons, congregations, presbyteries, trustees, foundations, estates, and any other sources. Any major capital campaign initiated by Bethel University with targets primarily Presbyteries, Synods, and Congregations of the Cumberland Presbyterian Church will be scheduled by mutual consent of Bethel University and the General Assembly Corporation through the Office of the Stated Clerk.

B. The General Assembly Corporation will provide financial support for the university by regular benevolent giving in accordance with an objective funding formula developed by the General Assembly Corporation.

The General Assembly Corporation will encourage support of Bethel University by Synods, Presbyteries, sessions and individual Cumberland Presbyterians through planned giving programs. The General Assembly Corporation pledges programmatic support to the university by encouraging use of personnel and facilities of the university for denominational events, emphasizing the opportunities afforded by church-related higher education in its youth ministry programs, and providing the specialized services of the denominational Board of Stewardship, Foundation and Benefits.

VI. REVIEW AND REAFFIRMATION OF THE COVENANTAL RELATIONSHIP

There will be a review, and if necessary, revision of the covenant relationship every five years. The General Assembly Corporation and the Board of Trustees of Bethel University will see that such a review is accomplished through appropriate committees. These committees will be appointed by the respective entities.

The review process will be initiated by the administration of the university and the review/reaffirmation process shall consist of an in-depth review of all aspects of the university. The review process will be designed by the administration of the university and a review committee elected by the General Assembly Corporation. The review shall include consideration of changes and/or amendments to the Covenant relationship, as well as any suggestions to the university and the General Assembly resulting from the review. The administration of the university and the General Assembly Corporation committee shall produce a joint written report of the review process to be signed by the General Assembly Corporation Committee and the President of the university and submitted to both the Bethel Board of Trustees and the General Assembly Corporation.

Responsibility for approval of any change in the covenant resides with the Board of Trustees of Bethel University and the General Assembly Corporation. This agreement may be modified or altered prior to the reaffirmation process only with the consent of both parties.

VII. COMMUNICATION BETWEEN COVENANT PARTNERS

Bethel University and the Church will communicate concerning the affairs of the university and the strength of the relationship at least every five years during the reaffirmation and renewal of the covenant. However, Bethel University is encouraged to submit information-only reports through the Stated Clerk to any meeting of the General Assembly Corporation.

VIII. APPROVAL OF THE COVENANT

This document establishes and contains the terms of the covenant relationship between the Cumberland Presbyterian Church and Bethel University. By formal action, the Board of Trustees of

Bethel University and the General Assembly Corporation adopt this Covenant and pledge themselves to carry out its provisions. Approved by the Board of Trustees Bethel University

_____
President, Bethel University
Board of Trustees

_____
President, Bethel University
Approved by the 187th General Assembly Of the Cumberland Presbyterian

_____
General Assembly Stated Clerk

_____
Date

Respectfully Submitted,
The Bethel University Covenant Review Committee," be adopted.

VI. THE REPORT OF THE BOARD OF TRUSTEES OF THE CUMBERLAND PRESBYTERIAN CHILDREN'S HOME

The Children's Home continues to be the arm of the Cumberland Presbyterian Church reaching out to broken families in crises. For 113 years, the Children's Home has fulfilled its calling to serve children and families offering healing and hope. The mission of the Children's Home is to be kept before the Cumberland Presbyterian Church in thought and prayer and in such tangible ways as Children's Home Sunday on March 18, 2018. Every five years the Children's Home's covenant relationship is reviewed. Renewal of the Covenant with updated revisions is recommended.

The Children's Home continues to need our help, our financial gifts and volunteer efforts are concrete ways that we can participate.

RECOMMENDATION 10: That the General Assembly urge presbyteries and in turn churches and other groups to support the Children's Home with volunteer help, financial assistance, as well as celebrating Children's Home Sunday on March 18, 2018.

VII. THE REPORT OF THE JOINT COMMITTEE ON THE COVENANT RELATIONSHIP BETWEEN THE GENERAL ASSEMBLY CORPORATION AND CUMBERLAND PRESBYTERIAN CHILDREN'S HOME

RECOMMENDATION 11: That Recommendation 1 of the Report of the Joint Committee on the Covenant Relationship Between the General Assembly Corporation and Cumberland Presbyterian Children's Home, "that the Joint Committee on the Covenant Relationship Recommends the Adoption of the Following Document:

The Addendum Number One 22 April 2017

I. HISTORICAL RELATIONSHIP BETWEEN THE CUMBERLAND PRESBYTERIAN CHILDREN'S HOME AND THE CUMBERLAND PRESBYTERIAN CHURCH

The Mission Statement of the Cumberland Presbyterian Children's Home has been revised to read: "In response to Christ's love and example, we serve children and families by providing healing and hope." The Children's Home is in its 113th year of operation as a ministry of the General Assembly. As the Children's Home entered the 21st Century, it maintained its core values while updating its delivery of services to fulfill its ministry. Today, CPCH is one ministry with four interrelated programs -- Long Term Residential Foster Care, Emergency Residential Foster Care, Single Parent Family residential and service program and Cumberland Family Services counseling.

II. . . . .

III. . . . .

IV. THE LEGAL RELATIONSHIP AND THE CORPORATE INTEGRITY OF EACH COVENANT PARTY

Separate Legal Entities.
a. Governance of CPCH. CPCH's Certificate of Formation and By-Laws provide that it shall be managed by a Board of Trustees, of which at least 10 of the 18 Trustees must be members of a local Cumberland Presbyterian Church or Presbytery.

VII. APPROVAL OF THE COVENANT

This document and subsequent Addendums establishes and contains the terms of the Covenant relationship between the Board of Trustees of the Cumberland Presbyterian Children's Home and the Cumberland Presbyterian Church General Assembly Corporation.

This Addendum Number One is signed on the _____ day of _____ 2017.
Cumberland Presbyterian Church Board of Trustees of the
General Assembly Corporation Cumberland Presbyterian Children's Home

_____   _____
The Rev. Michael Sharpe   **The Rev. Dr. Richard A. Brown**
Stated Clerk   **President, CEO & General Counsel**

Respectfully,
The Joint Committee on the Covenant Between the Cumberland Presbyterian Children's Home and the General Assembly Corporation," be adopted.

Respectfully Submitted,
The Committee on the Children's Home and Higher Education

THEOLOGY AND SOCIAL CONCERNS/ UNIFICATION TASK FORCE
(Appendix E)

I. REFERRALS

Referrals to this committee are as follows: The Report of the Ministry Council, Section 1.B.6; The Report of the Unified Committee on Theology and Social Concerns; and The Report of the Unification Task Force.

II. PERSONS OF COUNSEL

Appearing before this committee were: Reverend William Robinson (CPCA) and Reverend Joy Warren (CPC), representatives of the Unification Task Force; Elder Joy Wallace and Reverend Nancy Fuqua, representative from the Unified Committee of Theology and Social Concerns; and Ministry Council staff: Mrs. Edith Old, Reverend Milton Ortiz and Reverend Lynn Thomas.

III. CONSIDERATION OF REFERRALS

A. REPORT OF THE UNIFIED COMMITTEE OF THEOLOGY AND SOCIAL CONCERNS

RECOMMENDATION 1: That Recommendation 1 of the Report of the Unified Committee on Theology and Social Concerns, "that the General Assembly of the Cumberland Presbyterian Church commend Japan Presbytery for their diligent theological work in response to the social concerns that face them on a daily basis," be adopted.

RECOMMENDATION 2: That Recommendation 2 of the Report of the Unified Committee on Theology and Social Concerns, "that this paper be distributed to all presbyteries as a study document and that General Assembly direct presbyteries to use the resolution as a model for the work of presbytery committees on theological and social concerns in order that presbyteries might begin to use their declarative authority and speak theologically to the social issues that confront the Church," be adopted.

RECOMMENDATION 3: That Recommendation 3 of the Report of the Unified Committee on Theology and Social Concerns, "that the General Assemblies accept the papers, "A Question of Hermeneutics" and "Identifying and Addressing Elder Abuse-A Social Response" as study papers and that they be used to initiate thought and discussion within the Cumberland Presbyterian Church and the Cumberland Presbyterian Church in America," be adopted.

RECOMMENDATION 4: That Recommendation 4 of the Report of the Unified Committee on Theology and Social Concerns, "that the Office of the General Assembly of both denominations makes these papers available to churches through the stated clerks of the presbyteries," be denied.

The Committee offered the following recommendation in its place:

RECOMMENDATION 5: That the office of the General Assembly of both denominations make these papers available to the church (members) through the stated clerks of the presbyteries, denominational publications, all forms of digital media, and directing attention and traffic to www.cumberland.org/uctsc, which is the website for the Unified Committee on Theology and Social Concerns.

RECOMMENDATION 6: That Recommendation 5 of the Report of the Unified Committee on Theology and Social Concerns, "that the General Assemblies recommend to presbyteries the book "America's Original Sin" by Jim Wallis as a resource on addressing racism in America," be denied.

The Committee offered the following recommendation in its place:

RECOMMENDATION 7: The General Assemblies recommends to the presbyteries works such as; but not limited to "America's Original Sin" by Jim Wallis, "Race Rules: Navigating the Color Line" by Michael Eric Dyson, "Understanding Every Day Racism" by Philomena Essed, and "The New Jim Crow: Mass Incarceration in the Age of Color Blindness" by Michele Alexander as resources on addressing racism in America.

B. REPORT OF THE UNIFICATION TASK FORCE

The Committee was in support of the Unification Task Force.

RECOMMENDATION 8: That Recommendation 1 of the Report of the Unification Task Force, "that the General Assemblies encourage pastors, elders, sessions, churches, presbyteries and synods to continue their study and discussion of the Proposed Plan of Union, and that responses be directed to the UTF through the Office of the Stated Clerk of the CPC or Office of the Administrative Director of the CPCA, "be adopted.

RECOMMENDATION 9: That Recommendation 2 of the Report of the Unification Task Force, "that the fourth Sunday in June be set aside in the church calendars as Unification Sunday beginning in 2018," be adopted.

In light of the discussion on how to improve the process of unification the committee offered suggestions that embrace the global church.

RECOMMENDATION 10: That the General Assemblies encourage pastors, elders, sessions, churches, presbyteries, and synods to be more proactive in creating, diverse, meaningful shared community experiences world wide between CPC and CPCA. Recommended activities include pastor/choir swaps, sporting events, VBS, and revivals, and also more effectively utilize all forms of social media and digital communication to promote unification.

C. REPORT OF THE MINISTRY COUNCIL, SECTION 1.B.6

The CPC Commissioners met with members of the Ministry Council Staff who explained the importance of self-assessment, nature of missions, and expanding dialogue with the Unification Task Force. Unification Task Force representative, Reverend Joy Warren was invited back to speak to the commissioners. She indicated that the Unification Task Force welcomes feedback from all avenues.

RECOMMENDATION 11: That Recommendation 3 of the Report of the Ministry Council, Section 1.B.6, "that the Cumberland Presbyterian General Assembly instruct boards and agencies listed in the Unification Task Force's revised plan to provide a report to the next General Assembly (188th) asking these boards and agencies to provide: 1.) Their ideas with respect to the best ways to implement unification within their board or agency, 2.) Their assessment explaining if their board or agency needs structural changes as part of unification and what those changes should be, and 3.) What the board or agency anticipates will be the approximate costs implementing unification and or restructure of their board or agency," be adopted.

Respectfully Submitted,
Committee on Theological and Social Concerns/Unification Task Force

MINISTRY COUNCIL/COMMUNICATIONS/DISCIPLESHIP
(Appendix F)

I. REFERRALS

Referrals to this committee are as follows: The Report of the Ministry Council, except shaded section 1.B.5 which is referred to Stewardship/Elected Officers, section 1.B.6 which is referred to Theology and Social Concerns/Unification Task Force, and section II.C which is referred to Missions/Pastoral Development.

II. PERSONS OF COUNSEL

Appearing before this committee were: Ms. Edith Old, Director of Ministries; Reverend Tom Sanders, Represetive from Ministry Council; Reverend Elinor Brown, Discipleship Ministry Team; and Mr. Mark Davis, Communications Ministry Team.

III. CONSIDERATION OF REFERRALS

A. REPORT OF THE MINISTRY COUNCIL EXCEPT SHADED SECTION 1.B.5 WHICH IS REFERRED TO STEWARDSHIP/ELECTED OFFICERS, SECTION 1.B.6 WHICH IS REFERRED TO THEOLOGY AND SOCIAL CONCERNS/UNIFICATION TASK FORCE, AND SECTION II.C WHICH IS REFERRED TO MISSIONS/PASTORAL DEVELOPMENT.

We commend the Ministry Council on their hard work, continued exceptional stewardship of all their resources, and the creation of a cooperative and empowering environment, and make the following recommendations:

RECOMMENDATION 1: That Recommendation 1 of the Report of the Ministry Council, that the 187th General Assembly amend the Ministry Council Bylaws, ARTICLE III, BOARD OF DIRECTORS, AUTHORITY, AND MEETINGS, Section E., Meetings to add "5. Meetings. A special meeting of the Ministry Council shall be called when requested by five or more Directors. (Bylaws online at https://cpcmc.org/mc/bylaws/)," be adopted.

RECOMMENDATION 2: That Recommendation 4 of the Report of the Ministry Council, "that the 187th General Assembly continue to encourage congregations, presbyteries, synods, and

denominational groups to adopt and practice a written safe sanctuary plan; encourage presbyteries to maintain a copy of the safe sanctuary plan of every church and denominational entity within its jurisdiction; and encourage the Ministry Council to continue offering training and sample policies to congregations, presbyteries, synods and denominational groups about subjects to consider and include when writing a safe sanctuary plan," be adopted.

In hearing all the great work and programs being facilitated by the Ministry Council, we desire to hear the voice of the Council, presbyteries, and congregations about their perception and vision of our present and future Cumberland Presbyterian Church.

RECOMMENDATION 3: That the following questions be submitted to the Ministry Council to address, sample the local congregations, and report results to the Ministry Council Committee of the 188th General Assembly in 2018 and publish for the denomination to view for visioning on all church levels.
1. Where are the greatest opportunities for our congregations to thrive in the future that you see?
2. What do you see as the greatest threat(s) to continued, effective ministry in and through our congregations?
3. What can we do individually, collectively, and institutionally to overcome these dangers?

Respectfully submitted:
The Committee on Ministry Council/Communication/Discipleship

MISSIONS AND PASTORAL DEVELOPMENT
(Appendix G)

I. REFERRAL

Referral to this committee is as follows: The Report of the Ministry Council, section II.C.

II. PERSONS OF COUNSEL

Appearing before this committee were: Reverend Michael Qualls, Director of the Program of Alternate Studies and from the Ministry council: Mrs. Edith Old, Director; Reverend Milton Ortiz, Team Leader, Missions Ministry Team; Reverend T.J. Malinoski, Evangelism and New Church Development; Reverend Johan Daza, Cross Cultural Ministries; Reverend Pam Phillips-Burk, Women's Ministries; Reverend Lynn Thomas, Global Missions; Mrs. Jinger Ellis, Finance and Administration; and Reverend Lanny Johnson, Ministry Council representative.

III. CONSIDERATION OF REFERRAL

A. THE REPORT OF THE MINISTRY COUNCIL, SECTION 11.C

The Committee is grateful for the life and witness of Reverend Harry Boyce Wallace and we ask our denomination to pray for his family as well as future missionaries.

The Committee is grateful for the life and witness of Reverend Randy Jacob and we ask our denomination to pray for his family as well. Our committee was informed that because the life and ministry of Reverend Randy Jacob was chronicled so well in The Cumberland Presbyterian Magazine, it will not be duplicated in The Missionary Messenger as was reported in the preliminary minutes.

RECOMMENDATION 1: That Recommendation 5 of the Report of the Ministry Council, "that the 187th General Assembly encourages presbyteries in attendance to promote the Stott-Wallace Missionary Support Fund among the churches of their presbytery. That each presbytery stated clerk provides the presbytery with the promotional video to be shown at presbytery and brochures for presbytery delegates to take back to their churches," be adopted.

RECOMMENDATION 2: That Recommendation 6 of the Report of the Ministry Council, "that the 187th General Assembly calls the Cumberland Presbyterian Church to be in diligent prayer for new exploration initiatives (formerly known as Mission Probes), and new church development as a means of evangelism and denominational growth in the United States. For individuals, both lay and ordained, to answer the call to church planting and for all judicatories of the Church to emphasize starting new exploration initiatives and/or new churches by identifying individuals and geographical areas where a Cumberland Presbyterian presence is needed and desirable," be adopted.

The committee agrees in principle with the Report of the Ministry Council concerning Recommendation 7, however, the General Assembly's role is to work through presbyteries who in turn work through churches and other groups.

RECOMMENDATION 3: That Recommendation 7 of the Report of the Ministry Council, "that the 187th General Assembly encourages presbyteries, local churches, and individuals to support Intercultural Internship opportunities through praying for the interns, and also through financially support the ongoing internship opportunities throughout the country," be denied.

RECOMMENDATION 4: That the 187th General Assembly encourages presbyteries who in turn encourage churches, group, and individuals across the Cumberland Presbyterian Church to support Intercultural Internship opportunities through praying for the interns, and also through financially supporting the ongoing internship opportunities throughout the country.

B. THE REPORT OF THE BOARD OF TRUSTEES OF MEMPHIS THEOLOGICAL SEMINARY

The committee recognizes that the ordination of ministers is the function of the presbytery. As the presbytery is required to approve preparation for ministry the Alternate Studies route by a vote of two-thirds with the reasons for the exceptions noted in the minutes, the committee agrees that approval from another body is not necessary.

RECOMMENDATION 5: That Recommendation 4 of the Report of the Board of Trustees of Memphis Theological Seminary, "that the General Assembly approve discontinuance of the process of requiring PDMT to review exceptions made for candidates to prepare for ministry through the Program of Alternate Studies," be adopted.

Respectfully submitted,
Committee on Missions and Pastoral Development

CHAPLAINS/HISTORICAL FOUNDATION
(Appendix H)

I. REFERRALS

Referrals to this committee are as follows: The Report of the Board of Trustees of the Historical Foundation and the Report of the Commission on Chaplains and Military Personnel.

II. PERSONS OF COUNSEL

Appearing before this committee were: Ms. Susan Knight Gore, Archivist, Historical Foundation; Robin McCaskey Hughes, Representative, Historical Foundation; Ted Acklin, CPCA, Huntsville Presbytery, Olivia Brandon, CPCA, Huntsville Presbytery, Lawrence Greenslit, Director of the Presbyterian Council for Chaplains and Military Personnel, and Reverend Cassandra Thomas, representative to the Presbyterian Council for Chaplains and Military Personnel.

III. CONSIDERATION OF REFERRALS

A. REPORT OF THE BOARD OF TRUSTEES OF THE HISTORICAL FOUNDATION

1. HISTORY INTERPRETATION AND PROMOTIONAL ACTIVITIES

a. 1810 Circle - After hearing from Ms. Susan Knight Gore, the committee agreed that the 1810 Circle is a giving program that needs our continued support. After some discussion with our brothers and sisters from the Cumberland Presbyterian Church in America, we concluded that the name of the program would better represent both denominations if it were changed to the 1810/1874 Circle.

Upon further discussion, the committee agreed with the Historical Foundation recommendation concerning the 1810 circle noting that the General Assembly's role is to first work through the presbyteries who in turn work through churches and other groups.

RECOMMENDATION 1: That Recommendation 1 of the Report of the Board of Trustees of the Historical Foundation, "that the General Assembly make congregations and presbyteries aware of the 1810 Circle and encourage new members to support this endeavor annually," be denied.

RECOMMENDATION 2: That the General Assembly instruct presbyteries to make congregations aware of the 1810 Circle and encourage new members to support this endeavor annually.

RECOMMENDATION 3: That, in solidarity with our brothers and sisters of the Cumberland Presbyterian Church in America, the Board of the Historical Foundation change the name of the 1810 Circle to the 1810/1874 Circle.

b. Denomination Day Offering

The committee agreed with the Historical Foundation recommendation concerning encouraging congregations to have a special offering on the Sunday designated as Denomination Day, noting again that the General Assembly's role is to first work through the presbyteries who in turn encourage the support of their congregations.

RECOMMENDATION 4: That Recommendation 2 of the Report of the Board of Trustees of the Historical Foundation, "that congregations be encouraged to have a special offering on the Sunday designated as Denomination Day to help support the special project designated for that year," be denied.

RECOMMENDATION 5: That the GeneralAssembly instruct presbyteries to encourage their congregations to have a special offering on the Sunday designated as Denomination Day to help support the special project designated for that year.

2. PUBLICATIONS

Upon further discussion, the committee agreed with the Historical Foundation recommendation concerning the making others aware of the availability of funds to publish books on topics concerning the Cumberland Presbyterian Church and the Cumberland Presbyterian Church in America, again noting that the General Assembly's role is to first work through the presbyteries who then inform churches and individuals.

RECOMMENDATION 6: That Recommendation 3 of the Report of the Board of Trustees of the Historical Foundation, "that the General Assembly make presbyteries, congregations, and individuals aware that the Historical Foundation is interested and has funds to publish books on topics concerning the Cumberland Presbyterian Church and Cumberland Presbyterian Church in America," be denied.

RECOMMENDATION 7: That General Assembly make presbyteries aware that the Historical Foundation is interested and has funds to publish books on topics concerning the Cumberland Presbyterian Church and the Cumberland Presbyterian Church in America, and instruct them to share this information with the churches and individuals of their presbytery.

3. ACQUISITIONS

Following discussion, the committee agreed with the Historical Foundation, that the preservation of session records are vital to the work and ministry of each congregations. We also noted that there is no place better qualified, or equipped to do the work of preservation than the Historical Foundation. Likewise, we agreed with the recommendation encouraging congregations to preserve their session records through the Historical Foundation, once again only noting that the General Assembly's role is to first work through the presbyteries who in turn encourage their congregations.

RECOMMENDATION 8: That Recommendation 4 of the Report of the Board of Trustees of the Historical Foundation, "that the General Assembly encourage all congregations to preserve their session records by depositing them in the Historical Foundation," be denied.

RECOMMENDATION 9: That the General Assembly instruct presbyteries to encourage all congregations to preserve their session records by depositing them in the Historical Foundation.

The committee agreed with the Historical Foundation's report that, because the minutes of a body are the legal record of the actions of that body, it is vital that we maintain accurate, up to date records from our synods and presbyteries. The committee agreed that closing churches is never an easy thing, but preserving the history of those churches remains essential to understanding who we are as Cumberland Presbyterian.

RECOMMENDATION 10: That Recommendation 5 of the Report of the Board of Trustees of the Historical Foundation, "that the General Assembly instruct each synod and presbytery to deposit their minutes in a timely fashion with the Historical Foundation," be adopted.

RECOMMENDATION 11: That Recommendation 6 of the Report of the Board of Trustees of the Historical Foundation, "that the General Assembly instruct presbyteries to locate the session records when closing a church and then deposit them in the Historical Foundation," be adopted.

4. COMMENDATION OF HISTORICAL FOUNDATION STAFF

The committee was impressed with the passion and diligence with which the staff of the Historical Foundation works in preserving the heritage of the Cumberland Presbyterian Church and the Cumberland Presbyterian Church in America. Their efforts in preserving our historical records and artifacts and in educating our churches and individuals about their heritage should not go unnoticed. For that reason, the committee expresses its gratitude to the staff of the Historical Foundation for their tireless work in preservation of the heritage of the Cumberland Presbyterian Church and Cumberland Presbyterian Church in America.

B. REPORT OF THE COMMISSION ON MILITARY CHAPLAINS AND PERSONNEL

Having reviewed the report from the Commission on Military Chaplains and Personnel and having heard from Lawrence Greenslit and Reverend Cassandra Thomas, the committee would like to note that the ongoing support of all of our Military Chaplains and Personnel is a vital part of the ministry of the Cumberland Presbyterian Church, and we commend those members of the commission for their work representing the Cumberland Presbyterian Church and the Cumberland Presbyterian Church in America as a part of the PCCMP.

Respectfully submitted:
The Committee on Chaplains/Historical Foundation

STEWARDSHIP/ELECTED OFFICERS
(Appendix I)

I. REFERRALS

Referrals to this committee are as follows: The Report of the Moderator, The Report of the Stated Clerk; The Report of the Ministry Council, section 1.B.5., The Report of the Board of Stewardship, Foundation and Benefits; The Report of the Our United Outreach Committee; The Report of the Place of Meeting Committee; and The Line Item Budgets Submitted by General Assembly Agencies.

II. PERSONS OF COUNSEL

Appearing before this committee were: Reverend Robert Heflin; and Mr. Mark Duck (Board of Stewardship); Reverend Cliff Hudson (Our United Outreach Committee); Reverend Michael Sharpe, Stated Clerk; and Moderator of the 186th General Assembly, Reverend Dwayne Tyus.

III. CONSIDERATION OF REFERRALS

A. REPORT OF THE MODERATOR

We reviewed the Report of the Moderator. There were no recommendations in the report. We would like to thank the moderator of the 186th meeting of General Assembly, Reverend Dwayne Tyus, for his work and love of the Cumberland Presbyterian Church. Reverend Tyus was able to touch the heart of the denomination as he visited presbyteries and visited with clergy and elders around the world.

B. REPORT OF THE STATED CLERK.

We commend the excellent work of the Stated Clerk, Reverend Michael Sharpe. The report of the Stated Clerk was received and the following recommendation is made.

RECOMMENDATION 1: That Recommendation 1 of the Report of the Stated Clerk, "that the 187th General Assembly approve the following dates for the 2017-2018 Church Calendar:

CHURCH CALENDAR 2017-2018

July-2017
- 8 Children's Fest, Bethel, McKenzie, Tennessee 8 Program of Alternate Studies Graduation
- 8-22 PAS Summer Extension School, Bethel, McKenzie, Tennessee August-2017
- 1-Sept 30 Christian Education Season 5 Bethel University Commencement
- 6-Sept 24 Christian Education Season 19 MTS Fall Semester Begins
- 20 Seminary/PAS Sunday
- 21 Bethel University Fall Semester Begins 29 Bethel University Spring Convocation
- 30 MTS Opening convocation

September-2017
- 10 Senior Adult Sunday
- 17 Christian Service Recognition Sunday
- 17 International Day of Prayer and Action for Human Habitat

October-2017
- Clergy Appreciation Month
- 1 Worldwide Communion Sunday 8 Pastor Appreciation Sunday
- 22 Native American Sunday

November-2017
- Any Sunday Loaves and Fishes Program 1 All Saints Day
- 4 World Community Day (Church Women United) 5 Bethel University Sunday
- 5 Stewardship Sunday
- 12 Day of Prayer for People with Aids and Other Life-Threatening Illnesses 19 Bible Sunday
- 26 Christ the King Sunday

December-2017
- Any Sunday Gift to the King Offering
- 3-25 Advent in Church and Home
- 9 Bethel University Commencement 24 Christmas Eve
- 25 Christmas Day

January-2018
- 6 Epiphany
- 8 BU Spring Semester Begins 8-9 Stated Clerks' Conference
- 7 Human Trafficking Awareness Day
- 15 Deadline for receipt of 2017 Our United Outreach Contributions

February-2018
    Black History Month
    1   **Annual congregational reports due in General Assembly office**
    4   **Denomination Day**
    4   **Historical Foundation Offering**
    4   **Souper Bowl Sunday**
    11   **Our United Outreach Sunday**
    14   **Ash Wednesday, the beginning of Lent 14–March 31 Lent to Easter**
    18   **Youth Sunday**

March-2018
    Women's History Month (USA)
    18   **Children's Home Sunday**
    25   **Palm/Passion Sunday**
    25-31 **National Farm Workers Awareness Week 29 Maundy Thursday**
    30   **Good Friday**

April-2018
    1   **Easter**
    1-7   **Family Week**
    8   **One Great Hour of Sharing**

May-2018
    5   **Bethel University Commencement**
    6   **Friendship Day (Church Women United)**
    12   **MTS Closing Convocation & Graduation**
    20   **Pentecost**
    27   **Memorial Day Offering for Military Chaplains & Personnel for USA churches**

June-2018
    3   **Stott-Wallace Missionary Fund Offering/World penMission Sunday**
    17-21 **General Assembly, Norman, Oklahoma 18-20 CPWM Convention, Norman, Oklahoma**
    24-29 **Cumberland Presbyterian Youth Conference, Bethel University, McKenzie, Tennessee**

July-2018
    7   **Program of Alternate Studies Graduation**
    14   **Children's Fest**
    7-21   **PAS Summer Extension School, Bethel, McKenzie, Tennessee**

August-2018
    4   **Bethel University Commencement**
    5-Sept 30   **Christian Education Season**
    18   **MTS Fall Semester Begins (tentative)**
    19   **Seminary/PAS Sunday**
    22   **Bethel University Fall Semester Begins**
    25   **MTS Fall Semester Begins (tentative)**
    28   **MTS Opening convocation (tentative)**
    30   **Bethel University Spring Convocation**

September-2018
    4   **MTS Opening convocation (tentative)**
    9   **Senior Adult Sunday**
    16   **Christian Service Recognition Sunday**
    16   **International Day of Prayer and Action for Human Habitat**

October-2018
Clergy Appreciation Month
    7   **Worldwide Communion Sunday**
    7   **Pastor Appreciation Sunday**
    21   **Native American Sunday**

November-2018
    Any Sunday Loaves and Fishes Program
    1   **All Saints Day**
    2   **World Community Day (Church Women United)**
    4   **Bethel University Sunday**

    4   Stewardship Sunday
    11   Day of Prayer for People with Aids and Other Life-Threatening Illnesses
    18   Bible Sunday
    25   Christ the King Sunday

December-2018
    Any Sunday Gift to the King Offering
    2-24   Advent in Church and Home
    8   Bethel University Commencement
    24   Christmas Eve
    25   Christmas Day," be adopted

C. THE REPORT OF THE MINISTRY COUNCIL, SECTION 1.B.5

We are thankful for the work of our Ministry Council and their focus on the future of our denomination and its work around the world.

RECOMMENDATION 2: That Recommendation 2 of the Report of the Ministry Council, "that the 187th General Assembly calls for all future General Assembly sites to have high speed, hard-wired internet access in the main meeting room, and that this condition be included in the contract negotiations with the host venue," be adopted.

D. REPORT OF THE BOARD OF STEWARDSHIP, FOUNDATION AND BENEFITS

RECOMMENDATION 3: That the General Assembly instruct the presbyteries to inform the congregations and individuals of our endowment programs and encourage churches to open their own endowment accounts; emphasizing the average return on investments since 1981, has averaged 9.8%.

RECOMMENDATION 4: We request the Board of Stewardship explore opportunities for Cumberland Presbyterians in all states to be able to have a saving account through the Investment Load Program.

RECOMMENDATION 5: That General Assembly direct the Board of Stewardship to instruct the presbyteries to inform the congregations and individuals of the Ministerial Aid Program, in giving aid for retired ministers and surviving spouses.

E. REPORT OF THE OUR UNITED OUTREACH COMMITTEE

We express our thanks to Reverend Cliff Hudson the OUO Development Coordinator, and the Our United Outreach Committee for their council and service to our denomination. We have a problem with the Development Coordinator title in the allocations report. One would believe that this allowed money was a salary package, which it is not. It is the allotment for several personnel, and office.

RECOMMENDATION 6: That Recommendation 1 of the Report of the Our United Outreach Committee, "that General Assembly adopt the following Our United Outreach allocatsions for 2018,

The allocation is to be as follows:	$2,800,000.00		
Development Coordinator	92,044.00		
Legal Fees	25,000.00		
Unification Task Force	35,000.00		
		Sub-total 152,044.00	
(Amount to be allocated)	2,647,956.00		
Ministry Council	$ 1,323,978.00	50%	
Bethel University	132,398.00	5%	
Children's Home	79,439.00	3%	
Stewardship	158,877.00	6%	
General Assembly Office	211,836.00	8%	

Memphis Theological Seminary/ Program of Alternate Studies	185,357.00	7%
Historical Foundation	79,439.00	3%
Shared Services	436,913.00	16.5%
Contingency	13,240.00	.5%
(Next four items total 1%)		
Comm. on Chaplains	10,247.00 .	387%
Judiciary Committee	9,665.00 .	365%
Theology/Social Concerns	3,601.00	.136%
Nominating Committee	2,966.00	.112%
	2,647,956.00	

Our United Outreach Goal $2,800,000.00," be adopted.

RECOMMENDATION 7: That the General Assembly direct the Our United Outreach Committee to change: "Development Coordinator" to "Development Coordinator Office." This name change would reflect the reality of the work performed by those who make up the ministry, not just a Director.

RECOMMENDATION 8: That the General Assembly direct Our United Outreach Committee to extend a call to all congregations to pray and "rethink their giving" to Our United Outreach, by giving at least a tithe, if not more, to fund the denomination and its programs and ministries.

F. REPORT OF THE PLACE OF MEETING COMMITTEE

We are thankful for the work of the Place of Meeting Committee, which consists of the Moderator, Stated Clerk, and the representative of the Women's Ministry. This committee has worked hard to serve the people of our denomination and to ensure they have a wonderful experience at the annual General Assembly meetings. The report of the Place of Meeting Committee was received and concurred in.

G. LINE ITEM BUDGETS SUBMITTED BY GENERAL ASSEMBLY AGENCIES

This committee thanks the Reverend Michael Shape, Stated Clerk, for his help in explaining the line item budgets to this committee and answering questions that were a concern to members of the committee. No actions were required by this committee.

Respectfully submitted:
The Committee on Stewardship/Elected Officers

CHURCH CALENDAR 2017-2018

JULY 2017

8	Children's Fest, Bethel, McKenzie, Tennessee
8	Program of Alternate Studies Graduation
8-22	PAS Summer Extension School, Bethel, McKenzie, Tennessee

AUGUST 2017

1-Sept 30	Christian Education Season
5	Bethel University Commencement
6-Sept 24	Christian Education Season
19	MTS Fall Semester Begins
20	Seminary/PAS Sunday
21	Bethel University Fall Semester Begins
29	Bethel University Spring Convocation
30	MTS Opening convocation

SEPTEMBER 2017

10	Senior Adult Sunday
17	Christian Service Recognition Sunday
17	International Day of Prayer and Action for Human Habitat

OCTOBER 2017

	Clergy Appreciation Month
1	Worldwide Communion Sunday
8	Pastor Appreciation Sunday
22	Native American Sunday

NOVEMBER 2017

	Any Sunday Loaves and Fishes Program
1	All Saints Day
4	World Community Day (Church Women United)
5	Bethel University Sunday
5	Stewardship Sunday
12	Day of Prayer for People with Aids and Other Life-Threatening Illnesses
19	Bible Sunday
26	Christ the King Sunday

DECEMBER 2017

	Any Sunday Gift to the King Offering
3-25	Advent in Church and Home
9	Bethel University Commencement
24	Christmas Eve
25	Christmas Day

January-2018

6	Epiphany
8	BU Spring Semester Begins
8-9	Stated Clerks' Conference
7	Human Trafficking Awareness Day
15	Deadline for receipt of 2017 Our United Outreach Contributions

February-2018

	Black History Month
1	Annual congregational reports due in General Assembly office
4	Denomination Day
4	Historical Foundation Offering
4	Souper Bowl Sunday
11	Our United Outreach Sunday
14	Ash Wednesday, the beginning of Lent
14–March 31	Lent to Easter
18	Youth Sunday

March-2018

	Women's History Month (USA)
18	Children's Home Sunday
25	Palm/Passion Sunday
25-31	National Farm Workers Awareness Week
29	Maundy Thursday
30	Good Friday

April-2018

1	Easter
1-7	Family Week
8	One Great Hour of Sharing

May-2018

5	Bethel University Commencement
6	Friendship Day (Church Women United)
12	MTS Closing Convocation & Graduation
20	Pentecost
27	Memorial Day Offering for Military Chaplains & Personnel for USA churches

June-2018

3	Stott-Wallace Missionary Fund Offering /World penMission Sunday
17-21	General Assembly, Norman, Oklahoma
18-20	CPWM Convention, Norman, Oklahoma
24-29	Cumberland Presbyterian Youth Conference, Bethel University, McKenzie, Tennessee